JIM BRIDGER

JERRY ENZLER

JIM BRIDGER

TRAILBLAZER
OF THE
AMERICAN WEST

UNIVERSITY OF OKLAHOMA PRESS : NORMAN

Publication of this book is made possible through
the generosity of Edith Kinney Gaylord.

Library of Congress Cataloging-in-Publication Data

Names: Enzler, Jerry A., 1951– author.
Title: Jim Bridger : trailblazer of the American West / Jerry Enzler.
Other titles: Trailblazer of the American West
Description: Norman : University of Oklahoma Press, [2021] | Includes bibliographical
    references and index. | Summary: "A comprehensive biography on Jim Bridger, famed
    mountain man, explorer, fur trader and guide"—Provided by publisher.
Identifiers: LCCN 2020046404 | ISBN 978-0-8061-6863-0 (hardcover)
Subjects: LCSH: Bridger, Jim, 1804–1881. | Frontier and pioneer life—West (U.S.) | Scouts
    (Reconnaissance)—West (U.S.)—Biography. | Trappers—West (U.S.)—Biography. |
    Pioneers—West (U.S.) —Biography.
Classification: LCC F592.B85 E59 2021 | DDC 978/.02092 [B]—dc23
LC record available at https://lccn.loc.gov/2020046404

The paper in this book meets the guidelines for permanence and durability of the Committee
on Production Guidelines for Book Longevity of the Council on Library Resources, Inc. ∞

2 3 4 5 6 7 8 9 10

To Katherine Fischer,
my favorite editor,
who traveled back in time with me

CONTENTS

ACKNOWLEDGMENTS

I was captivated by the story of Jim Bridger many years ago, and I have been fortunate to work with so many talented people as I researched and wrote this biography. I am particularly indebted to the historians and editors who took on the task of reading the manuscript and guiding me in the process, including Jay Buckley, Katherine Fischer, Jim Hardee, Candy Moulton, and Lee Whittlesey.

I recognize the many colleagues, friends, and advisors who encouraged and informed me, including Stephen Ambrose, James C. Auld, Will Bagley, Kathleen Barlow, Edwin Bearss, Bruce Belason, Deanne Blanton, Doug Brinkley, Susan Badger Doyle, Thomas Steuart Fothringham, Dudley Gardner, Clint Gilchrist, Fred Gowans, Tom Gronski, Andy Hahn, Jim Hanson, John Jackson, Mark Kelly, Carol Kuhn, Clay Landry, Willie LeClair, William MacKinnon, Alan McFarland, Mike Pilgrim, Doyle Reid, Scott (Doc Ivory) Olsen, Daniel Smith, Lisa Strong, Robert Utley, Scott Walker, and others too numerous to name.

I am thankful for the tremendous resources and helpful staff at libraries and archives across the country, including the American Heritage Center, University of Wyoming, Laramie; Beinecke Rare Book and Manuscript Library at Yale; Belleville (Illinois) Public Library; Campbell House Museum and Mercantile Library, St. Louis; Church Archives, Church of Jesus Christ of Latter-day Saints; Colorado Historical Society; Council Bluffs (Iowa) Public Library; Denver Public Library; Dubuque County (Iowa) Historical Society & Captain William Bowell Library Fort Bridger Historic Site (Wyoming); Fort Laramie National Historic

Site Archives (Wyoming); Fur Trade Research Center, Tetonia, Idaho; Hudson's Bay Company Archives of Manitoba, Canada; Huntington Library, San Marino, California; Loras College Library, Dubuque, Iowa; Missouri Historical Society; Montana Historical Society; Museum of the Fur Trade, Chadron, Nebraska; Museum of the Mountain Man, Pinedale, Wyoming; National Anthropological Archives, Smithsonian Institution; U.S. National Archives; Nebraska Historical Society; New York State Library, Albany; Sheridan (Wyoming) Library; State Historical Society of Missouri, Columbia; Yellowstone National Park Research Library; Utah State Historical Society, Salt Lake City; Utah State University Library, Logan; and University of Wisconsin Library and Archives.

This biography of Jim Bridger could not be written without inclusion of the indigenous peoples who were so essential to Bridger's story, and I acknowledge the vital role they played in Bridger's life. Tribal names that appear in quoted material and other passages reflect nineteenth-century usage consistent with the periods covered in this biography.

I salute the expertise of the University of Oklahoma Press and affiliates, including acquisitions editors Chuck Rankin and Kent Calder, managing editor Steven Baker, copyeditor Leslie Tingle, cartographer Bill Nelson, marketing assistant Amy Hernandez, and publicity manager Katie Baker.

Finally, I express my heartfelt appreciation to Katherine Fischer, Rebekah Enzler and Jerod Bast, Jason and Carrie Enzler, James and Katie Enzler, Elizabeth Enzler and Colin Muenster, and Andrew Enzler and Katya Karaz.

TO FIND A HOME
1804–1821

James Bridger, Jim to all who knew him, left home for the west when he was eight years old. He had helped his parents, James and Chloe Bridger, keep a farm and an inn near Richmond, Virginia. Now he and his family were traveling nearly a thousand miles looking for a new life in Illinois Territory on the western edge of the American settlements.[1] For Bridger, a brown-haired lad whose eyes were "liquid hazel . . . bright almost to blackness," the move would change his life forever.[2]

By day they followed dusty roads and rain-swollen streams. By night they sought shelter and talked of dangers ahead. Daniel Boone's Wilderness Road through the Cumberland Gap was the best route across the Appalachians to a land the Iroquois called "Kentake" and a river called Ohiyo.[3] It was indeed a "good river," and travelers like the Bridgers boarded flatboats to float west. When the emigrants ran out of states, they crossed the territories—Indiana, the "Land of the Indians," and then Illinois, named for the Illiniwek people.

The year 1812 was a dangerous time for the family to travel. The United States was thirty-six years old and was at war with the British for the second time. As the Bridgers moved west, the war moved with them, and the British defeated the Americans in three significant encounters. In July British soldiers and four hundred Indians captured Fort Mackinac in Michigan. In mid-August the British and Tecumseh's Indian confederacy captured over a thousand American soldiers at Fort Detroit. Closer still and also in mid-August, the English and their allies, the Potawatomi and Winnebago Indians, captured Fort Dearborn at a place called Chigagou, an Indian word meaning "onion field." The Americans surrendered, but Potawatomi warrior Nuscotnumeg brought the Indians to a frenzy, shouting, "We have them within our grasp; we must kill 'em all."[4] The Potawatomis ambushed the surrendering Americans, killing and mutilating sixty-eight people, including soldiers, civilians, and children.

The indigenous peoples in the upper Mississippi River valley resented the Americans, who had appropriated three million acres of the land they had inhabited for thousands of years.[5] Even the name "Indians" that the Americans and British used to describe them was a misnomer. While the British and the French were content to trade with them, the Americans wanted to take their land to build towns, cultivate farms, and establish governments. By supporting the British in the War of 1812, the People hoped to drive the Americans back.

The Bridgers finally reached their new home in Illinois and settled at a place called the American Bottom near the Mississippi River. This was the place where eight years earlier, in the spring of 1804, Meriwether Lewis and William Clark had assembled their expedition to map a route across the vast land extending from the Mississippi River to the Pacific Ocean. That was the same time that Jim Bridger was born in Virginia, on March 17, 1804.

The flood plain was called "American" to distinguish it from land just across the Mississippi, which had been claimed by both France and Spain before 1803. It was called "Bottom" because it was rich lowland created by the flooding river. The Bridgers planted themselves at Six Mile Prairie, which lay that many miles from St. Louis. They were squatters like their neighbors and perhaps, like them, they wore hooded capotes or blue linsey hunting shirts cinched with colored belts. The Bridgers found the land fertile for crops and fecund for hunters, but they had few stores and even fewer schools.[6]

That year the settlements in the American Bottom were paralyzed with fear of Indian attack. Winnebago warriors to the north had recently killed two lead miners near Dubuque, cut them into pieces, and eaten their flesh.[7] In September 1812 Shawnee raiders massacred fifteen children and nine adults at Pigeon Roost in Indiana Territory, just twenty-five miles from the emigrant route along the Ohio. And now the Potawatomis who had killed so many Americans in Chigagou were threatening the American Bottom. Settlers had petitioned President James Madison for soldiers, forts, and muskets, but to no avail.

Many Potawatomis lived on the Illinois River at a place called Peoria. Their inspirational leader, Main Poc, was one of the most influential Indians west of the Wabash River. His name, a rough translation from French, meant "maimed hand." He had been born with no thumb or fingers on his left hand, and he claimed this allowed him to talk with spirits and escape injury in battle.[8] He was an alcoholic who wore several human scalps around his waist and had once scolded Thomas Jefferson, telling the president he had no right to interfere in Potawatomi affairs with other Indians, unless he wanted the Indians to interfere in U.S. foreign affairs.

Main Poc's followers moved stealthily south toward the American Bottom, boasting they would cut off the heads of the Americans, the "troublers of the Earth."[9] In the event of an attack, the Bridgers and other less fortunate families planned to gather in one of the larger houses or in one of the newly constructed blockhouses spaced about twenty miles apart. Governor Ninian Edwards sent his family to Kentucky for their safety. Settlers sounded the alarm when they saw the approaching attackers. The element of surprise now lost, the Potawatomis temporarily retreated, but then returned to wreak havoc on the Illinois settlements. The Illinois legislature soon required all white males between eighteen and thirty-five to join the volunteer militia and patrol the blockhouses. Each volunteer had to supply his own gun, ammunition, and knapsack.[10]

In the fall of 1812 several volunteers from the Bottom joined Governor Edwards in a counterattack on Peoria. In that raid the 362 volunteer soldiers found the scalps of six white women and children and many stolen horses, and in retaliation they burned the Potawatomi and Kickapoo villages and killed eighty Indians. The war moved even closer to the Bridgers. Two years later, when Jim was ten, Kickapoo Indians killed Rachel Reagan and six children at Wood River, just twenty miles north of Bridger's home.[11] The Illinois legislature authorized a fifty-dollar bounty for the capture or killing of every Indian guilty of murder or depredation. The legislature also offered one hundred dollars for every Indian male killed and for every woman or child captured in "hostile" Indian territory.[12]

Jim's father was a surveyor and was often away during the war.[13] There was plenty of newly acquired land to survey in Illinois and even more across the river, where Missouri had just become a territory. A man identified as James Bridges or Bridger, perhaps Jim's father, carried dispatches in Missouri during the war, travelling between Salina and Osage in 1812 and St. Louis and Arrow Rock in 1814.[14]

The final battle of the war occurred on January 8, 1815, when Gen. Andrew Jackson defeated the British at New Orleans. Whatever fears or emotions that young Bridger felt during the war were not recorded. But decades later Bridger enthusiastically praised Jackson's victory over the British, saying, "Old Hickry gin um the forkedest sort o' chain-lightening that prehaps you ever did see in all yer born days."[15]

The end of the war allowed Bridger to safely reconnoiter the American Bottom, an explorer's paradise. Young Bridger, now eleven, would have investigated the Cahokia Mounds, the huge, mysterious, flat-topped earthen pyramids just a few miles south of his home. The biggest mound, rising over ninety feet and about three hundred paces on each side, is the largest single extant Native American construction in North America.[16]

Bridger would have also seen the flying dragons painted on the majestic bluffs overlooking the Mississippi in the Piasa Hills a few miles north of his home. Long before Europeans had explored the region, earlier people had painted these frightening, four-legged dragons with bodies covered in fish scales, blazing red eyes, teeth like those of a ferocious tiger, and horns so huge they would be good for gouging. Their long tails wound forward over their backs, curved down over their heads, passed through their legs, and ended in fish tails. Explorers Louis Joliet and Jacques Marquette had seen these rock paintings 140 years earlier, and Indians told them that their warriors were afraid to even gaze upon the ancient demons.[17]

If his adult life is any indication, young Bridger was likely gregarious, enthusiastic, and resourceful.[18] But three tragedies interrupted his childhood in rapid succession. When he was twelve, his mother fell ill. Perhaps a doctor or healer gave her laudanum or applied leeches to draw out what were believed to be morbid elements. When Chloe Bridger breathed her last, her husband was away. Jim, his brother, and his sister had to cope with their mother's death alone.[19]

Jim's brother died the same year, and some sources say he suffered the same illness that killed their mother. Then, when Jim was thirteen, his father died. Now Jim and his sister were orphans. In less than two years they had lost their mother, brother, and father. An aunt on his father's side came to care for them.[20]

While some boys hunted wolves for seventy-five cents a scalp or helped on nearby farms, young Jim worked on a flatboat ferry to support himself and his sister.[21] There were nine licensed ferry operators in Madison County in 1817–18 and several more in St. Louis.[22] Working on the ferry, Bridger would have learned to read the currents and the eddies of the river. He would have also read the weariness on the faces of traveling families and seen the dangerous ways of the river rogues.

Previous biographers have written that Bridger apprenticed to a nondescript blacksmith in St. Louis, but Bridger actually apprenticed to a famous gunsmith named Philip Creamer in Illinois, one of the most skilled gun makers on the frontier. Creamer lived in the nearby village of Cahokia and was said to have a great natural genius for working in metal, able to make "all parts of a gun and put it together as if it had grown fast there by nature." A reliable person in those days was said to be "as sure as a Creamer lock."[23]

Creamer had enlisted in the Illinois militia during the war but was soon employed in making and repairing guns for the volunteers. A brace of Creamer's brass-mounted pistols cost forty-five dollars, a steel-mounted pair brought fifty to fifty-five dollars.[24] Creamer's pistols were the weapons of choice for a duel on Bloody Island in the Mississippi River, where the important and the insulted went to "restore their honor." Duelers seeking the best pistols went to the "celebrated gunsmith, who lived in an obscure place in Illinois, almost a secluded hermitage, a creature of whim and singularity."[25]

One of Bridger's first tasks under Mr. Creamer was to journey with him to the Illinois Indian agency in Peoria. After the war the Potawatomis were woefully short of working firearms, powder, and ball, and were thus unable to hunt. The United States established an Indian subagency in Peoria, and Illinois Indian agent Richard Graham hired Creamer and his apprentice Jim Bridger to take care of the Potawatomis' gunsmithing and blacksmithing needs.[26]

Agent Graham, Creamer, and Bridger set out in April 1817 for their new home in Peoria, 170 miles north. They brought anvil and bellows, steel and iron, and specialized tools needed for gunsmithing. Graham was expected to make his home at the agency but was crestfallen when he saw the remote Indian village, which he viewed as far "from any settled or civilized part of the World."[27] Graham's brother George, the acting U.S. secretary of war, ruled against the construction of a new residence, and Richard Graham decided to operate from his home in St. Louis, while Creamer and Bridger stayed at Peoria to staff the Indian agency.[28]

Creamer repaired the Potawatomis' guns, traps, kettles, and farming tools, while Bridger pumped bellows, hauled iron, and cleared ashes. Hot sparks flew in the shop when the hammer clanged against the red metal. While Bridger was helping shape iron, his life among the Potawatomis was undoubtedly shaping him. He had seen his family and neighbors live in fear of the Potawatomis and other Indians throughout the war. Now living among them and interacting with

them and their families, Bridger was introduced to a peaceful coexistence he
would come to embrace. He would have heard agency interpreter Antoine Le
Claire translate their language and seen passing frontiersmen use flying fingers
to make sign language.[29] Soldiers stationed at the agency and travelers passing
by undoubtedly shared their tales of the wilderness. He would have seen the
problems caused when traders brought large amounts of illegal alcohol to sell
the Potawatomis.[30]

Bridger also witnessed how authorities took advantage of native peoples. War
Department policy was to provide generously for Indians to keep them friendly,
and Illinois Governor Edwards favored giving them mainly guns, traps, and
ammunition that would allow them to support themselves and their families
so they would feel "a dependence upon their own industry."[31] Like many other
Americans of that day, Edwards felt they just had to keep the Indians "in a good
humor for a few years until they would be powerless, overwhelmed by the influx
of American settlers."[32] His prediction proved true, as the white population in
Illinois grew from 12,282 in 1810 to 55,211 in 1820.[33]

Bridger's services at the Indian agency when he was twelve and thirteen were
valued at fifteen dollars a month for seven months; added to that was a subsis-
tence allowance of twenty cents a day for a total of $147.80.[34] Creamer may have
been paid this to Bridger, but it was more likely that he kept it as compensation
for teaching his apprentice. Bridger may have also worked for Creamer at his
shop near Cahokia. One family history recalled, "When Joseph [Dickson] was
preparing to move [from the American Bottom] to the Sangamon country in
the spring of 1818, he drove his wagon to the blacksmith shop operated by Philip
Creamer located two miles east of Turkey Hill."[35] This recollection noted that
fourteen-year-old Jim Bridger lived and worked for Creamer at this shop near
Cahokia. The Creamers had six children, including Susan, who was the same
age as Bridger. The household also included Creamer's "feeble minded" brother
and a slave a bit younger than Jim. Three other Creamer children were buried
in the nearby Catholic cemetery.[36]

Creamer continued to excel as a master mechanic, and Bridger's skills grew as
well. Illinois became a state in 1818 when Bridger was fourteen, and the government paid Creamer eighty-five dollars to create the first state seal, fashioned after
the Great Seal of the United States.[37] Creamer is said to have made a pistol for
Secretary of War John C. Calhoun, who was so impressed he asked Creamer for a
sketch of his life. Creamer refused, saying he "was no showman or stud-horse to
be advertised."[38] Creamer also built surveyors' compasses with John Messinger

that were said to be "as well calculated and as well finished in workmanship as any made in the United States."[39] Messinger instructed young men on the principles of surveying, but Bridger may not have been invited.

Bridger may have lived for a time with his father's brother, William, in Illinois-town, directly across from St. Louis. James Haley White, a lad who knew Bridger at this time, recalled that Jim's new family consisted of a father, two daughters, and three sons, whom he remembered as "John the eldest, James the next, and Matthew the youngest."[40] The 1820 U.S. Census agrees, showing the William Bridger household having two girls and three boys—two boys aged sixteen to eighteen (John and James) and one boy under ten (Matthew).[41]

William Bridger may not have been the best father figure for his orphaned nephew. In 1813 William was arrested in one of the oldest indictments in Madison County, Illinois, charged with shooting at neighbor Elizabeth Carter at eighty yards. The indictment said that William "with force and arms [did] beat, wound and illy treat" her until her life was "greatly despaired of." Williams was found guilty and paid a fine of $7.50, the equivalent of many days' labor.[42]

When Bridger was seventeen, he was ready for the next phase of his life. Some young men were becoming merchants or farmers. Susan Creamer was marrying John Anderson in Kaskaskia.[43] But Bridger was drawn to the river again. Though the frozen Mississippi might look like an icy shroud, it still pulsed with life below. Spring would soon break the river free and start Jim Bridger in a whole new direction.

KEELBOATING
UPRIVER
1822

If Jim Bridger looked up the Mississippi, he could imagine the vast wilderness far above Fort Snelling, which guarded the confluence of the Minnesota and Mississippi rivers. Zebulon Pike and twenty men had searched for the source of the Mississippi, but they never found it. If Bridger looked down the Mississippi, he could imagine it flowing hundreds of miles south to New Orleans and the Gulf of Mexico. But he was destined to follow the chocolate snake called Missouri, whose fangs reached far into the Rocky Mountains.

Bridger couldn't read, so the words of the advertisement in the *Missouri Gazette* that February day in 1822 must have been read to him by another. But almost every boatman and trapper in St. Louis was talking about what the ad said: William Ashley and Andrew Henry were looking for one hundred enterprising young men to follow the Missouri to the far northwest to trap beaver.[1] They planned to travel by keelboat for fifteen hundred miles and then cover another thousand miles by horse and canoe.

St. Louis in 1822 was bustling with five thousand people. Merchants scurried over brick streets to shops and banking houses while traders bickered at fur depots. Townspeople spent their money at any of fifty grocery stores and taverns while boatmen played the game of pitching quoits at stakes driven into the sand. Enslaved blacks toiled at farms and factories.[2] The newspaper ad directed applicants to Andrew Henry's "diggings" in Washington County, so after Bridger crossed the Mississippi, he would have had to travel another seventy miles to reach the lead mines, where he would have seen miners lowered by windlasses into the earth, one foot in a wooden bucket, the other dangling free. The miners used blasting powder to separate valuable lead from the rock, just like Bridger hoped to use steel traps to separate valuable beaver from Rocky Mountain streams. Henry and Ashley might had hesitated at this tall and wiry recruit. He was young, and there was no blood on his knife. But he had worked a flatboat and knew some blacksmithing. Maybe he was "as sure as a Creamer lock."[3]

Henry and Ashley were revolutionizing the trapping industry, hiring trappers to work on commission and paying them half the value of the skins of the beavers they trapped. Their plan relied on trappers to help transport supplies up the Missouri to the mountains and build and defend a fort in Indian land. The Henry and Ashley Fur Company would provide Bridger with a gun, powder, lead balls, and traps. Anything else he wanted he would have to buy on credit from the company.[4] Could Bridger become one those enterprising young men? Would he survive on the frontier?

Like most who could not write, Bridger would have put his X next to his name in the ledger. His fortunes were now tied to the company, and he could make a dollar or more for every beaver he caught and skinned, more than the daily pay for rivermen or Indian interpreters.[5] He planned to send any money he earned back to the American Bottom to support his sister.[6] If he was sharp, he could make his pile. If he wasn't, he could make his grave.

Bridger's future was now tied to the success of Henry and Ashley's new company. Andrew Henry, who had crossed the Rocky Mountain twelve years earlier, would lead the newly hired trappers into the wilderness. William Ashley, the lieutenant governor of Missouri and brigadier general of the state militia, was hoping to make enough money from this trapping expedition to fund his run for governor, and he used his connections to raise $30,000 to underwrite their fur trade venture.[7]

Henry and Ashley's fur company and the rival Missouri Fur Company competed for knives, guns, traps, and boats. Ashley purchased all the knives available. He bought firearms, including several broken guns, and employed every blacksmith and gunsmith he could round up to fix them, perhaps Bridger among them. Missouri Fur had 150 beaver traps made, but they could not find the steel to make the springs. Ashley purchased the only two keelboats available in the region but then rejected one, and Missouri Fur Company snatched it up.[8]

The two companies also competed vigorously for men, and Ashley posted several newspaper ads to recruit them. Sometimes a company would lodge its men in rented houses to keep them engaged, providing bread from two bakers and "pork plenty, which the men had to cook for themselves." Indian interpreters were also in high demand, and a list of them circulated about town.[9]

Late March and early April would have been a busy time for Bridger and the other men as they loaded crates and barrels onto the keelboat. The goods came not only from St. Louis but also from Louisville and Pittsburgh, and the keelboat would carry them west to the Rockies to supply the trappers and trade with the Indians. The men hauled aboard rifles to hunt animals and brass kettles to cook their meat, lead balls to ram down gun barrels and powder to propel the balls out again. They loaded traps to snare beaver and scalping knives to separate the fur from their flesh, blankets and beads to trade with the Indians and whiskey to separate Indians from their beaver pelts.

Bridger may have frequented the well-known Green Tree Tavern in St. Louis, a popular haunt with a swinging sign in front and a dusty wagon yard in back. For three and a half dollars a traveler could also get a week's room and board.[10] Jim Beckwourth also may have been a customer. The son of a white man and an enslaved black woman, Beckwourth would figure prominently in Bridger's future. He was emancipated, had some education, and then became a blacksmith's apprentice in St. Louis. He had a romance that caused him to shirk some of his duties and led to an argument with master blacksmith George Casner. Hammers flew, and the constable tried to arrest Beckwourth. The apprentice pulled a pistol and ran, eventually going up the Mississippi to the lead mines at Galena, Illinois.[11] Beckwourth's older sister, Winney, whom James White labeled "a woman of the town," might have frequented Green Tree Tavern as well. So too would have legendary boatman Mike Fink and his companion, Pittsburgh Blue, who swore and spat like a man but left no doubt she was a woman, "an abandoned woman . . . fond of whiskey, and always full of it."[12]

Bridger normally might have attended a dance sponsored by a local Catholic church, but during Lent they held pancake "frolics" where old voyageurs recounted their frontier "hair breadth escapes" and "well dressed and well painted French girls" flirted with eligible men. Young couples mushed toward the pancakes, grabbing them with their hands and devouring them with molasses.

While Bridger was preparing for his journey west, Henry and Ashley were keeping an eye on the nation's capital, where Secretary of War Calhoun was considering their application for a license not only to trade but also to hunt and trap on Indian land. General Henry Atkinson, the military officer in charge of Indian affairs in the West, supported Henry and Ashley's application although he warned that two other trapping expeditions had recently been "cut up in detail" by the Blackfeet.[13] Indian agent Benjamin O'Fallon also supported hunting and trapping above the Mandan villages, which lay about a thousand miles up the Missouri River, noting that those Indians had already been turned against the Americans by the British fur traders.[14] However, Calhoun, who was positioning himself for a run for president, remained consistent with federal law and approved Henry and Ashley's license to trade but not to hunt or trap. Henry and Ashley ignored Calhoun's restrictions, as did the Missouri Fur Company and others.

William Clark, who had journeyed up the Missouri with Meriwether Lewis eighteen years earlier and was in St. Louis as superintendent of Indian affairs for the western tribes, also turned a blind eye to the traps and the trappers being assembled for Rocky Mountain expeditions. Millions of dollars in beaver fur scurried and swam about in those mountains. If the Americans didn't take their pelts, Britain's Hudson's Bay Company would. Britain and the United States jointly laid claim to the vast land from the Rockies to the Pacific, and whoever developed the strongest presence there would have the advantage when the territory's disposition would be decided.

William Clark kept an Indian museum at his house, displaying painted bison robes, wampum, peace pipes, and, according to one account, the bark canoe in which Sakakawea's son, Pompey, was born.[15] Pompey and Sakakawea had accompanied Lewis and Clark's expedition to the Pacific, and Clark subsequently raised Pomp as his own, sending him to school. Bridger may never have entered Clark's Indian museum; it was meant to be visited by "any person of respectability."[16]

St. Louis was alive with anticipation of the departure of Henry and Ashley's brigade. The St. Louis *Enquirer* wrote that the Three Forks of the Missouri contained "a wealth in Furs, not surpassed by the mines of Peru," and that many of the trappers came from "the most respectable employments and circles of society."[17] In contrast, a partner from Missouri Fur said Henry and Ashley's men were "untried" and "of evry description and nation."[18]

Some trappers saw themselves building their fortunes on beaver pelts. Wives and sisters saw their men disappearing to a land of Indians and grizzlies, perhaps never to return. Did Bridger sign up for such an adventure to escape the expectations and exclusions of civilization? Was it to make his fortune? Or was it to take the measure of the new land and make it his home?

Andrew Henry set out with their first boat and more than a hundred men on April 3, 1822. Mike Fink, known as king of the keelboatmen, commanded the men who stood on the narrow catwalks on either side of the boat, long poles in hand to use human muscle to move the boats upstream. Bridger was one of those boatmen, according to James White, who knew Bridger when they were young and also spent half a day with him in 1849. Bridger had narrated his history, and White recorded that Bridger was on the 1822 expedition from St. Louis to the mountains. Though some of the men accompanied the land company, "James Bridger . . . accompanied the boats."[19]

Fink, atop the cargo hold, would shout, "Set poles for the mountains," and they sank their poles into the river until they hit the oozy bottom; the other end of the poles rested snug against their shoulders. Then Fink would bellow, "Down on her now! Down on her!" They lowered their bodies and pushed against the poles with their shoulders, their legs churning in unison to force the boat upstream.

Fink, who ruled over Bridger and the other boatmen, was over fifty years old and still a spectacle. His hair shone raven-black, but his once-bronzed skin was sallow, as if he was "suffering from ague and fever."[20] Those who didn't laugh at his jokes might be in for an eye-gouging or teeth-cracking. Just a year earlier Fink reportedly spotted a Negro lad standing on the riverbank with a protrusion on the back side of his heel, and he shot it off. The boy fell in pain, and Fink's lame defense in court was that now the fellow could wear "a genteel boot."[21]

Jim Bridger's journey of more than two thousand miles was similar to the journey undertaken by Joseph Bridger, said by some to be Jim's ancestor, who in 1654 sailed 3,600 miles from Gloucester, England, to the Isle of Wight in Virginia. He too was looking for opportunity as he escaped the bloody reign of Oliver Cromwell. Joseph Bridger became one of the wealthiest men in the Virginia colony, serving in the House of Burgesses and commanding the colonial militia in the Indian War of 1675.

Three and a half centuries later, archaeologists investigating the Chesapeake colonists searched for Joseph's remains. In the dark crevices under the floor of the Old St. Luke's Church, one archaeologist squeezed under the ancient Bridger ledger stone and extended her arms into the small brick crypt. She passed dozens of bone fragments up to her colleagues—cranial bones, pelvic bones, parts of a femur, and other remains. Through forensic analysis, anthropologists determined that Joseph Bridger had been a big, robust man with a moderately protruding brow and a square, unusually prominent jaw.[22] Jim Bridger was said to also have "a full, square face."[23] Bridger family genealogists have suggested that Bridger's ancestor may have been this Joseph Bridger, whose descendants included two more Joseph Bridgers and three James Bridgers, the third being the subject of this book, born in 1804. DNA analysis may someday confirm this lineage.

Regardless of his antecedents, this Jim Bridger in 1822 was fighting the power of the Missouri River, which pushed millions of gallons of water every second against him and the other pole men on the keelboat. They needed to muscle the boat forward to not be swallowed into failure. For the first mile they were actually fighting two rivers flowing side by side, the Missouri's murky stew to the west and the Mississippi's lighter soup to the east. Neither river wanted to surrender to the other, nor to this ragtag band of adventurers. The boatmen used their poles to push away floating logs and snarly branches and to avoid snags and sawyers lodged in the river bottom that threatened to spear the hull. They cast their poles wide and braced off, while the patroon maneuvered the sweep and shouted, "Push off now! Push off!"

It was grueling work, staining their shirts with sweat and straining their hearts. They faced the back, or stern, of the boat and lowered their bodies with poles jammed into the clefts of their shoulders. They thrust the boat forward, using the force of their legs with each step they took toward the stern. When they reached the stern, they raised their poles, leaped to the top of the cargo hold, and ran to the bow to join the endless circle again. Assuming each man's step was two feet long, it would take more than four million steps from each man to reach the Yellowstone.

At the end of the day, they hauled their weary bones to shore and united with the land party that had traveled parallel to the river, all under Major Henry's command. They were careful to tie the keelboat far enough out so a drop in the water level wouldn't ground it. On any given night the river could rise or fall a foot or more depending on the amount of rain or snowmelt it received from upstream.

It was an arduous journey for both the boatmen and the shore party. It must have seemed only moments after falling asleep that they heard the command to rise—"Levee!"—and they were called to ache once more. On the keelboat the order again was "Lean on her, now! Lean on her!" and they pushed harder against the poles. Daylight finally broke in the east and shadows along the shore revealed themselves as trees. They argued with the river, and it argued back. In the early morning the river gave up wisps of fog like smoke from a thousand campfires.

When the winds were right the men stretched their sail and let the breeze push them. Sometimes they walked in the water or along cliff banks to pull the boat by the cordelle, a long rope used to tow the keelboat. God help any of the land party who kicked rattlers from the bluffs onto the men below.

The river that pushed against them stretched out before Bridger like a giant arm, its fingers ultimately reaching into the mountains to capture the snowmelt

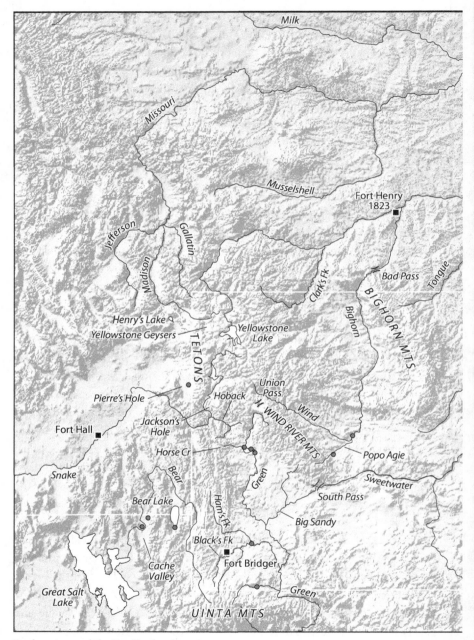

Exploration and the Fur Trade, 1822–1845

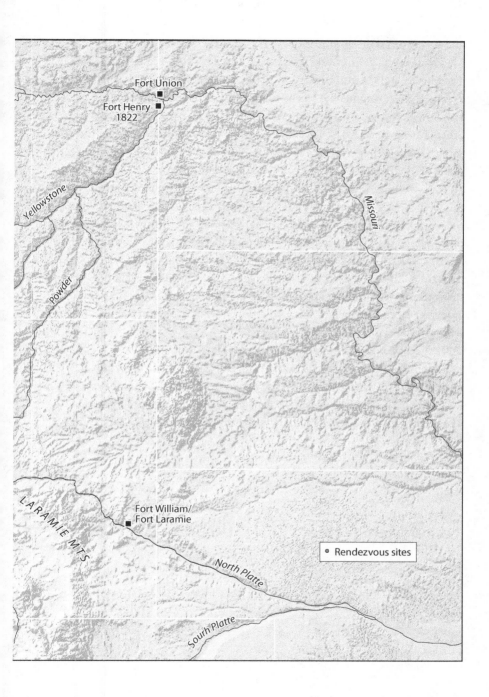

Fort Union

Fort Henry
1822

Yellowstone

Missouri

Powder

LARAMIE MTS

Fort William/
Fort Laramie

North Platte

South Platte

● Rendezvous sites

and rain from thousands of slopes. The Missouri begins where the Jefferson, Madison, and Gallatin rivers converge at Three Forks in present-day Montana. The Marias, Judith, Musselshell, and Milk rivers all join the Missouri. The Yellowstone River, augmented by the Bighorn, Tongue, Powder, and other rivers, also flows into the Missouri. Then the Little Missouri, the Platte, and dozens of other rivers join the Missouri as well. The boatmen could not conquer this fearsome beast, but they could move against it in sweat-soaked bursts. They became one with the monster, fighting it, drinking it, bathing in it.

From its headwaters the Missouri flows 2,500 miles to St. Louis, where it joins the lower Mississippi and continues its flow into the Gulf of Mexico, making it the third longest river in world. The river channel alters from side to side, and navigating it gave rise to a song: "A romping, dark brunette / As fickle and gay as any coquette / She glides along by the western plains / And changes her bed, each time it rains."[24] But music was incidental; it was muscle that proved, and Bridger's muscles tightened to iron and his skin tanned to bronze. The bluffs along the banks climbed higher and reddened with clay, and the land became wild with black bear, turkey, and deer.[25]

They reached Franklin, Missouri, just a dozen miles from Boone's Lick, where years ago the pathfinder's sons Nathan and Daniel had come to make salt. Their father had died just a couple of years earlier at ninety-six. A frontiersman in Franklin who had been upriver in Indian land saw Henry's men and predicted the Blackfeet would "attack, rob, and kill his hunting parties at every opportunity."[26]

THE BLOODY MISSOURI

1822–1823

The Upper Missouri was a new world to Bridger, and he must have been fascinated with the people and lands that he saw. By the middle of July the expedition had traveled five hundred miles, and the men were hungry. They carried no food, game was scarce, and they were glad to find even a stray dog to roast and eat. They were disappointed to find no food at Fort Cedar, the new outpost built by Missouri Fur Company in Dakota Sioux country. One recruit, Daniel Potts, was so discouraged he decided to "turn [my] tail up stream and bear my cours down in company with eight others."[1]

Bridger might have been as hungry as the nine who deserted, but he stayed with the party. They poled the keelboat into what was called the Grand Detour, a place where the Missouri River made a giant, thirty-mile loop, while the land party had to cover only a couple of miles to join with the boatmen again. From there the group traveled another eighty miles upriver and passed the two villages of the Arikaras, a powerful band that lived in what is now South Dakota who controlled trade in that stretch of the river.

Beyond the lands of the Arikaras lay the region occupied by the Mandans, a large band that had suffered greatly from smallpox decades earlier. One in five members of the tribe had blue eyes, a genetic trait contributed by French Canadian traders. Henry's men may have stopped in the Mandan villages to barter for favors from the women, and Bridger would have been amazed to hear of the spring ritual known as O-Kee-Pa.

A Mandan man painted his seminude body to play the role of the evil one, O-ke-hee-de, and harass the women until they broke his ceremonial wooden phallus. The triumphant women who had reclaimed the power of creation for the people then danced to lure men into their embrace as a way to call the buffalo to their land so the men could hunt them. Then some of the young men cut slits into their chests and suspended themselves from ropes in order to prompt vision dreams.[2]

The expedition traveled farther upriver to the area controlled by the Assiniboines. Henry posted men to guard their horses in a grove of timbers and then left to visit with the leaders to arrange for trade. As he parleyed, some of the Assiniboines rode to the grove, firing their guns in salute. The horse guards returned the signal, emptying their single-shot rifles. At that point the Assiniboines swooped down on them and stole twenty-five horses, valued at $1,440. These horses had been intended to carry the trappers into the mountains. The saddles, blankets, pistols, and other gear the expedition lost were valued at another $400. Although the trappers tracked the raiders and found several of their campsites, they never caught up with them.[3]

Given the hardships and dangers the expedition faced, Henry would have preferred to stay at home mining, reading, or playing the violin.[4] But he had been in debtor's court thirty times in the past six years and still owed $12,000, mostly for debt he had cosigned for friends. Rather than go to jail, he sold much of his land to pay the obligations. Another man might have just put his land in his wife's name, but Henry refused, saying he would rather "live a poor man rather than a dishonest one."[5] As a result he was now leading one hundred men back to Blackfeet lands to pay his bills.

Twelve years earlier, in 1810, Henry had built a fort at the Three Forks of the Missouri, in today's southwest Montana. He met fierce resistance from the Blackfeet Indians, who made several attacks on his trappers. One of his trappers, George Drouillard, who had been an essential member of the Lewis and Clark expedition, was warned of the danger of trapping alone, but he boasted, "I am too much an Indian to be caught by Indians."[6]

The Blackfeet killed Drouillard and two others, strewing their body parts across the scene of battle. Henry abandoned his fort at the Three Forks and built another Fort Henry on the Snake River, the first American trapping fort west of the Continental Divide. During this earlier expedition Henry had found several mountain passes that improved on Lewis and Clark's route, and he returned to the States a year later with about forty packs of beaver pelts.[7]

Henry, Fink, Bridger, and the others arrived at the confluence of the Yellow-stone and the Missouri in August 1822. Henry picked the spit of land between the rivers for the location of their fort and sent men out to cut timbers and set the logs vertically, securing them with horizontal bracing. They built lookouts on the corners and a log storehouse inside, and they named it Fort Henry.

Meanwhile the company's second keelboat, named *Enterprize,* had left St. Louis on May 8, some thirty-five days after the first boat.[8] About three hundred miles upriver, the current pushed the mast against an overhanging branch, and the boat capsized. Nobody drowned, but the boat and most of its cargo were lost at a cost of $10,000, not accounting for the loss of time and profit. Boxes of trade mirrors and other goods floated downstream.[9] Ashley quickly found a third boat and against his original plan went upriver himself with forty-six men and more trade goods.

Henry and Ashley and their men united at Fort Henry and traded tales of their losses. Bridger noticed that Daniel Potts, who had deserted at Cedar Fort, was among Ashley's men. Potts had been separated from the other deserters, and without a gun or provisions to make a fire, he tried to survive on birds, frogs, snakes, and any other animal he could eat raw. Indians found him and brought him back to health. After four days he set out again with three quarters of a pound of buffalo suet. He walked for six days until he found refuge with Ashley's keelboat coming up the Missouri.[10]

The company Bridger worked for had now lost almost $12,000 from the sinking of the keelboat and the loss of horses to the Assiniboines. But Missouri Fur was doing well, having just sent boats down the Missouri to St. Louis with $14,000 worth of pelts. Another Missouri Fur brigade passed Fort Henry on its way up the Yellowstone to trap more beaver. Ashley went back to St. Louis to get more men, horses, and supplies, leaving so late in the season that he navigated "along with the floating ice."[11]

Henry divided his men into three units, but it is not known which party included Bridger. One party stayed at the fort, trapping what they could and trading with Indians who came in with pelts to sell. Henry led the second party, who took the boat and canoes up the Missouri. John Weber (pronounced Weeber or Weaver) led the third party of trappers in canoes to ascend the Yellowstone to the mouth of the Powder, and then to follow the Powder upriver as far as they could. Weber was a large, powerful man with "an eye like an eagle and a voice like a trumpet."[12] He had run away to sea from his home in Denmark and held a financial interest in the lead mines along with Henry and Ashley.

The objective of all three parties was to amass beaver pelts. Bridger drew his equipment from the clerk, and the cost of beaver traps was marked against his account at roughly double their $2.75 wholesale cost in St. Louis.[13] A Sheffield knife with an eight-inch blade would be essential to skin the beaver and would also come in handy in close combat. Now he was ready to trap and scalp beaver.

Bridger searched for "beaver slides" and other signs. Beaver are the only animals other than humans that make dams. They gnaw tree trunks until they fall and dam up the streams, causing the upstream water to pool and create new habitat. As they gnaw, they simultaneously sharpen their curved incisors, which are mostly hidden deep within their gums. They are communal creatures and slap the water with their tails to warn other beaver of danger.

To set a trap, Bridger approached a spot where he saw sign and waded in the stream to mask his scent. He used a knife to cut a level bed about half a foot under the water; there he set the trap. He opened a small container of castoreum (an oil harvested from a sack near a beaver's anus) and put a bit of it on a small stick. Then he placed the stick so the castoreum hung directly above the trap. He carried the chain attached to the trap out into the steam and hammered a set pole through the other end of the chain, driving the pole into the streambed to secure it. Finally, he splashed water onto the bank to wash away his scent. If he spotted a beaver during this setup, he might just shoot it with his rifle.[14]

The next morning he would check his traps to see how many of these forty-to-fifty-pound rodents he had caught. He used his scalper to peel off the pelts and scrape away much of the muscle and fat; back at camp he laced the pelts onto circular willow hoops to dry. Often scores of furry disks hung on lines, their bloody sides facing the sun. At the fort the clerk would credit Bridger for half the value of his furs, which was used to pay any company debt he had accumulated.

None of the trappers working for Henry and Ashley knew then that death lay in wait for one of every five of them over the next few years. Some would be killed by Indians. Others would be smothered by cave-ins or winter storms. Some would starve or die of thirst. Others would be mauled by grizzlies or even shot by someone in their own company.

Evening campfires were come-alongs for stories. One classic tale concerned John Colter, who had journeyed west with Lewis and Clark and then stayed in the mountains for several years. In 1809 Colter was captured by the Blackfeet; they took his weapons, stripped him, and forced him to run for his life. He ran naked, his bare feet pounding on cactus and uneven terrain. The warriors chased him with their spears, but Colter outran all but one of them. This lone

Blackfeet rushed at him, and Colter broke the Indian's spear and killed him with the spearpoint. Colter dove underwater and hid from the other Blackfeet in the dry upper chamber of a beaver lodge. Miraculously he survived. The story of Colter's run became both a warning and an inspiration to the men.[15]

Winter took up residence in Bridger's bones as he waded through numbing streams. The trappers had no shelter other than what they built, no food except what they hunted, and no protection except what they could provide themselves. Eventually the rivers froze, and a certain beauty crept onto the icy landscape. They found beaver in their lodges by the absence of snow on top, the upper chambers warmed by the animals' bodies. Some of the trappers built the cabins against the cold while others hunted and laid up a supply of meat, mostly small game and the occasional antelope and deer.[16] Collectively this family of men continued their work of trapping the streams of the West.

Daniel Potts, a literate man, recorded their experiences up the Missouri that winter. The ice where the Musselshell joined the Missouri froze four feet thick, so solid that the shaggy buffalo began to lumber across the ice in abundance and soon surrounded the camp.[17] Potts challenged a bull in horn-to-tomahawk combat, and the men gathered to watch.

Potts approached and the bull snorted; he continued forward, and the beast charged. The odds definitely favored the hairier beast. Potts let fly with his tomahawk, but it bounced off the bull's thick matted hair. He grabbed a long spear and thrust it into the buffalo's eye, causing it to recoil in rage. Potts tried for the other eye but missed, and then thrust the spear deep into the buffalo's heart.

They roasted buffalo meat that evening, memorializing Potts and his duel. Nearly all parts of the buffalo made for good eating—the tongue, ribs, marrow, liver, hump roast, and the hump fat, which was called the fleece. They made a sort of sausage, called boudins, by turning the intestines inside out, washing them, and filling them with small cuts of loin and organ meat seasoned with pepper and salt, if they had it. The mountain goats were the next feast to walk into their camp with their pale buff coats, their creamy white bellies, and their huge circular horns. In just two hours the trappers killed twenty-six of them within one hundred square yards, a meat source that would prove invaluable during the cold winter ahead.

The weather grew colder still. The trappers' breaths clouded up, and their eyebrows caked with ice. Hearing trees explode during the night as their sap froze, the hunters were glad to be inside the fire-warmed cabin. They told stories, played cards, read books—or listened to those who could. Soon it was Christmas.

By the time 1822 gave way to 1823, Bridger was a seasoned hibernant, spending his first winter in the wilderness.

When the ice broke in April 1823, Bridger heard great moans and cracks as huge chunks began to wash downstream, and the river was born once more. Some of the trappers discovered that Indians had camped just one day's distance from them.[18] One of the trappers accidentally discharged his gun with the ramrod still in the barrel; it shot like a bullet through Daniel Potts's knees. They put him in a canoe and paddled down to Fort Henry, unsure if he would ever walk again.[19]

Eleven men continued to trap the upper Missouri tributaries that spring, and Blackfeet raiders stole four of their horses. At Great Falls the men saw the river plummet over five falls in a ten-mile stretch, cascades that ranged from six feet to eighty feet. The water catapulted over the ledges, sending glistening mists high into the air. But the Americans were after beaver, not beauty, and they moved to calmer waters to let the jaws of their traps have their fill.

There were three divisions of the Blackfeet people: the Piegans, also known as Piikánis; the Bloods (Kainais); and, residing farther north, the Siksikas. The Blackfeet had no intention of giving up their hard-fought land to the whites, whom they sometimes called "Big Knives." In the early seventeenth century, pressure from encroaching whites had driven the Blackfeet west from the eastern timberlands. The Blackfeet had taken the Shoshone lands on the Great Plains, and the land now belonged to them. Like most indigenous peoples, they saw no reason to parcel off small sections for individual family ownership. They claimed it collectively and preferred to roam at will to the best places for hunting or wintering. The American trappers saw it differently—a vast sparsely settled land open to trapping and trading. They were generally welcomed by the Crows and Shoshones. They were not welcomed by the Blackfeet.[20]

In that spring of 1823 Henry's men approached a huge butte standing out against the rounded foothills. This was near a former buffalo jump, a sacred cliff where the buffalo had given their meat to the People. The ancient People traditionally had young boys hide under buffalo skins and make the sounds of wounded calves to draw the cows. Then older boys wearing wolf robes ran at the herd from the sides, chasing them over the cliff to their death. The women waited near the bottom of the cliff to skin the broken bodies and take the meat for drying. This land where the buffalo had given up their meat to the ancient People was not for whites.[21] (Missionary Fr. Pierre De Smet once observed an Assiniboine demonstrate the call of the wounded buffalo calf, and he was indeed able to draw the cows toward him repeatedly).[22]

On May 4, 1823, the Blackfeet attacked Henry's trappers about ten or fifteen miles above the mouth of Smith's River. They killed four of the trappers, C. Mayo, Iyo, Lemai, and one whose name was not recalled. The seven remaining trappers hurried to safety, abandoning about 200 traps valued at $1,200—30 that had already been set plus another 172 traps stored in an underground cache.[23]

Missouri Fur company men also fell to the Blackfeet. In the early months of 1823, brigade leaders Robert Jones and Michael Immell negotiated with the Blackfeet to allow them to trap, and in late May they successfully negotiated for the right to build a trading post at the Great Falls of the Missouri. At the end of May, this same band of Blackfeet Blood warriors, now numbering in the hundreds, ambushed the Missouri Fur brigade on a narrow buffalo trace on the Yellowstone. Immell was in the lead and killed one of the attackers before he was slain and cut to pieces. Jones fought desperately and killed two of the Blood warriors before he too was slain by two spears to his breast. In all, Missouri Fur lost seven men; four others were wounded in the attack.[24]

In addition to the deaths of eleven men, these attacks caused significant financial loss. Henry and Ashley estimated their loss at $2,685 in horses, rifles, and sundries, and the loss to their business investments was much larger. Joshua Pilcher estimated Missouri Fur's loss at $15,000 to $16,000.[25] American blood would continue to redden the Missouri.

4

MIKE FINK AND HUGH GLASS
1823

In Bridger's first twelve months in the West, he learned that danger could come from within the company as well as from outside. In late winter 1823, Mike Fink was at Fort Henry demanding alcohol. Major Henry refused, and Fink left the fort to live in a nearby cave, joined by a younger trapper named Carpenter. One day Fink and Carpenter argued while at the fort, and Fink challenged Carpenter to "shoot the cups." Carpenter shot first, knocking the cup of whiskey off Fink's head but also grazing his scalp, causing blood to trickle down his forehead.

Now it was Fink's turn to shoot, and Carpenter nervously put his cup of whiskey on his head. Fink raised his gun, calling to Carpenter, "I taught you to shoot differently from that *last* shot! You *missed* once, but you won't again!"[1] Fink's shot pierced Carpenter's forehead, and he fell to the ground, dead.

Carpenter's friend, Talbot, thought it was murder and said so. Eventually Fink approached Talbot in the blacksmith shop saying, "I didn't mean to kill my boy." Talbot told Fink to stop, but he kept advancing. Fearing for his life, Talbot raised his pistols and shot Fink. The king of the keelboatmen was dead. Months later Talbot drowned while trying to cross the Teton River, a tributary to the Missouri. The saga of Fink, Carpenter, and Talbot became one of the most dramatic tales of the early West.

An even deadlier incident befell Ashley and his men in June 1823, a tragedy that would change the trade and travel in the West for years to come. Ashley was bringing two keelboats upriver with supplies and trappers. He was paying $200 a year instead of a share of each beaver trapped, and James Clyman had recruited men from "grog Shops and other sinks of degredation," writing that "Fallstafs Battallion was genteel in comparison."[2]

On the new recruits' first day on the boat, a man fell overboard and drowned. Then three men carting gunpowder from St. Louis to the keelboat at St. Charles were literally blown up, ignited by a laborer smoking a pipe. The explosion sent all three men into the air; two died instantly and the third expired a few moments after he landed.[3]

They desperately needed more horses, and Ashley stopped at the earthen lodges of the Arikara villages to trade for them. The Arikaras were upset that Missouri Fur Company had killed two of their people and took out their anger by killing one of Ashley's men visiting their village for female companionship. Then they fired on Ashley's men sleeping on the sand bar in front of the village. In total, the Arikaras killed fourteen of Ashley's men, wounded ten, killed or stole nineteen horses, and stole a boat and thirty-one guns.[4]

Half of Ashley's remaining men deserted, and he sent Jedediah Smith upriver to ask Henry for reinforcements. Soon Henry and twenty men were canoeing downstream, Bridger presumably one of them. As they paddled they could count with each stroke the number who had died: four trappers killed above Great Falls; Carpenter killed by Fink; Fink killed by Talbot; one man drowned; three blown up; and now fourteen more killed by the Arikaras. A total of twenty-four men from Henry and Ashley's company had died along the Missouri in the past nine months, never to drink at Green Tree Tavern again.

As they paddled, the relief party could also count the number of animals killed or stolen: twenty-four by the Assiniboines; four by the Blackfeet; nineteen by the Arikaras; seven by the Sioux. In all, they had lost fifty-four animals that could be carrying fifty-four men. Henry's party paddled past the Arikara villages and finally reached Ashley and his men laid up on a wooded island.[5]

Alarm and anger swept across the frontier. William Clark warned Secretary of War Calhoun that no American trader would be safe if the Arikaras "are not Chastised and the British Traders driven from the Missouri."[6] Colonel Leavenworth marched north with 220 soldiers and two six-pound cannons, preparing for the army's first battle against Indians west of the Mississippi.

The force assembled to take revenge against the Arikaras became known as the Missouri Legion, a combination of Leavenworth's soldiers, Ashley and Henry's

men, Missouri Fur trappers under Joshua Pilcher, and hundreds of Sioux warriors, who were always ready to fight their enemies the Arikaras. Several trappers
were assigned leadership positions, including Jedediah Smith and Hiram Scott
as captains, Edward Rose as ensign, Thomas Fitzpatrick as quartermaster, and
William Sublette as sergeant major.[7]

Twice Leavenworth issued orders to attack, then canceled them. An Arikara leader, Little Soldier, came out to talk, reporting that Grey Eyes, who had
led the original slaughter of Ashley's men, had now been killed. Leavenworth
was quick to offer peace, but Indian agent Joshua Pilcher and newly appointed
subagent Henry refused to draw up the treaty. Pilcher and Henry had come to
retrieve stolen arms and horses and to punish the Arikaras to prevent future
theft and murder. Leavenworth argued they had come to correct the Indians,
not exterminate them.

The Arikaras offered only three rifles, one horse, and eighteen robes. But
instead of forcing them to return all the stolen goods, Leavenworth dropped all
demands for further restitution, saying that "the Indians had been sufficiently
humbled" and "the blood of our countrymen has been avenged."[8] The trappers
planned for battle anyway, and the Arikaras deserted their villages, fearing they
would be annihilated. Leavenworth ordered all boats to loose cables and drop
downstream. As the force descended the river, they saw a cloud of smoke rising
from the Arikara villages: Missouri Fur Company trappers Angus McDonald
and William Gordon had set fire to them.

After the engagement the Arikara conflict continued to be fought nationwide
in official letters and newspapers. Pilcher accosted Leavenworth, writing, "You
have by the imbecility of [your] conduct and operations, created and left impassable barriers."[9] In contrast, the *New York American* wrote that the calamity was
caused by General Ashley and his trappers, who "armed and equipped for war"
had invaded "the territories of Independent Indian nations."[10]

The company Bridger worked for had lost over $16,000 in stolen horses and
goods in the last year and a half, and the Missouri River was damned and deadly
to them now. They had taken only twenty-three packs of beaver—about twenty-
three hundred pelts—which averaged out to only a few dozen pelts taken by each
man. They had also traded for another two packs.[11]

Then Henry and Ashley made a decision that would change the course of
Western history. They would abandon the Missouri River and travel by land
to the Rocky Mountains, beginning a pattern of traveling by overland routes.
Jedediah Smith led one contingent west toward the Bighorn River, and Andrew

Henry led the other group overland toward Fort Henry, planning to meet Smith's group on the Bighorn.

Of all the animals that Bridger and the trappers encountered, the grizzly bear was the most ferocious, and each of the westbound parties witnessed an attack by *Ursus horribilis* that summer. Jedediah Smith met his grizzly as he led a party of sixteen men through a brushy bottom near the Powder River. The grizzly took Smith's head into his mouth and "laid the skull bare."[12] Seeing Smith's broken body paralyzed the trappers. "Come take hold," one said. "Why not you," replied another.

Smith took charge of his own treatment and ordered: "One or 2 for water and if you have a needle and thread git it out and sew up my wounds around my head" James Clyman sewed the open gashes on Smith's face but said he could do nothing with his ear. "O you must try to stich up some way or other," commanded Smith.

So Clyman continued, "Stiching it [the ear] through and through and over and over laying the lacerated parts togather as nice as I could with my hands." They left Smith with two caretakers, and he soon recovered and resumed command.[13] From that time on, he wore his hair long to cover the scars on his face and ear.

Hugh Glass met his grizzly on the banks of the Grand River near the burned Arikara villages. Glass was one of a party of thirty men under Andrew Henry that had already been attacked by roving Mandan Indians, who killed two men, wounded two others, and stole two horses.[14] As they ascended the Grand River, Hugh Glass, who could not be restrained or "kept under Subordination . . . went off the line of march one afternoon and met with a large grizzly Bear."[15] Glass shot the bear but only wounded him, and the grizzly attacked. Fellow trappers came to his rescue, shooting at and distracting the bear. The grizzly attacked Glass again when the men continued to fire. Finally, the grizzly died and fell on Glass's body.

The story of Hugh Glass and the grizzly became an oft-told tale, each version becoming more dramatized. One faulty 1839 version seemed to implicate Jim Bridger when it suggested a seventeen-year-old lad named "Bridges" was left behind as a caretaker for the injured Glass. The summary that follows is based on Glass's account to fellow trapper Black Harris, who relayed it to a writer named James Hall. Hall's "The Missouri Trapper" was published in 1825 in the *Philadelphia Port-Folio* and reprinted by several St. Louis newspapers. Then several authors tried their hand at retelling it in later accounts.

After the grizzly attack Andrew Henry set up camp around Glass's comatose body, planning to stay one night and bury him in the morning, assuming he would not survive the night. But the next day a whisper of breath could be felt escaping Glass's broken body. Henry made the decision to leave Glass and called for a volunteer to stay a day or two and then bury him once he died. Only a lad of seventeen stepped forward. Uncomfortable leaving the youth alone, Henry offered a purse of eighty dollars, which motivated trapper John Fitzgerald to also step forward. Henry and the rest of the men went on their way, relieved that they were not the ones staying behind.

Fitzgerald and the youth began their vigil, and the second day was like the first. They stayed for a third day, wondering which band of Indians would be first to attack them—the Arikaras or the Mandans. They kept vigil a fourth day, watching over Glass's wretched body. Live or die, old man, they must have wished. Damn Hugh Glass for wandering off the path! Damn the others for not volunteering!

Finally, Fitzgerald announced they would leave. The boy refused. But Fitzgerald persisted, and nothing the lad could say changed Fitzgerald's mind. Henry had already determined that the young man could not stay alone, so the youth left with Fitzgerald, who took Glass's rifle and his shot pouch. Fitzgerald and the boy caught up with Henry and reported that Glass was dead. The seventeen-year-old did not contradict Fitzgerald's story.

Somehow Glass awakened from his coma and dragged himself to a stream. For ten days he kept himself alive eating cherries and buffalo berries hanging over the stream. He crawled toward the distant Missouri River and came upon wolves killing a buffalo calf. He scared the wolves away and ate the raw buffalo meat. He eventually found his way to Fort Kiowa, where he joined five engagés in a pirogue paddling their way up the Missouri. Glass left the boatmen for an overland route, and the next day the Arikaras slaughtered all five of his traveling companions. Two Mandans came to Glass's aid and gave him a fleet horse to continue his journey.

Glass made it to Henry's new fort at the confluence of the Bighorn and the Yellowstone River, but Fitzgerald was not there, having left to carry a dispatch to Fort Atkinson. The youth was there, but Glass did not want revenge on the boy, who was described as an "unwilling and overpersuaded accomplice."[16] Glass joined a few of Henry's men who were leaving for Fort Atkinson on February 29, 1824. This party was attacked by Arikaras and two of the trappers were killed, but again Glass survived.[17]

When Glass arrived at Fort Atkinson, he found that Fitzgerald had enlisted and was therefore protected from his revenge. The commanding officer ordered Fitzgerald to return Glass's rifle and also gave him "fixens" so he could again take the field. The return of his rifle and the gift of supplies surprisingly appeased the wrath of Hugh Glass, who seemed not as interested in revenge as in telling his story, "astounding, with his wonderful narration, the gaping rank and file of the garrison."[18]

Historians have debated who the youth was who volunteered to stay with Glass and then didn't contradict Fitzgerald when he reported that Glass was dead. Daniel Potts wrote of the event but gave few details. James Clyman, who knew Bridger well, wrote of Glass's story many years later but did not mention Bridger or Bridges. The first lengthy account, printed in 1825 by James Hall, was based on information from Moses "Black" Harris, who was with Henry, Bridger, and others during that period. Harris, who got the story from Glass, also did not mention Bridger, simply saying that Henry induced "two of his party to remain with the wounded man." Philip St. George Cooke published an account in 1830 that identified Fitzgerald and a youth of seventeen as the volunteers.

In 1839, sixteen years after the incident, an aspiring author named Edmund Flagg wrote an error-filled account that stated that the two who stayed with Glass were "Fitzgerald and Bridges." Some have taken that as proof that Jim Bridger was the youth. Flagg had come to St. Louis as an aspiring attorney and set up an office in the basement of the Planters House hotel. At the same time, he tried to establish a career as an author and poet, attending literary events and looking for interesting stories he might write.[19]

Flagg took charge of the Louisville *Literary Newsletter* in 1838 and the next year wrote and published his erroneous account of Glass titled "Adventures at the Head Waters of the Missouri." Flagg erred when he wrote that the Ashley/Henry party left St. Louis with two keelboats in March 1822, when actually one keelboat left April 3 and the other May 8. He placed Glass's encounter on the Cheyenne River, not the Grand River as consistently reported by others. Accounts up to that date said that Henry offered a reward of forty dollars or eighty dollars, but Flagg wrote that "a collection of the men" created a purse of three hundred dollars, although it's highly unlikely that the men would pay from their own pockets.[20]

Most egregious was Flagg's assertion that Henry and his trappers carried Glass for two days and on the third day left Glass with the two caretakers and "the same night arrived at the mouth of the Yellowstone." If they had been that close, there was no reason to leave Glass at all.

Flagg also falsely wrote that Glass rejoined the full body of trappers at the fort at the mouth of Yellowstone, when in fact the trappers had abandoned that fort months earlier. He also wrote that Fitzgerald turned over Glass's rifle to Henry to be auctioned off to the highest bidder, but most accounts report that Fitzgerald took Glass's rifle with him to Fort Atkinson. These errors cast serious doubt on Flagg's accuracy.

Flagg wrote that the lad was named Bridges, and there were at least seven men named Bridges in and about Missouri at that time.[21] Equally significant, by 1839 Jim Bridger was a well-known figure in Western history, having been described in Washington Irving's *The Adventures of Captain Bonneville* in 1837. If Flagg had heard "Bridger," he would have published it that way, not as "Bridges."

Flagg's erroneous account spurred others, and in 1882 Oregon emigrant Jesse Applegate crafted a wild account stating that Bridger was shunned by the trappers and had to live in exile with the Shoshones.[22] Eighty years after the Glass incident, steamboat pilot Joseph LaBarge "remembered" a "tradition" that James Bridger was the young deserter, but LaBarge's biographer, Hiram Chittenden, discounted LaBarge's statement, writing, "There is no other proof of it than this intangible tradition," and concluding, "Who the young man was is not known."[23]

James Stevenson, a scientist with the U.S. Geological Survey, gives the only word from Jim Bridger himself on the matter. Stevenson knew Bridger well, having hunted and tented with him between 1857 and 1860 as well as serving as his "reader" and "writer." In 1886 Stevenson received an inquiry about Bridger at his office at the Smithsonian and responded, "Bridger told me the story of your Glass; but there was no desertion," meaning no desertion by Bridger.[24]

Bridger may have been the young volunteer. But there is not enough evidence to state it as fact. History is sometimes slow to reveal its truths.

5

BRIDGER DISCOVERS GREAT SALT LAKE
1824–1825

After the trouble with the Arikaras, Henry led Bridger and the other trappers back to Fort Henry. They found that the corn they had planted had rotted, and the Blackfeet or Assiniboines had stolen twenty-two or twenty-three horses. They stole another seven horses after the trappers arrived. Henry abandoned the fort, and Blackfeet scavengers dug up the graves of Fink and Carpenter, hoping for clothing, blankets, or anything of value. But the bodies were too putrid to even search.[1]

In fall of 1823 the trappers traveled by boat and on foot up the Yellowstone, its course taking them southwest. The rapids at the mouth of the Powder River blocked passage of their boat, and the shortage of horses limited what they could move overland. Henry buried many of the precious bundles of goods and pelts along the Powder in underground caches, the name derived from the French verb *cacher*, to conceal. He intended to retrieve the goods the following spring, but Indians found the caches and took the "blankets, Strouds [cloth], Powder, Lead, Clothing, Kettles, etc." The Indians apparently destroyed Henry's keelboat, "as the steering oar was found floating by the Mandan Village."[2]

The trappers eventually met up with the Crows, and Edward Rose, who had once lived among them, served as interpreter. They traded for forty-seven horses, which they needed to carry their traps, goods, and pelts.[3] Now Henry and the trappers were able to continue up the Yellowstone, where they built a new Fort

Henry at the Bighorn River. The Crows were eager to get brass kettles, steel arrow points, beads, and other manufactured goods. More importantly, they wanted guns, powder, and lead balls to defend themselves against the Blackfeet, who were supplied by Hudson's Bay Company.

The trappers wintered with the Crows, and it must have reminded Bridger of his time with the Potawatomis when he was twelve and thirteen. Crow women were skilled at scraping beaver pelts and ornamenting and cresting shirts, leggings, moccasins, and blankets. They groomed their long black hair into a sheen with bear grease. They held liberal views on sex and often spent time with the trappers in exchange for bright mirrors and scarlet cloth. It was also not unusual for a Crow village to have one or more people "of two spirits," often a male who as a youth identified and dressed as a female.[4]

Now equipped with horses, Bridger and the other trappers could move more efficiently to beaver-bearing streams. They followed the Bighorn River south and eventually reached a thirty-foot waterfall and several thermal pools encrusted with darkened sediment, near present-day Thermopolis, Wyoming. They soaked their weary bodies in the warm waters, but it was beaver they were after, so they continued upstream through the Owl Creek Mountains. There the name of the river changed from Bighorn to Wind. Cottonwoods and willows gave shade, and water and grass fed their horses.

On the Popo Agie River in the Wind River valley, they found an oil spring with tar that made an ideal ointment to sooth the galled backs of their horses as well as their own aches and pains. The spring discharged "sixty or seventy gallons of pure oil per day" and had "the appearance, taste and smell of British Oil."[5] In crossing the mountains Daniel Potts, now recovered from his leg wounds, froze his feet and lost two of his toes to frostbite, making him unable to travel. A Crow chief took him into his lodge and twice a day stripped to his breech cloth and dressed Potts's wounds.

The Crows told the trappers that the beaver were so abundant on the other side of the Wind River Mountains that they did not even need traps—they could club as many as they wanted.[6] When the weather moderated in February 1824, some of the trappers attempted to cross the mountains near what is now DuBois, Wyoming. They climbed numerous switchbacks only to be blocked by deep snowdrifts. Finally they turned back, cold and disappointed.

James Clyman asked the Crows again how to cross the mountains, spreading a robe and using heaps of sand to represent the mountains. One of the Crows rearranged the sand piles, indicating that if they traveled south along the eastern front of the Wind River Mountains, they would find a level crossing. In early 1824 Jedediah Smith led a small team south, the majestic Wind River Mountains towering on their right. Wind needled their skin, cold numbed their hands, and they could barely hold flint and steel to start a fire. When they created a spark, the wind often blew it out, and when they did create a fire, they struggled to keep it lit.

The freezing trappers laid their blankets over the warmed spots where their fires had been, only to awaken hours later shaking with cold and holding onto their blankets. By day they separated into twos and threes to hunt for meat.[7] Finally they climbed a low, gentle pass fifteen miles across, just as the Crows had shown with the sand map. They were not even sure they had crossed the Continental Divide until they saw the westward-flowing streams.

Fur trader Robert Stuart and six companions from Fort Astoria on the Pacific coast had crossed this same pass traveling west to east a dozen years earlier. But its existence had been lost to mapmakers until the trappers learned of it again from the Crows. It became known as South Pass (in present-day southwestern Wyoming) and would be the main crossing for the next three decades for trappers, Oregon emigrants, and forty-niners.

It appears that Bridger, now under John Weber's leadership, crossed South Pass along with Caleb Greenwood, Ephraim Logan, Daniel Potts, Samuel Tullock, and some twenty others.[8] It had taken twenty-five months and more than twenty-five deaths, but now they were in a land where the beaver were plentiful. They trapped the waters of the Green River, which was called Río Verde by the Mexicans and Seedskedee by the Crows. Bridger was now in Mexican territory, west of the land Thomas Jefferson had purchased from France two decades earlier.

The Shoshones viewed it as their land and wanted to defend it from the Blackfeet and the Sioux. The tribe had been relying on the Hudson's Bay trappers for guns and goods but began to trade for guns with the Americans and accepted an American flag as a sign of peace and future trade. But some still pillaged the American traps and camps whenever they could. In the months ahead they would kill thirteen American trappers and plunder 180 American traps and a proportionate number of guns and knives.[9]

Bridger scouted every day for beaver cuttings and slides, wading knee-deep to set his traps and daub castoreum as a lure on a stick overhead. Soon the trappers' camp was dotted once again with bloody red ovals, pelts drying in the sun.[10] All did not come easy to Bridger. One night, while he was trapping with others along Green River, he heard a noise and saw eyes flashing, which often meant a wild animal had approached the campfire. Bridger raised his rifle and fired between the eyes—but it was not a deer or elk, only one of the company's mules, and he had to pay for it from his earnings.[11]

Winter warmed into spring, the pelts piled high, and the trappers cached them. They named the streams they found—Smith's Fork, Ham's Fork, and Black's Fork. LaBarge Creek was named for Joseph LaBarge, who had been slain there by Indians.[12] The Sweetwater was named for its refreshing taste, though some said it was because a trapper once allowed a sack of sugar to fall into it. Horse Creek was named as the place where the Shoshones stole several of Fitzpatrick's horses, although an alternate account says it was named for a wild horse that was found on its banks.[13]

Like other trappers, Bridger wore a leather hunting shirt that hung to his knees and leather leggings that sheathed his lower legs. Puckered moccasins made from animal hide covered his feet, and sometimes he wore a turbaned kerchief on his head against the heat and mosquitoes.[14] He usually had his rifle at hand and wore a powder horn and ball pouch strapped across his chest. A leather belt around his waist held his pistol as well as a sheathed knife in the middle his back. In his "possibles" bag he carried fire steels and tinder. Whatever else he owned he usually carried on his horse—traps, a hatchet, a cup and bowl, a buffalo robe, and maybe an extra shirt wrapped in a blanket. For his horse he had a saddle and saddle blanket, the latter called an apishamore.

That fall and winter of 1824–25, Bridger continued to trap with John Weber's group along the Bear River, which flowed north out of the snowcapped Uinta Mountains. They followed it north, exploring new lands and taking beaver every day—mostly laying traps but also shooting them when they saw them. Somewhere along that route, "Thomas, a half breed, was killed by Williams," and the stream became known as Thomas Fork.[15]

As they followed the course of the river, they came to a spring bubbling with carbonated water, a spot that eventually became known as Soda Springs. Here the Bear River turns west, and the trappers stayed with it, increasing their tally of pelts all along the way. The waterway then arched south and led them to beaver-rich streams and a beautiful hole called Willow Valley, which was surrounded by stupendous mountains that sported majestic robes of snow at their peaks and luxurious grasses and fruits at their feet.[16]

The course of Bear River is like a giant question mark in its route, and so it was in the trappers' minds. Where would it go next? Could it be the "Bonaventura," that mysterious river that rumor held might be the water passage to the west?

They argued among themselves about the course of the Bear, and some trappers made a wager. Twenty-year-old Bridger was selected to explore its course.[17]

Bridger mounted his horse and followed the Bear. He was going to see where the river flowed. This experience was different than setting traps in icy streams. He wasn't making money; he was making dreams. He studied what lay ahead, not knowing what he might find or if the Indians he would meet would be friends or foes. Bridger's reflection in still water showed a man far different in appearance than two years earlier. His skin browned from the sun, he could easily be mistaken for an Indian at a distance.

The Bear's winding course took him through Bear River Canyon, a deep, two-mile gorge. The towering rock walls could fill a person with both wonder and fear. It was also a perfect spot for an ambush. Even "friendly" Indians might kill a lone man for his horse and gun. But Bridger emerged from the canyon safely and continued to follow the Bear.

Then he saw it. The canyon walls fell away and the river flowed into a great expanse of water that extended for miles, its choppy waters dotted with whitecaps. He rode up to its shore and tasted it. It was salty, and a white rim of salt edged the shoreline. White seagulls and pelicans flew over the gray-green waters, and several hilly islands broke the surface. Salty spray stung his eyes, and even someone who couldn't swim could easily float in the brine. The land surrounding the water was arid, and few trees grew along the shoreline. An army general later recalled Bridger saying, "The valley was covered with the skeletons of animals that had perished in a terrible winter of a few years before."[18]

Great Salt Lake is the largest natural lake between the Mississippi River and the Pacific and the largest salt lake in the Western Hemisphere. Indigenous peoples had known of this lake for thousands of years. Trapper and trader Etienne Provost saw the southern portion of the lake from a distance in fall of 1824. Bridger made his discovery in late 1824 or early 1825. He went to the shore and tasted its waters, and became the first Euro-American to discover that it was a salt lake.

Bridger made his way back to Weber's camp and described what he'd seen. Some of the trappers supposed it "certainly to be the Gulf of California or the Pacific Ocean."[19] They were pleased to hear of a source for salt, since they had been short for some time and were tired of putting gunpowder on their meat.[20]

After his exploring expedition, Bridger and his companions were surprised to find a Hudson's Bay trapping brigade just eight miles upriver. Peter Skene Ogden was leading a group of British and Iroquois trappers who were well equipped with

The *"Devil's Gate"* (c. 1858–1860), by Alfred Jacob Miller. Devil's Gate, a day's travel west of Independence Rock, was a major landmark on the Oregon Trail, 1,500 feet long, 370 feet deep, and only 30 feet wide at the base. Bridger encountered many similar formations, including Bear River Canyon and Bad Pass. Scottish adventurer William Stewart hired artist Alfred Jacob Miller in 1837 to paint the spectacular scenery, the mountaineers, and the Indians of the Rocky Mountains. The works shown here were created much later from the artist's original sketches. *The Walters Art Museum, Baltimore*

horses, traps, and guns. The land west of the Divide and north of the Arkansas River was jointly claimed by England and the United States, and Hudson's Bay Company's plan was to kill all the beaver along a wide swath of territory along the border, purposely creating a "beaver desert."

The British wanted to stop American trappers from advancing farther west, just as burning a strip of forest would stop a fire from advancing. HBC North America leader George Simpson knew the country was a rich preserve of beaver, and for political reasons he intended to "destroy it as fast as possible."[21] Jedediah Smith learned at the HBC's Flathead Post that in the last four years the British had trapped and traded for eighty thousand beaver pelts from the Shoshone lands on both sides of the Rockies.[22]

Ogden and his trappers were flying the British flag, and the Americans swore they would tear down it down.[23] Johnson Gardner, a free trapper traveling with Weber's party, saw it as an insult, so he took the U.S. flag and marched with twenty-five Americans to the British camp. He intended to trample their colors, and he bellowed that the British were in U.S. territory. He told the free trappers in the HBC camp that he would buy their pelts at $3.50 a pound, far more than the British were paying. Fourteen HBC trappers deserted and came over to Gardner's side with their furs.[24] Many of them felt mistreated; George Simpson had once referred to them as a "worthless and motley crew . . . the very scum of the country."[25]

The next morning Gardner again hoisted the flag and led a march to Ogden's tent, where he demanded, "Do you know whose country you are in?" When Ogden stated it was under joint occupancy, Gardner replied, "Remain at your peril." Gardner then persuaded John Gray, whom HBC considered "a turbulent blackguard, a damned rascal," to have all the Iroquois take down their lodges as if to leave. Gardner and the deserting trappers cocked their guns in support of the Iroquois. The Iroquois hurled insults and obscenities at the British as they left with their furs, insinuating they might even pillage the British camp one night. Ogden set a double watch on his diminished camp.

The following day the Americans and Iroquois rode into the British camp once again. Three more free trappers deserted.[26] Ogden rode away with what was left of his brigade, having lost twenty-three men, seven hundred beaver skins, and nearly his life. Bridger later well remembered how the trappers "drove the Hudson's Bay Company from American soil."[27] This would not be the last time Bridger found himself in competition with the Hudson's Bay Company.

By the summer of 1825, Bridger and his fellow trappers wondered when they would be able to buy blankets and britches. When would they taste sugar or coffee? In the two years since the Arikara fight, Bridger had wintered with the Crows, crossed the South Pass, trapped the Seedskedee, discovered the Great Salt Lake, and nearly fought a war with the British. There had been plenty of losses—boats, horses, supplies, and men. But now they had found beaver, and they had gathered thousands of pelts that they needed to be paid for.

The previous summer Thomas Fitzpatrick, along with trappers Branch and Stone, had tried to take pelts down the Sweetwater River by bullboat, but rapids made it impossible to float the heavy furs in buffalo-hide boats. When the river abruptly took two of their guns and all of their lead, they had to rip the brass from their remaining gun and pound it into rifle balls in order to survive. They finally reached Fort Atkinson and sent a message to Ashley that they had crossed the Continental Divide at South Pass in 1824 and taken a large number of furs.

Weber, Bridger, and the others trapping Bear River country wondered when they would be able to sell their pelts. They were rewarded when Zacharias Ham and seven others searched them out and told them there was to be a rendezvous where the trappers could turn in their beaver skins and get credit for their work. Andrew Henry was no longer a leader of the company, and William Ashley had come out with plenty of supplies to sell to them in exchange for their furs.

In early 1825 Ashley had led an overland caravan of twenty-five men and fifty pack horses west from St. Louis—a laborious and troubling winter journey following the South Platte across the plains.[28] They finally reached the Front Range near present-day Fort Collins, cut northwest toward the Laramie plains, and then rounded the Medicine Bow Mountains to reach the North Platte River. From there they proceeded westward, crossing the Divide just of south of present-day Rawlins, Wyoming. They reached the Green River in April 1825, where Ashley set up camp. He sent trapping parties in every direction with the additional task of finding company men and free trappers and tell them of the summer gathering.

In a land where rivers and buffalo trails were the primary pathways, Ashley needed to find more than one hundred scattered trappers. In addition to sending Zacharias Ham to Bear River country, Ashley sent James Clyman and six men north up the tributaries of the Green River to find trappers there. Thomas Fitzpatrick and six men went southwest to the Uinta Mountains to search for trappers. Ashley himself took seven men and made a harrowing journey in bullboats down the Green River, shooting frightening rapids and cataracts that would later be known as Flaming Gorge, Ashley Falls, and Disaster Falls.

The message Ashley disseminated across the mountains invited the trappers to come to a rendezvous, at a yet-undecided place, on or before July 10. As he sent his scouts out, Ashley told them he would transport the goods down the Green River to a "conspicuous point not less than 40 to 50 miles from this place." He told them the place of rendezvous would be marked by trees peeled of bark near a junction of rivers. If there was no timber, he would "raise a mound of earth five feet high or pile rocks to that height and paint the top red with vermillion. Thirty feet northwest from the pile of earth or rocks he would bury a letter with any further instructions."[29]

It worked! By the first of July 1825, 120 trappers were gathered in a lush bottomland on Henry's Fork, twenty miles above the Green River (near present-day McKinnon, Wyoming). There was plenty of water and beaver sign as well as abundant willows and large timber along the banks of the stream.[30] The camp of the trappers who came to celebrate their survival and reap the rewards of their labors resembled a small village: tents, campfires, bales of beaver pelts, and herds of horses covered the landscape. Ashley's clerks set up scales to weigh the beaver pelts and stands to sell the products they had hauled out from the East.

The company men opened their bales of goods and took payment in beaver pelts (sometimes jokingly called "hairy bank notes"): coffee and sugar at $1.50 a pound; knives at $2.50 each. Bridger could buy flints for $1 a dozen, powder at $1.50 a pound, and lead at $1 a pound. Prices were three times what these goods cost in St. Louis, but Bridger and the other trappers relished them at any price, knowing the financial and human cost of freighting them across the country. The beaver pelts he had trapped these many months were recorded by company clerks and valued at $3 a pound. The eager trappers could buy axes, kettles, tobacco, sewing silk, needles, ribbons, combs, earrings, soap, and sleigh bells.[31]

This first Rocky Mountain rendezvous marked the beginning of a new way to supply American trappers and collect their hauls. Bridger and the others would remain full-time hunters, spending the whole year in the mountains instead of taking time to travel to and from St. Louis each spring and fall. A supply caravan would come west each spring laden with goods and return to St. Louis with beaver skins.

Rendezvous was not a new concept. The Shoshones had long held summer trade gatherings. In the 1770s French voyageurs, trappers, and traders paddled the rivers from New Orleans, Montreal, Quebec, and other locations to gather for an annual trading fair at Prairie du Chien, in present-day Wisconsin. Ashley's contribution was bringing the rendezvous to the Rocky Mountains, and it became the primary trading event for the mountain men for the next fifteen years.

Rendezvous was not just a time to swap goods. For Bridger it was a connection to the life he had left behind some twelve hundred miles to the east. It was also a time for him to learn what had happened to fellow trappers who had been hunting other regions and what had transpired within the leadership of the company during the past year. They talked of Henry, who had quit the fur trade, and Ashley, who had run for governor of Missouri, only to lose by about five hundred votes.

Ashley was intrigued to learn about Bridger's report of a salt lake, and Jedediah Smith told Ashley that the lake was a "free and easy passage and abounding in Salt." Smith gave some specimens to Ashley, who felt they "equal[ed] in appearance and quality the best Liverpool salt," referring to the salt works in Liverpool, New York.[32] Jim Clyman, who was thought to be dead, came in alive but with most of his hair cut off. The Indian who had saved him asked for his locks as a memento.[33] They talked of Johnson Gardner and others driving the British off, and they planned their trapping strategy for next year.

They brought their pelts to the scales, and it was an enormous haul. Weber's party, which included Bridger, had the largest taking—3,100 pounds of beaver fur. Jedediah Smith and his six men brought in 668 pounds. Zacharias Ham's party had 461 pounds. Caleb Greenwood's party brought in 202 pounds.[34] When Ashley's clerk finished tabulating the returns at rendezvous and the furs that had already been cached, he counted 8,829 pounds of beaver skins, worth nearly $50,000 in St. Louis.[35] The wealthy in St. Louis built their expensive mansions for a fraction of that amount.

BRIDGER BRAVES
BAD PASS
1825

After the rendezvous of 1825, Jim Bridger was one of fifty men who guarded Ashley and his furs on their way north to the Yellowstone River. If they could get past the Shoshones, Blackfeet, and Crows, Ashley intended to meet Gen. Henry Atkinson's boats on the Yellowstone and float his four and a half tons of beaver pelts back to the settlements. Atkinson's keelboats were fitted out with paddlewheels to be manually turned by boatmen, a miserable experiment meant to be a show of strength and power after the Arikara fiasco.

Ashley had picked Jedediah Smith to replace Andrew Henry as partner and field captain, and Smith led thirty of the men directly toward the Yellowstone while Ashley took the remaining twenty to dig up furs that were cached near the Sweetwater River. Ashley's men retrieved the valuable pelts and moved to rejoin the main group. But sixty Blackfeet attacked Ashley's group one morning at daybreak, and their wild screaming spooked the trappers' horses, even though they were closely hobbled. The Blackfeet wounded one trapper and made off with fifty-three horses, leaving the Americans with only two.[1]

Ashley and his men were stuck. Without horses they couldn't move unless they abandoned their heavy furs. Ashley sent a message to Smith, and two days later Smith's men arrived with horses to carry the packs. By nightfall they had covered ten miles. Thinking they were safe, they posted guards and turned in. Bridger and the other trappers thought of the Crows as friends, but about midnight a war party of Crows attacked the trapper camp. The trappers killed one of the raiders, wounded another, and drove the rest away.[2]

Crow leader Sparrow Hawk came to the trappers the next morning and asked them if they had any scalps. Caleb Greenwood, who spoke their language fluently, said no, while Jim Beckwourth hid the scalp and leggings he had taken from the dead Crow raider. The trappers accompanied the Crows to their camp, and there a woman, covered with blood from her mourning ritual of self-cutting, demanded that Sparrow Hawk avenge her son's death. Sparrow Hawk persuaded Ashley to give her presents, and then told the woman, "Now go to your lodge and cease your crying."[3]

The trappers noticed some of their stolen horses among the Crows, and Sparrow Hawk admitted his men had stolen them. He explained, "I was tired with walking. You would have given me tobacco, but that would not carry me. When we stole them, they [the horses] were very poor; they are now fat. We have plenty of horses; you can take all that belong to you."[4] The Crows now claimed peace with the trappers, and the Indians and trappers traveled together, moving north along the path adjacent to the Bighorn River. Bridger saw rock cairns along the way; the Crows sometimes added stones to the piles they passed.

They came to a deep, narrow canyon called Bad Pass, and the brigade stopped to discuss their options. Some men took the opportunity to hunt. Before long, one of their horses returned unexpectedly with fresh buffalo meat on its back but no one in the saddle. They found its owner, Baptiste, bleeding beside a small stream and surmised he had stopped to take a drink and was attacked by a grizzly. They patched his flayed body the best they could and brought him back to camp. Not long afterward Bridger was surprised to see the grizzly run right through their camp, stampeding the horses into a wild frenzy until several trappers brought it down with multiple shots.

Ashley had hoped to float their pelts down the river but could see it would be a frightful passage. In fact, in 1805 the Crows told a French Canadian trader named François-Antoine Larocque that there was a Manitou "dwelling in the falls and raising out of it to devour any man or beast that approached." Larocque gazed down the perpendicular wall at Bad Pass and wrote, "It is aweful to behold and makes one giddy . . . so that I did not dare to look down upon the river, [until] I could find a stone behind which I could Keep [stand behind] and looking over it . . . see the foaming water without danger of falling in."[5] Another traveler heard that the Crows spoke of a place "where the river plunged into a subterranean tunnel which gave forth dreadful sighings and groanings."[6]

Ashley wanted the river route explored before he committed to it, and Bridger volunteered to make the journey and soon set off on a makeshift wooden raft. As he drifted downstream, the Bighorn suddenly came alive, thrusting him through a narrow chute and crashing his raft into boulders, sending up great sprays of foam. The rapids thrust him up and down, swirling him between two perpendicular banks of stone towering nearly two thousand feet overhead. The canyon had been created by significant erosion as well as uplift, and the cleft was so narrow that the sun shone into the canyon's bottom for only a short while each day. Dark, looming walls engulfed Bridger, making his raft and paddle seem pitifully small. If he called out, his words bounced off the winding canyon walls.

The rapids held Bridger in their grasp, and the young trapper locked in his own resolve. When he could, he rested his aching fingers from their white-knuckle grip. His clothes were soaked and heavy with water. The river's path narrowed, and the current quickened again, tossing his raft like a leaf. Large boulders divided the flow. When he entered a chute, he might come out of it backwards.

Finally, the Bighorn calmed, ending its gauntlet. Bridger had taken all the river had to offer and survived. He was the first trapper to have run the rapids at Bad Pass, a feat unequalled in western travels, except perhaps by Ashley's descent of the Green River earlier that year and John Wesley Powell's voyage much later down the Green and Colorado.[7] George Gibbs's copy of the Jedediah Smith map states, "Here the river runs for 40 miles through the mountains, the Gap but just wide enough for the river—with few exceptions on both sides precipices [are] 1000 feet high. In 1826 [1825] J. T. Bridger passed through on a raft."[8]

Bridger reported to back to Ashley: it was impossible to float their pelts through the rapids. The water route ruled out, the trappers and their animals carried their furs and supplies overland, and only after they passed the lower canyon did they build bullboats to take their precious cargo to the Missouri. Ashley and Smith planned to take the pelts to St. Louis aboard Atkinson's keelboats, which they expected would be far up the Missouri by then, a floating and marching demonstration to show the Arikaras, Sioux, and others the power of the United States.

Meanwhile, William Sublette was to lead the majority of the men west for a fall trapping brigade.[9] For the past two years Bridger had trapped under John Weber, but when Jedediah Smith replaced Andrew Henry as Ashley's partner, Weber left the mountains with a sour heart, feeling he had been "beaten out of what was then a fortune by dishonest partners."[10] He committed suicide during a spell of neuralgia in 1859, but his name lives on through the Weber River in northeastern Utah.

This moment marked a decision point for Bridger. He could ride the keelboat down to St. Louis and rejoin civilization. Or he could ride his horse west under William Sublette's leadership and spend more years in the mountains. Which place was home to Bridger now?

The newspaper ad in 1822 had read "to be employed for one, two or three years." It had been three years and then some. Would he now go home to see his sister at the American Bottom and Philip Creamer at his gun works? Or would he stay with the nomadic trappers in search of adventure? Bridger decided that his home, at least for now, was in the mountains, and he rode west under Sublette's command.

Bridger trapped the Bear River and its tributary, the smaller Cub River, and then gathered in Willow Valley as they had the previous winter. It was a hard winter. Snow piled eight feet deep, so they moved to the Salt Lake where there was little snow and plenty of buffalo.[11] They sharpened their meat with salt and mingled freely with the Shoshones.

During that winter of 1825–26, the Bannock Indians raided their camp, stealing eighty horses. Bridger and Tom Fitzpatrick led forty trappers on foot to retrieve the animals. This was the first time that twenty-one-year-old Bridger assumed a leadership role in a fight against raiding Indians. It was also the first time for twenty-six-year-old Thomas Fitzpatrick.[12]

After several days the men reached the Bannock camp and spotted their stolen animals. Bridger led some of the men into the camp to reclaim the horses, while Fitzpatrick and the rest fired on the camp to provide cover. When the sounds of Fitzpatrick's assault filled the night, Bridger and his men rushed to the horses and cut their ropes, stampeding as many as they could, including some horses from the Bannocks' herd.

Bridger and his men galloped away with the stampeding horses, and the Bannocks gave chase. The trappers escaped with their own horses and some Bannock animals as well, and they reunited with Fitzpatrick. Jim Beckwourth, a notorious exaggerator, claimed he was in Bridger's party and the trappers killed six Bannocks but did not suffer a scratch.

The trappers had built two dozen lodges to house themselves, about four men to a lodge. When Bridger, Fitzpatrick, and the rest of the men returned with their recovered horses, they saw that a village of Shoshones had erected a large number of lodges surrounding the trappers' lodges.[13] The Shoshones had come in peace with their families, horses, and dogs to spend the winter, and the trappers presented them with an American flag that they treasured as a sign of renewed friendship.

In the spring of 1826, Bridger's brigade moved back to Willow Valley, their animals laden with seventy-five packs of fur. They dug a cache to store their pelts, their shovels creating a rhythmic sound. They had excavated a sizeable vault when they heard an ominous rumbling.[14] A great mass of rock and dirt fell into the chamber, burying a man named Marshall.

"His companions *believed* him to have been instantly killed, *knew* him to be well buried, and the cache destroyed, and therefore left him 'unknelled, uncoffined, ne'er to rise, till Gabriel's trumpet shakes the skies.'"[15] After that incident Willow Valley was called Cache Valley. Beckwourth partnered with Marshall's widow and was pleased that she was "smart, trim and active, and . . . of great service to me in keeping my clothes in repair, making my bed, and taking care of my weapons."[16]

Not long after, the friendship between the trappers and the Shoshones was put to the test. One of the trappers shot an antelope. But as he approached with his butcher knife, he was shocked to find he had not killed an antelope but a Shoshone hunter wearing an antelope skin as a decoy. The worried hunter hurried to camp, and an emergency council of the trappers determined their only recourse was to leave before the Shoshones discovered the crime. They quickly began to dismantle their tents and tie packs onto their mules.

The surprised Shoshone chief asked why they were leaving. The trappers said they were going hunting, but they had trouble maintaining the deception. Fitzpatrick eventually explained that one of his men had killed one of the Shoshones, to which the chief replied, "Oh, if that is what you are alarmed at, take off your packs and stay. The Indian was a fool to use the decoy when he knew the antelope came into the sage every day, and that the white men shoot all they see."[17] The trappers gave the chief a scarlet cloth to wrap the body in and all seemed well again.

When the weather warmed, Bridger stayed in the valley of the salt lake with Sublette and his group. Sublette sent four men in a skin canoe around the perimeter of the Great Salt Lake, looking for its outlet. The men, surmised to be Henry Fraeb, James Clyman, Louis Vasquez, and Black Harris, nearly died of thirst because all the water was salty.[18] Bridger recalled the men "went out hunting and had their horses stolen by the Indians. They then went around the lake in canoes hunting beaver and were three months going around it."[19]

That spring Bridger likely accompanied Sublette and David Jackson's brigade to trap the land north and west of the Great Salt Lake. There Bridger may have explored again. A map by Jedediah Smith, who relied on Jackson to describe this region, shows a waterway called Bridger's Fork. The map notes, "This country is extremely rocky & rough, the river running through cleft rocks." Bridger's Fork is drawn flowing northwest toward the source of the Owyhee River in present-day Idaho. Later explorer John C. Frémont and geographer and former treasury secretary Albert Gallatin corresponded about the direction of Bridger's Fork.[20]

Soon it was time for the 1826 rendezvous, and they all looked forward to the annual bounty of goods and good times at Cache Valley (near present-day Logan, Utah). Bridger was one of many trappers who arrived with packs of pelts. Ashley and Smith appeared with the trade goods after a harrowing winter crossing of the plains. The streams fingered their way through the tall grasses of Cache Valley, providing an abundance of water and forage.

Here Bridger could trade his furs for blankets, guns, powder, and ball. For work he could buy traps, scalpers, scrapers, and axes. For pleasure he could trade his furs for sugar, coffee, tea, and alcohol. All of these items were also available to the Indians, as well as bells, scarlet cloth, mirrors, and other trinkets. They celebrated with "dancing, shouting, trading, running, jumping, singing, racing, target-shooting, yarns, frolic, with all sorts of extravagances that white men or Indians could invent." Beckwourth commented, "The unpacking of the *medicine water* contributed not a little to the heightening of our festivities."[21]

News that the trappers had crossed South Pass had created a stir back East. The Rocky Mountains no longer presented an unsurpassable obstacle to reaching the waters of the Pacific. This rediscovery of the pass by the trappers was a significant moment in the history of the American West, giving credence to the notion that the United States might expand into those lands. Both the British and the Americans, including Bridger, were trapping and hunting west of the Continental Divide on lands that belonged to indigenous peoples, and doing so in contradiction of the U.S. Indian Intercourse law of 1802. But neither Indian agent William Clark nor Secretary of War James Barbour took a strong stance against trapping on Indian holdings.[22]

Information flowed as rapidly among the trappers at rendezvous as the rivers they traveled. Bridger and others learned what had happened in the nation while they were so distant from it. The Erie Canal had opened, creating a water connection from the Atlantic coast to the Great Lakes. That year marked the fiftieth anniversary of the Declaration of Independence, and on the Fourth of July the trappers celebrated by firing three rounds and drinking toasts.[23] Two thousand miles to the east, ninety-year-old John Adams died that day in Massachusetts, saying, "Thomas Jefferson still lives." But Adams was wrong: for just hours earlier, eighty-three-year-old Jefferson had also breathed his last at his home at Monticello, Virginia.

Under Henry and Ashley's direction, Bridger and his fellow trappers had been active participants in revolutionizing the fur trade. With free trappers, overland routes, and the annual rendezvous, there was no need for established forts. The men were free to hunt the mountains year-round, and by living in lodges each winter, they were able to set traps each fall and spring, the prime trapping seasons. They could be resupplied each summer and only paid when they brought in pelts.

The trappers had amassed 125 packs of beaver pelts for the 1826 rendezvous, significantly more than the year before. Ashley sold his share of the fur company, transferring his mountain operations, animals, and supplies for $16,000 to a new partnership led by Jedediah Smith, David Jackson, and William Sublette.[24] Ashley held on to the most lucrative part of the business, however, which was supplying the trappers with goods from St. Louis. Ashley returned to St. Louis and in October, married Eliza Christy, and planned to build a fine mansion on the site of one of the prehistoric mounds in St. Louis.[25]

Smith, Jackson, and Sublette prepared for their summer and fall hunts, sending out the first brigades under their control. Smith led a party of fifteen men to explore and trap the route to California. He would be gone for a full year. William Sublette and David Jackson led the rest of the men north into Blackfeet country, where they sent out many brigades and perhaps even split into two camps. It was then, if not before, that Bridger became a forward scout for the trappers' brigades.

7

PILOT FOR THE
BRIGADES
1826–1830

Following the 1826 rendezvous, Bridger became one of the leaders in William Sublette's foray into the dangerous but beaver-rich lands of the Blackfeet. Over the past two years Bridger had proven his reliability and self-reliance through his solo exploration of Bear River to Great Salt Lake, his solo shooting of the rapids at Bad Pass, and his leadership with Fitzpatrick in retrieving the stolen horses from the Bannocks. Though Bridger was only twenty-two years old, he had four years' experience and was now one of the "spies" who were sent several miles ahead to scout the terrain and report any danger or possibility of attack. He would then signal his discoveries or report directly to the brigade leader.

Like many of the trappers, Daniel Potts was concerned for his safety that fall, and he expressed his worry in a letter to his brother. "I took my departure for the Black-foot Country much against my will as I could not make a party for any other rout. We took a northerly direction abut fifty miles where we crossed the Snake river or the South fork of the Columbia. . . . At this place we were dayly harrased by the Black-feet."[1]

The Sublette party trapped their way to Pierre's Hole (in present-day eastern Idaho), which offered stunning views of the Teton Range and its three prominent peaks. This became one of Bridger's favorite places. These peaks had been called the Pinnacles, the Pilot Knobs, the Three Paps, and the Three Brothers; the Shoshones called them Hoary Headed Fathers. But the romantic name that prevailed was the French "Trois Tetons" (meaning "three breasts"). (The name had earlier been attached to a formation on the Snake River plain that came to be called the Three Buttes.)[2]

The trappers crossed the mountains west to east, either through Conant Pass or Teton Pass, and came to the stunning valley on the eastern slope of the Tetons soon to be known as Jackson's Hole, after David Jackson. But the beauty of the setting was countered by the cunning of the Blackfeet who harried the American interlopers. From that high valley the brigade trapped north along the course of the Lewis River, a tributary of the Snake River. The land kept rising, and soon they stood six hundred feet above the river. The brigade eventually came across a huge alpine lake, refreshingly cool and remarkably blue. They called it Sublette's Lake; it would later be known as Yellowstone Lake.

On the western shore of that lake, Bridger saw that the earth itself seemed to bubble up. Great boils of mud churned from the earth, painting rich palettes of red, yellow, blue, pink, and green twenty-five feet high. Fountains in the lake crusted over and spurted vapor and hot spray.[3] Bridger later described several places where he could hear "subterranean noises" and see steam and "sulphurous flames" escaping from the earth.[4]

Their horses were skittish, their hooves echoing on the earth's crust. The ground erupted unexpectedly, shooting boiling water in a column. At one large geyser-hole they felt thunder exploding below them. It was as if they were at the top of the world and the bottom of the world at the same time. Daniel Potts felt the ground trembling beneath him and saw a geyser of "pure sulphor" erupt from the earth. He barely escaped a scalding.[5]

Indigenous peoples had known of these wonders for millennia. In 1805 James Wilkinson, then governor of Louisiana Territory, sent President Jefferson an American Indian map on a buffalo hide that depicted a volcano on the Yellowstone River.[6] John Colter saw thermal activity on the Shoshone River in 1807 after he returned from the Lewis and Clark's expedition, and Alexander McKenzie saw boiling fountains hot enough to cook meat in 1818.[7] In 1826 Sublette, Jackson, Bridger, Campbell, Potts, and others in their party were the first known Euro-Americans to penetrate what would later become Yellowstone Park.[8] Bridger was destined to explore the region many times.

In the 1820s and 1830s, this band of adventures, which included Bridger, became the most significant group of explorers ever assembled in North American history. They called themselves mountaineers, and Washington Irving described them: "A totally different class has now sprung up, 'the Mountaineers,' the traders and trappers that scale the vast mountain chains, and . . . move from

Indian Hospitality (c. 1858–1860), by Alfred Jacob Miller. This scene shows a trapper inside a Shoshone lodge about to enjoy a feast. The trappers became accustomed to Shoshone ways of communicating, trading, and courtship. *The Walters Art Museum, Baltimore*

place to place on horseback . . . heedless of hardship; daring of danger; prodigal of the present, and thoughtless of the future. . . . There is, perhaps, no class of men on the face of the earth . . . who lead a life of more continued exertion, peril, and excitement."[9]

The trappers were a family, and they relied on each other for survival. When a trapper was killed, they lost one of their own, and that loss was deepened by the knowledge that any one of them might be next. Their larger family included the Iroquois, Shoshones, Flatheads, Nez Percé, and Crows who often traveled and camped with them. Many trappers paired with Indian women and became fathers to a new generation of mixed-race children.

The trappers were constantly on alert, but there was always time for humor. One day, as the party was trapping the headwaters of the Missouri, Bridger saw smoke ahead and reported it to Sublette. Soon Bridger, Sublette, and Campbell were spurring their horses toward the site to determine if the smoke had come

Bull Boating (c. 1858–1860), by Alfred Jacob Miller. When rivers ran high, the trappers built bullboats out of buffalo hides and willow poles to cross treacherous waterways or float downstream. Bridger became an expert at constructing this type of boat. *The Walters Art Museum, Baltimore*

from Blackfeet who might attack them. But this time it was a false alarm. The campsite had been abandoned several weeks earlier, and all that was left were some still-smoldering logs. For a long time the incident became known in camp as "the battle of the burned logs."[10]

Smith, Jackson, and Sublette needed to place their order for rendezvous with the St. Louis traders by March 1, 1827. So on New Year's Day William Sublette, known as "Cut Face" (for a scar on his chin), and Black Harris, known as a man of "great leg" (for his many long-distance journeys), prepared to set out for a thousand-mile walk to St. Louis. They suffered bone-chilling cold and had to eat their pack dog. On the ninety-fourth day they arrived in St. Louis. Although they had arrived three days past the agreed-upon date, General Ashley still filled their order for the summer rendezvous.[11]

There was always danger. The 1827 rendezvous was at Bear Lake, and as the parties assembled, 120 Blackfeet attacked and killed a Shoshone man and his wife. William Sublette led trappers and Shoshones in response, and they killed six Blackfeet and wounded several others. Samuel Tullock was wounded so badly his hand withered until he could no longer use it.[12]

Jedediah Smith and his party had not come in from California and "had been given up as lost." But Smith and two others from his group finally arrived on July 3 after a year's absence, greeted by the firing of a small cannon.[13] They had crossed the Mohave Desert, reached Pueblo de Los Angeles, and then gone north to San Jose, amassing 1,500 pounds of beaver skins. Smith had left the furs and most of his men in California, and his small party crossed the Sierra Nevada, Salt Desert, and Great Basin to reach the Bear Lake rendezvous. Smith was the first Euro-American to lead a party overland to California as well as the first Euro-American to cross the Sierra Nevada (from the Spanish, *sierra*, the term for a range of mountains, and *nevada*, or "snowy.")

Bridger continued to play an important role for the fur company. He knew the mountain passes, where to find beaver, how to treat with the Indians, and how to keep his wits when under attack. Under the brigade's leaders and with scouts like Bridger, the trappers brought 7,400 pounds of beaver pelts to the 1827 rendezvous as well as 102 pounds of otter skins and 95 pounds of castoreum.

But trapping was just one skill the company leaders needed to prosper. They also needed to have a head for numbers. The sum of $22,690 was credited against Smith, Jackson, and Sublette's debt to Ashley. Ashley sold them $22,447 of supplies at high prices, and Smith, Jackson, and Sublette sold them at prices higher still to the trappers. One of Bridger's companions, Daniel Potts, complained, "There is a poor prospect of making much here, owing to the evil disposition of the Indians and the exorbitant price of goods."[14]

Rendezvous ended, and the trappers and traders scattered in several directions. Smith recruited eighteen men for a return journey to California. Hiram Scott, one of the party carrying the pelts east to St. Louis, became delirious and wandered away from his caravan with two other men. Nearly dead, his companions left him in order to save their own lives, and Scott crawled two miles before dying at the bluff above the Platte River that now bears his name.[15]

Profit and peril were two sides of the same coin in the mountains; although beaver were plentiful, the attacks by Indians to steal horses and pelts were deadly. Over the next year the Blackfeet killed three men at Red Rock Creek near the headwaters of the Jefferson River, including an Iroquois trapper, Pierre Tevani-tagon, for whom Pierre's Hole was named. Blackfeet also killed three men on the Portneuf River, including William Sublette's sixteen-year-old brother, Pinckney, whom Sublette had brought to the mountains to improve his poor health.[16] Blackfeet attacked Robert Campbell's brigade as it neared the 1828 rendezvous, again held on Bear Lake. The "balls flew like hail" as Campbell and another trapper raced their horses through the Blackfeet raiders to bring back ammunition and reinforcements.

The Blackfeet and Shoshones killed at least ten other men employed by Smith, Jackson, and Sublette in 1827 and 1828, with encounters at Godairs River, Little Lake, Shoshone country, Bad Pass, and Bear River.[17] In 1828 the trappers and traders brought in 7,107 pounds of beaver worth $35,811 in St. Louis.[18] Jedediah Smith never arrived from California that year, and again the partners worried about him and his party.

In the fall of 1828 Bridger piloted Robert Campbell's twelve-man brigade to Crow country. They hunted along the Powder, Tongue, and Bighorn rivers and then wintered with the Crows on Wind River under Long Hair, an eighty-year-old chief whose hair measured just under ten feet long. His people had to carry it for him as he walked. Bridger likely guided Campbell's brigade to Crow country again in 1829. In January Beckwourth decided to leave the brigade and live with the Crows, but he embellished his departure with an implausible tale of Bridger reporting the "painful news" of his death and the trappers mourning his loss.[19]

The 1829 rendezvous was held on the Popo Agie near the Wind River, and Campbell traded for 4,076 pounds of beaver pelts that he hauled back to the States. A second rendezvous of sorts happened that year at Pierre's Hole, where the mountain men were finally reunited with Jedediah Smith. He told them how the Mohaves had killed ten of his men in the summer of 1827 as they tried to cross the Colorado River in two shifts, and how the Kelawatset Indians had killed fifteen of his party on the Umpqua River along the Oregon coast in 1828.[20]

Bridger may have piloted Jedediah Smith and William Sublette in fall 1829 as they traveled the Snake River, the Missouri River headwaters, and the Yellowstone River.[21] On their way to winter camp in 1829 they crossed the mountains from the Yellowstone to the Bighorn, where the snow was so deep they had to break a path for their horses and mules. The animals still sank to their haunches in the snowdrifts. They lost a hundred animals from starvation and from being trapped in the snow.

At one juncture, Smith sent Black Harris to the top of a high peak to see if he could spot a route out of the mountains. When Smith asked him what he had seen, the irreverent Harris gave a "shocking oath" and said, "I saw the city of St. Louis, and one fellow taking a drink."[22] Finally, they reached winter camp on the Wind River. The bitter weather continued. The trappers had taken copious pelts and anticipated more in the spring, so on Christmas Day Sublette and Harris once again set out on another long walk to St. Louis to put in an order for goods for rendezvous.

It had been a challenging two years. Any connection with the States was to be taken advantage of, so Sublette and Harris planned to carry letters to loved ones back home. Bridger was not able to write and probably had little communication with his sister by then, if she was even still alive. But the letters of Jedediah Smith help tell the story.

On Christmas Eve Smith scratched out a letter telling his mother and father. "I feell the need of the wach & care of a Christian Church. . . . Our Society is of the Rougest kind." He wrote his brother, "Many Hostile indans inhabit this Space. . . . We have Many dangers to face & many difficulties to encounter." Smith had done well financially and sent his brother a draft for $2,200 to give to charity or put toward their brothers' education, saying that he would "face every danger" so that he might help those in need.[23]

It was obvious to Bridger and the rest of the men on Wind River that they could not find enough forage for their horses and would soon be counting the animals' ribs. To reach a valley where their horses could survive, they would have to cross the mountains. On New Year's Day 1830 they began their journey, trudging through deep snow by day and huddling around fires by night. By mid-January they reached Powder River, the paradise they had hoped for.

Buffalo roamed thick in the cottonwoods and grazed into camp, a walking feast coming right up to the cook fires. They had to post double guards to keep the buffalo from trampling their lodges. Bridger and others regularly gathered cottonwood bark for their horses, carrying branches to camp, making draw knives to strip the bark, and bringing the shavings to the horses, which crowded each other to get to the nutritious peelings.[24]

They shattered the solitude of winter with the echo of axes, the braying of the mules, and the whoop of the mountaineers. They told epic tales of adventure and filled the night with stories, some of them true. Smoke floated in a haze above their fires as they tried to retell from memory the storylines of their favorite books. Joe Meek, a Virginian who had come to the mountains the previous summer, learned to read while sitting at the campfire, He labored over "an old copy of Shakespeare, which, with a bible, was carried about with the property of the camp."[25]

The ice broke in April, and the trappers set out to cross the mountains with Smith as their captain and Bridger as pilot. Bridger led them to the Tongue River and then the Bighorn. A heavy snowfall made travel difficult, and Bovey's Fork of the Bighorn River quickly rose from the runoff. They led their animals into the swift current, but it proved too strong for them and swept many away. The animals gasped for air and screamed in panic, and the mountaineers struggled to not be pulled away with them. Thirty horses drowned and three hundred traps went down with them, a significant loss to the trapping brigade.

Bridger led them west over a low range through Pryor's Gap to Clark's Fork, the Rosebud, and finally the Yellowstone River, which was still high in its banks. They made bullboats by stretching buffalo hides over willow frames and floated themselves and their gear across. Bridger then took them to the Musselshell and the Judith rivers, where Henry's men had trapped their first season in the mountains in 1822. As always, the Blackfeet were a constant presence, harassing the trappers and stealing traps and horses.

When they reached the Bighorn, a party of men under Samuel Tullock tried to excavate a cache of furs. The overhead soil caved in on Meek and a Frenchman named Glaud Ponto, who often spent his money on riotous behavior. Their companions dug the trappers out of the caved-in cache, only to find Meek seriously injured and poor Glaud Ponto dead. He was "rolled in a blanket and pitched into the river."[26] This was the same Ponto who two years earlier had returned to St. Louis from the 1828 rendezvous to find that his brother had died. He told his companions, "I am mighty glad my brudder died and I got his fine clothes."[27]

Despite the deadly accident, Tullock got his pelts and joined the other trappers as they headed for the 1830 rendezvous. Bridger looked forward to the gathering but had no idea of the good fortune that lay in his future.

PARTNER IN THE ROCKY MOUNTAIN FUR COMPANY
1830–1832

Bridger knew the 1830 rendezvous was planned for the junction of Wind and Popo Agie rivers, and he piloted Smith's trappers there with their loads of pelts and thirst for liquor, coffee, sugar, and other treats. What he likely didn't know was that he would be asked to become part owner of the company. Bridger was young and strong, forthright and determined. Now twenty-six years old, he had explored new lands, led men in battle, and piloted brigades.

William Sublette arrived from St. Louis with ten wagons and two Dearborn carriages, the first wheeled vehicles to cross South Pass to the west side of mountains. He also brought twelve head of cattle and a milk cow. Among the mail he carried was a letter to Jedediah Smith informing the homesick captain that his mother had died the previous winter. She may not have even seen his letter to her from the previous Christmas.

Davey Jackson's brigade came in from Snake River with more returns. Indians and free trappers camped nearby, also eager for whiskey and other delights. There were thousands of horses and hundreds of men. The grass was plentiful, and the streams offered ample water. Joe Meek put it plainly: "Beaver, the currency of the mountains, was plenty that year, and goods were high accordingly. A thousand dollars a day was not too much for some of the most reckless to spend on their squaws, horses, alcohol, and themselves. . . . Pure alcohol was what they 'got tight on'; and a desperate tight it was, to be sure!"[1]

Smith, Jackson, and Sublette had made Ashley enormously wealthy, and now they were generating wealth for themselves. But over the previous three years, they had lost forty-four men. Though they had lost nearly $44,000 in animals, traps, and furs, this year's profit was more than $17,500 for each of them.[2] But the American Fur Company, the brainchild of John Jacob Astor and one of the wealthiest companies in the world, was setting its sights on the Rocky Mountain fur trade. Jedediah Smith was leaving the Rockies, and William Sublette and Davey Jackson were of the same mind.[3]

They sold their business to Tom Fitzpatrick, the Irish entrepreneur; Jim Bridger, the trail-blazing Virginian; Milton Sublette, the bold Kentuckian; Henry Fraeb, the sturdy German; and Jean Baptiste Gervais, the energetic French Canadian. The new partners called their enterprise the Rocky Mountain Fur Company, and the new booshways would become better known as Broken Hand, Old Gabe, Thunderbolt, Frapp, and Jervey.

Fitzpatrick, originally from County Cavan, had come up the Missouri with Ashley in 1823. He was a fearless leader and an excellent businessman. Fitzpatrick would be the main navigator of their financial interests and would make several trips to and from St. Louis, leaving Bridger and the other partners to lead the trapping brigades.

By 1830 Jim Bridger was an eight-year mountain veteran. He knew the land better than almost all of them, and he knew how to treat with the Indians and keep company men and free trappers in line. What skills he lacked with words and numbers he made up in frontier knowledge, audacity, and bravery.

Milton Sublette, William's brother, had trapped the Santa Fe and Taos country and had defended himself against Comanches, Apaches, Mohaves, and Blackfeet. When Tom Smith was wounded by Indians and couldn't amputate his useless foot himself, he turned to Milt Sublette to cut through his Achilles tendon, thus helping Peg-leg Smith earn his new nickname.[4] Milt had come to the northern Rockies with his brother William in 1829 and led the previous fall's brigade with Fraeb and Gervais.[5]

Fraeb and Gervais seemed to travel in the same parties. Henry Fraeb was one of four trappers who had circumnavigated the Salt Lake in 1826. His heavy German accent colored every word he said. William Sublette had chosen him along with his brother Milt and Gervais to lead the previous year's hunt on the Bighorn.

Jean Baptiste Gervais, a French Canadian, had been with Northwest Company, moved to the Hudson's Bay Company, and then had deserted that enterprise under

Ogden in 1825. He was with American trappers in 1828 in the Snake River country and was likely with Campbell and Bridger when they trapped the Crow country[6]

The profits and losses of this new partnership were now theirs to own. They purchased horses, blankets, knives, traps, lead, powder, flints, liquor, and other goods from Smith, Jackson, and Sublette, agreeing to pay them $15,532 in fourteen months. Bridger was not just pilot now, but co-owner. He clearly saw the trail ahead and knew they had two opponents—the Blackfeet and the American Fur Company.

John Jacob Astor had chartered the American Fur Company in 1808 and was determined to control the entire trade. He partnered with Bernard Pratte and Company—which included Pierre Chouteau Jr., who was from one of the founding families of St. Louis—to gain a stronghold on the Missouri. By 1826 the St. Louis interests were operating Astor's western department. By 1830 Astor controlled most of the fur trade west of the Missouri, having bought out rivals or put them out of business through stiff competition. Bridger's company, the Rocky Mountain Fur Company, was now in his sites as "the opposition."

In the spring and summer of 1830, Chouteau sent Lucien Fontenelle, Joseph Robidoux, and Andrew Drips to the mountains with trappers and trade goods, intending to take the fur trade away from the Rocky Mountain Fur Company.[7] The thirty American Fur Company men crossed the Green River in bullboats, searching in vain for the rendezvous. They never found the gathering, so they cached their trade goods along Ham's Fork and set out trapping in three directions.

Bridger knew where to find beaver, and Fitzpatrick understood the free trapper and rendezvous system that Ashley and his successors had developed to near perfection. When rendezvous broke up, Bridger, Fitzpatrick, and Milt Sublette led eighty trappers toward the Three Forks, which lay in the heart of Blackfeet country, while Fraeb and Gervais led thirty-four men to the Snake River country.[8]

When they traveled, Bridger, Fitzpatrick, and Sublette typically rode at the head of the column, followed by the clerks and their pack animals loaded with small trunks on their flanks that contained company ledgers, accounts, and contracts. The brigade might stretch out for more than a quarter mile. Behind the clerks came the camp keepers, each leading several pack animals. Most animals carried a pack on each side and a third balanced in between on their backs.

The trappers and hunters rode next, leading additional animals that carried their traps and personal effects. Then came the Indian women and children of the trappers, riding their own mounts. A sharp lookout rode at the rear, alert for attacks and keeping stragglers in line. The mountaineers found plenty of beaver, but mosquitoes pestered them, and the Blackfeet stole their traps and horses. They retreated to the safety of the Yellowstone River, where they wintered.

As their predecessors had been doing for several years, Fitzpatrick and a companion set out for St. Louis in March 1831 to order supplies for that year's rendezvous, likely boating down the Yellowstone and then the Missouri. Bridger and Sublette took their men south to the Tongue River for the spring hunt. On their third night out, the Crows saw the trappers' horses feeding on dry grass in a little bottom and drove off fifty-seven head. Most of the remaining horses belonged to freemen (trappers not affiliated with any company). Several trappers, led by Antoine Godin, tracked the Crows on foot and recovered the stolen horses.[9]

From Tongue River, Bridger and Sublette took their trappers to the Powder, where the group separated. Sublette followed the North Platte, and Bridger led his men to the head of Laramie's Fork. Mornings typically began with one or two "spies" galloping out at full speed to check the ravines and gullies for distances of up to half a mile, making sure no raiders were lying in wait. When all was safe, Bridger called the camp to turn out. The men let their horses out to graze and the camp turned to breakfast and preparations for the day. Then they broke camp and dispersed into the wild to collect their beaver and lay new sets. As the main camp moved forward, the booshway continued to send spies to investigate thickets and defiles where an enemy might hide.[10]

In the summer of 1831 Bridger's and Sublette's parties met up again at New Park and moved west to Bear River, near Salt Lake, to wait for Fitzpatrick and the anticipated supply caravan.[11] But Fitzpatrick didn't appear. Bridger, Sublette, Fraeb, and Gervais all reported good hunts. Hundreds of free trappers and Indians had gathered at the rendezvous to trade. The partners had a year's worth of beaver to sell. But they worried about Fitzpatrick after several weeks passed with no sign of him.

Rocky Mountain Fur Company had few goods to induce the free trappers to part with their pelts. Blankets and knives were scarce. Tobacco had given out. They had no alcohol. They purchased what furs they could with leftover beads and shiny mirrors, but it was not much of a rendezvous. Fortunately for Bridger's company, their competitor American Fur was also late that summer and was not able to trade for the freemen's furs.

According to Joe Meek, Henry Fraeb traded horses to a Crow shaman, a holy man, to tell them where Fitzpatrick was. The medicine man spent several nights "singing, dancing, hopping, screeching, beating of drums, and other more violent exercises and contortions," and then fell asleep. When he awoke he told them that Fitzpatrick was not dead. He was on the road, but not the right road. Fraeb took a small party to search for the lost booshway.[12]

Under pressure to reduce their growing debt, Bridger and Sublette had no choice but to organize their fall hunt with poorly supplied men. Unable to write, Bridger would let the others worry about records and accounts. He would worry about the Blackfeet and the beaver. He led the trappers from Bear River to Gray's Fork, where they fought with the Blackfeet. They trapped the Snake and the Salmon rivers, from there pushed on to the Deer Lodge River, and then went north to the headwaters of the Flathead River, which they believed to be a fork of the Missouri but later learned was a tributary of the Columbia.[13] Every season the mountaineers learned more about the rivers and mountain passes.

As the leaves turned, Bridger brought the brigade back to the Salmon, and they reunited with Fraeb at the camp of the Flathead Indians. Fraeb and Fitzpatrick had found each other, and Fraeb took charge of Fitzpatrick's forty men and the pack-laden horses and brought the goods to the trappers in Cache Valley.[14] When Fraeb arrived, he relayed to Bridger and the other partners the story of Fitzpatrick's journey.

Fitzpatrick had left the previous March 1831 to purchase supplies for rendezvous, but he was late and only got as far as Lexington, Missouri, where he met Smith, Jackson, and Sublette. They had given up on him and were leading a caravan loaded with goods they intended to trade at Santa Fe. The best the traders could do was take Fitzpatrick with them to Santa Fe and let him buy what goods he might find there. Fitzpatrick had taken the road to Santa Fe—the wrong road, as the Crow shaman had said. The caravan ran out of water in the desert between the Arkansas and Cimarron rivers, and they scouted for water in various directions.

Smith and Fitzpatrick rode south together, but they too ultimately separated: Fitzpatrick to dig for water in a dry hollow and Smith to see if he could find water three miles farther on. Jedediah Smith was never seen again. Jackson, Sublette, Fitzpatrick, and the rest went on to Santa Fe. Mexican traders eventually showed up with Jedediah's pistols, saying they had gotten them from the Comanches. They said the Indians had been lying in wait for buffalo to come to a waterhole along the Cimarron when Smith wandered into their trap, and they killed him. Thirty-two-year-old Jedediah Smith, who had escaped so many harrowing events, was dead.[15]

Fitzpatrick purchased $6,000 of supplies from Sublette and Jackson in Taos, promising that he and his partners would pay them "good clean, well handled mountain fur" at Taos to be valued at $4.25 a pound.[16] Fitzpatrick hired forty men and started north, meeting Fraeb on the Platte River and transferring the men and goods to him. Fitzpatrick then headed back to St. Louis to prepare a supply caravan for next year's rendezvous.

Even though the caravan was late, trapper Warren Ferris recalled that the 1831 rendezvous "presented a confused scene of rioting, and debauchery for several days, after which however, the kegs of alcohol were again bunged, and all became tranquil. . . . We purchased all the dried meat the Indians could spare, together with robes, and '*appishimous*,' square pieces of robes used under our saddles in travelling, or under our beds in camp."[17]

Jedediah Smith was dead, but in 1831 another force entered Bridger's life, a twenty-one-year-old scrapper who had come up from Taos with Fitzpatrick. Like Bridger, he had apprenticed as a youth, in his case to a Missouri saddle-maker. He had run off before his apprenticeship was done, and his master fulfilled the legal requirements by posting a reward of one cent for his return in the Franklin *Missouri Intelligencer*.[18] His name was Christopher Carson, and he was five years younger than Bridger. He would trap and fight under Bridger for much of the next decade.

Carson had some schooling, but he abandoned it for a life of adventure, later telling Jessie Frémont, "I was a young boy in the school house when the cry came, 'Indians!' I jumped to my rifle and threw down my spelling book, and there it lies."[19] He went to the southwest, trapped the Colorado, sold beaver at Pueblo de Los Angeles, and used the skin of a dead horse to carry water across the desert.

During the winter of 1831–32, Bridger settled his mountaineers into quarters with the Nez Percé and the Flatheads. Chief Insula of the Flatheads, a skilled horseman, wore an eagle feather in his hair and was also known as the War Eagle's Plume or Red Feather. When Insula saw some of Bridger's men leaving their goods lying about the camp, he ordered that none of his people steal them. His men should steal only from other tribes, not from those who camped together. The Flatheads maintained that they had never killed a white man and did not fight except in defense, for they were taught "never to go out to hunt their own graves." They also were known for their faithfulness in marriage.[20]

The Euro-Americans called them Flatheads based on sign language that signified they did not deform their heads into a slope like Salish peoples on the Pacific coast.[21] The Flatheads and Nez Percé wanted peace and trade with the whites. They had just sent four men from their tribes to St. Louis to meet with William Clark and others to ask for instruction in the white man's religion.

In the spring of 1832 Bridger new exactly where to go and led the trappers to
Henry's Fork, up the Snake River, then to the Salt River and Grey's Fork, before
heading south to the Bear River.[22] He knew the beaver fields well, while the competing American Fur trappers, led by Henry Vanderburgh and Andrew Drips,
were at a loss to know what streams would produce the best hunts. With almost
unlimited financial resources and a trading post on the upper Missouri supplied
by steamboats, American Fur trappers had everything but the knowledge of
where to find beaver. So they figured they would just follow Bridger.

Bridger wanted to "shake the dust from off their feet" but found that Vanderburgh followed them everywhere. Two brigades crowded into beaver fields
only big enough for one. Vanderburgh used his abundant supply of goods to
attract the Indian trade and tempt some of Rocky Mountain Fur's men away.
They also tried to ferret out the location of the next rendezvous—a secret known
only within Rocky Mountain Fur.[23]

During their travels Milt Sublette got into a fray with John Gray, a former
Hudson's Bay Iroquois trapper who thought Sublette had insulted his daughter.
Gray stabbed Sublette so severely many thought he would die. They bandaged
him as best they could, but his wounds left Bridger to lead the brigade alone. Joe
Meek stayed with the ailing booshway, and, when Sublette was able to travel,
they set out to find Bridger. Sublette and Meek were captured by a rogue band
of Shoshones who wanted to kill them. A Shoshone known as Good Gotia and a
comely woman named Mountain Lamb helped the trappers escape. They rejoined
Bridger's camp, and Mountain Lamb became Milt Sublette's wife.[24]

When the Rocky Mountain Fur brigade arrived at Pierre's Hole for the 1832
rendezvous, American Fur was right behind them. Skin lodges and campfires
spread across the central portion of the valley, and the trappers saw the sun rising
each morning over the Tetons. Bridger was always energized in Pierre's Hole with
its snowcapped peaks and mountain streams. Years later, when Bridger guided
topographical engineer William Raynolds there, the captain wrote that Pierre's
Hole "almost deserves the extravagant praise bestowed upon it by Bridger."[25]

Rocky Mountain Fur Company had brought in enough pelts to make a substantial payment on their debt—if their supplies arrived first. Four of the five
partners were there—Bridger, Fraeb, Gervais, and the wounded Milt Sublette.
A hundred company trappers waited eagerly for the caravan. Vanderburgh and
Drips camped nearby with ninety American Fur trappers, hoping their caravan would arrive first. Free trappers were there as well, as were a few Hudson's

Bay men. The skin lodges of five hundred Flatheads and Nez Percé dotted the grassland on the outskirts.

Bridger and his partners were desperate for their pack train. They had already foregone last year's trading profits when Fitzpatrick was sidetracked on the wrong road. This year he was on his way overland from St. Louis with William Sublette and the trade goods. American Fur had shipped its goods by steamboat to Fort Union (near the confluence of the Missouri and the Yellowstone), and Lucien Fontenelle was packing them overland from there. Whoever got there first would reap the rewards. Bridger's personal fortune and the company's fate rested in the balance.

9

EAGLE RIBS AND THE BLACKFEET

1832

By the summer rendezvous of 1832, Jim Bridger and Tom Fitzpatrick were tired of being constantly followed. They rode to the American Fur camp and offered to split the mountains, each taking their own portion. Vanderburgh refused.[1] Vanderburgh, a veteran brigade leader, was known as fearless yet cautious, courageous but cool.[2] American Fur Company's goal, in Pierre Chouteau's words, was "écraser toute opposition"—erase the opposition—and they could withstand temporary losses in exchange for greater returns in the future.[3]

Meanwhile, change was underway in the east. The new Baltimore and Ohio Railroad had carried 80,000 passengers in the last year, and the railroads would soon cross the Alleghenies. President Jackson and Congress were forcing the Cherokee out of their Appalachian homeland to land west of the Mississippi. But in the mountains of the West, the world's hunger for beaver pelts kept men like Bridger and his partners distant from what was happening in the states.

The free trappers didn't care which caravan arrived at rendezvous first. They just wanted goods and whiskey.[4] Milton Sublette sent out two riders to find Rocky Mountain Fur's caravan. They returned in a few days, on foot and bereft, robbed by the Crows. It was another week before the Rocky Mountain Fur caravan arrived at rendezvous, but they were still ahead of American Fur's supply caravan.

As had happened the year before, Tom Fitzpatrick was nowhere to be found. He had gone ahead of William Sublette and the caravan but had not shown up at rendezvous. Fitzpatrick or no, the booshways began trading whiskey for beaver pelts. Four hundred mountaineers and one thousand Indians had gathered at this rendezvous, and many competed with each other in feats of horsemanship, strength, skill, and foolish behavior.[5] One trapper carried alcohol in a cooking kettle as if it was holy water and baptized a red-headed trapper. Another trapper touched a lighted stick to him, and he caught fire. Some laughed while others beat the flames with blankets and pack saddles until he was extinguished.

The gaunt figure of Tom Fitzpatrick finally arrived at rendezvous. He had been chased by the Gros Ventres and retreated up a mountain. With only one shot left for his rifle, he hid in a hole in a rock wall covered by brush. He crept out that night only to find that the Gros Ventres had camped all about him. Quickly sliding back into the hole, he watched in panic as the guard roamed close for the rest of the night. The Gros Ventres finally left the next morning, and Fitzpatrick set out for rendezvous, arriving several days later. His hair had turned white.

William Sublette brought not only one hundred stubborn mules but one hardheaded Yankee as well. Nathaniel Wyeth was a Boston ice merchant who had convinced two dozen New Englanders to join his Pacific Trading Company and take furs from the Rocky Mountains to the mouth of the Columbia River. He provided each of his emigrants with a uniform: "a coarse woollen jacket and pantaloons, a striped cotton shirt, and cowhide boots."[6]

Wyeth had invented a boat that could travel on wheels and built three of them, each thirteen feet long. Some laughingly called the contraption "a boat begot on a wagon—a sort of mule, neither horse nor ass." They transported these "Nat-wye-thiums" from Boston to St. Louis, where he realized they would not do and sold them for half their cost." The group joined William Sublette's caravan, but when they reached rendezvous, more than half deserted, disgusted with Wyeth's autocratic leadership. But Wyeth was thinking of a way to partner with the Rocky Mountain Fur Company.

The future of the company relied on three factors: surviving Indian attacks, stopping cutthroat competition from American Fur, and avoiding financial servitude to William Sublette. The last of these was where they were losing money. They had 169 packs of beaver pelts, roughly 13,000 pounds, which were worth over $58,000 in St. Louis. But even that was not enough to pay what they owed. They had the original debt of $15,532 from 1830, plus $6,000 for goods purchased in Santa Fe in 1831, plus another $15,620 for goods just received at the 1832 rendezvous. Added to that was $10,318 for back wages and notes, $7,070 to transport their furs to St. Louis, a $1,500 commission to William Ashley (now a congressman), and interest on their debt. When it was all calculated, they still owed William Sublette $5,400.[7]

Milton Sublette and Henry Fraeb led a brigade out from rendezvous, going nine miles south, which was far enough to keep the men away from liquor. At dawn Milt noticed the dust of a large party, and his spyglass revealed it was a traveling village of some two hundred Gros Ventres, led by Chief Biahoh. The hand sign naming these people was flowing hands, signifying that they came from the land of waterfalls. But when one made this sign in front of the stomach, it was misinterpreted as "big bellies," or "*gros ventres*" in French. Because the Gros Ventres spoke the Blackfeet language with strangers, the trappers mistakenly considered them part of the Blackfeet Confederacy.[8]

Biahoh rode forward wrapped in a bright scarlet blanket. Antoine Godin and a Flathead Indian rode out from the trappers' side to meet them. Godin had lost his Iroquois father to the Blackfeet two years earlier and saw this as his chance for revenge. His Flathead companion also wanted revenge: the Blackfeet had recently killed many of his people in a horse raid.

Godin asked if his companion's rifle was charged. The Flathead said that it was, and Godin told him to cock it and follow him. When Biahoh held out his hand in friendship, Godin grasped it and shouted the order for the Flathead to fire. The shot was point blank, and Biahoh fell. Godin grabbed the chief's scarlet blanket in glee and raced back to the safety of the trappers while shots rained about them. Soon both sides were shooting and looking for cover.

Milton Sublette sent a messenger back to rendezvous with a plea for help. His brother William armed himself several times over, and he and Campbell shouted their last will and testament to each other as they raced to battle. When they arrived, they saw the Gros Ventres had built a breastwork of logs, saddles, timber, and packs.[9]

William Sublette correctly assumed that these were the same Gros Ventres who had stolen their horses and tried to kill Fitzpatrick just a few weeks earlier. He addressed the forty or fifty trappers and the two small bands of Flatheads and Nez Percé. Campbell later recalled Sublette's stirring encouragement: "And now boys, here are the Black Feet who have killed so many of your companions;—who have probably been prowling around us for several days, waiting a favorable chance of attacking us, when they believed us unprepared."[10] They raised the war whoop, and a small group crawled to the breastwork on their hands and knees as bullets hailed around them.

A man called Sinclair called out, "I am shot!—oh God—take me to my brother." A trapper named Phelps was wounded in the thigh. William Sublette spied an Indian firing from a hole in the breastwork and tried to hit him whenever he peered through. "Watch that place," he said to Campbell, "and you'll have a fair chance." A ball fractured Sublette's left arm and passed out under the shoulder blade. That same ball may have hit another trapper in the head. Sublette tried to continue, then wheeled and dropped to his knees. Campbell carried him out of the thicket.[11]

Tom Fitzpatrick took up the charge and kept the fort under siege. Zenas Leonard and four others crawled toward the fort. Two of the approaching trappers were killed and another was shot through the foot.[12] One of Fraeb's men crawled flat on the ground toward the fort, pushing a great log in front of his head. The Gros Ventres shot rifle balls into the log until the man behind it was pinned behind a tree. A Canadian trapper crawled to the Gros Ventre wall and raised his head above the top. Two balls pierced his forehead, and he pitched off the wall with an agonizing scream.

The trappers retreated, and long-distance marksmanship became the game. Once in a while a Flathead or Nez Percé rushed up to the breastwork and dislodged a log or a buffalo robe as a trophy. The trappers began to collect dry wood and brush to burn the Gros Ventres out, but the Nez Percé argued that the fire would destroy the bounty of robes, blankets, and other plunder that was sure to be theirs. The Gros Ventres chief taunted them in this way: "So long as we had powder and ball, we fought you in the open field: when those were spent, we retreated here to die with our women and children. You may burn us in our fort; but, stay by our ashes, and you who are so hungry for fighting, will soon have enough. There are four hundred lodges of our brethren at hand. They will soon be here—their arms are strong—their hearts are big—they will avenge us!"[13]

This was translated through the trapper ranks, and somehow it got twisted into the message that the trappers still at rendezvous were being slaughtered. Fraeb immediately mounted his horse and raced back to rendezvous, and other trappers followed. When they arrived back at the main camp, they found it wasn't under attack at all. By the time they returned to the battle the next morning, the Gros Ventres had abandoned their fort, leaving the bodies of ten warriors. Thirty-two horses and several dogs lay as lumps, dead or dying. One Gros Ventre woman mourned next to the body of her husband. The trappers admired her courage and argued to save her, but a Nez Percé raised his ax and killed her.

Lead was valuable, so trappers used their knives to retrieve the flattened lead balls from the trees, working most of the morning on the pock-marked timber. They found Fitzpatrick's horses that had been stolen two weeks earlier. They returned to camp, buried their dead, and built horse pens around the graves to conceal the burials from Indian scavengers. Dr. Jacob Wyeth treated the wounded, applying a salve to and wrapping William Sublette's broken arm.[14]

Milton Sublette and Gervais packed up again for the southwest. Wyeth and his Oregon settlers set out in the same general direction. William Sublette prepared to leave for the States, carrying two years' haul of precious furs to sell for the struggling Rocky Mountain Fur Company. Bridger and Fitzpatrick and sixty men saddled their mounts for Blackfeet country as great balls of hail rained down on them. They took cover and watched the ice balls ricochet off their horses' backs. The hailstorm lasted a full hour, as if an omen of the coming trouble with the Blackfeet. From Pierre's Hole they rode north and cached their goods on the Salmon and then, according to Tom Fitzpatrick's reckoning, went farther north in Blackfeet country "than a company of whites ever has been before in search of beaver but found them much scarcer than I had any idea of."[15]

Meanwhile, Vanderburgh and Drips had gone to the Green River to get their supplies from Fontenelle. Then they picked up Bridger and Fitzpatrick's trail on the Dearborn River, a tributary of the Missouri in central Montana. They and their 112 men only caught five packs of pelts, and from that point on they followed and camped next to Bridger and Fitzpatrick.[16] There were no printed maps for the trappers. But the mountains and passes were etched in Jim Bridger's mind. His knowledge of the land was what American Fur Company did not have, and their only recourse was to follow him.

Bridger and Fitzpatrick led their brigade over the Divide, and American Fur followed. There were so many trappers they were stripping the streams bare and scaring the game. When a hunter shot a bear or an elk, the entire company had to pick the lone carcass to the bone, and they supplemented their food with beaver. Bridger and Fitzpatrick changed course. So did American Fur. Everywhere the Rocky Mountain Fur brigade went, American Fur followed. If Rocky Mountain Fur didn't make their hunt, they could go bankrupt.

Bridger and Fitzpatrick ordered their men to leave the campfires burning and slipped away. Vanderburgh's scouts figured it out and followed them. Fitzpatrick led the pack horses and camp keepers in one direction, while Bridger led the trappers another, wading through miles of streams to hide their tracks. But American Fur found them.

With little other recourse, Bridger and Fitzpatrick determined they would now lead American Fur on an unprofitable hunt. They rode to the Three Forks, deep in Blackfeet country, but did not stop to set a single trap. Vanderburgh and Drips hurried their trappers after them, not wanting to lose their guide; it was a wild goose chase, and Rocky Mountain Fur was the goose in charge. Snow fell over the September blooms, and sleet pelted their faces. One morning fifteen inches of snow clogged the trail, and it was deeper yet in the mountains. The sun melted the snow, overflowing the streams. Still, wherever Bridger and Fitzpatrick went, Vanderburgh and Drips followed.[17]

Finally, Vanderburgh and Drips understood they were gaining nothing by following. Vanderburgh struck out on his own with fifty men on the Madison River. Drips, traveling with his Indian wife, Mary, and their newborn, led the rest of their men to the Jefferson. That left Bridger and Fitzpatrick to trap on the Gallatin. Now there was a brigade trapping on all three forks of the Missouri, and there were two bands of Blackfeet close by, the Piegans and the Bloods.

Vanderburgh was the first to fall. On the Madison his party came across a smoldering fire and buffalo carcasses and immediately took caution. As they crossed a dry ravine, "suddenly the lightning and thunder of at least twenty fusils burst . . . from the gully."[18] They shot Vanderburgh's horse, and it fell on him, pinning him to the ground. Vanderburgh killed one of the attackers, but before his men could come to his aid, a Blackfeet smashed him with his tomahawk, and a volley of bullets finished the job. Led by a warrior named Eagle Ribs, the Blackfeet shot another horse, which threw its rider, and they killed him, too. A third trapper jabbed his spurs into his horse and cleared the ditch, but not before the Blackfeet wounded him in the shoulder. The Blackfeet fell on Vanderburgh with their axes and knives, howling at the thought that this invader would enter the next world without his hair or his weapons.[19]

Andrew Drips's party on the Jefferson was also attacked by the Blackfeet. They lost several horses in the first assault. In the second assault one trapper was killed and several more were wounded. Blackfeet bands had now killed American Fur trappers on the Madison and Jefferson forks of the Missouri. Events unfolding on the Gallatin, the third of the Three Forks, would involve the Rocky Mountain Fur Company.

The mountaineers spotted a small group of Blackfeet in a bend of a lake, and some of the more bellicose trappers shot their rifles in a circle around them, containing them in the water. But more Blackfeet arrived, and the tables were turned. The trappers raced to Bridger's camp, chased by numerous Blackfeet warriors. When the Blackfeet crested the hill, they pulled up abruptly, surprised to see such a large camp before them.[20]

Now the two rival forces faced each other, both sides well manned and fully armed for war. On the Blackfeet side were the Bloods, led by Eagle Ribs, also called Peh-to-pe-kiss, a highly decorated Blackfeet Indian.[21] Eagle Ribs carried

Peh-tó-pe-kiss, Eagle's Ribs, a Piegan Chief (1832), by George Catlin. Eagle Ribs was a Blood Blackfeet who boasted of taking eight scalps from the trappers and traders. In 1832 Eagle Ribs struck Bridger with his own rifle and then he and his men wounded Bridger with two arrows. *Smithsonian American Art Museum, Gift of Mrs. Joseph Harrison, Jr.*

not one but two medicine bundles as well as a burning hatred for the Americans, boasting of "eight scalps, which he [said] he has taken them from the heads of the trappers and traders with his own hand."[22] He was a member of the Blackfeet Buffalo Society which gave him the right to wear a pair of polished buffalo horns as a headpiece, an honor held "only by the bravest of the brave; by the most extraordinary men in the nation." Eagle Ribs and a small party advanced, bearing a pipe of peace. An equal group of trappers advanced to meet them, prepared for any number of ways this could end.

Traveling with Bridger and Fitzpatrick was a spirited Mexican free trapper named Loretto and a Blackfeet woman who had been captured by the Crows. Loretto had paid her ransom, so she traveled with the trappers as Loretto's wife, and she had not seen her family since she had been abducted. Bridger rode forward to meet with Eagle Ribs and his party and took the Blackfeet woman with him to serve as interpreter. Seeing movement among the chiefs and thinking it might be treachery, Bridger cocked his rifle.

Eagle Ribs, who was extending his hand, heard it and grabbed the barrel of Bridger's rifle. He twisted it downward, and the rifle discharged into the earth. Bridger struggled with Eagle Ribs over the rifle, and Bridger's horse turned. A Blackfeet drew his bow and let fly, the arrow driving deep into Bridger's lower back. A second arrow pierced his back. Eagle Ribs wrested the rifle from Bridger's hands and struck him with it, felling him to the ground.[23] He leaped onto Bridger's horse to make his escape. Bridger later recalled "being hit so as almost to break his neck."[24]

The Blackfeet woman who had rushed to her brother was now trying to get back to her husband and baby, but the Blackfeet wouldn't let her. Loretto heard her cries and ran toward the Blackfeet to give the child to his wife. Both sides ceased fire as Loretto raced across the open plain and placed the baby safety in his wife's arms. The Blackfeet chief, moved by the Mexican's bravery, ordered him to return to the trappers—he would be safe. The young Mexican hesitated, but the chief scowled. Loretto's wife, heartbroken, implored him to go and save his own life. He returned to the mountaineers, safe from Blackfeet bullets and arrows.[25]

When the Blackfeet had retreated, the trappers rushed to the wounded Bridger. His shirt was red with blood from the two feathered arrows protruding from his lower back. The steel arrowheads, supplied by the British, had razor-sharp edges, and the trappers needed to be careful as they removed them. The first arrow came out smoothly, but the second one was stuck. As they continued to pull, the shaft came out, but the three-inch point did not. A scalper might dig it out,

but it might also cut too much bone or muscle. Getting it out of him would take
more skill than the trappers had, and they left the second point in the wound.
A splash of whiskey probably helped clean the wounds and ease his pain. They
patched both wounds, though Bridger would suffer the effects of that remaining
arrowhead most of his life.

When night came the Blackfeet slipped away under cover of darkness. Bridger
suffered through the night, trying to find a position that didn't send lightning
pain through his body. He would never forget this day; the three-inch steel blade
in his back was a painful reminder. By their best estimate, the trappers killed
nine Blackfeet, but lost one of their party and almost lost Jim Bridger.

Fitzpatrick summarized the skirmish in a letter to Campbell: "In our fight
Bridger was shot in 2 places with arrows we lost one horse one squaw & the gun
which you sold Bridger."[26] This rifle taken by Eagle Ribs was likely the one made
by Philip Creamer that Campbell had recently purchased in St. Louis. Campbell
had noted it to be "for Self," but this suggests that he sold the Creamer rifle to
Bridger at rendezvous [27]

Years later, Joseph Brazeau at Fort Edmonton told how Black Harris, who
was on "baddish" terms with Bridger, saw Bridger sometime later. He cried out
mockingly, "Hulloa! Bridger, what's the matter now?" The stoic Bridger humorously replied, as if it was nothing, "Only some feathers in my ——."[28]

THE RACE TO
RENDEZVOUS
1833–1834

By the time the snow fell in the winter of 1832–33, Rocky Mountain Fur had accumulated twenty packs of beaver pelts, compared to five packs trapped by American Fur. But American Fur had learned the location of valuable beaver fields, and its brigades showed no signs of relenting in their efforts to drive competitors out. All five Rocky Mountain Fur Company partners wintered together on the Salmon River. They built their lodges near the Nez Percé and Flathead villages, and American Fur set up nearby.[1] As the winter's grip closed in, Bridger's wounds closed as well, though the cold seemed to sharpen the point still lodged in his back.

Sometime after Bridger's injury, he was inspecting the camp keepers' equipment and found that one of the men, Maloney, had a dirty rifle, a condition that could impact its accuracy. According to Meek, Bridger was exasperated and confronted Maloney: "What you would do with a gun like that if the Indians were to charge on the camp?" Maloney retorted with a comment referring to Bridger losing his rifle to the Blackfeet: "Be Jasus, I would throw it to them, and run the way you did."[2] Bridger was not used to sharp answers from careless camp keepers, but he allowed the men to laugh at his expense.

Rocky Mountain Fur Company desperately needed a successful spring hunt. As soon as the weather allowed, Milton Sublette and Gervais took a brigade to the Snake River country, while Fitzpatrick, Bridger, and Fraeb led a brigade into the Laramie country, where they split into smaller parties. Fraeb and his men trapped on a tributary of the East Fork of the Medicine Bow River in southeast Wyoming. There the Arikaras stole sixty of the party's horses, and the tributary became known as Frappe's Creek. Black Harris and his party, trapping for Sublette and Campbell, also lost their horses that spring to the Arikaras, who also attacked and killed Hugh Glass, Colin Rose, and Hilain Menard as they were crossing the Yellowstone near its confluence with the Bighorn. The Arikaras left a portion of each scalp mounted on three posts at the site.[3]

Fitzpatrick joined Bridger and Fraeb on the North Platte, bringing a total of sixty men together again. Fitzpatrick wrote to Campbell on June 4, 1833, that he had found "beaver much more plentiful than I have in any part last fall. We have done very well so far this hunt. I put in cache a few days ago about forty packs of good fur."[4] The other two partners, Milton Sublette and Gervais, led another thirty men in the Snake River country.

Fitzpatrick was late again in placing an order for the 1833 rendezvous, so he sent Fraeb east to see if he could find the annual westbound caravan on the trail. Fitzpatrick also enclosed a letter with Fraeb for Robert Campbell, imploring Campbell to not be "backward in assisting Freab. . . . I shall depend much on you; you are well aware of the incapacity of our agent."[5] Fitzpatrick didn't specify the nature of Fraeb's incapacity.

Campbell was indeed already approaching the mountains with a caravan of goods, and he sent Louis Vasquez and two others to hunt up the trappers. They were successful, and Fitzpatrick, Bridger, and Fraeb's party connected with Robert Campbell's caravan. Fitzpatrick purchased all of Campbell's goods, with the exception of ten mules, four cows, two bulls, and some liquor, all of which Campbell kept.

This one-day rendezvous of sorts is rarely recognized by historians. Since Bridger, Fraeb, and several other trappers were not going to the full rendezvous, held on the Green River that year, they had to do some trading here to replenish their supplies and larder. The men also wanted to celebrate. According to Campbell's clerk, Charles Larpenteur, "A big drunken spree took place. Our boss [Campbell], who was a good one, and did not like to be backward in such things, I saw flat on his belly on the green grass, pouring out what he could not hold in. Early next morning everything was right again, and orders were given to catch up and start."[6]

Two tourists had come west in Campbell's brigade. Dr. Benjamin Harrison, son of William Henry Harrison, the hero of Tippecanoe, had sent his son to the mountains "to break him from drinking whiskey."[7] The future president of the

United States was not aware that whiskey would be so prevalent there. The other tourist was Sir William Stewart, of Perthshire, Scotland, who had paid Sublette and Campbell $500 for the privilege of riding with Campbell's caravan to the Rockies. Stewart wanted to experience the adventure that James Fennimore Cooper had written about, and he found the embodiment of Cooper's heroes in Jim Bridger and his men.

Fitzpatrick, Campbell, and the two tourists set off for rendezvous on the Green River with a large group, while Bridger and Fraeb's brigade set out to trap the Laramie Black Hills that summer. Bridger had been at every rendezvous from 1825 to 1832 but missed this 1833 gathering. Rocky Mountain Fur Company's financial position was not strong, and Bridger and Fraeb needed to keep their men trapping.[8]

That spring in 1833 Bridger and his men, some of whom were Mexicans from the Taos area, found what he termed a "gold canyon" along the Chugwater River in the Laramie–Medicine Bow region. One of the men washed a small bit of gold, perhaps twenty-five cents worth, from a basinful of soil, and the finding was on everyone's tongues.[9] Bridger and his hands gathered gold dust from the banks of the canyon, and they found a "considerable" quantity. The first significant gold rush in the United States was in North Carolina in 1799; the second was in 1829, when thousands of miners rushed to Georgia. Bridger's find on the Chugwater was nothing like the North Carolina or Georgia rushes, and it was not worth interrupting their trapping. But Bridger would search for gold there again in 1850.[10]

American Fur was still one of the thorns in Rocky Mountain Fur Company's side. The latter company had sold fifty-five packs of beaver skins at the 1833 rendezvous, which was just a little better than American Fur's returns.[11] With Astor's money behind it, however, the company could choose to lose money for a year or two if they could drive Rocky Mountain Fur into bankruptcy. Fitzpatrick agreed at rendezvous to split the mountains with American Fur. Rocky Mountain Fur would take the eastern slopes—the Seedskedee, Three Forks, and the Yellowstone country. American Fur would take the western slopes—the Salt Lake, Shoshone, and Flathead country.

The other thorn for Rocky Mountain Fur Company was their debt to William Sublette. While Rocky Mountain Fur had about $21,000 worth of beaver, Sublette's goods cost them $15,000, which was five times their original cost. Then they had to pay for transporting their pelts to St. Louis. When all was counted, Rocky Mountain Fur still owed thousands of dollars to William Sublette, accumulating at interest. They needed capital, and Fitzpatrick entered into a contract between the five partners of Rocky Mountain Fur Company on the one part and St. Louis businessman Edmund Christy, who invested $6,608, on the other part. The partnership, known as Rocky Mountain Fur Company & Christy, existed for one year and little came of it.[12]

More significantly, Milton Sublette, Tom Fitzpatrick, and Nathaniel Wyeth agreed on a secret plan whereby Wyeth would supply Rocky Mountain Fur Company at the 1834 rendezvous with no more than $3,000 of goods at first cost in the States, plus $3,521 for markup and delivery, which was to be paid with beaver skins at $4 per pound, for a total cost of $6,521—far less than the $15,000 they paid William Sublette for 1833. Either party could cancel with a $500 payment. Secrecy was crucial. If William Sublette learned of the deal early, he could immediately call in the debt. Milton Sublette left the mountains to have his leg examined by a real doctor; he would also help select the goods for Wyeth to secretly bring to rendezvous in 1834.[13]

A band of young Crows robbed Fitzpatrick's camp near the Bighorn River when Fitzpatrick had left it in the charge of the Scottish adventurer William Stewart. The Crows took forty-three beaver skins, horses, traps, and even clothing. Fitzpatrick got the men's horses back only after threatening the Crows that he would leave their land and take all their trade with it. Samuel Tullock, now working for American Fur, purchased the furs that the Crows had stolen, and Fitzpatrick asked Congressman Ashley to investigate.[14]

Fraeb's party had its troubles as well. Several men had crowded into Fraeb's tent to avoid a downpour. A clerk named Guthrie, leaning against the lodge pole, was killed by lightning. According to raconteur Joe Meek, Fraeb thought Indians were attacking, but seeing no Indians, he exclaimed in his German accent, "Py Gott, who did shoot Guttery?" John Hawkins, nephew of the famed Hawken gunsmith brothers of St. Louis, spoke out in a drawl, "G—a'Mighty, I expect. He's a firing into camp."[15]

Another tale involving Hawkins said that he was once critical of a campsite Bridger had selected. Bridger said it was well positioned in case of attack, but Hawkins disagreed. Hawkins climbed a hill and rolled a rock down on the camp that went through a lodge, broke a gun, and injured a man's leg. The rock would have killed the man if it had not been stopped "by a nest of kettles and a bale of meat." Someone made a song about it, including the lines: "The rock rushed down with a mighty din / And broke a gun and a Frenchman's shin." Bridger charged Hawkins for the ruined equipment and added another ten dollars for hurting the man.[16]

Bridger's West was changing. The mountain men had been attacked that winter not just by the Blackfeet and Arikaras but also by the Shoshones and the Crows. More significantly, the beaver were getting scarce from overtrapping, and the competition between trappers became more intense. William Stewart first experienced rendezvous in 1833 and later wrote, "With 1834 came the spoilers—the idlers, the missionaries, and hard seekers after money."[17]

As if to mark these changes, a fantastic meteor shower stunned the Western Hemisphere, beginning about midnight November 12, 1833, and continuing for several hours. Called "The Night of the Falling Stars," the constant barrage of moving lights was the most remarkable celestial display that America had ever recorded. A Missouri traveler said it was an "innumerable quantity of vapors passing toward the earth"; the Kiowas thought it was "something ominous or dangerous"; and Lakotas drew it in their winter count to represent that year. The event also initiated the serious study of meteorites by scholars.[18]

Bridger and Fitzpatrick came together again by November 1833 on Ham's Fork. Between them they had twenty-three packs of beaver skins from their summer and fall hunts. Fitzpatrick wrote a letter to Milton Sublette mentioning their deal with Wyeth and changing the location of the 1834 rendezvous from Horse Creek to the mouth of the Sandy. He gave it to Black Harris to deliver.[19]

Bridger and Fitzpatrick led the trappers to winter quarters near the junction of the Little Snake River and the Little Bear River (now called the Yampa). When spring finally thawed their world, Fitzpatrick wrote their order to William Sublette for the upcoming summer. In March 1834 Kit Carson and a handful of trappers arrived at Bridger and Fitzpatrick's camp with Captain Richard Lee, first cousin to Robert. E. Lee. When Lee saw Bridger and Fitzpatrick's pelts, he arranged to buy them with the goods he was packing.[20] Fitzpatrick set out for a spring hunt with Carson. Bridger decided to go with Lee and his men to Taos.

William Stewart was not to be left out and went to Mexico, too. Stewart cut an impressive figure with his racing horses and prized shooting rifles. He was the second son at Murthly Castle in Perthshire, Scotland, and because his older brother received the title and inheritance during a time of primogeniture, he was spending his time and money on adventure in the Rocky Mountains. He had had a relationship with a laundress, Christina, and she became pregnant. He married her, but his family did not accept her well, so he had lodged her and their son, George, in a house in Edinburgh and came to America.[21]

Bridger, Lee, Stewart, and their men made their way to "a range of mountains [near the city of Taos] whose western slopes gave birth to the waters of

California," perhaps the San Juan Mountains.[22] The town was soon to become known for "Taos lightning" and other pleasures. Adobe saloons and stores lined the dusty streets, and lonely trappers seemed to be smitten with the idea of, and the actual sight of, senoritas with pretty dresses and soft Spanish voices. But it was furs they needed, and they left Taos to continue to trap. What happened next became the stuff of legend.

William Stewart had a prize race horse named Otholoho, which he must have raced at the 1833 rendezvous, for he claimed that the horse was "the swiftest in the West, beat the Snake nation, and would, had there not been foul play, . . . have beaten all the horses of the whites." Joe Meek recalled the horse as "a Commanche [sic] steed of great speed and endurance," and Beckwourth remembered the animal as "a fine iron-gray."[23]

One of Bridger's camp keepers, a young Ioway Indian named Marshall, wouldn't work, and Bridger finally fired him. With no horse and nowhere to go, Marshall followed the camp on foot. Stewart took pity on him and hired him, giving him a mule and traps to hunt with. But Marshall wouldn't do any work for Stewart either, and Stewart threatened to turn him adrift as Bridger had. At turnout the next morning, the camp keeper reported two horses missing: one of them was Stewart's beloved race horse, Otholoho. Also missing was Stewart's prized rifle, which he had left beside the fire. Most telling, Marshall was also missing. Stewart could scarcely believe the ingratitude and in a moment of rage, blurted his anger: "I'd give five hundred dollars for his scalp."

There was a trapper among them, Mark Head, whom Stewart thought was "one of the most successful beaver hunters in the west; though rather under the usual scale of intellect."[24] Head took Stewart's outburst seriously, and he and another man set out to earn the bounty. They found Marshall as he was taking meat from a dead buffalo that he had run down with Otholoho.

"What are you about?" asked Mark Head.

"The Captain sent me out for meat," said Marshall, who then started to put his cords to right to mount his horse. Head shot him dead.

That night the camp spied two riders approaching, silhouetted against the setting sun, leading two additional horses. Mark Head rode up to Stewart and returned his stolen horses and gun. Then he showed Stewart the scalp attached to the barrel of the rifle and said he wanted his bounty. Stewart was horrified and grabbed the bloody patch from the rifle and flung it away. Stewart swore he would not cross the back of his favorite race horse again. He gave Otholoho

Preparing for a Buffalo Hunt (c. 1858–1860), by Alfred Jacob Miller. Few occasions were as exciting as a buffalo hunt, and an experienced horse was essential. When meat was needed, Bridger was known to have killed twenty buffalo with twenty consecutive shots.
The Walters Art Museum, Baltimore

Hunting Elk among the Black Hills (c. 1858–1860), by Alfred Jacob Miller. Trappers and hunters relished the opportunity to add to their larder. The best marksman took the shot because more than one hundred hungry men awaited the results. Bridger was an excellent shot and in 1859 brought down a thousand-pound elk. *The Walters Art Museum, Baltimore*

to Bridger. The story of Mark Head and Marshall became a classic tale of the mountains, and Otholoho would figure in a later event.

Bridger led his party north to trap the Laramie, and they had a good hunt. Stewart recalled the story: "Somewhere south-west of the Medicine Bow Creek, the camp of Jim Bridger, that celebrated leader of the Free Trappers of the mountain wilds, had stopped to make meat. The ground was not bad for running, and there were vast herds of bison within range. At the evening fires the song and the tales went round, and the anticipation of the morrow's feast gave spirit to both."

The next day they ran the buffalo, and by evening "load after load of meat and tired hunters were coming in, and the fires glared to put out the sun; the hump rib was presiding at every blaze, and the fat pudding and the marrow gut were seething in every pan; the tongues, the trophies of they who kill, were yet hung to their saddles, and the pack-mules were rolling their blood-smeared coats in the dust."[25]

Kit Carson and his brigade soon joined them at the headwaters of the Laramie, and together they set out for the summer rendezvous on the Green River.[26] There the fate of the Rocky Mountain Fur Company would be determined. In the summer of 1833 William Sublette and Robert Campbell had begun building a string of forts along the upper Missouri, competing with American Fur Company for the ever-growing Indian trade. In response, American Fur raised the price their forts would pay for beaver skins to twelve dollars a pound, more than they were worth in St. Louis. Their goal was to force both Sublette & Campbell and the Rocky Mountain Fur Company out of business.

William Sublette had braved Blackfeet attacks, deserts, and starvation. He was not afraid of a business office, either. He went to New York City to meet with the leaders of the American Fur Company, making veiled threats that his friend, Congressman William Ashley, could make things difficult for them by reporting Kenneth McKenzie's whiskey still at Fort Union (which was illegal) and the Crows' theft of Fitzpatrick's furs and horses, allegedly instigated by McKenzie.

By the end of January, Sublette & Campbell had a deal. America Fur would purchase Sublette & Campbell forts along the Missouri and give the mountain trade to the company for the following year. In the words of Robert Campbell's brother, Hugh, Sublette also agreed to "[set] at rest all competition." William Sublette was in a unique position to make that offer, as he held the debt of Rocky Mountain Fur Company and could put them out of business.[27]

Sublette & Campbell had learned by early March 1834, perhaps through Dr. Harrison, that Rocky Mountain Fur had entered into an agreement with

Wyeth to be supplied at the 1834 rendezvous. If the deal held, Rocky Mountain Fur Company & Christy might cut its costs enough to pay off its debt and stay in business, and William would not be able to uphold his agreement to set all competition at rest.[28] Sublette & Campbell knew by February 28, 1834, that they were going call in the debt of Rocky Mountain Fur Company. On that day Robert Campbell tactfully wrote Bridger, "In case of any change in your affairs, it [is] my wish that you and [Fitzpatrick] would come in here and join us."[29]

Nathaniel Wyeth and Milton Sublette set out for rendezvous together. Sublette had been suffering for some time from a fungal infection in his leg, and the irritation of riding brought painful flare-ups. He was forced to turn back, casting "a gloom over the whole camp."[30] Wyeth headed west without Milton, one of the company partners and the brother of the man who held the company debt.

William Sublette had started just one week behind Wyeth and now was just five days behind. On May 12 Sublette passed Wyeth.[31] He reached the Laramie River on May 30, 1834, and he paused to begin construction of a fort to supply trappers and to trade with the Sioux and Pawnees. Sublette stayed long enough to see the first logs laid for Fort William on the Laramie, which was destined to one day to be the site of the iconic Fort Laramie.[32] But Sublette was now traveling light, having left some of his supplies at his new fort.

William Sublette arrived at Green River on June 13. Two days later Tom Fitzpatrick came to Sublette's camp and told him the camps would soon move a few miles south for rendezvous on Ham's Fork. On June 18 Wyeth and his men arrived with their goods, which Fitzpatrick refused, although he agreed to pay the $500 penalty. Edmund Christy arrived with several Shoshones and Nez Percé and presumably Gervais. Bridger was still a week away.

Also that day a Nez Percé Indian named Kentuck drove a buffalo right through the camp, as he had promised Sublette he would. The Americans, the French Canadians, and the Shoshones simultaneously cried out in their own language, "bull, un caiac, and . . . Oka-hey trodlum." The next day, Insula, a leader of the Flatheads, killed a large grizzly that ran through camp and into some willows.[33]

William Sublette called in the Rocky Mountain Fur Company's debts, and Fitzpatrick had no choice but to close shop. Rocky Mountain Fur Company was through, and documents of dissolution were drawn up June 20 at Ham's Fork. First, Fraeb sold his interest to Fitzpatrick, Milton Sublette, Bridger, and Gervais for forty head of "horse beast," forty traps, eight guns, and $1,000 of merchandise.[34] Gervais then sold his interest to Fitzpatrick, Sublette, and Bridger for twenty head of "horse beast," thirty traps, and $500 of merchandise. A new partnership was formed—Fitzpatrick, Sublette, and Bridger—but neither Milton Sublette nor Jim Bridger was even present. It was a short-lived company, soon to be merged with yet another firm.[35]

Bridger arrived with his brigade at Ham's Fork on June 25, 1834, just after Kit Carson and William Stewart, who had appeared the night before. It was all over but the telling, and Fitzpatrick delivered the news to Bridger. Strategy had defeated heart. Suppliers, bankers, and dealers had defeated them. As Stewart had noted, "1833 was the last good year."[36] Bridger and his partners had battled American Fur, not fully realizing that their real competitor was their supplier, William Sublette. They were some of the best leaders in the mountains. It was their accounting ledger that didn't add up for them.

BRIDGER'S FAMILY
1834–1835

By 1834 Jim Bridger had been in the mountains for twelve years. He'd trapped and explored for four years for Henry and Ashley and a year for Ashley and Smith. He piloted for Smith, Jackson, and Sublette for three years, and then was booshway and co-owner of the Rocky Mountain Fur Company for four years. He'd slept under the stars in summer and in temporary skin or log lodges in winter, all the while making his home among other mountaineers and Indians. He was only thirty and had mountain passes yet to explore.

Nathaniel Wyeth was upset that Rocky Mountain Fur had reneged on their deal, and Joe Meek recalled him saying, "Gentlemen, I will roll a stone into your garden that you will never forget."[1] That stone was Fort Hall, which he built on the Snake River above the mouth of the Portneuf, a location that made it a direct competitor to the rendezvous system. Wyeth wrote to Milton Sublette, who was nursing his ailing leg, "Business is closed between us, but you will find . . . that all you will ever make in this country will go to pay for your goods, and you will be kept as you have been, a mere slave to catch Beaver for others."[2]

When in the field, trappers tried to out-trade, out-trap, and outwit each other. But at rendezvous, "all past tricks and maneuvers [were] forgotten, all feuds and bickering buried in oblivion."[3] Horse racing was one of the main events at rendezvous, and on July 4 many of the men went to rival camps to compete. Isaac Rose described such a scene, with Bridger riding Otholoho, and trappers and Indians placing their bets and lining the raceway. After the starting gun, wild cheers erupted at every change in the lead, and Otholoho was the perennial winner. Rose claimed that Bridger made so much money betting on Otholoho that he valued his horse at $3,000.[4]

Several of the mountaineers had taken Indian wives. Milton Sublette had joined with Mountain Lamb, and when he left the mountains to care for his leg, Joe Meek stepped in, buying her a fine horse, a beautiful blue skirt, and a scarlet bodice and leggings. Meek thought she was as pretty "as the dawn," and he loved the sound of her Shoshone name, Umentucken Tukutsey Undewatsey.[5]

Bridger married a Flathead woman sometime in 1834 or 1835. A trapper was expected to protect his wife and provide for her. In return she would become a companion, a helper, a lover, and perhaps a mother. A woman was expected to give her husband children and raise them, to carry firewood, prepare meals, make clothing, dress skins, and much more. Even the daughter of a chief was expected to show she could dress buffalo robes, pack wood, and carry a heavy burden. Because of Bridger's status as leader of the trapping brigade, many of those duties would be done by the camp keepers. This marriage probably brought Bridger a sense of family that he had not experienced since he was thirteen.

To win the consent of the father of the bride, a man needed to present tributes to show his esteem for her and her family, such as one or more horses. Such a union often brought kinship, trade, and protection to both the mountaineers and the Indians. A wife would be respected and protected in the trapper camps. A husband would often provide his wife with a horse and bridle, perhaps decorated with fine cut-glass beads, porcupine quills, and tinkling hawk's bells.[6] Bridger's marriage brought him not only a wife but also a family of relatives and their traditions.

Little is known about Bridger's first wife. Grenville Dodge recorded a family tradition that she was the daughter of a Flathead chief, and some have leaped to the conclusion that the chief was Insula. Biographer Gene Caesar corresponded with a Bridger descendant in the 1950s who named the first wife as Cora but without citing a source.[7] These bits of family lore have not been otherwise documented.

William Sublette headed back to the States with the pelts on July 10, and the Fitzpatrick and Bridger camp moved up Ham's Fork fifteen or twenty miles two days later. The next day they traveled farther upstream to a fine bottom of grass where American Fur Company was camped. Fitzpatrick and Bridger wanted nothing more to do with William Sublette, and on July 19 they rode over to talk to their rivals, Andrew Drips and Lucien Fontenelle, to explore a partnership.

The Thirsty Trapper (c. 1858–1860), by Alfred Jacob Miller. An Indian woman gives a weary trapper a drink of water from a buffalo horn. *The Walters Art Museum, Baltimore*

All business was temporarily put aside when Shoshone leader Ma-wo-ma and his warriors rode into camp with five captive Ute women and several captive children, a common practice among some warring groups. Ma-wo-ma said he liked one of the women too well to bring her to his camp, for his wives would beat and kill her. A burly Irishman, William O. Fallon, purchased two of the Ute women, and they subsequently escaped from his tent.

While Joe Meek was away from camp, Fallon accused Mountain Lamb of helping them escape, and he chased her with a whip. She ran into her tent, and

Fallon bellowed for her to come out. Mountain Lamb snuck out the back, circled around, put a gun to his head, and said, "Coward! You would whip the wife of Meek. He is not here to kill you. But I shall do that for myself."[8] Fallon had no choice but to back down, and cheers of admiration rose from the mountaineers.

The trappers moved on to North Piney Creek, a tributary of Green River, and on August 3, the Fitzpatrick, (Milton) Sublette, and Bridger company entered into partnership with the Fontenelle and Drips company. The new name for the five partners would be Fontenelle, Fitzpatrick & Company.[9] They would get their supplies from Pratte, Chouteau & Company, who had just purchased American Fur Company's western department from millionaire John Jacob Astor. Astor withdrew from the American Fur Company that same year.

Bridger led fifty men to Blackfeet country, and Drips led the other brigade into the field, perhaps into today's Utah and Colorado. Fontenelle and Fitzpatrick set out for the settlements to buy more goods and hire more trappers. Milton Sublette, who had once helped Peg-leg Smith cut off his own leg, was already in St. Louis facing the same procedure from Dr. Farrar.[10] Bridger's party was constantly attacked by Blackfeet. Five of Bridger's men were killed, and Kit Carson remembered, "A trapper could hardly go a mile from camp without being fired upon. As we found that we could do but little in this country, we started for winter quarters," which meant following Pierre's Fork (today's Teton River) to the Snake River.[11]

Booshways and married men had lodges of their own. The rest of the brigade slept several men to a lodge, each having a central fire to gather around. As each day closed, they banked their fires for the night. As the winter solstice approached, darkness arrived sooner each evening and lingered longer each morning. The snow piled higher, and horses' hooves sank deeper. Sometimes the men had to go ahead of their horses and plow a path with their knees.

In the first weeks of 1835, Bridger moved the horses to an island for forage and containment. Blackfeet stole eighteen of the animals, including Bridger's famous racing horse Otholoho (the same horse Rose called Ogohoro and Meek called Grohean).[12] Bridger was said to be nearly wild over the loss of his magnificent horse. A hasty posse of twelve chased the Blackfeet, among them Kit Carson, Joe Meek, Mark Head, Isaac Rose, and Joe Lewis. They tracked the thieves and found them camped in a protected shelter, the eighteen horses corralled in a cleft of rocks behind them.[13]

They met to parley, but Meek said the Blackfeet talked a "tissue of lies."[14] They said they had intended to steal only Shoshone horses—thus the horses they had stolen must be Shoshone horses. The trappers broke for their guns, thrashing in snow up to their knees. The Blackfeet had the advantage of snowshoes and fanned out to strategic positions.

Mark Head was directly opposite a Blackfeet fifty yards in front of him. He spoke with a peculiar nasal twang and a Virginia drawl, making almost everything he said sound ludicrous. Head had an old flintlock, having loaned his percussion rifle to another trapper the day before. A Blackfeet warrior jumped up to shoot at him, and Head tried to fire back. Smoke curled up from his gun, but no ball came out. "Damn it" called out Head in his peculiar voice, wondering how he would ever get a shot at the Blackfeet.

The Blackfeet popped up again. Once more Head's gun failed to fire. "Damn," he said. A trapper imitated Head's nasal twang, calling out, "Here he is." Another trapper also imitated Head and shouted, "No, here he is." Twice more Head's shot was a flash in the pan. Finally, Head called out in his nasal drawl, "See here, one of you fellas that's got a good gun, come and shoot this red relic of barbarism." When the Blackfeet jumped up again, Joe Lewis finally shot him.[15]

Two Blackfeet had closed in to kill Mark Head, and Carson shot one of them. The other shot Carson, giving him a wicked chest wound. A second ball exited through his back. By nightfall three Blackfeet had been killed. The trappers suffered through the night with nothing to cover them from the bitter cold but their saddle blankets.

The blood from Carson's wound froze in a great clot. He suffered terribly and later remembered it as the most miserable night of his life. At dawn the Blackfeet were still there, and the ailing trappers had no recourse but to return to camp. Bridger immediately set out again with thirty men. As they neared the cedar thicket where the Blackfeet had forted, they found the raiders were gone.[16] Bridger's Otholoho was gone as well.

In August the mountain men gathered for the 1835 rendezvous at Horse Creek and the Green River, at a camp dominated by a tremendous view of the Wind River Mountains. They numbered several hundred strong: American and French, Dutch and English, Mexican and Portuguese. There were several hundred others as well—Shoshones and Utes, Salish and Nez Percé, Bannocks, Iroquois, and Delawares. They raced, rode, and rough-housed, awaiting the arrival of the supply train.

Fitzpatrick arrived with the caravan and a long line of pack animals to be unloaded; a straggling band of greenhorns to be acclimated; and two missionaries to bring God to Gehenna. Clerks set up tents and the trading began. Fontenelle sent greetings and a gift to Old Gabe. "Bridger has a fine coat, cap, pantaloons, etc. baled up for him among the goods. Present him if you please my respects."[17]

Bridger and Fitzpatrick apprised one another of the activities of the past year. In spring 1835 Fitzpatrick had purchased Fort William on the Laramie River from Sublette & Campbell for Fontenelle, Fitzpatrick & Company. It stood only twelve days' ride from the Green River and would be a convenient waystation for trappers and a trading post for Indians. The fort was one of the farthest-west locations where mail could be held to post either east or west. Fontenelle was at their newly acquired fort to establish trade with the Sioux, but he had continued his destructive drinking and was also slowed by cholera.[18] Fitzpatrick also brought news for the partners that the price of beaver in St. Louis had fallen steadily. Hatters were using cheaper materials, including a rodent called a nutria, to make "beaver felt." Fashions were changing, and more men were now wearing silk top hats instead of beaver hats.

The missionaries who arrived with Fitzpatrick's caravan were Presbyterian Marcus Whitman, an amiable follow who was also a doctor, and the Rev. Samuel Parker, a fastidious man "inclined to self-applause." On the journey out the caravan riders had ridiculed, tempted, and even thrown rotten eggs at them for their reluctance to travel on Sundays. Many of the caravan party suffered from cholera, and three men died. When Whitman insisted they move from the river bottom to higher ground and avoid bad water, their health improved quickly, and the western men quickly warmed up to him.[19]

Two great dramas dominated that rendezvous. The first featured Jim Bridger and Marcus Whitman, an arrowhead and a surgeon's blade. The arrowhead in Bridger's lower back had plagued him for nearly three years and "made ugly running sores all this time."[20] The muscle and scar tissue that had grown around the projectile made its removal a more severe cut than most trappers wanted to attempt. Finally, here was a doctor who might be able to operate. Bridger stripped off his shirt, and with little else to entertain them, the trappers, camp keepers, and Indians all gathered around to watch the doctor cut into Old Gabe.

Marcus Whitman was tall, muscular, and sinewy, a friendly sort with dark blue eyes and dark brown hair. He had undertaken two sixteen-week terms of study, at fifty dollars a term, to become a doctor. Then he studied under Dr. Ira Brant of Rushville, New York, going to patients' homes. Most doctors of that era knew very little about "germ theory," and few saw need for a thermometer. But they knew about bloodletting. On the journey to rendezvous, Whitman had bled himself to relieve the pain from pushing wagons over swollen streams.[21]

Bridger lay on the ground, flat on his belly, and steeled himself against the pain. There was no ether then, but whiskey might do. Whitman approached Bridger's back, cutting blade firmly in hand, and pierced the skin. Blood spurted, and Whitman cut deeper. The doctor probed and finally found the arrow, now enmeshed in a cartilaginous substance. Bridger lay as still as possible; a sudden move by either man could cause serious injury.

Jonathon Keeney, who had come out to the mountains in 1831 to work under Bridger, remembered the operation. "The Doctor cut deep into the sores and around the arrow points [point] with a sharp knife and inserted some instrument like a pair of pincers." The "point had struck a bone" and "had partly clinched around a rib and required the strength of two men to pull it out, and Bridger had to be held down. He bore the operation with only a slight groan or two, and the point actually straightened out when it gave way"[22] It was done, and Reverend Parker recorded that Whitman "pursued the operation with self-possession and perseverance; and his patient manifested equal firmness."[23] Bridger's wounds healed fast, and soon he was able to travel.

William Stewart wanted the arrow point, "which had been for years wandering about Jim Bridger's back and hip." He carried the souvenir with him even at Murthly Castle, Scotland, as a memory of his time in the west. Nineteen years later, as he wrote his semiautobiographical novel *Edward Warren* and described Whitman's operation, Stewart had the arrowhead in his pocket as he wrote.[24] Whitman also removed an arrowhead from another man's shoulder that had been there for a year and a half and used a penknife, typically used to sharpen a quill pen, to cut a small hole in a man's chest to express fluid.[25]

The other drama paired Kit Carson against a trapper named Shunar, or Chouinard. On the third day of rendezvous, this huge French Canadian bully from Drips's party bellowed that he could whip every man he chose. He flogged a couple of his countrymen to prove the point. Then he put the challenge to the hundreds of men gathered, proclaiming he could easily "take a switch" to any American, Spaniard, or Dutchman. Some say Shunar and Carson were rivals for the affections of a young Indian woman. Carson remembered, "I told him I was the worst American in camp. There were many who could thrash him . . . and that if he used such expressions any more, I would rip his guts."[26]

Shunar raced for his rife and rode forward for all to see. Carson seized a pistol, the first weapon he could grab, and galloped hard forward. He stopped nearly on top of Shunar, his horse's flank rubbing against the French Canadian's horse and crowding his rifle. He asked Shunar if he was "the one he intended to shoot."

"No!" Shunar bellowed, but he raised his rifle as he said it. Carson pulled his pistol as their horses collided and both shots sounded as one. Shunar's ball creased Carson's head, cutting a groove in his hair, the powder burning one of his eyes. Carson's ball struck Shunar at the wrist, passed through his arm, and lodged in his upper arm. Carson recalled, "We had no more bother with this French bully."[27] Some accounts claim Carson killed Shunar; others say he just wounded him. The suggestion that this disagreement was over a woman may be true. Carson married an Arapaho woman named Waanibe that year; her name meant "Singing Grass" or Singing Wind." They soon had a daughter named Adaline.[28]

After rendezvous Bridger put his fall brigade on the march, leading them toward the Tetons. Missionary Parker rode with them, as did a group of Flatheads. The brigade traveled in a loose order—booshways, clerks, trappers, camp keepers, and then Indians. The Flatheads traveled in a proscribed order as well, with Insula followed by the lesser chiefs, who were in turn followed by the male tribe members, and then the women and children. The brigade settled for a time at Jackson's Little Hole, a beautiful valley at the source of the Hoback River near present-day Bondurant, Wyoming. There they could give the horses time to recoup and Bridger's men time to trap.

Samuel Parker hoped to establish a mission among the Flatheads. On their first Sunday he called as many as would come to church services. He did not want to upbraid them for their sins, but he did want to show them they were unfit for heaven. He had observed that many mountaineers disdained commonplace vulgarities and had manufactured their own phrases and used them to express anger, joy, hope, and grief. He had heard that one trapper sold the Indians "Bibles," at high prices, that were actually decks of cards.

The service was already going poorly for Parker, and then buffalo were sighted at far end of the valley. Shouts of excitement echoed throughout the camp, and the men hurried for guns and horses. Later, Parker disparaged them for hunting on the Sabbath, particularly in the middle of Sunday service, but afterward the trappers watched as he ate heartily of the tenderloin.[29] The Flatheads eventually split off from the brigade, and fortunately Parker went with them.

By September Bridger and his trappers were on Henry's Lake, just west of Yellowstone, along with about twenty Flatheads, perhaps his extended family. Henry's Lake was thirty miles in circumference and bordered by pine forests all around except for a small prairie on the south end. Fourteen trappers, including Kit Carson and Joe Meek, left Bridger's camp and met up with Wyeth and several men trapping for him on the headwaters of the Madison Fork. Some of their guns were broken, and they had little ammunition.

The next morning they were attacked. Blackfeet warriors fired down on the trappers from both sides of the bluffs above them. The trappers took cover, so the Blackfeet set fire to the dry grass. Soon the wind caught the fire and whipped it into a towering blaze that consumed the pine trees in columns of flames. A circle of flame and smoke united over the trappers' heads, and "death seemed almost inevitable." To save their lives, "all hands began immediately to remove the rubbish around the encampment and setting fire to it to act against the flames that were hovering over our heads." The trappers were forced to take cover behind their dead and wounded horses. "The Blackfeet blood was up—the trapper blood no less."[30] Several men on both sides were wounded. Finally, the Blackfeet leader stood on a high rock and struck the corners of his robe three times to the ground, the signal to cease fighting and move off.

When the mountaineers made their way to Bridger's camp, one of them still had a ball in his shoulder. Bridger, who had just had the arrowhead removed from his back, tended the injured man. He probed the wound with a trimmed pine stick and found the ball near the back of the man's shoulder. Making an incision with his knife in the man's back, Bridger used a wire to find and pry the ball out. Then he covered the pine stick with cloth and ran it all the way through the wound to remove any poison that might have been on the ball. Bridger bandaged the wound and put the man's arm in a sling, and the trapper quickly recovered.[31]

They trapped their way to the Continental Divide, where one of their French Canadian trappers was killed and scalped. They descended to Stinking Creek, where the trappers went both upstream and downstream.[32] Each party was attacked by Blackfeet. Responsibility of leadership fell heavily on Bridger, but now at least he had Cora to bolster his spirits.

He led the brigade northwest, and they came to a large village of 180 lodges of Flatheads and Pend Oreilles (Hanging Ears) on Beaver Head Creek in present-day southwest Montana. Hudson's Bay traders under Francis Ermatinger were among the Flatheads, buying every beaver skin as fast as the Indians could pull the animals from the water and skin them. Then the whole cavalcade moved twelve miles and camped with another village, which added 130 more lodges to their encampment.

Bridger's brigade had been traveling with men from Nathaniel Wyeth's group who were short of horses and supplies. Joseph Gale, the leader of this Wyeth band, instructed one of his camp keepers named Osborne Russell to go to Fort Hall alone for horses. Even though Russell was not one of Bridger's party, he and some of his men strenuously warned Russell that the journey was too dangerous for one man. Russell went anyway and regretted it: he got lost, went two days without water, and awoke one night surrounded by a full circle of hungry, howling wolves just thirty paces from him and his horse.[33]

By this time Bridger's wife Cora was pregnant, and she may have followed the Flathead tradition of eating plenty of bitterroot to aid in lactation. An expectant Flathead mother was "urged to ride her horse at rapid gaits to harden herself and to make the expulsion of the afterbirth easy."[34] No one expected the delivery to delay the trapping brigade, as Indian women were known for traveling soon after giving birth. After Mountain Lamb had a baby, she rode fifteen miles the same day, carrying her newborn in a basket hung from the pommel of her saddle.[35] In 1835 or 1836, Jim and Cora Bridger had a girl, and they named her Mary Ann.

THE SIEGE
1836–1837

In the winter of 1835–36, Bridger ordered his brigade to camp on Blackfoot Creek in what is today southeastern Idaho. Fat buffalo cows crowded the valley, and to preserve the grass for their horses, some of the hunters inadvertently drove the buffalo over the mountain to the head of the Missouri. The snow fell so deep the cows could not return during the winter. The hunters killed plenty of bulls but "they were so poor that their meat was perfectly blue."[1] This poor meat required slow cooking, and their winter camp was usually dotted with heaps of burning ashes, each tended by a camp keeper with an old club.

Bridger's camp keeper, Simon, cooked the meat for hours in mounds of smoldering ash to make it palatable. Finally, he rolled the ponderous mass out of the embers, and when he beat it with his club to knock off the ash, it made the charred meat bounce several feet into the air like a "ball of gum elastic." Simon drew his butcher knife and called, "Come Major, Judge, Squire, Dollar Pike, Cotton and Gabe won't you take a lunch of Simon?"[2] Major was Joe Meek; Judge may have been Osborne Russell; Squire was George Ebberts; Cotton was Cotton Mansfield; and Gabe was Jim Bridger. Come they did, and Simon hacked huge slices from the bull ham for them, calling, "Who will take this cut?"

Winter finally released its hold, and Bridger broke camp on March 28, 1836. They trapped several tributaries of the Snake River, all running high with snowmelt. Bridger then took them south to Bear River, where they united with Andrew Drips and his ninety trappers. They caravanned together to rendezvous, joined by several hundred lodges of Shoshones, Bannocks, Flatheads, and Nez Percé. That year's trading fair was held at the junction of Horse Creek and the Green River, amid clear streams, plentiful grasses, and stunning views of the snow-capped Wind River Mountains.[3]

Tom Fitzpatrick arrived six days later with forty men, supplies, and a mangled left hand. He had accidentally discharged his rifle the previous winter when chased by the Blackfeet, and the ball had shattered his hand. From then on, Indians called him "Broken Hand." He was now the fourth of five partners saddled with a challenging physical condition. Bridger was still bothered by the two arrow wounds he'd gotten in 1832. Fontenelle had a serious drinking problem. What remained of Milton Sublette's left leg had turned cancerous. The fifth partner, Andrew Drips, had narrowly escaped injury at the battle of Pierre's Hole in 1832 when he was shot though his hat and lost a lock of his hair.[4]

Five missionaries bound for Oregon arrived at rendezvous with Fitzpatrick that summer—Dr. Marcus Whitman and his wife Narcissa, Henry and Eliza Spalding, and William Gray. Narcissa Whitman and Eliza Spalding were the first white women to cross the Rocky Mountains and the first white women to attend the Rocky Mountain rendezvous. Narcissa, a pretty, auburn-haired woman with an "attractive sparkle" in her eye, had agreed to marry Marcus Whitman so that she would be allowed to go on the mission. She wore a common black dress to her wedding and later confided, "We had to make love somewhat abruptly and must do our courtship now that we are married." To further complicate the dynamic between the missionaries, Narcissa had rejected Henry Spalding as a suitor some years earlier, and Spalding still harbored a "wicked feeling" toward both Narcissa and Marcus.[5]

Back east Henry Spalding had met artist George Catlin, who warned him that the "fatigues of the journey . . . will destroy" a woman and that the "enthusiastic desire" of the Indians to see a white woman may result in "unrestrained passion [and] consequently in her ruin." Eliza Spalding was not fazed, however, and replied that she would trust in God "and go forward without fear." She did suffer on the journey, though, and fainted as they crossed the Continental Divide at South Pass. As they laid her on the ground, she told her husband, "Don't put me on that horse again. Leave me and save yourselves."[6] But once she had recuperated, the group pushed on.

Many of the trappers hadn't seen a white woman for quite some time; it had been fourteen years for Bridger. Joe Meek reported that some of the trappers raced out to see the female missionaries, greeting them with whooping, hollering, and shooting. Most if not all Indians at rendezvous had never seen a white woman either, and the men tied their scalp locks, inserted eagle plumes, painted their faces, and raced their horses forward until they were just a few yards from the approaching caravan. The Indian women combed and braided their hair and lined up to greet the female missionaries with kisses.[7]

Bridger and his four partners in Fontenelle, Fitzpatrick & Company had important business to conduct. Since forming the company two years earlier, Bridger and Drips had led most of the trapping brigades, while Fitzpatrick delivered trade goods to rendezvous and beaver pelts to St. Louis. The partners also owned Fort William on the Laramie River, and Fontenelle managed the post. Built by William Sublette in 1834 with blockhouses on two corners, it could by defended from all four directions.[8] Fontenelle, Fitzpatrick & Company had captured such a significant portion of the trade with the Lakotas there that Pratte, Chouteau & Company sent their agent, Joshua Pilcher, to buy the fort from them. When Pilcher met with Fitzpatrick at Fort William, Fitzpatrick had refused his offer.

Pilcher was determined to close the deal and "put a period to this business." He persuaded Pratte and Chouteau to increase their offer, warning that if they did not "compromise with those *fools* you will have opposition *heavy*."[9] Pilcher rode with Fitzpatrick to rendezvous to keep up the pressure, and finally they came to terms. Pratte, Chouteau & Company bought out Fontenelle, Fitzpatrick & Company in 1836, not only purchasing Fort William but also securing the services of their key leaders, Bridger, Drips, and Fitzpatrick. This gave Pratte, Chouteau & Company virtually complete control of the fur trade on the American side of the Rockies.

Bridger, for his part, would be paid over $3,300 for his work over the next two years. Lucien Fontenelle was dropped, however, as he had embarrassed himself and his partners by excessive drinking and by abandoning his work for "sleigh riding" and "frolicking."[10]

Two of Bridger's partners, Fitzpatrick and Sublette, had a falling out. Milton Sublette kept working for Pratte, Chouteau & Company, managing the fort on the Laramie, and he was short of tobacco, whiskey, blankets, and other goods that the Fitzpatrick had promised to send. Sublette was so concerned that he complained to company headquarters in December 1836 that Indians were taking their buffalo robes and beaver skins to the forts on the South Platte River. Sublette wrote that Fitzpatrick "would have nothing more to do with me . . . though we were partners." He then concluded, "I shall [never] have any thin more to do with him."[11]

The 1836 celebration of trade, friendship, and survival ended in mid-July, and the parties set out in their different directions. The missionaries moved on to Walla Walla in the Oregon country under the protection of the Hudson's Bay Company. Fitzpatrick left with their furs, which had been weighed, pressed, and packed for delivery to St. Louis. Bridger led the major party of sixty trappers toward Blackfeet country, and Drips led a small brigade to the Snake River country.

Bridger took his trappers through Two Ocean Pass, a rare discovery that the trappers had made early in their explorations. Here, just south of the Yellowstone thermal area, a twelve-inch trout could actually swim across two streams that were joined at the Continental Divide. A single stream splits in two: one part flowing west to the Pacific, and the other flowing east to eventually join the Gulf of Mexico and the Atlantic. It amazed Bridger, and in future years his description of this wonder was shared with thousands of people.

As Bridger and his men rode through the thermal regions of Yellowstone, the land "seemed to be all on fire . . . below the surface." Their horses' hoofbeats sounded like they "were traveling on a plank platform covering an immense cavity in the earth." One horse's hind leg broke through the earth's crust and a "blue steam rushed forth from the hole."[12]

As captivating as Yellowstone's wonders were, it was still a dangerous land, and the trappers' brigade continued east down the Yellowstone River. Blackfeet raiders killed a French Canadian trapper named Bodah, and one of Bridger's trappers accidentally shot a friendly Delaware Indian through the hip. In early September Joe Meek and Dave Crow rode into camp with dried blood on Meek's horse.

When asked where they had been, Meek responded, "Gabe, do you know where Prior [Prior's Fork] leaves the cut bluffs going up to it?" Bridger said he knew the place. "Well sir . . . I heard a rustling in the bushes within about 5 steps of me. I looked around and pop pop pop went the guns covering me with smoke so close that I could see the blanket wads coming out of the muskets." Meek said that "a ball struck [my] horse, Too Shebit, in the neck and just touched the bone." Horse and rider both "pitched heels overhead but Too Shebit raised running and I on his back . . . raised a fog for about half a mile till I overtook Dave."[13]

Two days later, at the confluence of Rock Creek and Clark's Fork of the Yellowstone, the Blackfeet surprised two men setting their traps and shot one of them, a man named Howell, through the chest with two fusee balls. The trappers rode out, found the attackers, and drove them to an island. In the process they lost a Nez Percé man who was fighting to avenge Howell. Howell suffered an agonizing twenty-hour-death, and they named the place Howell's Encampment.[14]

Later that fall Joe Meek was captured by the Crows as he trapped on the Rocky Fork of Clark's Fork, near today's Red Lodge, Montana. Meek remembered, "They had the prairie, and I war forced to run for the Creek bottom; but the beaver had throwed the water out and made dams, so that my mule mired down." Meek raised his gun, "old Sally," to shoot at them and then die, for he figured the fight meant death for sure, but the Crows took him prisoner instead.

After a smoke of three hours, the chief, "The Bold," called Meek into the ring and said, "I have known the whites for a long time, and I know them to be great liars, deserving death; but if you will tell the truth you shall live." Then he demanded. "Tell me whar are the whites you belong to; and what is your captain's name."

"Bridger is my captain's name, or, in the Crow tongue, *Casapy*, Blanket Chief," said Meek.

"How many men has he?" asked the chief.

Meek considered telling the truth and living, but he said "Forty," which was a tremendous lie, for there were many more than that.

The Bold laughed. "We will make them poor," he said, "and you shall live, but they shall die."

On the fourth day they crested a hill and saw Bridger's camp three miles distant along the Yellowstone. Seeing the size of the camp, the surprised chief turned to Meek with a scowl: "I promised that you should live if you told the truth; but you have told me a great lie." The warriors gathered around Meek, tomahawks in hand. But The Bold didn't want Meek, he wanted Bridger, and so told Meek to call Bridger's guard over to talk to the Crows. Meek shouted to the guard that he should ride to Bridger and tell him the Crows were going to kill him. The horse guard raced to camp, and Bridger quickly surveyed the position of the Crows. The bottomland between them was rolling plains crisscrossed with creeks.

Bridger gave instructions to five men and then rode out alone to a spot about three hundred yards from the Crows. He shouted that The Bold should send a subchief out alone to smoke with him. Little-Gun rode out on behalf of the Crows and stopped a hundred yards from Bridger and dismounted. Little-Gun stripped off his clothes, according to the Crow laws of war, and Bridger did the same. Unarmed and unclothed, they moved toward each other and embraced.

While this was going on, the five men Bridger had selected had crawled through the ravines as Bridger had instructed. They circled behind Little-Gun, separating him from his camp. When they raised up with their rifles, they cut off any chance for Little-Gun to retreat, and Bridger now had a prisoner of his own. "It war kill or cure, now," Meek remembered. The Crows howled threats and grabbed their weapons but then saw a hundred of Bridger's trappers appear in a line on the other side of the plain, ready for battle.

Bridger shouted that he would trade Little-Gun for Meek. Meek explained the offer, and the chief sullenly agreed, saving face by saying he would not give up a chief for one white dog's scalp. Joe Meek was sent towards Bridger, and Little Gun was sent back to the Crows. That evening The Bold agreed to a truce and a mutual pact of defense against the Blackfeet, and he returned Meek's mule, gun, and beaver packs, telling him he could even "out-lie the Crows."[15]

The streams iced and the snow fell. At Christmas 1836 Bridger led his traveling village about four miles down Clark's Fork to the Yellowstone. Thousands of buffalo made their situation "fat cow" again, meaning there was plenty of meat, and the bottoms had plenty of sweet cottonwood for the horses. The trappers' main duties were to hunt buffalo for food and to gather cottonwood for their horses to eat. The camp keepers guarded the horses, kept the fires going, and cooked for the trappers. Bridger and his family likely had their own lodge. At night, groups gathered to debate, argue, and spin yarns in what some called "The Rocky Mountain College."[16]

In February 1837 the Blackfeet shot a ball through Isaac Rose's right elbow; the ball exited his right forearm.[17] Rose screamed, dropped his rifle, and barely escaped with his life. Bridger and an Indian healer traveling with Bridger's brigade looked at Rose's swelling wound and concluded he had been shot with a poison ball. The Blackfeet made these by enticing a rattlesnake to strike a piece of buffalo meat and then rolling grooved lead balls in the poisoned meat. Rose's arm ballooned so large that his skin peeled off up to his shoulder, and Rose believed his profuse bleeding helped wash the poison out.[18]

A few days later some of the trappers spied several Blackfeet crossing the frozen Yellowstone below them. As usual, Carson, Meek, and a handful of others were the first to rush to battle, excited to know that the Blackfeet were in a vulnerable position. The mountaineers fired on them from above, and the Blackfeet took shelter in abandoned wooden fortifications on an island. The vengeful trappers surrounded them, and the two sides shot at each other in the bitter cold.[19] The Blackfeet shot a trapper named Manhead, a Delaware Indian, in the knee and wounded another man with a ball through the hip. The trappers returned to

Bridger at sunset; Manhead still had the ball lodged under his kneecap. It, too, was a poison ball, and his knee swelled to enormous size before he died.[20]

The next morning Bridger led a large party across the ice to reconnoiter. The Blackfeet were gone, but Bridger examined the battleground and concluded the Blackfeet carried seven or eight wounded away on travois and dragged the bodies of several dead Indians over the ice and into the river. Bridger knew the Blackfeet did not mutilate bodies of the dead that lay in water, and perhaps the Blackfeet felt their own dead might be free from mutilation if they were left in the water.[21] Bridger warned the trappers: "Now, boys, the Indians are close by, and in a short time a party of five or six hundred will return to avenge the death of those we have slain, and we will have to keep a sharp lookout."[22]

The mountain men's ultimate test with the Blackfeet had begun. February 22 was cold and wintery. As he had done every day, Bridger climbed a high butte to gain a broad view of the terrain, "to look out for 'squalls' as he termed it."[23] He was alarmed to see hundreds of Blackfeet coming across the hills about ten miles below and assembling at the timberline on a large island. Bridger descended the butte and described to the camp the enormous force preparing to attack them.

The trappers were well aware that Santa Anna and thousands of Mexican soldiers had surrounded Davey Crockett, James Bowie, William Travis, and 184 others a year earlier at the mission in San Antonio, Texas, called the Alamo. Now Bridger, Carson, and eighty trappers were facing a similar challenge, surrounded by a force many times larger than their own. After fifteen years of skirmishing over beaver, would Bridger and his men soon be annihilated on this frozen plain?

Bridger sent a man up the butte to track the Indians' movement and directed most of his men to gather logs and brush to build a barricade around their camp. They drove forked logs into the ground and laid heavy logs horizontally into the forks. They then put logs vertically against the horizontal barricade six feet high, leaving just enough gap to allow rifle barrels to fit through. Soon a rough fort emerged, two hundred fifty feet on each side. In the center they built a blockhouse for the traps and other property. This was also a place of refuge for Indian women and the wounded. As they worked, more and more Blackfeet gathered. When Bridger returned from a reconnoiter on the butte, the breastwork was completed, and he posted double guards at each face and had them serve three-hour watches. Bridger roamed the perimeter of the fortification, rifle in hand, and at night peered into the darkness.[24]

The next day marked the one-year anniversary of the beginning of Santa Anna's thirteen-day siege of the Texians at the Alamo. Bridger put his men to work cutting additional timbers, some as thick as eighteen inches, and braced them close together against the inside of the wall for added protection. From his lookout high on the bluff, he was pleased to see his men had doubled the thickness of the palisade. He selected six men to join him as he rode closer to the Blackfeet encampment to determine their numbers and plans. The Blackfeet were now only three miles downstream on the frozen riverbank. They had only a few horses, so their attack would be on foot.

When Bridger returned to camp, he had 150 to 200 trade guns distributed to his eighty men so they could shoot several times before reloading. The Delaware and Flathead Indians with the trappers painted their faces red and black. Osborne Russell guessed that 1,100 Blackfeet were "intending to rub us from the face of the earth" Kit Carson believed there were 1,500 Blackfeet and counted 111 small fortifications for defense. Isaac Rose estimated there were 1,500 to 1,600 warriors ready to charge. The trappers were outnumbered by more than ten to one.[25]

That night the temperature plummeted. It was an unusually clear night, and the moon and stars shone brightly, lighting up the trappers and their makeshift fort. Fifteen hundred Blackfeet warriors were ready to annihilate them. The Blackfeet staged a war dance, and the mountaineers could hear their war songs. For Bridger and his trappers, there was no escaping.

About ten P.M. the sky took on a strange luster, then the heavens lit up with darting bursts. It was the northern lights. The colors flashed in an amazing spectacle, an army of colors scattering helter-skelter. Above the Blackfeet the heavens were the color of blood. Was it a foreshadowing of the great death that the Blackfeet would bring to the mountain men's brigade? The spectacle lasted nearly two hours, and when it was over the sky bled a deep red across the entire northern horizon. Then the color gradually faded. The trappers, wrapped in blankets, continued to huddle near their fires.[26]

The next morning a lone Blackfeet crept close to the trappers' fort and shot at Bridger's cook, Jim, as he was gathering wood. Was this the beginning of the attack? Bridger ordered Maselino, a Mexican, to climb the butte and assess the situation. At the top Maselino was surprised to meet a Blackfeet warrior spying on the trappers. Maselino turned to run, and the Blackfeet shot him in the heel. Maselino made a fifty-foot leap down the bluff, then slid on the snow the rest of the way down. The camp rose to arms, but still the attack didn't come. The trappers paced back and forth.[27]

Soon sentries called out that the Blackfeet were advancing on the frozen river, more than a thousand strong. When they were within four hundred yards, they halted, still in a compact group. A chief wearing a white blanket came forward and gave the sign to Bridger that they would not fight that day. Then they began their retreat. Some of the more reckless trappers like Carson called out and dared the retreating Blackfeet to make an attack. Fortunately for the trappers, the Blackfeet stuck to their plan. They retreated a mile and sat in council. Then they arose and divided, half going toward Crow country and the other half returning to their villages.[28] The mountaineers and their families were saved, though they did not know why. Was it the fortification they had built or the stunning display of northern lights?

13

KNIGHT OF THE
ROCKIES
1837–1838

After near annihilation on the Yellowstone in the early months of 1837, Bridger led his brigade on to the Bighorn. It was fat cow again, and their meat scaffolds groaned under the weight. Disagreements within camp arose often and were usually quickly settled. Bridger's challenge as captain of the brigade was to keep incidents between the whites and Indians from escalating into a battle. An argument within a group remained an argument, but the same incident between people of different loyalties lead to bloodshed. Such conflicts had been flaring up in the Rockies for several years and would continue in 1837.

The Crows came to Bridger's camp to trade in the spring, and bargaining began. A belligerent Crow man promenaded about the camp, rummaging from bundle to bundle. As he passed Mountain Lamb, he raised his whip and struck her because she was a woman and a Shoshone. When Joe Meek saw his wife whipped, he instantly shot the Crow, who fell dead. The camp erupted in confusion. The Crows saw this as a sign of war and raced for their rifles. Bridger's men raised their rifles in defense and shot two more of the Crows. The Crows shot back, killing one of Bridger's men. Bridger finally brought his men under control and told the Crow chief that the fighting was over. The chief did not fully accept the explanation of how it started, though, and he led his people away.

Meek recalled that Bridger chastised him, saying, "Well, you raised a hell of a row in camp."

"Very sorry, Bridger, but couldn't help it," answered Meek. "No devil of an Indian will strike Meek's wife."

"But you got a man killed," said Bridger.

"Sorry for the man," Meek replied. "Couldn't help it, though, Bridger."[1]

Bridger hurried the brigade away from these Crows, and over the next several months the trappers ranged to the Stinking River, then the Wind and the Popo Agie River, then southwest to South Pass and the Green River. There they awaited the arrival of the trade caravan for the 1837 rendezvous. The Bannocks were camped three miles away, and among their herd were horses they had stolen from French Canadians and Nez Percé the previous fall. These aggrieved trappers rode into the Bannock camp and took back their horses, bringing them to Bridger's camp for protection.[2]

That afternoon thirty Bannock warriors charged into Bridger's camp, rifles raised. The Nez Percé passed their horses to the trappers to hold and gave a particularly fine horse to Bridger. The Bannocks wanted no fight with Bridger, and many started to leave. But one agitated warrior fiercely called out to his fellow Bannocks: "We came to get horses or blood and let us do it." Osborne Russell understood some of the Bannock language and warned the mountaineers to be ready for an attack. The hot-headed Bannock rushed through the crowd and seized the bridle in Bridger's hand, trying to jerk it free. He was oblivious to the "cocked rifles that surrounded him. . . . The moment he seized the bridle two rifle balls whistled thro. his body."[3]

Arrows flew and rifle balls rained down. Meek's wife, Mountain Lamb, was struck by an arrow in the breast, which killed her. Several mountaineers chased the Bannocks, forcing them onto an island. At daybreak an old Bannock woman came out and chided the trappers: "You have killed all our warriors. Do you now want to kill the women? If you wish to smoke with women, I have the pipe." At that the trappers fell back.[4]

Tom Fitzpatrick finally arrived with the supply caravan for the rendezvous. Mountaineers, Crows, Flatheads, Shoshones, and Nez Percé spread out along the banks of the confluence of Horse Creek and the Green River. Letters were distributed from families and friends. Alcohol was available at $4 a pint.[5] The law had allowed earlier supply caravans to carry a small amount of spirits for "each boatman"—even after there were no boatmen. A recent federal law had barred liquor in the Indian country for boatmen and disallowed alcohol for trade in the mountains altogether. Yet American Fur Company continued to bring their kegs past Fort Leavenworth, and Kenneth McKenzie at Fort Union had built a still and traded with the Mandans for corn to produce his own alcohol far up the Missouri.[6]

The day after Fitzpatrick's caravan arrived, the serious trading began. Beaver pelts and St. Louis goods changed hands under the tents. Men bet on horse races, and the winners bought more alcohol and trade goods. They even packed dried buffalo meat in smoked buckskin to take to William Sublette in St. Louis. On the second night after the traders' arrival, William Stewart hosted an "entertainment" for twenty-five of the leading mountaineers under a large tent. He served choice old liquors to complement an ample supply of fresh buffalo meat. David Brown, who had come west to be one of Bridger's trappers, later recorded one of the first and most complete descriptions of Bridger, which was eventually published in the *Cincinnati Atlas* in 1845.

> On the right of Captain Stewart sat, or rather squatted in oriental fashion, one of the most remarkable men of this remarkable assemblage. This was Mr. James Bridger, or "Jim" Bridger, . . . [who was] engaged . . . to fill the difficult and hazardous position he now held as partisan or leader of beaver hunting parties, for which he was admirably adapted from his wide and thorough acquaintance with the whole mountain regions from the Russian settlements to the Californias, and every hidden nook by hidden lake and unfrequented stream.[7]

Brown was awed with Bridger's "absolute understanding of the Indian character in all its different phases" and wrote

> His bravery was unquestionable, his horsemanship equally so, and as to his skill with a rifle, it will scarcely be doubted, when we mention the fact that he has been known to kill twenty buffaloes by the same number of consecutive shots.
>
> The physical conformation of this man was in admirable keeping with his character. Tall—six feet at least—muscular, without an ounce of superfluous flesh to impede its force or exhaust its elasticity, he might have served as a model for a sculptor or painter, by which to express the perfection of graceful strength and easy activity. . . . His cheek bones were high, his nose hooked or aquiline, the expression of his eye mild and thoughtful, and that of his face grave, almost to solemnity. . . . One remarkable feature of this man I had almost omitted, and that was his neck, which rivaled his head in size and thickness [goiter], and which gave to the upper portion

of his otherwise well-formed person a somewhat outré and unpleasant appearance.

To complete the picture he was perfectly ignorant of all knowledge contained in books, not even knowing the letters of the alphabet, but put perfect faith in dreams and omens, and was unutterably scandalized if even the most childish of the superstitions of the Indians were treated with anything like contempt or disrespect; for in all these he was a firm and devout believer.

Scotsman William Stewart was equally impressed with Bridger and his men, likening them to King Arthur and the Knights of the Round Table. He purchased a unique gift for Bridger, ordering it from Britain, shipping it to St. Louis, and then carrying it carefully boxed to the rendezvous. It was a polished steel helmet and a cuirass: a breastplate and backplate fashioned after the ceremonial armor worn by the English Life Guards of the sixteenth century. It was as if Bridger was a legendary knight—stately, brave, and ready to do battle. He cut a dashing figure in the armor and created a sensation when he mounted his steed and rode through the camp.

Stewart also brought an artist to the 1837 rendezvous—Alfred Jacob Miller, who had trained in Paris and Rome. Miller painted a dramatic scene, titled *Rendezvous*, that featured Jim Bridger in armor in the foreground of a grand panorama of the Wind River Mountains. Miller described the scene: "The whole plain is dotted with lodges and tents, with groups of Indians surrounding them; in the river near the foreground Indians are bathing; to the left rises a bluff over-looking the plain whereon are stationed some Braves and Indian women. In the midst of them is Capt. Bridger in a full [partial] suit of armor. This gentleman was a famous mountain man, and we venture to say that no one has travelled here within the last 30 years without seeing or hearing of him."[8]

Miller also created a closeup, a pen-and-ink sketch entitled *Jim Bridger, in a Suit of English Armor*. For that Miller wrote: "Capt. Bridger, a celebrated Leader or Bourgeois in the Rocky mountains, was a great favorite of Sir Wm Stewart who imported a full [partial] suit of English armor & presented it to Bridger, who donned it on all special occasions & rode so accoutered at the head of his men."[9]

Joe Meek, who had been frequenting the alcohol kettle mourning the loss of Mountain Lamb, put on Bridger's armor and strutted about as if a king of old, shouting, "A horse, a horse, a kingdom for a horse." The irascible Bill Williams

Rendezvous 1837 (c. 1858–1860), by Alfred Jacob Miller. Jim Bridger is in the left fore-ground (on horseback) wearing a polished steel helmet with plume and a cuirass given to him at the 1837 rendezvous by Sir William Stewart. *The Walters Art Museum, Baltimore*

replied, "For what king, Besonia, speak or die." They were paraphrasing Shake-speare's *Richard III* and *Henry IV,* respectively.[10]

While George Catlin and Karl Bodmer had painted many important scenes of life and trade along the Missouri River, Alfred Jacob Miller painted hundreds of scenes documenting the lives of the mountaineers and the American Indians interacting with each other at rendezvous and in the wilderness. Miller's well-known paintings include *The Buffalo Chase, Taking the Hump Rib, Lassoing Wild Horses, Indian Female Running a Bull Buffalo, The Trapper Takes a Wife, Stampede by Blackfeet,* and *Trappers Dancing around the Camp Fire.*

Missionary William Gray, who had attended the 1836 rendezvous on his way to Oregon, showed up at the 1837 rendezvous as well. The disgruntled Gray was quite disturbed by the sinful ways at rendezvous—the trappers drank and swore constantly, and one man had a wife in each of three villages. Gray was so anxious to escape that he prepared to leave for St. Louis early, taking with him a few Flatheads and Shoshones.[11]

Bridger told Gray that his plan was suicide; he had seen too many people die because of poor decisions like this. Crossing Sioux lands with other Indians was an insult to the Sioux, and driving extra horses along without enough men to defend them was just asking for an attack. Gray claimed he had God for his protection. Bridger slapped his hand on the breech of his rifle and declared, "Sir, the grace of God won't carry a man through these prairies. It takes powder and ball."[12]

After the rendezvous, Fontenelle, who must have redeemed himself to his employers, led the main brigade to the Yellowstone with Bridger as pilot. Carson recalled, "We trapped the Yellowstone, Otter, and Musselshell rivers and then went up the Bighorn and on to the Powder where we wintered." The trappers experienced one of the coldest winters in memory. They had to corral their horses and feed them bark cut from cottonwood branches. The buffalo had depleted the nearby grazing lands, and Carson remembered, "We had to keep the buffalo from our camp by building large fires in the bottoms. They came in such large droves that our horses were in danger of being killed."[13]

The trappers had camped that winter near a Crow village, and they learned that smallpox had broken out among several tribes. This horrible disease, introduced to North America by European explorers and colonists, was devastating to indigenous peoples of North America. In 1837 the steamboat *St. Peters* brought the deadly disease up the Missouri River and infected three Arikara women who boarded. When the steamboat arrived at the Mandan village, passengers and Indians gathered for a great celebration, and the disease spread among them like wildfire. The Mandan villages were hit the hardest, the smallpox killing almost all of them. Only thirty people survived.[14] The smallpox virus was most often spread person to person, and the notion that the disease was spread by infected blankets or had been purposely spread by U.S. citizens has since been debunked.

The indigenous peoples in the Americas had once numbered in the millions. Over the course of the sixteenth, seventeenth, and eighteenth centuries, their population declined at a devastating rate because of smallpox and other diseases. The United States was not totally indifferent to their plight. Congress, which included Rep. William Ashley, allocated $12,000 in 1832 to vaccinate all the Indians in America. But the money ran out on the Missouri before the doctors ever reached the Mandans. Mandan chief Four Bears, whose image had been painted by George Catlin a few years earlier, was among those who died. He purportedly said he did not fear death but was horrified "to die with my face rotten, that even the wolves will shrink from horror at seeing me."[15]

The Blackfeet were infected with the disease when one of their men boarded the steamboat *St. Peters* at the mouth of the Little Missouri River, then transferred to a keelboat bound upriver for Fort McKenzie with goods to be traded to some five hundred families of Blood and Piegan Blackfeet gathered there. Within weeks, twenty-six Blackfeet died at the fort and many more died as the Bloods and Piegans went back to their villages.[16]

Bridger piloted the trappers to Three Forks of the Missouri in spring 1838, and as they crossed from the Gallatin Fork to the Madison Fork, they discovered the trail of a Blackfeet camp three or four days ahead. The next day they came upon an Indian lodge that held nine dead bodies scarred by smallpox. Bridger took an alternate course up the mountains to avoid any attack on the Blackfeet by the mountaineers. This detour caused a significant rift between Bridger and the free trappers. Carson, Meek, Russell, and many others protested so vigorously that Bridger resumed the path that followed the Blackfeet tracks.[17]

The next morning the trappers caught up with the village, and several free trappers wanted to attack them. Bridger opposed this and refused to give orders for an attack, instead directing the men under his immediate command to protect company property. Fifteen of the free mountaineers rode off to attack the Blackfeet village, which included men, women, and children. Russell said they climbed a one-hundred-foot ledge, "crept to the edge and opened a fire on the Village which was the first the Indians knew of our being in the country."[18] Carson, who was also part of the attacking party, wrote, "We were determined to try our strength to discover who had the best right to the country. . . . We soon reached the village, attacked it, and killed ten Indians . . . taking several scalps."[19]

The free trappers rode back to Bridger's camp, chased by a much larger contingent of mounted Blackfeet warriors. Cotton Mansfield fell and was trapped under his horse. As six Blackfeet rushed toward him, Mansfield cried, "Tell old Gabe that old Cotton is gone."[20] But his comrades rallied and saved him. When the Blackfeet reached the trapper camp, they took the high ground on broken rocks that rose a hundred feet on each side.

Shots were exchanged for two hours or more with little effect. The mountaineers finally charged up the hill and attacked the Blackfeet "muzzle to muzzle." Russell wrote, "They retreated from rock to rock like hunted rats . . . whilst we followed close at their heels loading and shooting."[21] The Blackfeet retreated with their dead, except for two bodies that they threw into the river. They carried their wounded back to their camp slowly, making a mournful cry.

Bridger led the brigade away from the Madison River and crossed an undulating plain south to Henry's Lake (now Raynolds Pass), where they found a small

Blackfeet village of about fifteen lodges.[22] Some of the trappers prepared to attack that village as well, planning to "smite it without leaving one to tell their fate."[23]

Six men from the village came out in peace and supplication, skeleton-thin and weaponless, and finally calmed the hatred of the trappers who had wanted to attack them. They were the Piegan band of Blackfeet, and Bridger met with their chief, Little Robe, who told him they were dying from smallpox. Both sides agreed to peace and traded for horses and skins.[24] Before the pandemic was over, six thousand Blackfeet died, almost two-thirds of their entire population.

The rest of the season was relatively peaceful. Bridger's brigade trapped the Snake River and Pierre's Hole, and then crossed the Tetons to Jackson's Hole before eventually heading out for rendezvous. The summer gathering for 1838 had been scheduled for Horse Creek, but a hand-scrawled note on an old trading house at Horse Creek announced, "Come on to the Popeazua [Popo Agie River]; plenty of whiskey and white women."[25]

Andrew Drips had brought out the summer caravan to the Popo Agie, where that river joined the Wind to become the Bighorn River. Nine missionaries attended the gathering: Elkanah and Mary Walker, Cushing and Myra Eells, Asa and Sarah Smith, William and Mary Gray, and Cornelius Rodgers.[26]

Bridger arrived at the Popo Agie on July 5 with one hundred men, sixty Indian women, and many mixed-race children.[27] The mountaineers with Bridger who instigated the attack on the Blackfeet paraded on horseback to the tents of the missionaries, firing rifles, beating drums, and hoisting a Blackfeet scalp as their colors. Missionary Sarah Smith was disgusted to hear of the assault on the Blackfeet. "The Indians made no attack on B's [Bridger's] party but this party [the free men] attacked them & shot 15 of them dead without excuse but to please their wicked passions." One of the mountaineers told how a wounded Blackfeet "grasped the limb of a white man . . . begging for his life . . . while others dragged him away & cut his body in pieces."[28]

William Gray, who had been at the rendezvous in 1836 and 1837, was there again, this time to return to the mountains with his wife. As Bridger had predicted, Gray's ill-fated departure the previous summer had been devastating, and the Sioux had not let Gray pass. They killed all the Indians traveling with him, making widows and orphans out of their families back in the mountains. Somehow Gray was spared. Some of the mountaineers at rendezvous swore bloody oaths against Gray, suspecting that he had given up the Indians for his own life.[29]

Also arriving with the caravan was a Swiss immigrant named Johann Sutter (pronounced "Sooter"), who would go on to California to build Sutter's Fort. Ten years later one of his laborers would make a discovery that changed the course of history in the United States and the world.[30]

The economic panic of 1837 had swept the nation, and the depressed economy eventually hurt the fur trade. Fortunately, Bridger had done very well financially. On July 12, 1838, Chouteau & Company gave Bridger a draft for $3,317 in payment for his previous two years' work. This may have included payment for Bridger's share of the company that he and his partners had sold to Chouteau in 1836. Bridger had little use for money in the wilds of the Rockies and authorized William Sublette to cash the draft and deposit the money for him in St. Louis.[31]

Several forts had been recently established in the mountains to purchase beaver pelts and sell supplies to the trappers, and during the 1838 rendezvous there was talk that the Chouteau Company would no longer bring supplies to the mountains. Many longtime trappers left the firm, "owing to the Company being so hard. Some ran off, Stole horses traps and other articles of value."[32] Carson and seven men went to Brown's Hole and Fort Davey Crockett (in present-day northwest Colorado), where Carson joined a trading expedition to the Navahos. He became a hunter for the fort, keeping twenty men well supplied with meat. By then Andrew Sublette, the fourth of the five Sublette brothers, and Louis Vasquez had built Fort Vasquez, one of the many forts on the South Platte River.[33]

After the 1838 rendezvous Bridger and Drips led their hunters up the Wind River, crossed the Divide to Jackson's Hole, and then crossed the Tetons to Pierre's Hole.[34] Chouteau ultimately did send out a caravan for the 1839 rendezvous, and that summer Bridger and Drips again took their men to the junction of Horse Creek and Green River to meet the traders. Rows of Indian lodges built of poles and hides extended for a mile along the Green. The mountaineers, "knights without fear and without reproach," made a singular impression on newcomer F. A. Wislizenus: "No rock is too steep for them; no stream too swift. Withall, they are in constant danger from hostile Indians [and] victims fall each year."[35] Several Indian women were engrossed in the game of "hand," their gambling songs rising above the din as they passed a small stone or wood ball from one hand to another behind their backs and then bet on which hand held the token.

Finally, a rifle shot boomed above the clamor. It was Black Harris, the man of great leg, this time riding a horse and bringing trade goods from the settlements. Mules pulled two-wheeled carts, and pack mules carried more goods. The party was just twenty-seven people—Harris and nine employees, accompanied by more missionaries, free trappers, and travelers. Their trade goods included woolen shirts, coffee, tea, chocolate, tobacco at a dollar a twist, and alcohol.

Harris brought disturbing news to the 1839 rendezvous. The company would no longer hire a trapping brigade that fall. Jim Bridger had survived the worst of what the mountains had to throw at him—wounds, starving times, river torrents, and Blackfeet raids. Now he was out of a job. For all of those years, he had stayed in the mountains, never once going back to the States. What would he do now?

SEVENTEEN YEARS
WITHOUT BREAD
1839–1841

Jim Bridger was a mountain man, "the proudest of all the titles worn by the Americans who lived their lives out beyond the settlements."[1] And he was one of the best of the mountain men, with courage and skill, knowledge and determination. He lived a life wild and free, and he embodied an American ideal, as Daniel Boone had a generation earlier. Bridger had not set out to be a hero. What had mattered to him, as it happened, mattered to the nation: exploring the Rockies, discovering the Great Salt Lake, opening the routes to Oregon and California, and forging alliances with the Shoshones, Salish, Nez Percé, and Crows.

By the late 1830s the fur trade was changing. The competition for pelts had decimated the beaver population. Changing fashions meant more people were wearing silk hats instead of beaver, and fur collars and cuffs were being made from another animal—nutria. The decreasing market led many trappers to skip the rendezvous entirely and go directly to the forts on the South Platte to sell their pelts.

Some of the mountain men had turned to theft. In 1836 Peg-leg Smith and Jim Beckwourth went to California with Ute chief Walkara to steal animals from ranches and missions near Pueblo de Los Angeles.[2] In 1839 Peg-leg Smith, Jim Beckwourth, Bill Williams, Phil Thompson, Ute leader Walkara, and several others went back to California to carry out a huge raid in the vicinity of the mission at San Luis Obispo, midway between San Francisco and Los Angeles. They used mares in heat to lead more than three thousand horses away from the Mexican ranches, making the raid the largest livestock theft in California history. Peg-leg Smith admitted, "I came near going under. . . . Them Spaniards followed us and fought us in a way that the Spaniards were never before known to do."[3] Honest mountaineers looked down on the practice of stealing horses, and Doc Newell recorded, "Shuch thing never has been Known till late."[4]

Buffalo hunting or horse stealing was not for Bridger. At thirty-five, he had spent his first eighteen years in the States and the following seventeen years in the West. Maybe it was time to see the settlements again. His wife Cora may have mused about the spirit that led Bridger to make this journey. She may have been aware that when some whites went home they never came back.

That summer of 1839 Bridger joined Andrew Drips in bringing the furs caravan back to St. Louis. If Bridger paused along a stream to slake his thirst, his reflection would have shown a very different person than the one who came upriver by keelboat in 1822. What had happened to Daniel Potts and Captain Weber? They had lost Jedediah Smith, Milton Sublette, and so many more. Who was next?

In the settlements Bridger found cities where prairie grass once grew. By September they reached St. Louis and delivered the pelts and account books to Pierre Chouteau's company. Bridger's personal account at Chouteau's was credited for $408 on September 17, far less than the $3,317 he had received for the two years prior.

The settlements seemed strange to Bridger, as foreign as an Indian village might seem to a greenhorn. St. Louis had grown immensely. Pierre Chouteau was constructing massive new stone offices and warehouses on Laurel Street overlooking the river levee, as well as a four-story salesroom and office. Bridger must have reveled in the bread he tasted in the States, for he later told Capt. William Raynolds that he had once gone seventeen years without tasting bread, which would have been from 1822 to 1839.[5] Bridger likely meant he hadn't tasted leavened bread, as Robert Campbell recalled: "The trappers would make a feast of batter fried in melted buffalo tallow to make a sort of fritter and call their friends around to partake."[6]

Bridger's weathered face and confident demeanor gave proof he was a frontiersman. He cradled his rifle in his arms and carried his knife behind his back, stuck into his belt. Bridger was not too concerned about street toughs lurking in alleys. The cutthroats he had to worry about were the financial ones who could scalp him with words on paper.

A man named H. J. Clayton struck up a brief friendship with Bridger at the Union Hotel and later described him:

Bridger was tall—fully six feet high—erect, thin, wiry, and sunburnt almost to the complexion of an Indian—a light olive—with a face noble and expressive of generosity, dark brown hair and liquid hazel eyes, bright almost to blackness. . . . In form he was straight as an arrow, wore moccasins, and, as an Indian, turned his toes as he walked slightly inward, so strikingly did his manners conform to those of the wild denizens of the forests. So also when walking in the streets of St. Louis with Mr. Dripps he followed him in single file—never at his side, never leading.[7]

Bridger wanted to see his old home, so he crossed the Mississippi to Illinois by boat, retracing a journey he had taken many times when he was young. No bridge yet crossed the Mississippi River anywhere along its length. The river lapped against the sides of the boat, evoking memories of his ferryboat days more than twenty years earlier. After they docked, Bridger explored the American Bottom again, each step carrying him back to an earlier time, each landmark sparking a memory of a younger self. For years his very existence had depended on stealth, but now, walking the American Bottom, he could break twigs under his feet as he had done as a lad, not caring how much noise he made. The Creamers still lived there and had become even more prominent.[8] The man could still feel the heat of the forge and the weight of the coal bucket that the boy had known so long ago.

Memories of his youth must have flooded his mind—perhaps the slosh of a pail of milk or the smell of the forest as he roamed. If his mother and father had lived, perhaps he never would have gone to the mountains. He might have become a surveyor like his father or a gunsmith or blacksmith like Creamer. If he visited his brother's grave, a twelve-year-old's tear might have welled up. If he had lived, would the two Bridger brothers have trapped and traded in the West together like Joe and Stephen Meek, Kit and Moses Carson, or the five Sublettes?

But his brother had died as a boy and lay in his grave far too early. He must have wondered what became of his sister. Words would not have come easily in this place, but perhaps he was putting something to rest, finding a place for unknown things in his heart.

Bridger was despondent after his visit to the American Bottom. He wandered the brick streets of St. Louis like a homesick boy and told Clayton he wished "to go back to his free life in the mountains." Chills and fever plagued him in the turgid air of the Mississippi River valley, which made him long even more for the mountains.[9] Cooped up in a sleeping room was not Bridger's way to suffer through a sickness. He had no mountain roots to boil, no medicine man to smoke over him, and no high, dry air to breathe. It was obvious that the mountains had trapped Bridger just as Bridger had trapped the beaver in the mountains.

St. Louis was too crowded for his comfort. He told Clayton he had never before "seen two houses joined as one." Clayton was intrigued that Bridger "had no fixed residence, but as a hunter led a roving life, and changed his camp as he pleased." Bridger invited Clayton to come west with him, but Clayton said he was too young and too poor. "Go with me now," Bridger said. "You will have no need of money there. . . . You will never go if not now; for you will never have so good an opportunity." Clayton promised that if he lived long enough, he would see Bridger in the mountains.

Henry Fraeb was also in St. Louis, and he too was anxious to return to the mountains. After leaving Rocky Mountain Fur Company in 1834, he had trapped the Snake River country with Jean Baptiste Gervais, and they sold their pelts at Fort Hall. In 1837 Fraeb and Peter Sarpy established Fort Jackson on the South Platte, which they eventually sold to Charles Bent and Ceran St. Vrain.[10] Fraeb and Edmund Christy were sued for debt in 1839 by Sublette & Campbell. Fraeb did not appear in court, and a judgment was awarded against him, but the court could find "no good chattels, land or tennement" of Fraeb's to confiscate.[11]

Bridger and Fraeb became partners again in 1839, starting a new business under the name "Fraeb and Bridger." They obtained a license to trap and trade on the waters of the Columbia and talked of building a fort at Brown's Hole on the Little Snake, a tributary of the Green River.[12] They would be competing with Forts Lupton, Vasquez, and Lookout, as well as Bent's Fort, Fort Hall, and Fort John (later to be known as Fort Laramie). Bridger had been in the city since mid-September, and now it was mid-March. He would soon be thirty-six—time to visit Chouteau's and buy equipment and supplies for the mountains and make beaver "come to medicine."

The setting-off point for western caravans had moved west from St. Louis and now lay across the state at Westport, a settlement on the Missouri that would be the future site of Kansas City. Bridger and Fraeb assembled their men, mules, wagons, and goods. Drips was already at Westport assembling the rendezvous caravan, and Bridger and Fraeb planned to travel west with him. A third contingent of the caravan comprised Fr. Pierre-Jean De Smet and several other missionaries, trappers of souls.[13]

As always, Bridger was an extraordinary asset to the party. He dropped a buffalo near the forks of the Platte, and hump ribs were soon roasting over the campfire. The Sioux approached with rifles and bows, demanding a payment to let the party continue crossing their land. Drips calmly signaled for a council, and Bridger strode forward to parley with them in sign language. Bridger offered a few presents but made it clear that there would be no payment for crossing. He flatly refused to let the Indians search the carts or packs. With that, the Sioux let them pass.

Twice more bands of Sioux blocked their path. They were "thicker than bees" in the words of twenty-one-year-old Jim Baker, an adventurous youth with long, curly blond hair and blue eyes who was part of the caravan. "Thanks be to James Bridger," he wrote years later. "His great knowledge of, and ability to treat with [Indians] . . . was never excelled by any scout of the Plains."[14]

In what is now western Nebraska, the caravan approached Chimney Rock, a solitary spire reaching 350 feet into the air that had become a beacon for travelers over the years. But something didn't look right to Bridger's keen eye. It was shorter than when they had passed it the previous fall. Confirming Bridger's observation, they found broken pieces on the ground nearby. Thirty feet or more had broken off the top.[15]

On the Sweetwater they came to Independence Rock, which rises from the plains like a giant turtle in Wyoming. William Sublette had named it in 1830 when his caravan celebrated the Fourth of July there. In the ensuing years the huge rock had become a visitors' log as passing travelers wrote names, dates, and messages on it with buffalo grease and powder.[16] A day later they saw Devil's Gate, where the Sweetwater rushes through a tremendously narrow chasm. Fr. Pierre-Jean De Smet heard it called the "Devil's Entrance," but preferred to call it "'Heaven's Avenue' for the scene to which it leads."[17] On June 19 they caught sight of the Wind River Mountains. On the twenty-fourth there was snow, and six days later they reached the 1840 rendezvous on the Seedskedee (the Green River). Soon reunited with his wife and daughter, Bridger was likely amazed to see how much Mary Ann had grown.

Cora may have witnessed the Flatheads' First Roots ceremony, which had been handed down over centuries. Tradition said that in the earliest times, the Salish were starving, and an emaciated Salish woman sang a death song for her starving sons as she sat in the shadow of the Red Mountains. The rising Sun heard her cries and sent a red spirit-bird to her to promise that a new plant would grow from each of her tears, and they would know it because it would be white, like her hair, and rose, like the bird's feathers. The People were saved because the plant's nutritious root could be made into food called *spetlem*. Every spring when the grass greened, no bitterroots could be harvested until the elder women had conducted the First Roots ceremony, or the roots would shrivel.[18]

At rendezvous De Smet took particular notice of the Flathead Indians performing their rituals with the pipe as they passed it one to another. The motions of the Catholic Latin Mass would have seemed equally ritualistic to the Flatheads.[19] On July 5, 1840, Fr. De Smet celebrated the first public Catholic Mass in the Rockies at a point overlooking Horse Creek and the Green River, speaking in Latin, English, and French, as translators interpreted it for the Shoshones and Flatheads.[20] De Smet admired Bridger, thinking he was "one of the truest species of a real trapper and Rocky Mountain Man." Once De Smet asked Bridger if the wounds he had received from the Blackfeet had been "long suppurating." Bridger humorously replied, "In the mountains meat never spoils."[21]

The Shoshones put on a grand welcome, galloping in full costume and then dismounting to greet the arriving caravan. The greenhorns were awed by their painted bodies, feathers, wolf tails, animal teeth, and human scalps on poles. The Shoshones were preparing for a war party against the Blackfeet, packing their bows, arrows, and rations. Thirty of the principal Shoshones met with Bridger and the other leaders. The evening before the Shoshone warriors left, the chief came to each Shoshone lodge to perform his war dance and receive tobacco or some other ceremonial tribute to ensure success in the battle. The warriors talked of counting coup on their enemies and taking their women as prisoners.

Doc Newell, who had trapped with Bridger and then trapped out of Fort Hall, was at the 1840 rendezvous and made an agreement to guide the missionaries and settlers on to Oregon. Black Harris, who thought the guiding job had been promised to him, fired his rifle at Newell at seventy or eighty yards. Drips sternly rebuked Harris, saying if he had hit Newell, he would have hanged him.[22]

When Drips announced there would be no rendezvous the following year, some of the mountaineers were angry. Bridger, who had been to every rendezvous except that of 1833, knew which way the wind was blowing. So many trading forts had been established that the trappers could do just as well selling to them instead of waiting for summer rendezvous. Some mountaineers chose to go into the buffalo robe trade. As early as 1831 the Sioux had sold fifty thousand buffalo cow hides in one year to American Fur Company posts, far more than the number of beaver pelts typically taken in a year.[23] A Mackinaw flatboat had come down the Platte from Fort Vasquez in 1840 with seven hundred buffalo hides and four hundred buffalo tongues.[24]

Newell and Meek said they were leaving the mountains, done wading in icy beaver streams and fighting Indians. "Let us go down to the Willamette and take farms," they said.[25] Some mountaineers figured they might hire out as guides, while others went to California to steal horses. Bridger and Fraeb stayed with beaver trapping.

After the final rendezvous Fraeb, perhaps Bridger, mountaineer Joe Walker, and a dozen trappers went to Alta California to trap beaver and trade for horses. Jedediah Smith had spent three years in California (mid-1826 to mid-1829) to great tragedy, and Joe Walker had gone there in 1833, when he saw the Yosemite Valley. Hale, stout, eagle-eyed, and now gray-haired, the veteran mountaineer Walker had long wanted to raise a party to descend the Green River onto the Colorado to see "the canions of that river" and the "high table lands."[26] But this trip was overland, Bridger's and Fraeb's first visit to the Pacific.

Mexico had declared its independence from Spain in 1821 and in 1824 designated Alta California as one of its territories, thus claiming all of present-day California, Nevada, and Utah and portions of Arizona, New Mexico, Colorado, and Wyoming. Inhabited by indigenous peoples for thousands of years, the region had several missions and towns, including Pueblo de Los Angeles, which was founded in 1781.

Walker had already arranged for a passport, which was issued by the Mexican charge d'affairs, don Montoya, in Washington. The permit allowed him to visit California for two months to purchase horses. The small group rode south into present-day Colorado and then west, reaching Pueblo de Los Angeles by February 1841. The City of Angels had been a Spanish mission for sixty years and now boasted a population of three thousand—indigenous people, Spanish settlers, and missionaries.[27]

Aerguello, the prefect in Los Angeles, was suspicious when Walker, Fraeb, and Bridger arrived. Walker presented his passport, and the prefect told them that the Mexican government was well aware that Americans came from Santa Fe to Los Angeles to steal horses. Walker explained that those men were renegades, and he promised to bring Mexico's concerns to the government of the United States. They were ultimately given permission to trade.

They stayed in Los Angeles from February 10 to April 17 and established credit with local merchant Abel Sterns by selling him 417 pounds of beaver at three pesos a pound for a total equivalent of $1,147. They purchased animals from Juan Bandidi, a prominent ranchero: one hundred mares at two dollars each, two stallions at ten dollars each, and seventeen mules for twelve dollars each. They also purchased sugar, coffee, tobacco, beans, soap, and *aguardiente* (a potent liquor).[28] The trappers returned to the Rocky Mountains in mid-1841 with their animals and supplies.

FORT BRIDGER
1841–1843

Bridger and Fraeb returned from California and started construction on Fort Bridger, consisting at first of several log cabins, intending it to be a place to trade and live year-round. They chose a location on the west bank of the Green River a few miles below the Big Sandy. For eighteen years Bridger had slept under the stars or in a temporary lodge and wore or carried nearly everything he owned. He was now thirty-seven years old and his wife was pregnant with their second child. The time was right to settle down and have his first home in his adult life.

Tom Fitzpatrick arrived in the Rockies that summer guiding the Bartleson-Bidwell party, the first major emigrant train bound for Oregon and upper California, an event that signaled the beginning of the Oregon Trail. Fraeb, his trappers, and their Shoshone women and children were out hunting buffalo and drying the meat, and the wagon train stopped at their camp.

John Bartelson and others who had alcohol hidden in their wagons sold it to Fraeb and his men.[1] Even diluted four parts water to one part whiskey, it made a strong drink, and Fraeb and his men celebrated. The dour preacher Joseph Williams, also traveling with the emigrants, described Fraeb's party as "half breeds, French and Dutch, and all sorts of people collected together" who were a "wicked, swearing company of men." The wagon train also included Father De Smet, two other priests, and three novitiates.[2]

The wagon train continued west and the Cheyennes, Arapahos, and Sioux rode into Fraeb's camp, angry that the Americans were hunting and trading with the Shoshones. Fraeb gave them whiskey, which appeased them at first, but later they raided Fraeb's camp and swept away a number of cattle. When Bridger heard of the attack, he sent Jim Baker and two other men to tell Fraeb to abandon his camp immediately.

Even though he had women and children with him, Fraeb stayed out "making meat." On August 21, ten days after the first attack, the Sioux, Cheyennes, and Arapahos came back in large numbers to attack them close to the confluence of the Little Snake River and Battle Creek near today's Savery, Wyoming. Fraeb sent the women and children to shelter on a nearby mountain and ordered his men to the corral.

They fought off the Indian's first charge but lost many of their horses. Fraeb called for them to fort, and the party's dead horses became their breastwork, arrows protruding from their flanks. They led their remaining horses to gaps in their barricade and slit their throats to complete the defense. The Indians attacked the corral again, riding as close as fifteen feet. Fraeb kept shouting, "Don't shoot until you're sure. One at a time."[3]

The trappers fired in turns, half of them shooting while the other half reloaded. The battle raged through the day, the sun blazing down on the sweaty hunters. Fraeb was shot, and he fell back dead against a stump. Baker said Fraeb was "the ugliest looking dead man I ever saw . . . all covered with blood . . . rotten front teeth and a horrible grin."[4]

When it was over, Fraeb and four or more of his men were killed. About one hundred horses were stolen or killed, forty or more were wounded, and only five mounts were still healthy. The toll on the Sioux Indians was even more devastating; the heavy losses galvanized the Sioux to continue bringing war to the Shoshones and any Americans with them.[5]

Bridger had lost his friend and partner. The death of a company leader in battle was all too common—Jedediah Smith in 1831, Milton Sublette in 1837, and now Henry Fraeb in 1841. Their deaths were stark reminders of how fragile life could be amid the Indian factions who regularly engaged in mortal combat. The loss of his partner posed a practical setback for Bridger as well, for Fraeb was the only one of the two of them who could read and write.

That summer of 1841 the Bridgers sent their daughter Mary Ann to the Whitman mission in Oregon, probably as much for her safety as for her education. Fitzpatrick and his wagon train already included two families with small children and may have taken Mary Ann as far as Fort Hall.[6] Hudson's Bay Company's Francis Ermatinger, an acquaintance of Bridger's, was going from Fort Hall to

the Whitman Mission and may have taken her the rest of the way. Mary Ann
Bridger arrived at the Whitman Mission in August or September 1841, and there
she stayed to be schooled.[7]

Mary Ann had been gone only a few months before another child came into
the Bridgers' lives. In December 1841 Cora and Jim Bridger had a baby boy, Felix
Francis Bridger. Bridger's great-granddaughter, Mrs. Billie Duncan, remembered
(or surmised) years later that Jim Bridger's middle name was Felix.[8]

James Douglas, one of the HBC leaders, worried that the American trappers
might become shiftless and cause trouble as the fur trade economy declined
and they lost the Chouteau organization's stabilizing leadership. He proposed
to company management that American trappers "be formed into parties under
their own leaders and pushed, in Boats, down the Rio Colorado where they
might have opportunities for benefiting both themselves & the Company, as it
abounds in Beaver, particularly near its discharge into the Gulf of Calefornia."[9]

George Simpson, the head of HBC's North American operations, took this
a step further. In November 1841 he wrote to HBC governors in London revealing his desire to hire Bridger to join the British company. "An arrangement is
at present contemplated with Captain Bridger, the principal man among these
[American] trappers, by which it is hoped their entire hunts may next year fall
into the hands of the Company."[10] Simpson cautioned HBC governors that if
Americans did lead a brigade for the British, HBC would have to advance the
costs, and the Americans might just abscond with the goods. Simpson suggested
even that would be a positive outcome, because "we should in that case benefit
by their absence."[11] But it was a moot point. Bridger had no intention of trapping
for Hudson's Bay.

Richard Grant had replaced Henry Ermatinger as the chief factor or trader
for Hudson's Bay at Fort Hall, and he was determined to beat Bridger in the race
for furs. Fort Hall was just two hundred miles from Fort Bridger, at the confluence of the Snake and Portneuf rivers, and it had already captured much of the
American trade. The British had replaced Nathaniel Wyeth's original log pickets
with a twelve-foot-high wall made of "cakes of mud baked in the sun."[12] From
Fort Hall, HBC kept a close eye not only on American fur traders but also on the
emigrants heading to Oregon, "from the child in arms to the huge Mississippi
Yahoo, six feet 4 or 5 inches on his stocking-soles."[13]

Grant was focused on trapping southern California and wrote about the region
as "Queaterra." Americans called it Coyoterra, named after a western Apache

group that lived along the Colorado River near the Gulf of California.[14] Bridger had organized and equipped a trapping brigade to Coyoterra that summer of 1841 and hired Peg-leg Smith to lead it.[15] Peg-leg brought back twenty-four packs of pelts from Coyoterra in 1842, but then he argued with Bridger over his wages. Ultimately Peg-leg stole what he thought should be his pay in beaver and sold those pelts to Grant at Fort Hall.

Richard Grant immediately hired Peg-leg as a brigade leader for Fort Hall, knowing that as an American, he could more easily trap areas like the Coyoterra, which was far from British-claimed land. Grant gleefully wrote his HBC superiors that having Peg-leg Smith working for him was "a severe thorn in the side of Bridger."[16] Grant then pleaded with George Simpson for a bigger budget, noting that Peg-leg had only hunted part of the Queaterra country and only for a short time. "If from 35 to 40 Good Staunch men . . . with a leader as above mentioned, could be raised to hunt the Queaterra Country thoroughly I have not the least doubt but the result might prove profitable."[17]

Discord between Bridger and Grant went beyond the race for beaver. As early as 1839 Cheyenne Indians had stolen more than one hundred horses from the trappers at Brown's Hole. American mountaineer Phillip Thompson and a man named Michel chased the thieves but could not apprehend them, so they stole fourteen horses from Fort Hall instead. Thompson left a note threatening to kill the absent factor and stating that American "fathers fought for the country and the [Hudson's Bay] Company shall not possess it."[18]

Horse-thievery was rampant: Thompson's group also stole thirty horses from the Shoshones, and several mountaineers, including Joe Walker, Joe Meek, William Craig, Doc Newell, and Kit Carson, stole the horses back again for the Shoshones.[19] Renegade Americans then stole horses from Hudson's Bay men who were at Brown's Hole trying to collect debts from American trappers.[20]

None of the thieves were Bridger's men, but in the summer of 1842 Richard Grant at Fort Hall charged that Bridger's company had stolen goods that belonged to Hudson's Bay. Bridger vociferously denied the charge, and Grant responded with dreadful oaths against Bridger. That Grant would spout appalling oaths was no surprise. His supervisor, George Simpson, thought his employee was "not Steady, would Drink if not under constraint, speaks at random and is scampishly inclined."[21]

Meanwhile, Bridger had accumulated thirty packs of beaver pelts he needed to transport to Fort Laramie. With the Sioux, Cheyennes, and Arapahos vowing to make the plains flow red with blood, he decided to abandon his fort on the Green and send his wife Cora and their son Felix to stay with her Flathead relatives or with American and Indian families with whom he worked. When travelers passed Bridger's first fort on the Green River, all they saw were "three little, starved dogs" and "the grave of an Indian woman, who had been killed by the Shiennes [Cheyennes]."[22]

Accompanied by Tom Fitzpatrick, Bridger set out for St. Louis with a large party of trappers and traders traveling with beaver skins and other furs to sell. Two parties had already been stopped by the Sioux that spring. To avoid the raiding Indians, Bridger led the party on a little-known route through the Laramie Black Hills, so called because of the dark appearance of their slopes, created by thick stands of cedars and pines.

They arrived at Fort Laramie on July 3, 1842. Traders and trappers had been calling the site Fort Laramie for some time, after the river by which it stood, which had been named for J. Loremy, who had been killed by the Arapahos in 1821.[23] Bridger found that a new post had been built out of adobe to replace the original fort, which had been made of wood and was deteriorating.

At the fort they encountered a wagon train of 110 emigrants bound for Oregon, captained by Dr. Elijah White. Because of the Indian activity, the emigrants were afraid to go on, and they hired Tom Fitzpatrick to guide them to Fort Hall, paying him the attractive sum of $250. When Fitzpatrick led them out from Fort Laramie, 350 Sioux followed, and their chief swore to "kill the first whites on his path."

The Sioux overtook Fitzpatrick and the emigrants near Independence Rock, and the majority of Sioux wanted to kill them all. Fitzpatrick's skill and resolve secured their safe passage, but the Sioux swore that the trail was no longer open and that any whites they found on it in the future "would meet with certain destruction."[24]

Bridger and his party continued east across the Nebraska plains. It was a drought year—much of the water had dried up, and grasshoppers had destroyed most of the grass. On the trail they met a westbound party of cartographers and astronomic observers traveling "scientifically" with compasses, a barometer, a sextant, and horizon to map the land. They were the main body of John C. Frémont's first westward expedition, and when they saw the wild-looking riders approaching, they ran for their guns and checked their bullet pouches, exclaiming "Indians, Indians."[25] But their guide, Kit Carson, put them at ease, for the approaching riders were led by his friend Old Gabe, Jim Bridger.

Frémont himself was away from the party, exploring a side route with three of his men and three Cheyennes. It was five o'clock by the mapmaker's chronometer, and Bridger said there was a fine patch of grass not far back where they could eat and talk. After supper, the tablecloth was removed, and Charles Preuss, a dour cartographer from Germany, listened carefully to the talk so he could record it in his diary.

The objective of Frémont's expedition was to put on paper the route that Bridger, Carson, and hundreds of other mountaineers already knew—the Oregon Trail from Westport, Missouri Territory, to South Pass. Bridger told them they should not go beyond Laramie with such a small force. The Sioux, Gros Ventres, and Cheyennes were openly hostile to whites and had recently killed several people at the Red Buttes. If Frémont couldn't hire more men, they should turn back. Bridger offered to guide the party as far as the headwaters of the Sweetwater near South Pass and treat with the Indians if needed. But in Frémont's absence they had no authority to hire him.[26]

Bridger's warning had thrown the Frémont party into panic, and they worried about their fate. The French Canadians exclaimed, "*Il n'y aura pas de vie pour nous*" (There will be no life for us).[27] The next day Preuss and the others were dispirited and agitated. Preuss thought it was "ridiculous to risk the lives of twenty-five people just to determine a few longitudes and latitudes and to find out the elevation of a mountain range."[28]

There had been frequent discord between Frémont and Preuss. Preuss kept a diary even though Frémont had forbidden it, wanting no competition when he published his own record. Preuss expressed great disdain for Frémont in his secret diary, calling him a blockhead. He must have delighted in recording, "There was such a hurry this morning that Fremont became angry when my horse urinated [on him. It] whipped its tail when it had only half-relieved nature."[29]

Carson, Preuss, and the main body of men reunited with Frémont at Laramie. The Sioux at the fort confirmed that the threat Bridger had described was real. "Our young men are bad, and if they meet you they will believe that you are carrying goods and ammunition to their enemies, and will fire upon you."[30] Carson fully supported Bridger's warnings and, to Frémont's consternation, did something that spread more fear than anything else. He made his will.

Carson trusted Old Gabe, and according to Frémont "openly expressed his conviction that we could not escape without some sharp encounters with the Indians." Frémont's draft manuscript quotes Carson saying, "All of us should never see the fort again."[31] A number of Frémont's men requested to be discharged.

To ease their fears, Frémont hired Joseph Bissonette from nearby Fort Platte, and he helped interpret for them until they reached the Red Buttes. He was friendly with the Sioux and that helped them avoid any attacks. When Bissonette was ready to leave them, he told Frémont, "The best advice I can give you, is to turn back at once."[32] Frémont ignored the warning and persuaded his party to continue. Fortunately they survived.

When Bridger reached St. Louis, he found business was bad. Several banking and commercial houses had failed, and credit was hard to get. Bridger sold his thirty packs and paid off his men. Because Fraeb had died, Pierre Chouteau wondered whether Bridger would pay the entire debt of the company or just his share. Bridger quickly settled the partnership's account in full on September 3, paying sixty-five dollars in silver and gold.[33]

Bridger talked to his old friend, William Sublette, and told him there was still money to be made in the beaver trade. Sublette & Campbell asked to borrow money from William Stewart and, perhaps based on Bridger's optimism, promised Stewart that "there is the handsomest opening now for trade there ever was."[34] Stewart immediately loaned Sublette and Campbell $4,000 through a bank in New York.

Bridger found a new partner in Louis Vasquez, the youngest of twelve children from one of the finer families in St. Louis. Vasquez had been with Bridger in the mountains in 1822 and was one of the four trappers who had circumnavigated Salt Lake in 1826. Vasquez and Andrew Sublette had operated Fort Vasquez for seven years on the South Platte, where they had an impressive view of Vasquez Peak, which was later renamed Long's Peak. But lately they had made what William Sublette called a "stinking business of it," and Sublette & Campbell sued them for $2,751.77.[35]

Vasquez had to sell his land in St. Louis County to pay toward the debt. Vasquez was determined to earn back what he had lost on the Platte, vowing to his brother that he would "make money or die."[36] Bridger, having just lost Fraeb as a partner, was more interested in staying alive. Bridger and Vasquez hired thirty men, many of them French Canadian. They bought merchandise from Chouteau on credit at 50 percent advance on New York prices and set out for the mountains in September 1842.

They intended to build a new Fort Bridger, and they selected a site that was two days' ride farther west than Bridger's 1841 fort, locating their new log houses on a bench overlooking Black's Fork of the Green River. Richard Grant at Fort Hall observed, "My nearest American neighbors are Vasquez and Bridger traders established on Blacks Fork, a branch of the Green or Colorado River, their establishment was in 1842 on Green River but in 43 fearing the Shyans [Cheyennes] and Sewes [Sioux] Indians, removed to Blacks fork a couple days riding from Green River."[37]

Like Bridger's first fort, his second home was on land that had been claimed by the Shoshones for generations, and the Shoshones welcomed them. Because the fort stood west of the Divide, it was in Mexico. Located on a long-standing north-south Indian trade route, it was to be a base from which Bridger could launch beaver brigades. For a couple of months each year, it would also serve as a supply stop for emigrant trains. Bridger and Vasquez did not prosper as they started their new venture. They sent an express to Chouteau & Company asking for more supplies, but they had few beaver to show for their efforts to date. Hudson's Bay Company trappers had proven to be strong opposition.[38]

In the spring of 1843, the Bridgers and Vasquez abandoned their fort on the terrace and built the third and final Fort Bridger on the grassy lowlands below. It was an oasis—shady, grassy, and well-watered by several gurgling streams of Black's Fork that were alive with mountain trout. One traveler described it as "beautiful out of all reason, like a charming but improbable stage setting with the snow-topped Uinta Mountains to the south provide a magnificent backdrop."[39] Here they would stay.

They built two double log houses, each forty feet long, one for the Bridgers and one for Vasquez.[40] They also built a blacksmith shop, so emigrants could shoe horses and repair wheel rims, and a separate room for trading. They constructed a stockade by setting hewn logs upright side by side and attached a corral for horses and other livestock. The buildings had no wooden floors, just packed dirt sunk slightly below ground level. Archeological excavations have identified the location of the log houses, blacksmith shop, trading post, and fort perimeter. Artifacts dating to the Bridger-Vasquez period or earlier include a "two real silver coin" made in Mexico City.[41]

Archeological evidence shows that women were essential to the trading and trapping economy at the fort, and they had a significant presence within the fort itself. Women tanned hides and made clothing, ground flour, and did much of the actual trading on the perimeter of the fort. Excavations have discovered "manos [to grind food], sewing needles, hook and eyes, thimbles, decorative buttons, shoe parts, and prepared leather." Residents at Fort Bridger depended on Native Americans for food. "Indian Rice Grass was found in one of the storage pits within Bridger's Trading Post."[42]

Pollen and floral analyses and other studies have helped document the changing landscape at Fort Bridger. At one time the location was a wet meadow, but by

1843 the meadow had been replaced by "a grassland marked by sage and grease-wood [shrubbery]." Cottonwoods, pines, and junipers grew nearby, which were probably cut down to build the fort. The grass near Fort Bridger was overgrazed, often leading to blowing sand and dust.[43]

Bridger chose to live frugally, housing Cora, Felix, and himself in two rooms. His fort was much simpler than Fort Laramie or Fort Union. He lived the life he wanted, dwelling among the Shoshones and sending whatever money he made to increase his account. Fort Bridger was his home in the wild, and it allowed him to roam several times a year knowing that his wife and children would be safe and comfortable with their people.

For more than a century, some historians have marked a distinct period of exploration dating from the expedition of Lewis and Clark in 1804–6 to the establishment of Fort Bridger on the Oregon Trail in 1843. Jim Bridger played a significant role in that period and the next as well.[44]

16

THE OREGON TRAIL
1843–1844

By late 1843 Bridger's financial future was in peril. His last significant income had been earned from Chouteau & Company in 1838. Since then he had gone to St. Louis, partnered with Fraeb, traded in small amounts in California, lost Fraeb and several men and horses, and partnered with Vasquez. Now Bridger and Vasquez owed $4,500 to the Chouteau Company at Fort Pierre and needed money or furs to pay that debt.

Fort Bridger was a small trading post with limited inventory, but travelers on the Oregon Trail welcomed the supplies and blacksmith shop, and the chance to trade for well-rested livestock. Bridger and Vasquez both did the trading. Bridger also led trapping and trading brigades, while Vasquez spent more time keeping track of sales, orders, and accounts. One or both of them would take furs to Fort Laramie each year. Unfortunately, Bridger and Vasquez had only a few hundred pelts to show for the winter of 1842–43.[1] Richard Grant at Fort Hall kept a keen eye on them and reported that Bridger and Vasquez "like ourselves have done but very little this year, and in all likelihood they will do far less the next."[2]

Bridger's old friend William Stewart had returned to America and organized a commemorative rendezvous of fifty men to set out from Independence, Missouri, and ride to the Green River once again. He was now Sir William Drummond Stewart, as his older brother, John, had died, which made Sir William the heir.[3] Stewart hired William Sublette to lead the caravan, and Sublette was amazed at the "doctors, Lawyers, botanists, Bugg Ketchers, Hunters, & men of nearly all professions," who participated, half or more hired by Sir William.[4] On July 26, 1843, Stewart sent three men to Fort Bridger with an invitation for Bridger and the Shoshones to come to the Green River rendezvous once again and race horses.

Stewart also prepared a note to Bridger to leave on a pole at the site of the old Green River rendezvous: "The compliments of Sir Wm Stewart to Capt. James Bridger. Come and see us. We have been expecting you for several days, and shall wait for you a few days more. Come to camp. We have commenced an extensive game of ball, and we want you to come and 'Keep the ball in motion,' come. Our racing sports commence tomorrow. Come; and a steed is at your service. Come,—hurrah!"[5]

But Bridger had his hands full. In late July seventy-five Cheyennes led by a white renegade named Louis Reveire and his companion, Tesson, launched a daring synchronized raid on Fort Bridger. Most of the Shoshone men were away bow hunting. Vasquez was gone to Fort Laramie, and Bridger was inside the fort with a cook and a clerk. The Cheyennes surprised a hunter, John, who was out hunting with Bridger's gun, and forced him to tell how many were at the fort and where the guards were posted.

The Cheyennes then advanced covertly through the streams and willows until they were two hundred yards from the fort. There they split into two groups: one party to steal horses from the fort and the other to steal horses from the camp of the Shoshones and mountaineers.

The Cheyennes who raided the fort killed and scalped the Flathead horse guard, speared an Indian woman and a boy, and took a girl prisoner. They ran off with seventy horses belonging to the fort before Bridger even had a chance to respond.

The Cheyennes who raided the Shoshone and mountaineer camp speared a sleeping Shoshone boy and "dashed through the village, lancing, spearing and striking down all and everything in their way."[6] They got away with almost two hundred horses. Miles Goodyear, Jack Robinson, and five or six Shoshones gave immediate chase, and they were soon joined by several returning Shoshone hunters.

The Cheyennes rode in a dramatic crescent formation, driving the stolen horses at full speed before them, "zig-zagging, or as it is called, 'making snake,'" along the line "to prevent their pursuers from breaking it."[7] The Shoshones recovered almost all their horses, and nearly all the horses the Cheyennes made off with belonged to Bridger, Vasquez, the mountaineers, and the three messengers from Sir William Stewart.[8] The Cheyennes killed six to eight Indians from the fort that day, and it was considered "the most desperate affair known for many years in the mountains."[9]

On August 16, 1843, Tom Fitzpatrick led a portion of Frémont's second expedition along the Green River near Big Sandy River and saw old houses that had been part of Bridger's first trading post. Two weeks later Fitzpatrick and Frémont's party rode under a bluff along Black's Fork and saw the abandoned log homes of Bridger and Vasquez, the second Fort Bridger. They finally reached the third and last Fort Bridger, located on the well-watered bottom land of Black's Fork, a lush oasis of grass and willows.[10]

Vasquez, who had been hunting in the Uinta Mountains, welcomed Fitzpatrick and the party, telling them that Bridger had started with a party of forty men to trap the Wind River and then the Milk River. One of Frémont's mapmakers, eighteen-year-old Theodore Talbot, was disappointed at not meeting Bridger. Even though he was traveling that year with Kit Carson and Tom Fitzpatrick, he described Bridger in his journal as "the most celebrated trapper of the Rocky mts."[11]

Bridger's financial challenge continued. The goods he received from Chouteau & Company that year were damaged, the tobacco was inferior, the flannel shirts were too small, and the coffee was so rotten that people wouldn't even take it as a gift. The men that Chouteau sent to Bridger were so undependable that he was afraid to take them with him into dangerous territory. In addition, a competing entrepreneur named Joseph Morris arrived at Bridger's camp with two mules laden with trade goods supplied by Chouteau, and Bridger's free men traded their pelts to Morris. Bridger said it was impossible for him to do business "when opposed in his own camp and by his own people."[12]

After a meager hunt that fall of 1843, Bridger led his thirty men to Fort Union, at the confluence of the Yellowstone and the Missouri. They pitched their camp against the cold about a half mile from the fort.[13] Fort Union was easily accessible by steamboat from St. Louis and was well stocked with goods, something that Bridger could only hope for. The fort had become a popular place for artists and others to see and experience Indian life. George Catlin had painted portraits of Eagle Ribs and other Indians there in 1832, and Karl Bodmer had painted several portraits of Indians there in 1833.

With the increase in emigrants passing his fort, Bridger knew he could do very well if Chouteau & Company would resupply him, so he asked Edward Denig, the clerk at Fort Union, to help write a letter to Chouteau. This was a much simpler task than the one artist John James Audubon had asked of Denig six months earlier. Wishing to draw the head of an Indian who had been interred in a tree, Audubon persuaded Denig to climb on his shoulders to reach the elevated coffin of an Indian chief called the White Cow, who was now "three-years-dead." Denig tried to lower the coffin to the ground, but it tumbled down. "Worms innumerable were all about," wrote Audubon. "The head had still the hair on, but was twisted off in a moment, under jaw and all" so that Audubon could sketch it.[14]

On December 10, 1843, Denig took pen in hand and scratched out Bridger's request to Pierre Chouteau & Company, trying to put a positive face on Bridger's letter. "I arrived here some days ago from my Beaver hunt having been particularly unsuccessful owing to the lateness of the season and caught only about three packs. But I believe that a good hunt could be made in the same country and will therefore try it next spring when, I hope to do more than the present appearances would justify."[15]

Bridger reported that Vasquez "has traders with the Pannacks [Bannocks], Nez Perces, Flatheads, Cyuses [Cayuses], Pocans, Pend d'Oreilles, and other nations. . . . He will make satisfactory returns. . . . I have fair prospects of a hunt next spring, and a perfect reliance on Mr. Vasquez for his success in the trade. I send you my order hereby for an equipment for next year . . . to realize a profit to you, but for myself also." Bridger also had to explain the recent difficulties of his new partner. "The conduct of Mr. Vasquez at the Platte was not such as it should have been considering the recommendation he had in St. Louis, and I was sorry for it."

Then Bridger described his fort:

I have established a small store with a Black Smith Shop, and a supply of Iron in the road of the Emigrants, on Black's Fork, Green River, which promises fairly. They, [the emigrants] in coming out, are generally well supplied with money, but by the time they get there, are in want of all kinds of supplies. Horses, Provisions, Smith work, &c. brings ready Cash from them and should I receive the goods hereby ordered [I] will do a considerable business in that way with them. [At] the same establishment [I am] trading with the Indians in the neighborhood, who have mostly a good number of Beaver among them.

Bridger then described his future plans: "My present intention is to make a spring hunt and deliver up my returns, and after receiving the inclosed equipment, to make an expedition into the California, which country is now the only one remaining unexplored and is rich with Beaver. I shall take from 30 to

40 men for that purpose to trap it thoroughly and make also a large return of Horses, Valuable shells, &c." He requested of Chouteau: "Should it be necessary for us to have our license renewed you will be so good as to have it done, and forwarded by the equipment as also a passport to travel in the California and return therefrom."

While Denig was generous in writing the letter for Bridger, William Laidlaw, the commander at Fort Union, was just the opposite. A competitor of Bridger and Vasquez's, Laidlaw, who was also deep in debt to Chouteau, wrote an attachment to Bridger's letter with little appreciation for Bridger and an explanation of Vasquez's bad conduct on the Platte: "Bridger . . . is not a man calculated to manage men, and in my opinion will never succeed in making profitable returns. Mr. Vasquez, his partner, is represented to be, if possible, more unable than he, as by drinking and frolicking at the Platte, he has neglected his business."[16]

General agent Honoré Picotte wrote to Pierre Chouteau on January 4, 1844, objecting to furnishing either Bridger or Laidlaw with new equipment. The balance due by them was more than they could pay, and "their order [was] too heavy!"[17] This rejection of Bridger's order would have a significant negative influence on their fledgling company. The competition or ill-feeling that Laidlaw held for Bridger was shared by others at Fort Union and nearby Fort Mortimer. Fort Union clerk Charles Larpenteur wrote that "much of Bridger's conversation was his brave men, his fast horses, and his fights with Blackfeet."[18]

A large war party of Sioux raided Fort Union a few days before Christmas, wounding a horse guard with buckshot in the leg and stealing six horses. Bridger's men and men from nearby Fort Mortimer gave chase. They all pulled up when they saw the Sioux had crossed a ravine and assembled on a hill the other side. Gardepie, an old Creek Indian from Fort Union, was enraged at their insults and foolishly whipped his horse forward and shouted for all to join in his charge. Ellingsworth, the bookkeeper at Fort Mortimer, followed him, but Bridger's trappers and the rest of the Fort Mortimer men wisely held back.

It was a trap! Sioux warriors were hiding in the ravine, and they fired from behind cover, killing Gardepie and injuring Ellingsworth's mare. The Sioux, now greatly reinforced, increased their taunts, and the rest of the men retreated. According to Larpenteur, "Bridger became very much dissatisfied with his men, who dispersed in all directions."[19]

Bridger led a party of thirteen to the Salt Lake valley in April 1844 to collect salt and trap beaver. According to Samuel Allen Rogers, who was among the men, Indians killed two of their party and wounded Rogers in his shoulder and his knee. The two killed were buried between Big and Little Mountain east of Salt Lake. No other accounts corroborate this incident.[20]

The 1844 summer emigration was larger than 1843. Fifteen hundred travelers assembled at Westport, split into four wagon trains, and started cross country, the wagons full of possessions and the families walking alongside. When the emigrants rolled their wagons up to Fort Bridger, there was a holiday atmosphere. By the time they reached Bridger's fort, they and their animals were exhausted, but with rest they soon recovered. Some couples strolled arm-in-arm, and the women, trim in their pretty but worn dresses, were an unusual sight for the mountaineers and Indians at the fort.

Emigrants crowded the trading room, wanting first chance at the blankets and foodstuffs. They delighted at fishing for spotted mountain trout in the streams of Black's Fork and found ample shade and firewood among the cottonwoods, though some suffered from mountain fever caused by high altitude and heavy exertion. The children loved to play in the knee-deep grasses.[21] Blacksmiths and

Fort Bridger (c. 1860–1870), by William Henry Jackson. This fort, built in 1843 by Jim Bridger and Louis Vasquez, was an oasis for weary travelers on the Oregon and California trails looking for supplies and well-rested animals. *L. Tom Perry Special Collections, Harold B. Lee Library, Brigham Young University, Provo, Utah*

wheelwrights were in great demand and were happy to use Bridger's blacksmith shop.

Most emigrants wanted to purchase fresh stock, and Bridger and Vasquez had plenty of well-rested oxen, cows, young cattle, horses, twenty-five or thirty goats, and sheep to sell them. They branded their stock with the BV mark and sold oxen at forty dollars per yoke, if they could get it, mules at forty dollars each, and horses at twenty-five dollars each.[22] Bridger might trade one well-fed animal for two tired ones or swap out horses for mules. Competing traders from the Arkansas River and Taos set up wagons near Fort Bridger and sold moccasins and buckskin shirts and pants. And Miles Goodyear brought plenty of Taos Lightning to sell to parched emigrants.

The Oregon Trail was one of the longest roads in human history, formed and reformed by animals, Indians, trappers, rendezvous caravans, and now wagon trains. Emigrants came west to escape debt, build a better future, forget a romance, or start again. They learned how to survive on the trail, including how to pull Conestoga wagons into a tight circle, locking their front wheel into the rear wheel of the wagon ahead. They carved their names on three locations in Wyoming—at Independence Rock (south of Casper), Register Cliff (near Guernsey), and Names Hill (about a hundred miles north of Fort Bridger). "James Bridger 1844 Trapper" can still be seen carved into the rock at Names Hill at La Barge Creek on the Green River.

Emigrating was not for the weak of heart. The travelers fought mud, dust storms, and prairie fires. Beetles, "muskitoes," and buffalo gnats tormented them. Their mules suffered galled backs from poor packing, and violent storms leveled their tents and wagons. Some families lost hope, turning back. The wagon trains were too large for the Indians to attack; instead they demanded payment to cross their land. Some emigrant women did their own bartering on the trail, trading calico shirts to Indians in exchange for meat or fish.[23] Mending was a valuable and tradable skill for women on the trail. Emigrating was not for the poor of purse, either. Each wagon cost hundreds of dollars. Hiring a guide or wagon train leader cost $250 to $500, paid for by an assessment from each wagon. Then there was the loss of a half year's wages or the annual crop that farming would have brought.

One emigrant was John Minto, a twenty-two-year-old unemployed coal miner who served as a steamboat deckhand from Pittsburgh to St. Louis. Originally bound for the lead mines of Dubuque, he heard that a wagon train was leaving for the west and hoped he might get free meals if he helped with the wagons. He whirled his cap and said, "Boys, here is the fellow that goes to Oregon, or dies in a sand bank."[24] Minto joined a wagon train, agreeing to help a family named Morrison. When they reached Fort Bridger, Minto saw trappers with Native wives. The festive atmosphere was enlivened by card playing and shooting matches.

Minto mentioned to Mrs. Morrison the sad state of his clothing, and she agreed, saying, "Yes, John, and if you can trade anything at the fort here, and get some deerskins, I'll fix your pants for you." Seeing his bewilderment, she explained, "That means sewing buckskin over a pair of old pants before and behind. One big skin will be enough, and it will be almost good as a new pair. But if you can get three skins I'll make you a new pair, of skins only, besides."[25]

Minto entered the fort and found Bridger himself doing the trading, "a powerful built man . . . quick and sharp at a bargain." Minto showed Bridger his gun, the hammer missing off the right cock, and told him he wanted deerskins for it.

"Young man, I can't do it. We get few deerskins here," said Bridger. "I'll give you ten goat skins; that's the best I can do." By goat skins Bridger meant antelope skins. Minto made the deal with no dickering and brought back the ten antelope skins, dressed but not smoked. Minto was strongly attracted to the life of the trapper and trader and wanted to join Bridger, but Mr. Morrison talked him out of it. It might have been just as well, as Bridger was planning a trapping trip to California.

The Sager family of nine, traveling in the same group as Minto, suffered one of the most tragic experiences on the Oregon Trail. The father, Henry Sager, died of "camp fever" on the west bank of Green River on August 28, and, because they had no boards, they buried him in two troughs dug out of the body of a tree. The party reached Fort Bridger, where the children found streams full of fish. But their mother was mortally ill, and she asked that the children be given to the care of Marcus and Narcissa Whitman.[26] It must have occurred to Bridger that the seven children would soon be orphaned, just as he and his sister had been when they were young, and that the children were going to the Whitman Mission, where his own daughter Mary Ann was.

COYOTERRA AND THE
GULF OF CALIFORNIA
1844–1846

On the last day of August 1844, Bridger and his men set out for "the California," as Bridger termed it, a vast Mexican territory called Alta California that extended from Texas to the Pacific and from Oregon to the Sea of Cortez. He wanted to trap beaver, but he might have been just as eager to see new lands. On the journey south he followed the general path of Green River on horseback, as much of the route was too rough for wagons and too turbulent for boats. The lower Green River flowed into the "Red River," or to use the Spanish names, the Río Verde flowed into the Río Colorado. In Bridger's words:

> The Green River runs through [the Colorado Plateau] about 400 miles [and] in some places rocks [are] 5000 feet high—nothing can go down safe—persons have been [down] both sides of the River over the mountains, but cannot [go] by the water. It is a level high country—full of crevices—a black rock [looks] glazed [and it] rings like Pot metal. [It] would destroy horses feet. About the middle of the rocks comes in the Río Colorado. It winds & twists round. [The rocks] look like old castles burnt. Nothing but brush grows [and] Soap Weed and Prickly Pear—We call them Lancers. [The ground] is covered with musqeet, some willows.[1]

This was rugged country, and the junction of the Green and Colorado rivers would not be officially discovered for another twenty-five years, when John Wesley Powell explored and charted the Grand Canyon in 1869.

Farther south Bridger and his party reached the land called Coyoterra, which lies in present-day Arizona. The Apaches west of the Rio Grande were called Coyoteros because they hunted the coyote for food. This was where Bridger had sent Peg-leg Smith to trap and trade three years earlier.[2] Bridger and his men set their traps, but the Indians stole them almost as soon as they were set. They explored two hundred miles of tidewater where the Colorado drains into the Gulf of California. Bridger found it barren, but they were able to collect a large quantity of California shells, the largest and most beautiful being the abalones, which were popular trade items in the Rockies.[3]

Bridger saw several different bands of Indians on his journey and may have been describing the Hopi when he recalled: "There is a tribe of Indians in that country who are unknown to either travelers or geographers. They make farms and raise abundance of grain of various kinds."[4] Two years later Bridger told Brigham Young and his pioneering party, "Southeast of the Colorado—if there is a promised land, that's it. The Muscalaras Indians are very wild. The Mohavey Indians live on a mountain. There is a tree, like a cedar, [that produces something] like a juniper berry [with] a spicy taste. You may gather 100 bushels off one tree. You can eat twice the full of your hat. A man may go [there] with pack animals in about 20 days."[5]

Bridger left the Gulf of California and did not stop for winter. He traveled north toward Utah by a different, more westerly route than his journey down to the gulf. South of the Great Basin he crossed a desert in January 1845 with sand so hot it burned their horses' feet and he "was obliged to travel nights and lie by daytimes where he could find water."[6]

The mountain man didn't return to Fort Bridger until after the 1845 summer emigration had passed by the station, so Vasquez, busy with trade, was unable to take the partnership's deerskins and pelts in to Fort Laramie.[7] Instead, in September 1845 Bridger rode through the gates of the fort under the two brass swivel cannons guarding the entrance. He traded 25 horses, 24 mules, 840 dressed beaver skins, castoreum, and 675 deerskins, a good share of which was accumulated by Vasquez, and their account was credited for $5,000. Bridger's most unusual commodity was the 1,400 California shells, which were in high demand by the Indians for their pearly luster and could be used to make buttons, jewelry, and ornamental work. The traders promised to give him credit for shells as soon as they could assign a value.[8]

Bridger and his two French Canadian trappers delayed their return to Fort Bridger because the Sioux and Cheyennes had again vowed death to the Shoshones and "every person white or black they should meet."[9] Bridger was anxious to

Fort Laramie (c. 1858–1860), by Alfred Jacob Miller. Bridger and his partners owned this fort on the Laramie River for about twelve months in 1835–36. Originally built in 1834 as Fort William by William Sublette, it later became known as Fort Laramie. *The Walters Art Museum, Baltimore*

return to his fort and agreed to take a party of ten men with him as far as Fort Bridger, provided they all agreed to travel a difficult alternate route through the Wind River Mountains to avoid the Sioux. He surely told them to bring plenty of rope.

Among the group was a twenty-six-year-old lawyer from Ohio, Lansford Hastings, who had gone to Oregon and then California in 1842 and 1843. Based on that one journey, he wrote what would become a popular book, *The Emigrants' Guide to Oregon and California,* just published that year, 1845. His book endorsed a route that he had never taken, telling would-be emigrants that the most direct route would go by way of Fort Bridger, Salt Lake, and then cut west across the desert to the Sierra Nevada. It was just guesswork gleaned from a map. He was unaware that Jedediah Smith, Frémont, Carson, Bridger, and numerous others had already traveled some portion of that route.[10]

Bridger took Hastings and the other travelers by way of his little-known passage through the Laramie Black Hills and then headed toward the snow-covered peaks of the Wind River Mountains. He led them through canyons so narrow the men seldom saw the direct rays of the sun. They climbed precipitous slopes and then skidded downhill, using ropes to stop their animals from falling into deep chasms. One of the travelers said it was "the worst [trail] on the American Continent."[11] When Bridger finally brought them out of the mountains, they saw fresh sign indicting they had narrowly avoided unfriendly Indians. In all, it took them twenty grueling days to get from Fort Laramie to Fort Bridger, nearly twice the normal time. But they made it.

Though it was already October, Hastings announced he was still going on to California. Bridger encouraged him to winter at his fort, but Hastings intended to show the world that the Sierra Nevada could be crossed at any time of year. He was lucky. That winter there was little snow where he traveled, and he crossed the mountains and reached Sutter's Fort on Christmas Day.

Hastings returned from California in the spring of 1846 and crossed the Salt Desert to Fort Bridger with nineteen men, three women, and three children. They were guided by Bridger's former associate, James Clyman. They arrived at Fort Bridger on June 7, disappointed to find the fort empty and wondering at the cause of Bridger's and Vasquez's departure. Hastings went on to South Pass to begin promoting his new cutoff.[12]

Sometime in 1845 or 1846 the Bridgers had their third child and named her Mary Josephine.[13] Now they had two children in the mountains: newborn Josephine and four-year-old Felix. But all was not right for their mother—Bridger's wife Cora—and she was not able to spend much time with her newborn. Bridger's granddaughter remembered the family story. "She was bit by a wolf, and . . . must have suffered from rabies, she was taken ill. And one night she disappeared and no one ever knew what became of her."[14] Years earlier, Bridger had likely brought horses to her father to honor her family. She had given birth to three children, and now she was gone. Bridger either found another Indian woman to care for Felix and Mary Josephine, or he brought them to her family among the Flatheads.

The Sioux and Cheyennes continued to make war against the encroaching whites. In the late spring of 1846, Bridger and Vasquez traveled to Fort Laramie to turn in the past winter's returns. Arriving about May 7, they were fortunate to report all was quiet as to Indian difficulties near Fort Bridger.

Vasquez was carrying a Sioux scalp fully a yard long that the Shoshones had taken after killing a band of ten Oglala Sioux warriors. Learning that one scalp belonged to the son of the chief known as The Whirlwind, the Shoshones had entrusted it to Vasquez with a small parcel of tobacco attached as a peace offering. But The Whirlwind wouldn't accept it and instead called for a massive raid against the Shoshones. The rejected scalp was nailed to the wall next to a brass crucifix in the booshway's apartment, and Bridger and Vasquez hurried to load their wagons and get home to warn the Shoshones.[15]

During the summer of 1846 the number of emigrants on the westward trails continued to grow—an increase sparked in part by Hastings's new book. While many were headed to Oregon, many others were bound for California by way of the Fort Hall/Sierra Nevada route. The newest route, hotly debated, was Hastings's route over the Wasatch Mountains and across the Salt Desert to the Sierra Nevada.

James Reed was one of those who was infatuated with Hastings's shortcut. At Fort Laramie, he met up with Clyman, with whom he had served during the Black Hawk War of 1832. They stayed up late talking of the Hastings route. Clyman did not favor it, perhaps because he disliked the long stretch without fresh water. To add to his doubts, the Clyman-Hastings eastbound party had made a wrong turn crossing the Wasatch Range, which added many days to their journey. But Reed had made up his mind and told Clyman, "There's a nigher route, and it is of no use to take so much of a roundabout course."[16]

Lawyer Abraham Lincoln had helped Reed file for bankruptcy and sell his land and property in Springfield, Illinois. But he declined Reed's offer to join them on the journey west, planning a life in politics instead.[17] The Reed family had a trio of wagons—one of them, built for his ailing mother, was two stories tall and pulled by four yokes of oxen rather than three. Spring-cushioned seating took up much of the first level, and beds filled the second.

The built-in iron stove had a vent pipe running through both floors and the wagon top, and steps provided entry on the side instead of the end. George Donner, father of fifteen, also had a trio of wagons, as did his brother Jacob, father of seven. Then there were the Stantons' wagons and the Murphys' wagons. Collectively they became known as the Donner party, and they were headed for disaster.

Emigrants wanting to cross the Sierra Nevada before the snows blocked their path were advised to be at Independence Rock by the Fourth of July, but the Donner party was nearly a week behind. Regardless, they foolishly stopped for two days instead of one to celebrate the nation's birthday. They took another day off at Independence Rock, while many parties just hurried on. Now they were eight days behind the cautionary calendar.

A messenger on horseback delivered a letter from Hastings addressed to "To all California emigrants now on the road" that extolled the virtues of his new route. It also said Hastings himself would be at Fort Bridger to give further information and personally guide them. The road soon forked and many emigrants took the right fork, called the Greenwood Cutoff, which was a shortcut to Fort Hall that required a forty-five-mile desert crossing. The Donner party took the left fork instead, planning on taking the well-watered route to Fort Bridger and then Hastings Cutoff with its eighty-five-mile desert crossing.[18]

Some of their oxen died from poisonous water pools on the dry Sandy, and more died on the Little Sandy where they stopped for another day of rest. When they rolled into Fort Bridger on July 27, they needed to purchase more oxen. Reed said that "Bridger and Vasquez are the only fair traders in these parts" and called most of the other mountaineers near Fort Bridger "as great a set of sharks as ever disgraced humanity."[19]

Bronzed and bearded Joe Walker passed through with several hundred high-spirited California horses that he, Solomon Sublette, and others had obtained in Los Angeles. Traders from Taos loafed about, selling buckskin shirts and pantaloons for outrageous prices. Old Bill Williams's gun burst and knocked him to the ground. They poured whiskey down his throat, and he woke up saying, "Thought I was dead? Waugh! Since I come to these-here mountains, I been wounded a hundred times, and struck by lightnin' twice, and no god-damn mean gun can kill me!"[20]

The first group to take the Hastings Cutoff that year was the Russell-Bryant party, who were on mules and packhorses and had no families to care for. Edwin Bryant wrote a letter to James Reed and the Donners, who were following several weeks behind, advising them to avoid the cutoff and take the old road to Fort Hall. Bryant entrusted the letter to Louis Vasquez. The Russel-Bryant party left Fort Bridger and completed the Hastings Cutoff quickly, crossing the Sierra Nevada on August 26.

The second group to travel the Hastings Cutoff was the Harlan-Young party, guided by Hastings himself. They started west on July 20 with a train of forty wagons, which eventually grew to fifty-seven. A third contingent left Fort Bridger during the next week in small groups of wagons. They followed Hastings's tracks, many of them catching up and traveling with Hastings. The second and third groups of travelers crossed the Sierra around October 7.[21]

The fourth and last party to take the Hastings Cutoff that year was the Reed-Donner party. Even though they were seven days behind Hastings, who was himself behind the optimum time for the crossing, they still stayed three days at Fort Bridger, not leaving until July 31. On the day the Donner party left Fort Bridger, Reed wrote to a relative in Springfield, strongly advocating the route he had chosen, just as he had done earlier at Fort Laramie when talking to Clyman. Reed discussed the route with Bridger, who was known for giving extensive commentary whenever he was asked about a route.

Bridger very likely discussed the pros and cons of the entire trail section by section commenting on terrain, water, foliage, Indians, and other features, since such detailed advice was his custom. Indeed, Reed acknowledged in his letter that they would have to cross a formidable desert and would need to carry water in barrels in their wagons to keep themselves and their animals alive. Reed wrote, "Mr. Bridger informs me that the route we design to take is a fine level road, with plenty of water and grass, with the exception [of the desert] before stated."[22]

Bridger's statement was accurate; that portion of the route was indeed a fine level road. T. H. Jefferson, a cartographer in the party just ahead of the Donners, made a map of the route that is considered one of the great American maps. Jefferson, like Bridger, described the desert portion as "Road good, a level plain." Jefferson summarized the entire route this way: "The journey . . . is attended with some hardships and provocation—nothing, however, but that can be overcome. . . . The most difficult portion of the whole journey is the passage of the Californian Mountains, and particularly the descent on the western side."[23]

Some novelists and historians have treated the few words that Reed put is his letter as the entirety of Bridger's remarks and suggest Bridger was misleading the Donners. Bridger would have explained the difficulties of crossing the Wasatch Range and the Sierra Nevada, particularly in light of Reed's oversized wagon. He would have warned them that they were behind the prudent timetable and that they should hire a guide. Reed may even have asked Bridger to guide them, for Reed included in this letter that Bridger intended to "go to St. Louis this fall and return with the emigration in the spring."[24] The allegation that Bridger was trying to deceive the Donner party to keep emigrants on the Fort Bridger route is not consistent with his record of prudence and honesty.

The Donner party led their wagons out from Fort Bridger on July 31, following Hastings's tracks. They had twenty wagons and eighty-seven people—adults, children, servants, hired hands, mule skinners, and even cooks.[25] They were leaving eleven days after Hastings. One of the biggest challenges they faced was the size of their wagons and the difficulty of getting them through the Wasatch Mountains. Though Hastings had warned all trains to keep their wagons light, Reed's two-story wagon delayed them considerably.

In addition, Hastings had tried to find yet another route across the Wasatch Mountains and confused his party and the Donners as well by leaving a note on a stick, warning the Donners not to go the way he had gone. Hastings had never traveled this newer route and admitted that his choice was poor. If Hastings had taken the same route that he and Clyman had used just that spring, they would have made quick work of the road building and tree clearing. The Donner party floundered in the woods, and Reed wrote in his diary, "It took 18 days to gett 30 miles." They were now twenty-three days behind.[26]

The second major obstacle the party faced was the loss of James Reed. On October 5, four hundred miles west of Fort Bridger, Reed got into a fight with a hand named Snyder. When Snyder raised the handle end of his bullwhip, Reed stopped him with his hunting knife, killing him. Reed was banished from the train, and he crossed the Sierra Nevada well ahead of the slow-moving Donner party.[27] This loss of leadership undoubtedly contributed to the group's fate.

The final obstacle was the weather and Sierra Nevada range. The Stephens party crossed it in November 1844, and Hastings crossed in late December 1845. But conditions in 1846 were far different. The first winter storm hit the Sierra on October 16, when the Donner party was just fifty miles from the summit. They should have traveled on. But they camped at Truckee Meadows to rest for five days. They finally forged ahead only to be hit by another big storm on October 30, and eight inches fell that night.[28]

Less than a day's journey to the summit, they stopped and camped in late afternoon, thinking they would start fresh in the morning. But the snow continued to fall, until five feet of snow accumulated and drifts reached twice that height. The next day they tried to ascend the summit, now just three miles ahead, but they couldn't find the road. Their wheels slipped, and they had to turn back.[29] Snow blocked their path the next day as well.

These storms marked the beginning of the worst winter ever recorded in the Sierra Nevada. After 2,500 miles and seven months on the trail, they were stranded. The early snowfall and their extended rest-stops along the way had done them in. Some determined to spend the winter at Truckee Lake, while others decided to abandon their wagons and continue on foot.

But they floundered in a quagmire of indecision. Should they take bags of silver or bolts of calico, a crate of tobacco or a container of food? Some were so flustered by the decision that they again tried to cross with their wagons and failed. The group comprised forty men, twelve women, and twenty-nine children, seven of them still being breastfed. They built cabins, counted their standing meat, and measured their livestock against the days until spring. It was hopeless.

As the winter progressed, they exhausted their food supplies. Then they ate their animals. Then they boiled their leather. Then, as some began to die, they ate each other, marking packages of flesh so that no one would unknowingly eat the flesh of his or her own family. Thirty-six of the eighty-one emigrants died: two-thirds of the men and one-third of the women and children. They struggled valiantly and, in most instances, compassionately with each other.

Any one of a handful of decisions could be blamed for their calamity. They set out late; they took too many breaks; they had plenty of money but did not hire an experienced guide or trailsman to keep them moving; they banished James Reed; they stayed and rested for five days before trying to cross the final summit. Mormon Sam Brannan, one of the first to see the disaster of the Donner camp in spring 1847, described them as people "who by quarreling & fighting among themselves, delayed time until they got caught in the Snows in the Mountains last fall & could not extricate themselves."[30]

Twenty-five years after the tragedy, Reed wrote, "Several friends of mine . . . had left letters with Mr. Vasquez . . . directing me to take the route by way of Fort Hall and by no means go the Hastings cutoff. Vasquez being interested in having the new route traveled, kept these letters."[31] That may or may not have been true. But Reed had very early decided on the Hastings route.

Just one year after the ordeal, Reed wrote: "The disasters of the company to which I belonged, should not deter any person from coming who wishes to try his fortune. Our misfortunes were the result of bad management. Had I remained with the company, I would have had the whole of them over the mountains before the snow would have caught them; and those who have got through have admitted this to be true."[32]

"OLD BRIDGER IS DEATH ON US"

1847–1849

Jim Bridger had intended to visit Robert Campbell in St. Louis during the winter of 1846–47 and then return to the mountains leading a train of emigrants in the spring.[1] But instead, according to James Gemmell, he led a group of men on a trapping and trading expedition to the Crow and Sioux camps. They left Fort Bridger in August 1846, ascended the Green River, and camped near the Tetons. From there they followed the trail over the Divide to the streams that flow into Yellowstone Lake.

They camped near the west arm of the lake, and Bridger showed them geysers, Shoshone Lake, the stunning upper and lower falls of the Yellowstone, and Mammoth Hot Springs, where they camped several days to enjoy the baths and allow their animals to recuperate. They wintered at the mouth of the Bighorn and traded with the Crow and Sioux Indians, who were at the time friendly toward each other. In the spring of 1847, they returned to Fort Bridger with their furs.[2]

Bridger and two of his men were on their way to Fort Laramie when they saw a large party approaching near the mouth of the Little Sandy. Little did he know that this encounter would start a chain of events that would threaten his home in the West. Brigham Young, who could be likened to an American Moses, was leading a pioneering group of 143 church members to find a place where they would be free of persecution. They were an advance party of the Church of Jesus Christ of Latter-day Saints.

Young had planned to meet Bridger at his fort, but Bridger told him he was on his way to Fort Laramie to settle a dispute because his men had not delivered beaver pelts by the promised date. Bridger told them, "The Upper Gentry . . . want to take advantage of me."[3] Bridger's animals needed grazing anyway, so he suggested that they turn off the road a bit to talk. Though the Mormons had traveled less than two miles since nooning, they gladly agreed. They established a camp near the Sandy River about a quarter mile distant. That evening, the twelve leaders and several others went to Bridger's camp.

In the 1820s New York farmer Joseph Smith professed that the angel Moroni visited him several times, revealing that an ancient record engraved on plates was buried in a hill near his home. Smith "translated the record by the gift and power of God" and published the translation as *The Book of Mormon*.[4] The number of Smith's followers grew rapidly, but so did his detractors. The fledgling religion moved to Kirtland, Ohio, but townspeople accused them of running a banking scheme and forced them to leave. Smith and his followers then went to Jackson County in western Missouri, but local leaders ousted from there as well. They purchased most of the land in a small town of Commerce, Illinois, in 1839 and renamed it Nauvoo. They elected Smith mayor and, either to protect themselves or give themselves more autonomy, they made it illegal for law officers from other jurisdictions to serve arrest warrants in their city without his approval.[5]

Smith had taken multiple wives by then and encouraged other church leaders to quietly do the same. In 1844 some disenchanted Mormons started a newspaper called the *Nauvoo Expositor* to reveal and oppose polygamy and other Mormon practices. The Mormon-controlled city council declared the paper a public nuisance and ordered its press destroyed after publishing only a single issue. This was an assault on the freedom of the press, and Joseph was charged with rioting. Joseph Smith and others ultimately turned themselves in to the jail in nearby Carthage, where an angry mob stormed the jail and killed Smith and his brother Hyrum.[6]

On March 1, 1845, the council confirmed Brigham Young as President Joseph Smith's successor and "prophet, priest, and king to this kingdom forever after."[7] Young, and Smith before him, felt they needed a place of their own. Illinois governor Thomas Ford, who was not a supporter of the new church, agreed and advised, "Your religion is new, and it surprises people. . . . However truly and sincerely your own people may believe, . . . the impression on the public mind everywhere is that your leading men are imposters. . . . If you can get off by yourselves, you may enjoy peace."[8]

Young told Bridger that they were interested in settling in the Great Basin and had been studying the reports and maps of John Frémont's explorations for almost four years. Frémont's praise for the Great Basin was effusive, and Young and members of his quorum used to read parts of the report aloud.[9] They were well aware that the valleys of the Great Salt Lake and Bear River were part of Mexico, not the United States. Yet even so, Brigham Young sent a statement of intent to President Polk: "Resolved, that as soon as we are established in the Great Basin we design to petition the United States for a territorial government, bounded on the north by the British and south by Mexican dominions, and east and west by the summits of the Rocky and Cascade Mountains."[10] They carried an American flag, which they planted shortly after they arrived in the basin.

However, Frémont's map had a significant error: it showed Salt Lake and Utah Lake as one continuous body. Frémont had never seen this connection, yet his text claimed that the Utah Lake was the southern limb of the Great Salt Lake and called it a mystery why the northern segment of the lake was salty and the southern segment fresh. The Mormons were looking for this multifaceted lake, and Bridger pointed out that the two lakes were thirty miles apart, connected by a river.[11] He spoke freely, saying he "was ashamed of the maps of Fremont, for he knows nothing about the country, only the plain traveled road."[12] Bridger added that he had not yet seen a map of the mountains that was right. He could make corrections on every one. This must have given pause to Young and his men. Who was this illiterate trader telling them that Frémont's report was in error?

Frémont's maps were a boon to travelers and made a significant contribution to western cartography, including his conclusion that the Great Basin was "closed" and did not drain to the sea or other bodies of water. But he could be proud and possessive. When presidential advisor Albert Gallatin asked Frémont about routes over the Sierra Nevada, he curtly responded, "There are several . . . points at which that great range may be crossed, but a knowledge of these is confined to my own party."[13] To the contrary, Bridger told Young in 1847 that he personally knew of five or six places where he could pass over the Sierra Nevada to the California settlements in one day.[14]

The Latter-day Saints also noticed differences with what Bridger told them and what Black Harris had told them the previous day. Latter-day Saint Howard Egan heard Bridger talk, and he unwittingly concluded, "From his appearance and conversation, I should not take him [Bridger] to be a man of truth. . . . He said Harris knew nothing about that part of the country. He says there is plenty of timber there; that he had made sugar for the last twenty years where Harris said there was no timber of any kind. But it is my opinion that he [Bridger] spoke not knowing the place."[15]

William Woodruff, a future president of the Church of Jesus Christ of the Latter-day Saints, had a more positive opinion of Bridger's knowledge, writing that he "found him to be a great traveller, possessing an extensive knowledge of nearly all Oregon and California. . . . He said it [the basin] was his Paradise, and that if these people settled in it he would settle with them; and that there was [only one] thing that could operate against it becoming a great grain country, and that would be frost, as he did not know but the frost might affect the corn."[16]

Young wanted to plant potatoes and corn, and Bridger said, "I would give a thousand dollars if I knew that an ear of corn could be ripened in these mountains." He warned the emigrants that "it would not be prudent to bring a great population to the basin until [they] ascertained whether grain would grow or not."[17] Samuel Allen Rogers, who said he had hunted for salt and beaver with Bridger in Salt Lake valley in 1844, claimed that after Bridger met Young, he confided his worry, saying, "I am sorry for the women and children; they will get into that valley and starve to death."[18]

Bridger warned them that "the Indians 'round Uta Lake will strip a man, if they don't kill him. The Root Diggers use bow and arrows, are very wild. You can see their smoke and backs and that is all."[19] Bridger also referenced the Ute and Mexican practice of capturing and selling Indian children as slaves. The Mormons soon witnessed this themselves when a Ute strongman named Batiste threatened to kill a boy and girl taken from another band of Utes unless the Mormons purchased them as slaves, which they did to save the children's lives.[20]

The next morning, the Latter-day Saints laid out the food, and Bridger remarked, "There is more bread on the table than I have before seen for years." Brigham Young was surprised and asked, "But, Mr. Bridger, how do you live?" "We live entirely on meat," said Bridger. "We dry our deer and buffalo to eat, and also cook fresh when we can obtain it. We usually have our coffee, for that is easily obtained."[21] Bridger invited Young and his group to stop at his fort, and though his blacksmith shop had burned recently, he told them the anvil was there for them to use for their horses and wagons. He also noted that it cost as much as $4,000 to $5,000 to keep up his business, which presumably would be both annual income and annual expense.

Young moved on the next day and wrote Bridger a pass for the ferry that the Mormons had set up to cross the Little Sandy. In Young's note he expressed interest in hiring Bridger to guide them over the Wasatch Range, but Bridger did not make it back to Fort Bridger in time.[22] The Latter-day Saints stopped at Fort Bridger to shoe horses and repair wagons and then went on. They struggled through a difficult crossing over the Wasatch, and Young came down with a debilitating fever, sometimes called "mountain fever" and presumed to be Colorado tick fever. He was confined to a carriage, and when he arrived at the spot where his men had already viewed the valley, he confirmed, "This is the place, drive on."[23]

Brigham's brother, Lorenzo, was heartsick at the sight. Lorenzo's wife said she would gladly travel a thousand miles more to get to where "a white man could live." A third Mormon called it an interminable waste of sagebrush: "The paradise of the lizard, the cricket, and the rattlesnake."[24]

Jim Bridger returned to his fort to trade that summer with the Oregon-bound travelers. Invariably emigrants commented on how many of the mountaineers had a Shoshone wife, who often did much of the trading. One diarist wrote in 1847, "At night, having a fiddle & fiddler, we went up with our wives to the Fort & danced until 2 o'clock. I showed Bridger's wife and other[s] . . . how to dance U.S. dances. There was some wild romance in this."[25]

This was roughly the time when Bridger joined with a Ute woman named Chipeta, which means White Singing Bird (the same name as the future wife of Ute leader Ouray).[26] Some traders paired with an Indian wife in order to establish kinship with her people for increased trade or mutual protection. Bridger's marriage appears to have been based on a desire for a mate as well as the need for help in raising Felix and Mary Josephine.

Louis Vasquez had met his wife, Narcissa Burdette Land Ashcraft, a year earlier at Fort Laramie. A widow from Kentucky, Narcissa was traveling to Oregon when she was abandoned by a man she was traveling with. Some on the wagon train called her "a skinny widow with two children" and "a worthless white woman." But Francis Parkman, who was at Fort Laramie in preparation for his book *The Oregon Trail*, felt sorry for her for becoming something of a scandal and a burden to feed and care for.

Vasquez needed a cook and brought Narcissa and her two children to Fort Bridger, and soon they were married. They had six children together, including their first born, Louis, who was born twelve or thirteen months later in July 1847. Vasquez loved to read and paid for novels to be brought to him in the mountains. One acquaintance observed that Vasquez "put on a great deal of style, [and] used to ride around the country in a coach and four."[27]

The winter of 1847–48 was severe for Bridger. The Mormons suffered on the other side of the Wasatch as well, as fifty-foot-deep snow drifts enveloped Yellow

Creek. In spring 1848 the Mormons planted nine hundred acres of wheat. That summer, large, black crickets "came swarming from the foothills literally by millions" and fell on their crop. The settlers prayed for an answer, and seagulls came by the thousands and devoured the crickets. The gulls ate the crickets until "the plague was stayed and the crops of the pioneers saved."[28]

The Mormons transformed the valley, and Young occasionally encouraged them on with Bridger's statement: "I'd give a thousand dollars to know that corn could be raised in that basin." In one sermon he mistakenly claimed that Bridger offered to give one thousand dollars for *every* bushel they could raise in the valley.[29]

Brigham Young had brought his flock to the Great Salt Lake to escape persecution in the United States, but President James Polk ushered in an era of tremendous expansion. The Mexican-American War, which started over a Texas border dispute, ended with the Treaty of Guadalupe Hidalgo in February 1848. Mexico ceded territory that included half of New Mexico, most of Arizona, and all of California, Colorado, Nevada, and Utah (as these states are known today) to the United States in exchange for $15 million. Jim Bridger's fort and the Mormon settlement were now part of the United States.

The leaders of the Latter-day Saints cherished great dreams of empire and intended to unite with the Indians against the United States, if necessary. Even before Young and his pioneering party set out for the Rocky Mountains, he said: "When we go from here we don't calculate to go under any government but the government of God. There are millions of the Laminates [Indians] who, when they understand the law of God and the designs of the gospel, are perfectly capable of using up [killing] these United States. They will walk through them and leave them waste [dead]."[30]

One year after the Mormons' arrival, Bridger learned that Young was charging him with encouraging Indians to attack the new settlers. On July 16, 1848, Bridger had someone write a letter for him addressed to "The President of the Salt Lake Valley." It said:

> I am truly sorry that you should believe any reports about me having said that I would bring any Indians or any number of Indians upon you or any of your Comunity. Such a thought never entered my head and I trust to your knowledge and good sense to know if a person is desirous of living in good friendship with his neighbours [he] would [not] undertake such

a mad project. . . . Believe Mr President I am desirous of maintaining an amicable friendship with the people in the valley and should you want a favour at my hands at any time I shall allways think myself happy in doing it for you. From your Friend and well wisher James Bridger.[31]

This may have calmed Young, for in December he wrote Bridger and Vasquez that he was open to advice from them. On April 7, 1849, Vasquez took him at his word and cautioned Young against sending families out to establish new settlements. The Indians "are badly disposed toward the Whites. . . . They have been fighting with some Americans in the direction of Taos, and there have been sum of them kild, and to mind the matter, you have killed four this Spring. Last October, Mr. Bridger was at the Uinta for the purpose of staying the winter with them. Their conduct allarmed him so that he had to return to this place [Fort Bridger] to winter."

In May 1849 Vasquez wrote another letter to Young, warning that the Bannock Indians believed a Mormon named Barney Ward had murdered one of the Bannocks and stolen two horses, and they intended to cross the mountains and invade Salt Lake City. Vasquez urged Young to do what was necessary for the safety of his people and all other whites in the country. After Vasquez's letter was read aloud at council, Young surprisingly said. "I believe I know that Old Bridger is death on us, and if he knew 400,000 Indians were coming against us, and any man were to let us know, he would cut his throat."

Young had good things to say about Vasquez, believing he was a different sort of man. But Young seemed to have chosen Bridger as a target for Mormon wrath, and it is not known if it was justified. Young continued speaking to his council: "I believe Bridger is watching every movement of the Mormons, and reporting to [Senator] Thomas Benton at Washington. As to the affair [murder and stolen horses] it is a backhanded man [Bridger] that can't be understood. That letter is all bubble and froth."[32] Young continued, "Bridger and the other mountaineers were the real cause of the Indians being incensed against the Saints, if they really were incensed."

Several weeks later, Peg-leg Smith, who was also on difficult terms with Bridger and wanted to be on good terms with Young, wrote to the church leader that it was a Shoshone Indian who was killed, not a Bannock. Smith did not think Bridger and Vasquez killed the Indian, for they "were not brave enough, but they may have caused it to be done, to bring on a fuss between the Indians and our people, Bridger and Vasquez being jealous of them [Mormons] trading with the Indians."[33]

In 1849 an additional 1,500 Mormons passed Fort Bridger on their way to Salt Lake City, one of the fastest growing settlements in America. By 1850 the city had gristmills, stores, schoolhouses, sugar factories, woolen mills, and iron mills and offered blacksmithing, dentistry, flour, hard bread, and general merchandise.[34] Mail service began in 1850 with monthly pickups and deliveries at Salt Lake City, Fort Bridger, Fort Laramie, Fort Kearny, and Uniontown on the Kansas River. Emigrants could even flag down the mail wagon to add their own mail to the delivery bags.

For his part, Bridger welcomed Mormons to his fort, often inviting visitors in for treats. One young Mormon wrote they were "treated kindly with raisins and sugar."[35] In 1848 Bridger hired eighteen-year-old Mormon Homer Brown to carry furs and goods between Fort Bridger and Fort Laramie.[36] He also hired young Joshua Terry, giving him his keep and a promise of oxen, food, and clothing for his parents when they arrived for the rest of their journey." Terry would later become a raider for the Nauvoo Legion, which rode against the United States in 1857.[37]

On Young's first full day in the valley, he had declared, "We do not intend to have any trade or commerce with the gentile world. . . . I am determined to cut every thread of this kind and live free and independent, untrammeled by any of their detestable customs and practices."[38] But Young's threats were more extreme than his actions. He allowed gentile merchants Louis Vasquez and Livingston & Kinkead to open stores in Salt Lake City in 1849. Vasquez open his branch store in Salt Lake City in November 1849, and the newspaper reported that he was selling "sugar at three pounds for $2."[39] While Vasquez continued to be welcomed by the Mormons, Bridger was viewed with suspicion.

19

MARY ANN, CHIPETA, VIRGINIA, AND MARY JOSEPHINE

1847–1848

In the fall of 1847 Mary Ann Bridger was about twelve-years-old and had been living with Marcus and Narcissa Whitman for six years at their mission near present-day Walla Walla, Washington. She was about to experience the most horrific event in her life. She hadn't seen her exploring father and her Indian mother since she was six and probably did not know that her mother had died a year or two earlier. She was accustomed to her new guardians and followed their religious beliefs, saying prayers every morning and evening. Marcus Whitman was often away on missionary pursuits, and Narcissa took comfort in the children at the mission and particularly referred to two of them as "my two little half-breed girls, Mary Ann Bridger and Helen Mar Meek." Helen, two years younger than Mary Ann, was the daughter of Joe Meek, who named her after a heroine in Scottish literature.[1]

Narcissa loved caring for the girls and told her sister how much she enjoyed getting "my little girls' supper," "putting my little girls to bed," and "hearing my children read."[2] Narcissa's only biological child, a daughter, had drowned when she was two, and the missionary would point to a nearby grave and say, "All the child I ever had sleeps yonder," taking solace that the child's burial site lay "so close to the door."[3]

Mary Ann and Helen Mar did household chores and attended school. Narcissa made dresses for them with hickory shirting from Hudson's Bay stores. The girls went barefoot in the summer and swam every day before dinner in the Walla Walla River in a spot Narcissa picked to protect their modesty.[4] The girls often carried small boards or sticks on their backs as if they were babies, so Narcissa rolled up pieces of cloth as makeshift rag dolls, marking the eyes, nose, and mouth with a pen, and they caressed and carried them about the room as happy as could be.[5]

Dr. Whitman "loved to romp with the children, and they missed him when he was away, sometimes saying, 'Will father come home to-day?'"[6] Narcissa was also lonely when Marcus was gone, and she turned to Mary Ann for comfort. She wrote her sister, "Jane, I wish you were here to sleep with me, I am such a timid creature about sleeping alone that sometimes I suffer considerably, especially since my health has been not very good. . . . Good night, J., for you do not come to sleep with me, and I must content myself with Mary Ann."[7]

Narcissa said Mary Ann had "a mild disposition and [was] easily governed and makes but little trouble," but she was challenged by Helen, who "wants to rule every one she sees." Narcissa kept them isolated from the other Indians at the mission: "We confine them altogether to English and do not allow them to speak a word of Nez Perces. . . . I keep them in the house most of the time to keep them away from the natives, and find it difficult to employ their time."[8]

Mary Ann well remembered the day the Sager children arrived in 1844. She was nine years old and was washing dishes when Narcissa entered the kitchen with the children and asked cheerfully: "Well, Mary Ann, how do you think you will like all these sisters?" When Mary Ann learned they had just arrived from Fort Bridger, she must have wondered how her exploring father and Indian mother were doing. Helen wore a "green dress, white apron, and neat sunbonnet" that day, and Mary Ann was probably dressed similarly.[9]

The Whitmans had only intended to take in the five orphaned girls, but the couple eventually agreed to take the two Sager boys as well. The seven newcomers ranged in age from six months to fourteen years. Catherine, the oldest girl, was nine, the same age as Mary Ann. Twelve emigrant families also stayed with the Whitmans that winter of 1844–45, and school was held daily for the nine children in the Whitman household and sixteen from the emigrating families.[10]

On wash day the household would assemble the tubs at 4 A.M. Mary Ann and other older girls and women did the rubbing, while the males, wearing long aprons, carried the water and "plied the pounders." The hard work was made more pleasant because "jokes were current and all were in good humor." The wet clothes were hanging on the line just in time for school.[11]

In the fall of 1847 an emigrant train brought measles to the Oregon country, and it raged through the Indian populations. Dr. Whitman did what he could, but the Cayuses who lived near the mission had limited immunity and half the tribe died, including most of the children. The deaths generated great anger among them and led to rumors that they were being poisoned. They recollected that Whitman had once injected watermelons with an emetic to discourage the Indians from stealing them. In addition, his assistant had once set out poisoned meat to kill wolves; some Indians ate the tainted meat and almost died. It was not uncommon for the Cayuse and Walla Walla tribes to kill their own medicine men when they were unsuccessful in saving their patients; they reportedly shot seven of their medicine men in five years near Fort Vancouver.[12]

November 19, 1847, was a foggy day, and Mary Ann was alone in the kitchen washing dishes from the noonday meal. Dr. Whitman sat reading in the living room, and Narcissa was bathing two of the Sager children in a tub on the floor. Several boisterous Cayuses barged into the kitchen, and Tomohas, a younger man with a long face and wide mouth, demanded medicine. Dr. Whitman got it for him and led him into the kitchen, bidding that Narcissa lock the door between the kitchen and the living room, leaving Mary Ann and Dr. Whitman alone with the Indians.[13]

Cayuse chief Tiloukaikt, with his high cheeks and prominent nose, sat at the kitchen table distracting Dr. Whitman, and Mary Ann then saw Tomohas step behind the doctor and draw a pipe tomahawk from under his blanket. Suddenly he struck the doctor twice on the head. More Cayuses rushed in, and one of them shot Whitman in the neck. John Sager, the eldest of the Sager children, rushed into the kitchen with a gun and shot at the Cayuses. One shot back, wounding John in the neck. John stuffed his scarf into his wound to staunch the bleeding.

Mary Ann escaped through the exterior kitchen door and ran around the house to the living room, too frightened to speak. Narcissa grabbed her and asked, "Did they kill the doctor?" Mary Ann eventually stammered "Yes." Narcissa cried out, "My husband is killed and I am left a widow."[14] The Cayuses left the house and joined their tribesmen who were attacking other white men at the mission.

Narcissa rushed to the kitchen and found her husband lying in a pool of blood. He was alive, but barely, and she did what she could to stop the blood spurting from his neck. Several women burst into the kitchen, and they helped carry and drag the doctor to a settee in the living room. The women hurried Mary Ann, Helen, and four other children with them to the attic. Another family with three children hid under the floorboards in a three-foot crawl space. From their hiding places they could hear the marauding Cayuses and the screams and groans of the dying men.

The Cayuses broke into the schoolhouse, killed the school master, and lined up the children outside to be shot, excusing only the mixed-race children because of their Indian blood. Their chief, though, was moved to pity and ordered that all the children should be spared and taken captive. The Cayuses returned to the house and killed Narcissa and the other adults on the first floor. They captured Mary Ann, Helen Mar, and the other girls in the attic, moving them to the emigrant house with all the other survivors.[15]

The Cayuses killed fourteen people over the course of several days and took forty-seven captives—men, women, and children. Several Cayuses wanted to kill them all, while others pleaded to save them. They held their prisoners for a month, and some of the Cayuse men abused the girls, taking them against their will. Mary Ann was terrified. Helen Mar Meek and two other children suffering from measles died for lack of care.[16]

Hudson's Bay Company's Peter Skene Ogden finally bartered the release of the captives, buying their freedom by giving the Cayuse Indians fifty blankets, fifty shirts, ten guns, ten fathoms of tobacco, ten handkerchiefs, one hundred lead balls, and gun powder. He also gave smaller numbers of the same items to the Nez Percé for their role in safe delivery of the captives. One of the rescuers trying to arrange the captives' release heard that one motive of the Cayuse attack was to avenge the death of the Nez Percé chief, The Hat, who had been killed when he traveled with William Gray across Sioux lands against Bridger's strong warning.[17]

Mary Ann, the Sagers, and the other captives were told on Christmas Day that they would be saved, and on December 29, one month after the massacre, they set out in wagons. They had not gone far when a native woman told them to hurry because other natives were coming to kill them. They hurried along in fear, and when fording the Touchet River, high water washed over the sides of the wagon and drenched several of them, including Mary Ann. They had no time to change clothes or dry off, for they heard the stern warning, "Hurry, hurry. No camp, get to the fort." It rained on them all afternoon and they shivered from the winter cold. In her weakened state after a month's captivity, Mary Ann became deathly ill.[18]

In April 1848 Joe Meek arrived at Bridger's fort, having worn the red belt and Canadian cap of Hudson's Bay at times to travel safely because some of the Indians were determined to kill any Americans they saw. He told Old Gabe of the attack on the Whitman settlement and of Helen Mar's death, and he relayed that Mary Ann was in questionable health but was still alive. Meek and his companions were on snowshoes on their way to Washington City, swearing that justice would be done, and Bridger gave them four mules for their journey. Meek believed that President Polk would take action since he was married to Meek's cousin.[19] When Meek visited Bridger in April, he did not know that Mary Ann had died about the same time, undoubtedly due to poor treatment while in captivity, the lack of medical care, and extreme exposure to the elements she suffered while escaping the threat of another Indian attack.[20]

A few months after Mary Ann's death, Bridger's wife Chipeta gave birth to a daughter, Virginia, probably on July 4, 1848. Historians have taken Virginia at her word that she was born July 4, 1849, but as Virginia grew older, the birth year she claimed on census records kept making her seem progressively younger. The 1850 census shows her birth year as 1847. Her 1854 baptismal record and the 1860 census show her birth year as roughly 1848. The 1870 census shows her birth year as 1849, and the 1880 record shows her birth year as 1850.[21]

Chipeta may have suffered a difficult birth. Virginia remembered the family tradition: "I was quite young when Mother died, only nine days old. So you can imagine what little I knew of her. But all I know is the love of a father's care to me, and he taken all responsibility on himself for the care of me. When I was a little babe, he gave me Buffalo and mare milk in a bottle [to] nurse through a quill."[22] Drinking milk from buffalo was not unheard of. Dr. Wislizenus and his party had killed a buffalo cow ten years earlier whose udder was full, and they "sucked out the milk and found it refreshing and palatable."[23] But buffalo no longer existed near Fort Bridger by 1848.

Bridger's first wife, said to be named Cora, had given birth to three children: Mary Ann, Felix, and Mary Josephine. His second wife, Chipeta, gave birth to one child, Virginia. With an infant to feed in 1848, this may have been the time when Bridger married his third wife, a Shoshone woman. Bridger called her Mary and in the next decade she would give the family three more children: John, Elizabeth, and William.

Long after Bridger's death, somewhat dubious family stories cropped up. One claimed that Bridger's first wife, said to be named Cora, was a daughter of a Flathead chief, and that his third wife, Mary, was a daughter of Chief Washakie, and her Shoshone name meant Little Fawn.[24] Virginia recalled hearing a family tradition that her father offered six horses and three blankets to the father of his Shoshone bride as a marriage tribute.

---20---

THE GOLD RUSH AND
THE MAPMAKERS
1848–1849

California's gold had lain hidden in the earth for eons. Its discovery near Sutter's Fort in 1848 would unleash tens of thousands of miners, entrepreneurs, and settlers who crossed the country to claim it, many of them going way by way of Fort Bridger. Johann "John" Sutter was a con man who throughout his travels had bilked investors of their money: in Switzerland, along the Santa Fe Trail, and in a failed hotel effort in Westport, Missouri. He had portrayed himself along the way as a former officer in the Persian guards, an adjutant to the crown prince, and former officer in the Swiss Guard.[1] Bridger would have seen Sutter at the 1838 rendezvous, as the would-be entrepreneur had traveled west with the rendezvous caravan and before moving on to Mexico.

In Alta California, Sutter obtained Mexican citizenship and a land grant of 48,827 acres along the American, Sacramento, and Feather rivers where he built Sutter's Fort.[2] On a fateful afternoon in January 1848, James Marshall was building a mill for Sutter and noticed yellow specks in a ditch along the American River. He scooped up the gravel and swished it with water and found more glittering flecks. Marshall kept looking, and the next day he found a yellow nugget about half the size of a pea. The next month the United States acquired California and other lands from Mexico for $15 million. By May 1848 a miner celebrated his way through San Francisco with a quinine bottle filled with nuggets, and the word was out. President Polk announced the news of gold in California in his message to Congress on December 5, 1848, and the California Gold Rush had begun.

Meanwhile the beaver trade continued to diminish. By January 1849 Bridger and Vasquez buyers wrote, "Beaver has become almost worthless, bringing only 75 cts. per lb. . . . Wolf Skins are only worth 50 cts. for the largest, while the smaller ones can hardly be sold at all."[3] The Indians were no less forgiving. Charles Chouquette recalled that he was one of Bridger's men attacked by Blackfeet at Great Falls on the Missouri that winter of 1848–49.

Chouquette and two others had chanced upon a large party of trappers on the Bighorn led by a "broad shouldered, flaxen-haired and blue-eyed man riding as fine a saddle animal as I ever saw."[4] Chouquette asked him his name, and the leader replied, "My name is Bridger. Maybe you've heard of me." Chouquette may have viewed at this as humorous or humble, as "there wasn't a man west of the Mississippi who did not know him or know of him." They trapped together and wintered on the Yellowstone. According to Chouquette, Bridger was sick that winter and constantly doctored himself with various roots he gathered.

In spring 1849 they trapped the Musselshell River, the Snowy Mountains, the Judith River, the Big Belt Mountains, and Great Falls on the Missouri, where they spotted a large village of Blackfeet, four hundred men according to Chouquette. Knowing an attack was likely, Bridger ordered double guards to watch the camp that evening and took his turn at midnight. At first daylight the Blackfeet charged, and Bridger hollered, "Don't get excited, boys, and be sure of yer aim. Take it easy now."[5]

The trappers repelled the Blackfeet charge, but men on both sides were wounded. At the second charge, more men fell. According to Chouquette, "One great tall fellow had his horse shot out from under him and when he struck the ground he made for Bridger with a wicked looking war club in his right and a knife in the other. . . . When they met, the Indian aimed a blow at him with his war club, but Bridger caught it on the barrel of his rifle and it flew away off to one side. Then the Indian tried to knife him and Bridger just punched him with his rifle barrel so the fellow couldn't close in, and all of a sudden he hit him square in the forehead and smashed his skull as cool and easy as could be."[6] The Blackfeet charged once more with little effect and then left.

After the bloody fight with the Blackfeet, Bridger returned to his fort to deal with the huge flux of emigrants, swelled by the droves of forty-niners rushing to California. Vasquez was on his way to Fort Laramie that spring of 1849, and the first wave of gold seekers who met him on the trail purchased all of his spare animals on the spot: horses sold as high as $150 and oxen brought $125 a yoke. He sent a rider back to Fort Bridger for 130 more animals. Wagons lined up at the ferry crossings waiting in turn to pay five dollars for every wagon crossed. While emigrants waited, they visited gambling tents, including a regular Monte bank game brought up from Mexico after the recent war. At the beginning of June blacksmiths charged five dollars to shoe horses or oxen; they raised their price to eight dollars by mid-June and to twelve dollars before the month was out.

Bridger and Vasquez both operated ferries on the Green River, and W. H. Homen remembered how Bridger accomplished crossing the horses and cattle. After the boats took the wagons across, Bridger sent out a young Indian to guide the teamsters to a place where it was best to ford the animals. The Indian tied an emigrant horse to his pony's tail and then swam across, leading his horse and the entire herd behind them across the river.[7]

Emigrants now called the trail west the California Road, and miners filled the route, saying they were "going to see the elephant," an American colloquialism that meant embarking on a great adventure to see all there was to see. They invariably overpacked and eventually threw their excess along the trail; the heavier the item, the faster they jettisoned it. Anvils, plows, and ovens were usually the first to go, followed by grandma's dresser and clothing. They used logs and trees as post offices, holding messages for later travelers, and emigrants drew skulls and crossbones on buffalo skulls to warn of poisonous water. If a mother died in childbirth, the family would carry the newborn wagon to wagon, hoping to establish a network of nursing mothers to keep the baby alive. If a regretful traveler turned back after seven hundred miles, it might be said he "had seen the elephant and eaten its ears." [8]

Vasquez set up temporary tents near South Pass to trade with emigrants and to persuade them to go by way of Fort Bridger instead of the shorter desert route first called the Greenwood Cutoff and now known as Sublette's Cutoff. Vasquez aggressively warned the latter trail "would be a grave mistake, as a desert of considerable extent, destitute of water and fuel, had to be crossed." The portly Vasquez took paper and pencil and sketched the two trails, piling argument upon argument in favor of the Fort Bridger route. Most took the cutoff, but plenty of travelers took the slower but safer Fort Bridger route, though not all were satisfied with their choice. Emigrant William Johnston felt that Vasquez was making his argument simply to profit from the emigrants and wrote, "The deception practiced by Vasquez . . . was now painfully apparent"[9]

While Vasquez the trader was mainly interested in sales, Bridger the explorer reveled in talking with emigrants about the routes ahead. He stayed at Fort Bridger and laid down the route for many travelers, readily grabbing a charcoal and drawing the path right on his door. To emigrant William Kelly he pointed out a new line that would cut off thirty miles, but then warned him it had not yet been attempted with wagons—he didn't think they should run the risk. Kelly remembered that Bridger "had more experience as a mountaineer than any other [and] . . . was in the habit of leaving his partner as the home manager and . . . roaming through the fastnesses of the wilderness, by which means he became intimate with every practicable route or locality."[10] Several felt they had been steered wrong by lesser men, and one traveler wrote that almost every man who tried to answer questions "proves himself a fool or a liar," concluding they were "asses, asses all."[11] But Bridger was reliable and loved to describe the route.

Travelers wanting to buy supplies or use the blacksmith shop overwhelmed Bridger and his assistants. Bridger had a reputation for honesty and was quick in his motions. With his long hair and eyebrows lightened by the sun, he traded sharply, wearing tanned deerskins and a soft hat with a band made of two otter tails. He often was at the corral, trading his smaller, well-rested horses for the emigrants' larger but trail-worn animals.[12] Bridger and Vasquez had retail competitors. A Mormon family offered a public house with food, buckskins, and provisions. Peg-leg Smith, who had argued with Bridger over pelts, was running a trading post called Smith's Fort at Big Timbers on the Bear River north of Fort Bridger.[13]

The number of emigrants headed west climbed from fewer than five thousand in 1847 to twenty-five thousand in 1849. Many died along the way, mainly from disease: cholera, whooping cough, measles, mumps, smallpox, ague, and pneumonia, which was called lung fever. They often drowned, and "Shot himself accidentally" was a common epitaph.[14] Emigrants often concealed the burial sites from foraging animals by driving wagons over them repeatedly, but those following behind sometimes still saw snarling wolves fighting over body parts pulled from a grave. Wolves learned to gather when men were digging, their howling nearly drowning out the words of those gathered at the burial.

When William Johnston and his wife arrived at Fort Bridger, they saw a group of log buildings surrounded by a high picket fence and guarded by a heavy wooden gate. They enjoyed the beautiful and fertile valley at the foot of the Uintah Mountains and recorded that Mrs. Vasquez had "entertained us in an agreeable and hospital manner, notably by inviting us to *sit upon chairs*," which they hadn't enjoyed for quite some time. Johnston, who was not overly welcoming to Indians, also described a women he thought was Mrs. Bridger as "a stolid, fleshy, round-headed woman, not oppressed with lines of beauty. Her hair was intensely black and straight, and so cut that it hung in a thick mass upon her broad shoulders."[15]

In a corner of Mrs. Vasquez's room was a churn filled with buttermilk, and Mrs. Vasquez, dipping from it with a ladle, "filled and refilled our cups, which we drank until completely satisfied." Mrs. Johnston had lost a skillet but kept the lid, and she gave it to Narcissa Vasquez, who had a skillet but lost its lid. As the Johnstons turned to leave, Narcissa gave them "a roll of freshly churned butter, of a rich golden yellow, and glistening, as it were, with drops of dew." The Johnstons found the trading rooms depleted by the onslaught of emigrants. After looking at one keg of whisky, one jar of tobacco, one box of clay pipes, and St. Peter's pipestone (Catlinite), Johnston bought a buffalo robe with long silky hair for five dollars and the company purchased a steer for $20 for meat.[16]

After the emigrant traffic had passed in late summer, Bridger had several visitors. An acquaintance from St. Louis ten years earlier, H. J. Clayton, arrived on August 11, 1849. Bridger was sitting on a log in front of his house and rose to greet him. Clayton put out his hand and said, "I promised you ten years ago that I would see you in the Rocky Mountains and I am here to keep my word." Bridger remembered the face but told him he did not remember the name, and then added, 'I remember you well; I met you at the Union Hotel."[17]

They walked into Bridger's rooms, and Clayton was taken with the appearance of a Shoshone woman, a "great beauty . . . about twenty-two years of age. She was sitting in a plain rocking chair, sewing a garment of unbleached cotton cloth, while with her foot she was rocking a cradle made of the half of a hollow log . . . in which was a young infant cozily ensconced in a downy white wolf skin. Around the room, three other children, all girls, were playing all together forming a simple, beautiful domestic scene." The infant might have been a newborn baby, recently named John, who was born in 1849 or 1850. The three "girls" may have been one-year-old Virginia, three- or four-year-old Josephine, and seven-year-old Felix, perhaps misremembered or mistaken for a girl because of long hair.

Clayton was impressed with the "rich, musical, flowing cadences" that Bridger and his wife expressed in the Shoshone language. Bridger told Mary how he met Clayton in St. Louis, which caused her to smile, laugh, and chat in the liveliest manner. She prepared a sweet and savory meal of "fresh trout and delicious venison, with hard bread obtain from California immigrants, and excellent tea." Bridger had perhaps a thousand beaver skins packed and shelved along one side of the main room, no longer worth what they had once been valued.

Bridger was aware of his goiter and asked Clayton, "How did you know me?" noting that ten years earlier he didn't have "this great swelling on my neck." But Bridger's neck had already been enlarged at time of the 1837 rendezvous (as noted by David Brown). It likely came from a swelling of the thyroid gland caused by the lack of iodine in snowmelt streams. It was so large that the Sioux knew Bridger as "Big Throat." Despite his goiter, Bridger was in excellent health, and Clayton said he "was active as a boy and had a lot of endurance."

Clayton was on his way to the California gold fields and had traveled from Fort Leavenworth, Missouri, to Fort Bridger with an expedition of the U.S. Army Corps of Topographical Engineers. Capt. Howard Stansbury and Lt. John Gunnison led the sixteen-member team—cartographers, illustrators, scientists, and soldiers. Captain Stansbury, round-faced and round-bellied, had fourfold orders: to recommend a site for a military post in the area; to explore a potential route for a transcontinental railroad; to improve the wagon road between Fort Bridger and Salt Lake; and to survey the Great Salt Lake basin. The soldiers' broad-brimmed hats shielded them from the sun, but their heavy coats and trousers burdened them, and they reveled in the cool breezes that swept over the branches of Black's Fork. As they rested and enjoyed the climate, they made good use of Bridger's blacksmith shop to repair their wagon wheels.[18]

Besides making maps, Stansbury also studied the natural history of the places he encountered. He examined several specimens of fossils a few miles upstream from Fort Bridger, and he found them consistent with evidence that prehistoric life had once thrived in the land, a view that was becoming increasingly more common throughout the world. He also looked at a rock found in Black's Fork nearby that glimmered with specks of gold, concluding it was volcanic rock washed down from the snowcapped Uinta Mountains.[19]

The U.S. government envisioned a string of forts along the emigrant road. The United States had purchased Fort Laramie in June and had recently built Fort Kearny along the Platte River in Nebraska, which was under command of Capt. Benjamin Bonneville, who spoke highly of Bridger and his location. Stansbury strongly favored Fort Bridger for the site of a new government post, noting it sat on neutral ground between the Shoshones and the Crows to the north; the Oglalas and Sioux to the east; the Cheyennes to the southeast; and the warlike tribe of the Utes to the south. Stansbury reported that "a competent force established at this point would have great influence in preventing the bloody collisions which frequently occur between these hostile tribes, and would afford protection and aid to the great tide of emigration."[20]

Lt. John Gunnison, second in Stansbury's command, also strongly favored Fort Bridger for its central location among many tribes and noted, "If a humane policy is the proper one then here is the place for a pacificator." Gunnison not only endorsed Fort Bridger's location but Jim Bridger himself, concluding, "No more influential person could be found . . . than the enterprising man already connected with them by marriage." Indeed, Bridger had married first into the Flathead people, then the Ute people, and now the Shoshone people.[21]

Gunnison looked at Bridger as a bridge between two eras. He wrote that Bridger was

> one of the hardy race of mountain trappers who are now disappearing from the continent, being enclosed in the wave of civilization. . . . Major Bridger, or "old Jim" . . . has laid aside a [financial] competence; but the mountain tastes, fostered by twenty-eight years of exciting scenes, will probably keep him there for life. . . . With a buffalo skin and piece of charcoal, he will map out any portion of this immense region, and delineate mountains, streams, and the circular valleys called "holes" with wonderful accuracy. . . . As a guide for explorers the services of that man would be invaluable.[22]

Pertaining to a possible route for the railroad, Stansbury was excited when Bridger told him he knew a shorter, faster route across the Continental Divide. It was at a lower elevation and south of South Pass, which would eliminate the northern and southern swings of the Platte River/South Pass route. Stansbury immediately began planning for Bridger to guide them there the following year.[23]

Stansbury was also keenly interested in a more direct route from Fort Bridger to Salt Lake and observed that the Fort Hall road made a northing of nearly two degrees on the map before heading southwest toward the Sierra Nevada. He also determined that the Mormon road went more than a full degree south to Salt Lake, then turned north along the east side of the Salt Lake, then veered northwest to intersect with the southwestern portion of the California Trail.[24] Bridger drew a quick map to show Stansbury a much more direct route, and the captain immediately asked Bridger to lead him.

This encounter marked the beginning of a new career for Bridger, one that would engage him through the rest of his professional life. Though he had been pilot and booshway for countless trapping expeditions, he had never guided cartographers, surveyors, and scientists. It must have reminded him of his father's profession as a surveyor and the fine surveying compasses that Philip Creamer had made back in Illinois.

While Lieutenant Gunnison commanded the main party moving to Salt Lake, Bridger led Stansbury, Dr. Blake, and two other men to chart a new route across the Wasatch. A day or two after Bridger and Stansbury left, newly appointed superintendent of Indian affairs John Wilson arrived at Fort Bridger. Wilson was excited that Bridger and Stansbury had already traced out a more direct route from Fort Bridger to Salt Lake. He also agreed that Fort Bridger was an ideal spot for an Indian agency and wrote to the secretary of interior, "You will see at once the importance of the position of Fort Bridger, and the inevitable propriety of making it the great military post of this country." Vasquez and Bridger "are gentlemen of integrity and intelligence, and can be fully relied on in relation to any statement they make in regard to the different tribes, claims, boundaries, and other information."[25]

As Bridger led Stansbury west from Fort Bridger, he insisted that everyone was well armed. They rode horseback and led a couple of pack mules, traveling light with no elaborate instruments and carrying just flour, bacon, and ground coffee, and allowing only one blanket per man. Bridger left the regular Salt Lake route and crossed a dividing ridge that brought them to Medicine Butte, so named, he told them, for the Indian medicine men who built their lodges there. The trout were abundant, and as they caught them, Stansbury noted that those on the western side of the Divide had black speckles, while those east of the Divide had yellow speckles. An ox that wandered away from an earlier emigrant train provided an evening feast. They gave the extra meat to a small encampment of Shoshones whose teepees dotted the other side of the stream. Stansbury marveled at the skill the Indian women showed as they butchered the leftover meat, even cleaning the paunch and the entrails for food.[26]

Bridger knew the land well, having made more than fifty crossings of the Wasatch Range by various routes.[27] He led the small contingent across the bottomlands of the Bear River, a stretch of ground that was four or five miles wide. Stansbury was impressed, but Bridger cautioned him that the land lay under nearly four feet of snow every winter, and it flooded every spring. Stansbury was disappointed to learn it would never be a railroad pass, and Bridger told him if he wanted a railroad pass, he should go farther north to Cache Valley and Blacksmith's Fork.[28]

They crossed over a bluff into one valley, then crossed over another ridge and followed that to its head. They should have followed a long ridge running southwest, but Stansbury wanted a route that would provide more immediate westing and ignored Bridger's directions. Instead they crossed over several more valleys. Stansbury's choice led them to a dizzying, precipitous climb several hundred feet high where he feared a single misstep would drop them to "the yawning gulf beneath."[29]

The captain ultimately recognized that the valley of Pumbar's Creek would not make a good wagon road. They eventually saw a broad valley on their left, and Bridger announced that this was the other end of the valley that Stansbury had disregarded the day before. They saw a variety of trees there—oak, blackjack, aspen, wild-cherry, service-berry, and large box-elder. Stansbury was pleased with the moderate descent, which would require little labor.

It must have been difficult for Bridger to hold his tongue as Stansbury satisfied his curiosity by roaming around an area Bridger already knew well. Stansbury's insistence on following his own routes forced them to go through country that Bridger knew was unsuitable for wagons.[30] Stansbury was stubborn and a stickler for protocol: when he had arrived at Fort Laramie earlier that summer, he refused to come to the fort for open mess because it was the fort commander's duty to visit Stansbury's camp first.[31] Bridger's role as a guide was to suggest a route, but the final decision rested with the military leaders, and he would find such men sometimes discounted the mountain man's advice, perhaps because he was illiterate or they were trying to make a name for themselves as Frémont had.

Stansbury had not traveled on the Sabbath since he had left the Missouri and wanted to remain in camp that Sunday as well. But their provisions were nearly exhausted, and Bridger told him just over the ridges they would find a valley with excellent grass, wood, water, and game. That was enough to convince the captain to move on. As they entered the valley, Bridger pointed out that a sizeable number of Indians had been on this route a day or two earlier eating cherries. He saw the columns of smoke rising from the hills and knew the Indians were signaling each other about them, and he ordered a strict watch day and night.

They escaped the valley without trouble and entered Ogden's Hole, the winter and summer gathering spot for trappers and Indians. They came upon eight or ten Indian women and girls collecting grass seeds in baskets, all of them naked. They were root diggers, or, as Bridger called them that day, Snake-diggers, and when they saw Stansbury and his men, they scattered and hid in the tall grasses. Bridger called out loudly in their native tongue, asking them to stop, but they ran away with their baskets on their backs. As the men rode on, they almost trampled two girls about sixteen or seventeen years old who had hidden behind a large tree. They stood and gazed at the riders for a time, then waved them on and fled.[32]

Finally, Stansbury's group glimpsed the Great Salt Lake in the distance, and they were taken by the view of its waters shimmering in the sun that peeked through misty clouds above. This lake had once been nearly as large as Lake Michigan and much deeper, a freshwater lake that extended over the entire basin. At Brown's settlement in Ogden's Hole, formerly Miles Goodyear's ranch, Stansbury wanted to purchase food for the night, but the man wouldn't even sell them a cup of milk or an egg. They later learned Brown had served in the Mormon Battalion during the Mexican War, and he feared a visit from civil authorities concerning unsettled public accounts. They remounted and bivouacked within one hundred yards under some willows, careful not to let their animals roam. If a neighbor hadn't provided for them, they would have spent the night hungry.[33]

The following day they reached Great Salt Lake City and found Gunnison's party and their camp. Stansbury, with Bridger's guidance, concluded that the preferred railroad route from Fort Bridger to Salt Lake valley ran twenty-five miles west to Bear River, followed the Bear River valley upstream to the headwaters of the Weber River, and then followed these sources fifteen miles downstream, near Kamas Prairie. From Kamas Prairie the road could fork, one branch descending the Wasatch Range by Golden Pass to Salt Lake City and the other fork following down the Timpanogos [Provo] River toward Utah Lake.[34]

Bridger's work was done, and he met up with Clayton again before he set out for home. According to Clayton, Bridger was frustrated with Stansbury and "quite disgusted with his experience, and severely reproached himself for his act in offering to pilot Uncle Sam's men, and declared he would never do the like again."[35]

In Salt Lake City Brigham Young was disturbed that the government would send a survey party so soon after the Mormons had built their settlement and told Stansbury they had been following his progress since he left Fort Leavenworth. Their worry was not without cause, as a rumor was circulating that a member of Indian agent Wilson's party had boasted (incorrectly), "General Wilson had come clothed with authority from the President of the United States to expel the Mormons from the lands which they occupied, and that he would do so if he thought proper."[36] The fact that it was Jim Bridger who guided Stansbury to Salt Lake probably irked Young as well.

Young allowed Stansbury to survey the lake but only if he hired his secretary, Albert Carrington, so that he would know their movements and discoveries. The Later-day Saints community generally treated Stansbury and his team with hospitality. Stansbury's survey of Great Salt Lake and Utah Lake was one of the first in North America to use triangulation. They established fourteen stations, in some cases hauling wooden poles twenty miles to build their towers. They circumnavigated the lake as the trappers had done in 1826 and collected flora and fauna. But Stansbury and Gunnison were also worried. Stansbury wrote, "It had been darkly hinted that if I persevered in attempting to carry it on, my life would scarce be safe."[37]

BRIDGER PASS
1850

One of the first emigrant parties to show up at Fort Bridger in the summer of 1850 was a small group that included a miner named Charles Ferguson. He found Bridger very accommodating and eager to have his son and daughter read for them. At that time Felix would have been eight and Mary Josephine four. Ferguson remembered the children reading, even if only a little bit. Perhaps they had been tutored by Narcissa Vasquez or another person at the fort.[1] Narcissa was fond of Jim Bridger and often wanted him to come to dinner with Louis and her, but she did not care to have his Indian wife join them.[2]

In 1850 the census taker came to Fort Bridger, now part of the Green River precinct, and counted eleven households and forty-six people. He recorded Bridger as age forty-one, though he was actually forty-six, and Mary, his Shoshone Indian wife, as twenty, which was not considered young for a married Shoshone woman with a child. James Carson, age twenty-four was listed as an Indian trader and part of the Bridger household. Louis and Narcissa Vasquez, fifty and forty-one, were listed as a separate household. The Bridger children were listed as Felix, Elizabeth (Mary Josephine), and Jane (Virginia).

There were nine other households at Fort Bridger: eight of them listed white men as heads of household, and five of those had Indian wives. One white woman was listed as head of household. Twenty-six children in the eleven households were listed as "Indian." The census did not enumerate the many other Indians who lived near the fort.

That year the emigrant register at Fort Laramie recorded that 39,000 men and 2,000 women and children had passed by the fort as of mid-August 1850, and many of them took the trail past Fort Bridger. That was larger than the population of the cities of Chicago or Washington, D.C. They came in approximately 10,000 wagons with 36,000 oxen, 23,000 horses, 7,000 mules, and 7,000 cows.[3] Some Indians called the trail the Great Medicine Road and wondered if the whites left a great void in the east.

Bridger and Vasquez had replenished their storeroom and also had a good supply of oxen, mules, and horses. Emigrants generally stopped at a nearby tar spring to fill tar buckets for their wagon wheels. One traveler was smitten with Fort Bridger and recorded, "Upon the whole, this high mountain vale is one of the most romantic spots that have as yet fallen under my observation."[4]

No sooner had the great tide of emigration passed beyond Fort Bridger but Captain Stansbury and his men arrived at the fort on September 5, 1850. Within a few days they learned that President Zachary Taylor had died two months previously. While the president's death was shocking news for the soldiers, it was celebrated by Brigham Young, who proclaimed, "Zachary Taylor is dead and in hell, and I'm glad of it. . . . Any President of the United States who lifts his finger against this people, will die an untimely death and go to Hell!"[5]

As to the railroad route across the plains, Stansbury had entertained the thought of exploring the Arkansas River on his way east. But he quickly came back to the route Bridger had suggested the previous year, which would cross the Continental Divide south of South Pass and travel through today's southern Wyoming to the Medicine Bow Mountains. Stansbury knew this would cover some difficult terrain, so while still at Salt Lake, he had sold all their wagons and purchased pack-mules to carry their baggage.[6] Bridger agreed to guide them and insisted they be well armed with plenty of ammunition, as they would be going through Sioux country.

Bridger led them east out of Fort Bridger along Black's Fork, enjoying the black and white currants that were ripening. They quickly diverted from the regular path, using a pendulum odometer strapped to a cartwheel to count the number of revolutions. The number of rotations multiplied by the circumference of the wheel gave their distance each day. The odometer allowed one or two of the men to ride. Lieutenant Gunnison recorded, "Today I rode a little distance on the 'Odom'—& shortly after getting on, the wheels ran on a sage sand knoll & overturned to the left, spilling out myself and [Albert] Carrington."[7] Along the way they observed the star Altair to chart latitude, recorded daily temperatures, took lunar observations, and observed for time.

They came to "The Church," a green-brown butte of fantastic and picturesque forms, then headed toward Pilot Butte, a huge landmark visible from forty miles away. These valleys were once full of buffalo, Bridger told them, but the range of the great bison herds was continuing to shrink. He pointed out the road to his old fort on the Green.[8]

Stansbury could readily see the remarkable change in the landscape between the Great Basin and the Green River valley. The Green River region had once been submerged in a giant sea or lake. Bands of blue and green strata—some a foot thick, some knife thin—angled horizontally. Stansbury imagined the vast lake had been bottled up by a barrier in Brown's Hole, which then broke and drained quickly. The ground was strewn with white and yellow quartz, obsidian, and flint.[9]

They forded the Green, only three feet deep that September. On their fourth morning, Stansbury and his men were frightened by a company of Indians charging toward them, and they drove their pack mules and loose animals back into the bush and prepared for battle. The Indians were riding fast, intent on achieving a surprise attack, but as they got closer, they saw Bridger and immediately eased up. They were Shoshones and had mistaken Stansbury's company for Utes. Now they were friends all around. The main party of Shoshones moved on, but two or three followed Bridger and Stansbury's party down Rabbit Hollow ravine, perhaps planning a horse raid. Bridger insisted on increased vigilance that night so they wouldn't lose any horses.[10]

After six miles of *mauvaise terres*, bad lands, they again came to level ground and followed Bitter Creek, where they enjoyed an abundance of black currants and buffalo berries. They spotted antelope, grouse, and an occasional bear, but no buffalo. Large strata of coal were visible in the rock, and one broken-off chunk was as large as a man. Bridger told them there was another bed of coal south of the mouth of Black's Fork that he had used, and it burned freely with a white, clear blaze.[11] They skirted the Red Desert and soon neared the pass over the Continental Divide that Bridger meant to show them.

They came to the first fork of Muddy Creek (not to be confused with Muddy Creek of Black's Fork near Fort Bridger), and Stansbury named it Bridger's Fork.[12] Bridger's Fork flowed west toward them, so they knew they were still west of the Divide. They were now in range of buffalo and eagerly anticipated the hunt, but perhaps became less eager after an old buffalo bull blundered into their camp that evening, stampeding several horses who broke free. Bridger's Fork opened to a rolling prairie between two high cliffs colored in shades of red and green. Finally, they reached the main flow of Muddy Creek Canyon. Stansbury found petrifications of shells there, further evidence of the great sea that had once covered the valley. Bridger ordered the men to keep their guns close and even sleep with them, as they now traveled a common battleground for many bands of Indians.

As they rested around the campfire, many enjoyed a pipe while Bridger regaled them with the dramatic story of how the Sioux, Cheyennes, and Arapahos attacked his partner, Henry Fraeb, just two miles distant in 1842, eight years earlier. The attackers numbered in the hundreds, and most of Fraeb's men were away hunting. Two men and two Indian women were killed in this attack, and the raiders made off with several animals. When Bridger heard of the attack, he sent a strong warning to Fraeb to abandon the country, but Fraeb continued. Ten days later the Sioux, Cheyennes, and Arapahos attacked Fraeb again, killing Fraeb and three or four more of his men.

Before noon the next day the expedition passed the spot where Oglala Sioux had attacked Louis Vasquez and fourteen fur traders, keeping them forted behind their barricade for four hours. One of Stansbury's hunters, who was part Indian, had been in the fight and pointed out the specific places where the bloody incidents of the siege occurred.[13]

The next day Bridger led them up the Muddy and showed them a beautiful pass about a mile and half long with a gradual ascent. From there Bridger led them another four miles and then announced they were on the dividing height between the Atlantic and the Pacific, and the men erupted in a universal shout. The pass was almost twenty miles long and, like South Pass, mostly level. The elevation was 7,350 feet, about the same as South Pass. It did not look like a mountain crossing at all, but a stretch of level land. Stansbury named it Bridger Pass, and he named the nearby mountain Bridger Peak. They had come 207 miles in the eight days since they left Fort Bridger.[14]

They rejoiced when they reached Sage Creek, happy to be where the water flowed east "almost to the very feet" of their loved ones. Bridger showed them several battered lodges or "forts" made by Indians for battle. The veteran mountaineer and hunter Auguste Archambeau dropped several buffalos for food, and they butchered them in "mountain fashion," which meant taking the choice pieces like the hump, hump ribs, fleece, side ribs, thigh bone for marrow, and the tongue.[15]

One morning they saw three buffalo bulls, and Gunnison, needing new lash ropes, thought one of the buffalo hides would serve that purpose; he handed his rifle to Bridger and rode off with a six-shooter. He galloped between the beasts, but when he rode into a gully his horse fell. Gunnison was thrown and hit the ground hard, cutting his face and stunning him for several minutes. His pistol discharged as he fell, killing his horse with a bullet through the neck. They found Gunnison wandering about "crazy as a loon" and brought him back to camp.

Bridger showed them Frappe's Creek and told how the Arikaras had stolen sixty horses from Fraeb there back in 1833.[16] The Medicine Bow range was their eastern beacon now. The mountains looked like brawny shoulders from a distance, but when viewed closer, they thrust up fists and fingers into the sky. As the party got closer yet, they saw pockets of snow just twenty feet from late summer flowers. When the occasion allowed, Bridger entertained them with descriptions of Yellowstone, obviously energized as he told of trees turned to stone and a mountain made of rock that was as black as night and shiny as glass. Stansbury had heard of obsidian, knew it was formed by volcanic eruption, and was convinced that Bridger's wild descriptions were scientifically possible. Gunnison also wrote of Bridger's fantastic narratives in his report.

> He gives a picture, most romantic and enticing, of the head-waters of the Yellow Stone. A lake sixty [twenty] miles long, cold and pellucid, lies embosomed amid high precipitous mountains. On the west side is a sloping plain several miles wide, with clumps of trees and groves of pine. The ground resounds to the tread of horses. Geysers spout up seventy feet high, with a terrific hissing noise, at regular intervals. Waterfalls are sparkling, leaping, and thundering down the precipices, and collect in the pool below. The river issues from this lake, and for fifteen miles roars through the perpendicular Canyon at the outlet. In this section are the Great Springs, so hot that meat is readily cooked in them, and as they descend on the successive terraces, afford at length delightful baths. On the other side is an acid spring, which gushes out in a river torrent; and below is a cave which supplies "vermilion," for the savages in abundance.[17]

As they continued their journey, Bridger noted Indians on the hills tracking their movements. Seeing that they were hovering at a distance, Bridger shouldered his rifle and walked out alone to meet them. As he neared, he made sign to the advance party of Indians that they should come out and meet.[18] They relaxed when they saw that they were white men, and many of them knew of Bridger.

Soon a steady stream of Indians galloped to the soldiers, shaking hands with everyone. They were Oglala Sioux and Cheyennes, and an old chief named Buffalo Dung wanted to trade. He complained that his eyes were bothered by the sun, and Stansbury brightened and searched his pack for an old pair of sun goggles with dark green glass, presenting them to the elder chief. Buffalo Dung wore them about camp with great pride even though it was nearly dark.[19]

Bridger began to talk to the Sioux in sign and held them entranced using this universal language. His stories caused the Indians to burst into simultaneous exclamations of surprise, interest, and spontaneous laughter. Bridger was a master storyteller with his hands, and he kept the band "listening" with their eyes for nearly an hour.[20]

Near the Chugwater River and Horse Creek, they came to Cheyenne Pass. Here Stansbury's official report said, "I sustained a severe injury by a fall, which not only incapacitated me from mounting my horse, but confined me altogether to my bed until our arrival at Fort Leavenworth."[21] The journals of his companions revealed that Stansbury severely sprained his leg when he tried to kick his dog out of his tent. They had to send to Fort Laramie several miles away for an ambulance.

Bridger had prospected for gold here seventeen years earlier, and he used the time to look again. He searched for the valley that held his "gold kanyon." The next day he found it, but it held no gold. Two hundred yards above their campsite, they found earthy marl and boulders with black iron oxide but no gold.[22] When the ambulance arrived to take Stansbury to Fort Laramie, Bridger prepared to ride back to Fort Bridger. He left them on the Chugwater River about fifty miles from Fort Laramie.

From the notes, recordings, maps, and measurements the expedition had made, Stansbury and his team put together a voluminous report. It described the routes, peoples, minerals, fossils, birds, and reptiles, including the horned frog or horned lizard, several salamanders, and other discoveries.[23] (Stansbury died of heart disease just thirteen years later at fifty-seven, caused by overexertion during his Rocky Mountain expedition.)

The new trail from Fort Bridger to Laramie was 347 miles, which was 61 miles shorter than the South Pass route, and the trail promised even more cutoffs with further exploration.[24] Bridger and the older mountaineers had been aware of this route for decades, as William Ashley had traveled some of it in 1825 when he brought goods out to the first rendezvous. In 1849 Capt. Lewis Evans led 130 people, including several Cherokees, by that or a similar route when they traveled from the front range of the Rockies (near present-day Denver) on their way to the California gold mines.

Congress ultimately appropriated funds to survey Bridger Pass for a wagon road, and six years later Lt. Francis Bryan surveyed the pass, guided by several

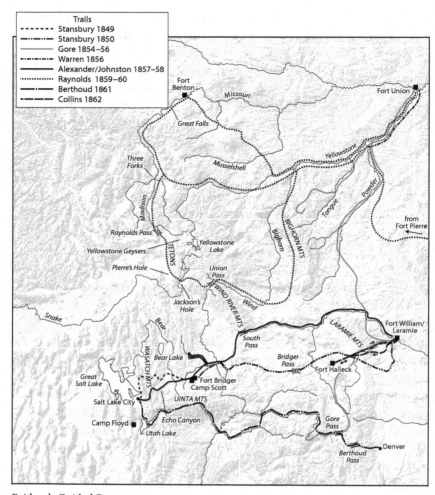

Trails	
- - - - -	Stansbury 1849
—·—·—	Stansbury 1850
————	Gore 1854–56
—··—··—	Warren 1856
————	Alexander/Johnston 1857–58
··········	Raynolds 1859–60
—·—·—	Berthoud 1861
- — - —	Collins 1862

Bridger's Guided Routes, 1849–1862

mountaineers who had explored that country for many years. Though the guides were experienced, none had been through Bridger Pass and had difficulty finding the place that matched Stansbury's report. They finally found it after climbing a nearby hill and seeing the open smooth plateau gently sloping west before them.[25] The route officially became known as Bridger Pass and the Overland Trail. Way stations soon dotted the route, and it became the general path of the overland stage, the transcontinental railroad, and Interstate 80 across Wyoming.

HORSE CREEK
TREATY
1851–1852

In the late summer of 1851, Thomas Fitzpatrick, now an Indian agent assisting with the great Indian treaty of 1851, was assembling the tribes in his district along the Oregon and California Trails. This would be the largest assembly of American Indians in recorded history. Congress appropriated $100,000 to fund the endeavor, mostly to buy goods to entice the Indians to agree to a treaty.

Fitzpatrick and Col. David D. Mitchell, superintendent of Indian affairs in St. Louis, circulated notices to Indians and enlisted emigrant trains, traders, and army detachments to spread the word to every plains tribe—the Sioux, Assiniboines, Crows, Hidatsas, Mandans, Arikaras, Arapahos, and Cheyennes.[1] Bringing them together was a big gamble, for the Indians might decide to fight each other or to unite to overcome the army.

The Shoshones were planning to attend, and newly appointed Ute Indian agent Jacob Holeman wrote Gov. Brigham Young requesting permission for the Utes to attend as well. Without any orders to the contrary from Washington, Young concurred and stipulated the Ute Indians should "go as privately as possible, in civilian dress, such as white men wear . . . in carriages or covered wagons, and when they shall arrive at Laramie, have a room where they can remain in safety."[2]

Subagent Stephen Rose purchased two horses from Bridger and Vasquez for $218, and Subagent Henry Day purchased a carriage and harnesses to transport Ute war chief Walkara and civil chief Sowerette, as well as Grose-Pinés, Arra, and Pinés, as they were all "hostile to the Snakes & Crows."[3] But the chiefs would not come, believing it a trap set by the Mormons to kill them. Day believed the Ute Indians were upset with Mormons for moving them off their land and wrote to the commissioner of Indian affairs in Washington that their civil chief, Sowerette, had raised himself up to his full height and said, "American good! Mormon no good."[4]

The Latter-day Saints had occupied and cultivated some Ute land, while the "American" mountaineers were merely trading there, without trying to claim permanent residence. Soon after arriving in the basin, Young talked of the Mormon Elders "marrying wives of every tribe of Indians so that the Lamanites would become a 'White & delightsome people'" through their offspring. Young hoped one day to "lead forth the armies of Israel to execute the judgements & justice on the persecuting Gentiles & that no officer of the United States should ever dictate him in this valley, or he would hang them on a gibbet as a warning to others."[5]

Chief Washakie set out leading the Shoshones to the council, and when they passed the Sweetwater, they found two of their men killed and scalped by the Cheyennes. Washakie sent the women and children back, and the enraged warriors rode swiftly toward Fort Laramie. Bridger rode ahead to see where they should camp. Among the throng of Indians and whites, Bridger heard the Irish brogue of his former partner and good friend Tom Fitzpatrick. Now older and grayer, Fitzpatrick had married Margaret Poisal in 1849, the sixteen-year-old daughter of French Canadian John Poisal and his Arapaho wife.[6]

Fitzpatrick told Bridger he had no money to dispense gifts to the Shoshones or even a place for them to stay, because the conference was for the Indians under the St. Louis superintendency, and the Shoshones lived west of the mountains in Brigham Young's superintendency. Bridger made the case for them just the same. The Shoshones also had to deal with emigrants on the Oregon, Mormon, and California trails, and they were under repeated assault by the Sioux, Cheyennes, and Arapahos.

Fitzpatrick reluctantly agreed to make room for them and told Bridger where they should set up camp. Washakie led the Shoshones toward a grassy plain on the edge of the encampment, sitting astride his finest war horse decorated in rich costume. The recent slaughter of two of his men was foremost on his mind. His warriors rode behind him in near-military formation, each man carrying his rifle. The approach of their traditional enemy alarmed the Sioux. Their leaders called their own warriors to be ready, and Sioux women moaned in anguish over husbands and sons lost to the Shoshones.[7]

As the situation escalated, the army bugle sounded "Boots and Saddles," and troopers hurried to their posts. Comprised mostly of a motley collection of boys and foreigners, the troopers typically dressed in white caps, white pants, and roundabout shell jackets.[8] A Sioux warrior leaped to his horse and raced towards the Shoshones with his bow and arrow in hand. Washakie continued to ride forward, stoically ignoring the Sioux. His Shoshone warriors raised their rifles in a defiant cry. This was high drama—a Shoshone chief pitted against a Sioux warrior—and it could blossom into full-scale war.

A quick-thinking French Canadian interpreter assigned to the Sioux quickly leaped to his horse and chased after the crazed Sioux. Washakie continued riding forward resolutely. The Sioux kicked his horse ahead, notching his arrow in his bow as the gap closed between them. The Shoshones and the Sioux taunted each other with words and gestures, and jeering rose even louder. Would the Sioux shoot his arrow at Washakie? Would Washakie, who had now raised his own rifle, fire at the Sioux? Or would the French Canadian overtake the Sioux and stop him?

The interpreter made a wild leap and pulled the Sioux off his horse. Washakie looked forward again and continued to ride toward the encampment. The Shoshones and Sioux kept shouting at each other, and interpreters were hard pressed to make sense of the babble. Finally, the story emerged: Washakie had killed the father of the Sioux who had just tried to kill him. Peacemakers attempted to get them to smoke the peace pipe, but the Shoshones refused until the scalps of their two recently killed men were returned and offerings made.

A young corporal, Percival Lowe, had been ordered to show Bridger where the Shoshones should camp, and he "galloped off with the great mountaineer whose fort I had seen dotted on my atlas in school a few years before."[9] After the standoff Bridger allowed the eager young man to stay with the Shoshones until their camp was formed and told him, "These are the finest Indians on earth. Stay with me and I'll show 'um to you." After the Shoshones were settled, Bridger explained to Lowe what had happened.

Well, you seen that fool Sioux make the run didn't you? Well,———saved that fellow from hell; my chief would 'er killed him quick, and then the fool Sioux would 'er got their backs up, and there wouldn't have been room to camp 'round here for dead Sioux. You dragoons acted nice, but you wouldn't have had no show if the fight had commenced—no making peace then. And I tell you another thing: the Sioux ain't goin' to try it again. They see how the Snakes are armed. I got them guns for 'um, and

Washakie (c. 1870–1871), photographed by William Henry Jackson. Shoshone leader Washakie and Jim Bridger were friends for many years, and together they attended the 1851 gathering at Horse Creek, where an Indian peace treaty was signed. *Collection of the Jackson Hole Historical Society and Museum (1958.3371.001)*

they are good ones. It'll be a proud day for the Snakes if any of these prairie tribes pitch in to 'um, and they are not a bit afraid. Uncle Sam told 'um to come down here and they'd be safe, but they ain't takin' his word for it altogether. They'll never be caught napping, and they're prepared to travel anywhere. Awful brave fellows, these Snakes; got the nerve; honest, too; can take their word for anything; trust 'um anywhere; they live all about me, and I know all of them.[10]

Colonel Mitchell invited "Captain" Bridger to the headquarters tent, where he spent several hours with the commissioners. They no doubt discussed the logistical problems of feeding large numbers of people and their animals. The presents for the Indians had not yet arrived, and the huge number of Indian horses soon depleted the forage around the fort. Moreover, there were no buffalo to hunt. The commissioners decided to move the entire assembly from Fort Laramie to Horse Creek, thirty miles east, where the Indians set up new camps. (This was a different Horse Creek than the trappers' rendezvous site on the upper Green River.)

Soon after this move, Robert Campbell arrived to serve as a commissioner, along with Father De Smet. The Indians called De Smet "Black Robe," and he was very popular with many of the tribes, ultimately recording 1,586 baptisms. De Smet estimated that there were a thousand skin lodges at the gathering and ten thousand Indians. He saw so many Indians boiling fat dogs in giant kettles, skins and all, that he called it "one of the greatest slaughters of the canine race." He sampled the dog meat and found it as tasty as suckling pig.[11]

The gifts for the Indians still hadn't arrived, and Mitchell had to begin discussions with the assembled tribes without that inducement. Interpreters translated to the assembled Babylonia as Mitchell welcomed the gathered leaders, telling them: "Your Great Father has appointed Major Fitzpatrick ('White Hair') with me in making this treaty; you will respect him as such." Mitchell also told them that if he knew the names of the "bad white men" in their lands, the U.S. government could punish them. He told them the ears of the Great Father were open to their complaints, and he wanted to compensate them for the buffalo and game that were driven off and the grass and the timber lost by the passing of emigrants through their countries.[12]

Not everyone was happy with the efforts to compensate the Indians. It is true that Mitchell appointed several lower-ranking Indians to act on the behalf of their tribes without the approval of the respective nations, but that was so "binding" decisions could be made by those who were present.[13]

Bridger's knowledge of the mountains and traditional tribal regions proved invaluable to the commissioners. To get their annuities, the Indians had to agree to abide by geographic tribal boundaries, cease warring, and select a chief to sign the treaty for them. Mitchell designated Bridger to work with Fitzpatrick to designate the boundaries. He asked De Smet to accurately sketch the terrain and draw the borders for each tribe as described by Bridger and Fitzpatrick, a near-impossible task given that these were lands they had been fighting over for decades.

During this mapmaking enterprise, De Smet also made a map of the Yellowstone thermal region based on firsthand knowledge from "the most famous trapper of all," Jim Bridger. The map identified all the primary features still cherished today, particularly the "volcanic country" (meaning the geyser basins of Firehole); "Sulphur Mountain" near "Gardener's Creek" (Mammoth Hot Springs); a large lake with "Hot Springs" and "Great Volcanoes" written alongside (i.e., Yellowstone Lake); "Falls 290 Feet" depicting the Grand Canyon of the Yellowstone; and "Volcanic country Steam Springs" (what is today known as Hayden Valley).[14]

De Smet said this was "the most marvelous spot of all the northern half of the continent," and he added that the maps were based on the travels of one "who is familiar with every one of these mounds, having passed thirty years of his life near them." He meant Jim Bridger. The map shows "Gardener's Creek," which is presumably how Bridger would have pronounced "Gardner's" with his Virginia drawl. Other features Bridger identified for De Smet's maps included Two Ocean Pass, Jackson's Lake, and Colter's Hell on Stinking River. One map even shows a body of water named "Bridger Lake" southeast of the thermal features.[15]

B. Gratz Brown, a correspondent who was covering the treaty council for the *Missouri Republican,* wrote this story for publication in St. Louis:

> The commissioners [had] the assistance of Mr. JAMES BRIDGER, the owner and founder of Bridger's Fort, in the mountains. This man is a perfect original . . . and has traversed the mountains East and West, and from the Northern Boundary to the Gila River. He is not an educated man, but seems to have an intuitive knowledge of the topography of the country, the courses of streams, the direction of mountains, and is never lost, wherever he may be. It is stated by those who have had him in their employ, that in the midst of the mountains, when the party of trappers wished to move from one stream to another, or cross the mountain to any

stream or place, or when lost or uncertain of the proper direction, they would always appeal to Bridger.

He would throw his gun carelessly over his shoulder, survey the country awhile with his eye, and then strike out on the course, and never fail to reach the place, although he had several hundred miles to traverse over a country which he [had] never traveled, and to places he had never seen. To this seemingly intuitive knowledge of the country, he adds the singularly retentive memory of peculiarities and of every incident in his own history and that of his companions.

In his own rude way, he can lay down nearly every stream that empties into the Missouri, or Yellowstone, or that flows down the western slope of the Rocky Mountains, and describe how the streams interlock with each other. He showed us, and his information in this respect was confirmed by others, how it was practical to go by water from the Missouri River into the Columbia River, or from the Atlantic to the Pacific Ocean, without portage at any place except where the rivers are impassable because of rapids. There is a lake in the Rocky Mountains from which the waters flow on the one side into the Missouri, and on the other side into the Columbia River. Every thing Bridger has seen, he recollects with entire precision, and in his wild life (he is now advanced in years) he has traversed the whole country in many directions.[16]

Corporal Lowe was with Bridger when the Shoshone holy man began to speak, and Bridger told Lowe, "Now, I don't know nothing about religion as I used to hear it in the states; but me and the Snakes don't have no trouble believing what he says."

Bridger pointed out to Lowe a brave Shoshone who had once followed some Sioux who had stolen their horses. He trailed them for a week and came back with all the stolen horses plus six more, and six Sioux scalps. "Now," said Bridger, "how many fellers can you pick out of your troop that could do what that Indian did, and make no fuss about it."

Bridger shook hands with Lowe and eyed him keenly, saying, "Young man, don't you stay in the army no longer than your times out, but come right up to Bridger. There's more money in the mountains than in all the rest of the world— gold till you can't rest, and I know where some of it is. Now be sure to come."[17]

Telling the Indians to stop stealing and warring was an almost impossible demand. Stealing horses, counting coup, and engaging in battle were the primary ways for many Indian men to win honor and realize their sense of worth. Finding an envoy to speak for each tribe presented another impossible demand. The tribes' and bands' allegiance to their leaders was not determined by seniority but by the decision of the people. Eventually, the tough decisions were hammered out, and the treaty was agreed to by the Indians. In return for their concessions, the proposed treaty promised to provide $50,000 a year in goods for the next fifty years.[18]

On September 11, Fitzpatrick set out for St. Louis with eleven Indian chiefs and subchiefs. From there they embarked on a sightseeing tour on their way to Washington, D.C. They arrived in the capital in late November and toured the city. Then, in full Indian regalia, they met President Millard Fillmore at the White House and squatted on the floor as if it was a teepee. They expected to smoke the peace pipe with the president but were told that it was not appropriate for white men to smoke in the presence of the ladies.[19]

Unfortunately, before it would ratify the treaty, the U.S. Senate reduced the payments proposed at the Horse Creek Treaty (also known as the Fort Laramie Treaty of 1851) from fifty years to a possible fifteen years. All the participating Indians consented except the Crows. While intentions were good, this treaty would be ignored by the whites and by the Indians, leading to decades of war.

From 1822 to 1848 Jim Bridger had lived free of almost all government control. But that was about to change. The Latter-day Saints had petitioned Congress in 1849 to bring their region into the Union as the State of Deseret. Their population numbered only 12,000 instead of the required 60,000, yet they proposed an enormous territory that encompassed much of the land recently acquired from Mexico, including some or all of eight present-day states.

The proposed boundaries of Deseret extended from the Continental Divide to the Sierra Nevada and from Oregon to Mexico; they had even included an outlet to the Pacific Ocean at San Diego.[20] The fact that the Saints were applying for statehood that year didn't deter Brigham Young from telling his people, "God Almighty will give the United States a pill that will puke them to death. . . . I am prophet enough to prophesy the downfall of the government that has driven us out."[21]

On September 9, 1850, Congress established the Territory of Utah as part of the Compromise of 1850, rejecting statehood and the name "Deseret" and greatly reducing the proposed boundaries to encompass present-day Utah, most of Nevada, and portions of Colorado and Wyoming. The Utah territorial legislature established Green River County in 1852, and Bridger's fort fell under the jurisdiction of the sheriff of Great Salt Lake County. Authorities in Salt Lake City passed several acts to protect citizens, including one that required brands on livestock had to be reversed when sold. If authorities found someone in possession of a horse whose brand was not registered to him, they could confiscate the horse as stolen property.[22]

In 1852 four men—James Pullen, John Keller, S. A. Warner, and Marion Wheeler—purchased horses at Fort Bridger without the brand reversed, and when they arrived in Salt Lake City, territorial officials seized their horses, which delayed their journey to the California gold mines. Their only recourse was to sue Bridger and Vasquez for damages. The first three sued for $5,000 each, and the last sued for $20,000. Fortunately, court arbitrators did not agree with $35,000 in damages for four horses, but they did assess Bridger and Vasquez $904, almost three times what the horses were worth.[23] But far more serious charges would someday soon be brought against Bridger.

In the late summer of 1852, Louis Vasquez moved his family to Westport, Missouri, the future site of Kansas City. He purchased a comfortable house with enough land to keep livestock fed and rested until it was time to take them to the mountains each spring. At Bridger's request Vasquez took Felix and Mary Josephine Bridger as far as Westport. His nephew, Augustus Pike Vasquez, then traveled with them from Westport to St. Louis so they could be enrolled in school.[24] Father De Smet wrote Father P. J. Verhaegen, superior of the order's residence in St. Charles, Missouri:

> Captain Bridger, an old Rocky Mountain friend of mine, has sent his two children (half-breeds) to the States to be educated. . . . He has left means with Colonel Robert Campbell for their education and clothing. Inquire of Madame Hamilton [Mother Superior at the Academy of the Sacred Heart] whether she will admit the little girl? and at what price? Will Madame Barada admit the boy as a boarder, pay for his schooling at your school [St. Charles Borromeo Catholic School], and for how much a year. Please answer without delay. I am afraid Protestants will try to get them; the sooner they are away from here the better.[25]

By October the children were living and learning at their respective schools in St. Charles. The Bridgers still had four-year-old Virginia and two-year-old John at the fort, and the family made a strong impression on Elizabeth Ferris, who arrived at Fort Bridger in September 1852 with her husband, Benjamin Ferris, President Fillmore's new secretary of the Utah Territory.

Elizabeth Ferris wrote, "Bridger came out and invited us in, and introduced us to his Indian wife and showed us his half-breed children—keen, bright-eyed little things." She added, "This man Bridger strongly attracts my attention. There is more than civility about him—there was native politeness. He is the oldest trapper in the Rocky Mountains; his language is very graphic and descriptive, and he is evidently a man of great shrewdness." His wife "was simplicity itself. She exhibited some curious pieces of Indian embroidery, the work of her own hands, with as much pleased hilarity as a child; and gave me a quantity of raisins and sauceberrys—altogether, it was a very pleasant interview."[26]

Just that summer Bridger had paid $400 to Charles Sagenes to purchase five houses on Black's Fork a mile and a quarter from Fort Bridger, and Bridger offered one of those houses to the Ferrises, telling them that Benjamin's assistance in business would more than compensate for the cost of lodging.[27] Bridger told them heavy storms were coming, but Elizabeth felt that Bridger was just being kind, and they went on to Salt Lake City. Bridger's prediction of heavy snows proved true. Several Mexicans on their way to Fort Bridger from the Colorado River froze to death that winter within twenty miles of the fort. An advance party for Benjamin and Elizabeth Ferris, who were returning to the States, was trapped in deep snow in April 1853 and nearly starved as they crawled for miles to the fort.[28]

With Bridger and Vasquez now living far apart, they relied on Robert Campbell and his banking house in St. Louis to keep track of their affairs and their individual and partnership accounts. In 1852 Campbell's office transferred $2,796 from Bridger's account to the Bridger-Vasquez partnership. Also that year Campbell received a $6,600 draft from merchants Livingston and Kinkead, payable to Bridger's account in July 1853, probably for purchased livestock.

Father De Smet kept Bridger informed as well, writing him in April 1853 that Felix and Josephine had been sick with ague during the winter but had recuperated well. In April 1853 Campbell sent blankets, beads, and other presents for Bridger to give to Flathead chief Insula, and he included a Colt revolver and a Bowie knife from Father De Smet to give to Insula. In June Campbell informed Vasquez that Bridger had done well in trading and needed more goods. He also reported that Fort Laramie had suffered a severe winter and their trade in buffalo robes was down.[29]

23

MORMONS TAKE FORT BRIDGER

1852–1853

When Fort Bridger became part of Utah Territory, Bridger's troubles with Brigham Young only escalated. The disputes revolved around the right to freely operate ferry boats on Green River and the right to freely trade with the Shoshones, Utes, and other Indians. Young was governor of a theocracy, not a democracy, and he levied taxes to raise money to support church efforts. Church leaders announced their preferred candidates for territorial offices, and they were elected unanimously by a public show of hands. Even when written ballots were adopted in 1853, the votes were marked to record how each person voted.

Most pertinent to Bridger's future was that many of the legal officers in Utah Territory were appointed by the church. This included the attorney general, county marshals, deputies, and probate judges. The probate courts in each county were vested "with civil and criminal jurisdiction, powers never intended by Congress. The inventive 1852 law emptied district benches of standing, left the federal judges with no cases to hear, and touched off a continuing struggle over court jurisdiction."[1] As to the governorship, Brigham Young reportedly said, "If they send [another] governor here, he will be glad to black my boots for me."[2]

The Latter-day Saints felt they had been unfairly treated by people in the states, and it seems they responded by reading people's mail so it would not happen again. Indian Agent Jacob Holeman complained to the commissioner of Indian affairs in Washington that the Mormons opened and examined "all letters coming and going."[3] When Holeman had mail pertaining to Mormon character or conduct, he sent it from either Fort Bridger or Fort Laramie so it would not be prematurely opened. Maj. William Singer claimed that Mormons destroyed letters containing anything derogatory about them, while another account said that "no letters deposited in the post office, by either gentiles or Mormons, ever left the valley without its contents being known."[4] According to Holeman, Mormons "boldly assert that, if Brigham was to tell them to cut any man's throat, they would do it without hesitation."[5]

The rift between Latter-day Saints and federally appointed officials was a major issue, and fault lay with both sides. Judge Perry Brocchus, appointed by President Fillmore, addressed three thousand Mormons in 1851 and chastised them for saying that "the United States were a stink in our nostrils" and were "going to hell as fast as possible."[6] Brocchus spoke against polygamy and insulted Mormon women, saying they should "become virtuous."

The bowery erupted in protest, and Governor Young rose in anger, pledging allegiance to the government and the constitution, but not to "the damned rascals who administer the government." He said, "All we care about is for [federal leaders] to let us alone, to keep away their trash and officers so far as possible."[7] Brocchus and the other appointees left the territory in haste and presented their complaints to the president.

As the number of westward emigrants grew from 25,450 people in 1849 to 60,000 in 1852, the stakes increased for the profitable Green River ferries. Bridger and Vasquez had been operating two boats at the crossing with long ropes, tackle, and other equipment. They employed several men to manage and conduct the crossings. Many mountaineers had established ferries on Green River through friendship or marriage with the Shoshones. But on January 16, 1852, the Utah territorial legislature gave ferry rights on Green River to Thomas Moor for one year. Moor was to remit 10 percent of revenues to the territory, and anyone else operating a ferry there would be fined $1,000.

A year later, on January 7, 1853, the Utah legislature upped the ante by granting an exclusive three-year charter for Green River ferries to Daniel Wells, a close friend of Brigham Young. Wells's rights required him to pay 10 percent of all proceeds to the Perpetual Emigrating Fund Company.[8] Now the church-controlled territorial legislature had decided that the mountain men who had lived and traded among the Shoshones for years were no longer allowed to run the ferries.[9]

Wells sold his exclusive rights to Hawley, Thompson, and MacDonald—all Mormons. Hawley and Company realized they had little chance of successfully operating ferries at Green River unless Bridger was associated with the effort, and on May 21, 1853, the company proposed that Bridger and Vasquez run these ferries for them and pay 50 percent of all receipts to the company and an additional 10 percent to the Perpetual Emigrating Fund to help the church grow.[10] If Bridger and Vasquez took in $20,000 total revenue, for example, they would pay $12,000 "off the top" to Hawley and Company and the Emigrating Fund, leaving only $8,000 to pay for their boats, ropes, labor, and other expenses.

It is clear that Brigham Young was directing the ferryboat negotiations. Daniel Wells later wrote to Hawley concerning the ferries: "I have never proposed anything to you except it was in accordance with President Young's wishes." Young also personally certified the receipts paid by ferry operators to the Perpetual Emigrating Fund.[11]

The unlicensed mountaineers continued to operate their own ferries on Green River, and on June 16, 1853, James Ferguson represented the partnership of Bridger Hawley Thomson & Co. in a suit for $20,000 against the mountaineers. Ferguson was not only Utah Territory's first attorney general but also a sheriff and a major in the territorial militia. Bridger, knowingly or unknowingly, was now part of a civil suit on the side of church members against mountaineers Jerry Dennis, D. Dennis, Jacob Sweeney, William Shortridge, John Livermore, William Clark, Taylor, Elisha Ryan, and William Davis, and others.[12]

Sheriff Louis Robison went to Green River on June 30 and took possession of their boat and fixtures. Fifty mountaineers raised their rifles in protest and told the sheriff to release the boat and leave immediately. Robison reported this to the court on July 18: "The law cannot be executed . . . without an armed force. . . . There appeared to be a determined resolution to resist the laws, and they expressed themselves that they did not care a damn for any laws." The Utah court ultimately decided in favor of Bridger Hawley Thompson & Co in the amount of $13,500 plus $112.75 in costs, but it seemed unlikely they would ever collect.[13]

The summer of 1853 also saw animosity grow between the Utes and the church settlements in southern Utah. Ute strongman Walkara led a series of attacks on southern Mormon settlements, and even though the war was focused on central and southern Utah, Young then revoked all licenses to trade with Indians. He also revoked the two Tavern Keeper licenses that had been granted by Holeman for Fort Bridger and Green River for the accommodation of travelers.

By August 6, 1853, Bridger had erected a sign about a mile and a half from his fort requesting emigrants to keep a mile away from his place.[14] This may have been because emigrant stock were overgrazing the land. Granville Stuart, who passed Fort Bridger in 1852, commented that the stock from wagon trains had "devoured the grass year after year till it has quit growing out." He noted the loss of "the most numerous clusters of wild roses that ever I saw, . . . the beautiful groves of cottonwoods that once fringed its banks, and . . . the fine growth of willows that once lined the stream."[15] Another reason may have been Bridger's impending conflict with Brigham Young and his militia.

Bridger was no supporter of Ute Indian treachery. Yet Judge Leonidas Shaver issued a writ for his arrest on August 17, 1853, charging that Bridger, "on the 1st day of August 1853 unlawfully aided and abetted the Ute Indians, and supplied them with arms and ammunition for the purpose of committing depredation upon and making war on the citizens of the United States." It was a charge of treason and the marshal was instructed to bring Bridger in.[16] Bill Hickman, who by 1854 was sheriff, tax assessor, and tax collector for Green River County, remembered it this way: "It was rumored that Jim Bridger was furnishing the Indians with powder and lead to kill Mormons. Affidavits were filled out to that effect, and the sheriff was ordered out with posse.[17]

Brigham Young was the master planner for the "Ft Bridger and Green River Expedition," and he specifically instructed James Ferguson to "raise fifty men fully equipped for service with rations for twenty days." He told Ferguson to take "two or three good spy Glasses and keep a vigilant lookout that you be not taken in ambush" and also to "take into your charge all such guns and ammunition and spill upon the ground any and all spiritous liquors that you shall find in or about the premises." Young signed his order as "Governor and Superintendent of Indian Affairs and Commander in Chief of the Militia."[18]

Four years earlier Brigham Young had said, "I believe I know that Old Bridger is death on us." Now Young was finally acting on it.[19] Historian Fred Gowans writes, "Underlying each of these issues was Brigham Young's growing desire to control the Fort Bridger–Green River area. . . . Some of the Mormons were not content to see this lucrative business go to the enrichment of the mountain men."[20]

Bridger was certainly the best known of the traders at Fort Bridger. But there were many other independent Indian traders at Fort Bridger, and he had little influence on them. Bridger may have sold arms and ammunition to the Utes. But it is also possible that he did not. As historian John Gray surmised, the "warrant for his arrest [was] in order to force him to sell."[21]

Ferguson's posse of fifty men had grown to seventy-nine by August 21. Salt Lake City was in a state of high excitement. William Kimball raised another forty-two men, because he had heard an erroneous rumor that Bridger had gathered a force of two hundred to defend himself and the fort.[22] Bridger had gone into hiding and watched the fort from a concealed spot with his spyglass, somehow keeping in touch with his wife Mary.[23]

Ferguson rode to Fort Bridger and reported to Young, "There are here some 4 or 500 head of Bridger's stock together with some few dry goods. You have marked out our course in regard to the contraband stores. What should we do with the rest? and what with the fort?"[24] Ferguson's questions seem to indicate that their goal was not just to arrest Bridger but to take his fort and possessions. The Mormons inventoried the guns, powder, anvil, iron, and steel they confiscated as well as foodstuffs taken, oxen slaughtered for food, and the cost of two months of their occupation of the fort; the list totaled $2,736. Then someone forged Bridger's name to the document statement that "the goods are charged at the established [prices] of this county given under my hand this the 25th day of February 1854. James Bridger." But Bridger was unable to sign his name at all—and certainly not on that day because in February 1854 he was in Washington, D.C.[25]

Young had told the posse to "spill upon the ground any and all spiritous liquors," but Bill Hickman recorded that they destroyed the whiskey and rum "by doses: the sheriff, most of his officers, the doctor and chaplain of the company, all aided in carrying out the orders, and worked so hard day and night that they were exhausted—not being able to stand up."[26]

On August 27 Elisha Ryan, one of the rebellious Green River mountaineers, unwittingly rode to Fort Bridger with several Shoshones. The Mormon posse arrested him and confiscated his animals—forty-seven cattle, five calves, one horse, two mares, and one colt—taking them in payment for damages due Bridger Hawley MacDonald & Co, for Green River ferry infractions. The animals were later sold at public auction for $1,820.75, just enough to cover court costs and posse fees.[27] As expected, neither Bridger nor his ferry partners received any payment from the proceeds. Hickman and three others were to escort prisoner Ryan to Salt Lake City, but after they rode and drank for several miles, Ryan was able to slip off his horse and escape.[28]

Kimball suggested that the posse set a trap for Bridger by making it look as if they had gone back to Salt Lake City. Young agreed and instructed Ferguson and Kimball to "leave Bridger property undisturbed . . . at Bridger and Green River. It is more than probable that Mr Bridger will return and We May have a good chance to get him by throwing him off his guard."[29] But Bridger was not easily decoyed, and the posse never captured him.

Seth Blair, the U.S. attorney for Utah Territory, proposed a scheme to Young where they would set up several people to sue Bridger for damages. If Bridger was not found, they could then confiscate his fort in payment. Blair offered: "I can draw up declarations and forward them in & the Surpoenas can be Sent out & coppys left at his Residence & it is most probable—that judgement [against Bridger] will go by default," meaning that the court could then just take Bridger's property.[30] Young checked into this scheme with Judge Shaver, who said the current writ would not justify taking the fort, but that it might be seized if they could charge Bridger with selling spiritous liquors or rum to Indians. Young also encouraged Ferguson to befriend Washakie so he might be "influenced to bring Mr. Bridger in, or give some information concerning his whereabouts."[31]

Some of the posse rode on to the Green River ferries, and Bill Hickman, one of the posse, remembered it was a bloody job that left him scarred in mind and body. They killed two or three of the mountaineers and confiscated property, livestock, and whiskey, again destroying it "in small doses." The posse returned to Salt Lake City, reporting that "Bridger was either gone for good or, if he returned, his influence would be diminished."[32] With Bridger gone, the Mormons tried to occupy Fort Bridger, but the angry mountaineers resisted the move, so instead they established Fort Supply about twelve miles southwest of Fort Bridger.

Word of the Mormon posse spread to the states. To some Americans, Bridger was a national icon. The Independence, Missouri, *Messenger* suggested that a band of mountaineers would go to war to protect him, and "the first thing the Saints know, the mountain men will bring such a storm about their heads, the like of which they never knew in the States." The *St. Louis Intelligencer* inaccurately printed that the Mormons killed Bridger at Green River.[33]

But Bridger was not dead. In fact, he hired government surveyor John Hockaday to survey his property, and the boundaries totaled about six square miles. Then Bridger set out east with Mary and his children for Westport, Missouri, possibly with their newborn, Mary Elizabeth. Coincidentally, Vasquez took the September mail coach east to Independence, sharing the ride with Dr. John M. Bernhisel, Utah's territorial delegate to Congress.[34]

When Bridger and his family arrived in Westport in fall 1853, they tried to find a place to live close to the Vasquez residence. The Westport area was home to several families similar to the Bridgers, with a white father, an Indian mother, and mixed-race children. By December Bridger was on his way to St. Louis and then Washington, and he left Mary and their children at the home of Westport pioneer Church Dyche.[35] Tom Fitzpatrick was also on his way to St. Louis and eventually Washington, and the two of them traveled together. They arrived at Robert Campbell's office on December 17 and prepared to go to Washington, D.C.

Several days of snow brought travel delays, and Bridger and Fitzpatrick waited a week to begin their journey. They finally set out on Christmas Day. Campbell saw Bridger's trip to Washington to plead his case against the Mormons as a worthy attempt, although he wrote Vasquez: "Mr Bridger left with Fitz last Sunday (Christmas day) for Washington. . . . I do not know that he can do much yet he may effect some change and as he had no business to keep him here I have recommended it but for him to go on—the expense will not be great and it may be of benefit to you."[36]

Fitzpatrick was traveling to Washington to secure approval for treaties he had forged with the Comanches, Kiowas, and Plains Apaches.[37] Fitzpatrick's company on the trip was no doubt helpful to Bridger, who had been in the mountains his entire adult life, except for his trip to St. Louis in 1839–40. There was no bridge yet anywhere across the Mississippi, so they would have ferried across the river to Illinois and then boarded a train or stage there.

Bridger and Fitzpatrick arrived in Washington on January 4, 1854, and checked into Brown's Hotel, a nationally known establishment on Pennsylvania Avenue midway between the Capitol and the White House and close to the stage and steamboat office.[38] One can only wonder at Bridger's reaction to the nation's capital. He was undoubtedly equipped with letters of introduction and support from Robert Campbell, by this time one of the wealthiest and most prominent men in the West.

Bridger petitioned Secretary of War Jefferson Davis to submit a claim for Fort Bridger to the president. Bridger's lawyer stated, "Mr. Bridger utterly denies that he has, in any instance, violated the laws in question, and alleges that the process of the [Utah] Court was improperly obtained, irregular in form, and illegal in substance."[39] Davis forwarded the request to C. Cushing, the attorney general of the United States.

While Bridger navigated the halls of Congress just a short walk from Brown's Hotel, Fitzpatrick went to New York on other business.[40] On his return to Washington, Fitzpatrick contracted a severe cold that deepened into pneumonia. Bridger stayed at Fitzpatrick's side, but there was little he could do to help his old friend. Campbell hurried in from Philadelphia, where he was transacting business, and both men were with Fitzpatrick when he died on February 7, 1854.[41] The three men had known each other for thirty years, as trappers, brigade leaders, partners, and friends.

Bridger pressed his case to members of Congress, declaring himself innocent of the charges and lobbying for the return of his fort. Most notably, he implored

Sen. Stephen Douglas, whose committee was debating the Nebraska territorial bill. On February 13 Utah territorial delegate to Congress John Bernhisel warned Young that Bridger was "telling marvelous stories about his being driven from his home in the mountains," and his statements were "the cause of the attempt to curtail our boundaries, so that he will be without [outside] the jurisdiction of Utah."[42]

Senator Douglas's committee was considering a bill that would reduce the eastern boundary of Utah by stopping it at Bear River and the Wasatch Mountain Range while transferring the Fort Bridger and Green River country to Nebraska. The bill was expected to pass the Senate and then go to the House.

Young was livid. On April 29 he wrote Douglas that he had heard "James Bridger, from Black's Fork of Green River, has become the oracle to Congress in all matters pertaining to Utah, not only civil & political, but even historical & geographical." Young threatened that the Mormons already had a majority population and warned that they "contemplated making several settlements there [Nebraska] in a short time, & you see that we stand every chance for having two Territories in lieu of one."[43]

Young wrote Bernhisel on the same day: "If one James Bridger must be the only inhabitant worthy of belief & patronage by Congress," then Congress should "organize still another Territory designed directly for the benefit of the illustrious James Bridger." Young was astounded "that a man of Bridger's appearance, ignorance, & folly . . . could have any influence with the professed wise men of our nation. . . . It only goes to prove how many characters are at Washington who prefer lies to the truth. . . . Please say to all who advocate such policy, 'Kiss my ass, damn you.'"[44] (The earthy insult was crossed out in the draft and not included in Young's final letter.)

Young also ranted to Bernhisel that he wanted to tell Congress to "keep your pet Bridger there, if you wish to preserve him, for if the legal officers [of Utah] get hold of him, & just laws of your own making are enforced, he may be strung up between the heavens & the earth."[45]

Surveyor John Hockaday supported Bridger's and mountaineers' rights to the Green River ferries and wrote the commissioner of Indian affairs on June 17 that the Shoshones claimed "they have given the said river [Green River] and the right of erecting ferries on the same to the white men that have married squaws of their tribe, and have children among them. . . . There has been no treaty made with the Indians, and that the land, timber, river, etc., legally belong to them, until purchase of them by treaty with United States government, and that the legislature of the territory of Utah have no right or authority to grant such charter on Indian lands."[46] Officers at Fort Laramie were also concerned that Mormons were claiming land to which Indian title had not been extinguished.

Attorney General Cushing advised Jefferson Davis on March 23, 1854, that the case belonged in the Utah courts and did not call for the interposition of the president. On June 26, 1854, Secretary of War Davis wrote to Bridger concluding that the president had no authority to entertain his claim.[47] The Kansas-Nebraska Act passed without removing Fort Bridger and Green River from Utah Territory.

Bridger returned to Westport and tried to make sense of his place in the world now that he had been forced to flee his livelihood and his home. His lifeline to the West now appeared to be as a scout. Though the mountaineers still prevented the Mormons from occupying Fort Bridger, it was not safe for Bridger to return.

Back in Utah Territory, Joseph Busby brought suit against Bridger and Vasquez in May 1854 on a matter relating to the Ham's Fork ferry, which they had jointly operated in 1853. The case was dismissed for lack of a material witness.[48] Shoshone chief Washakie missed Bridger and in June 1854 showed his anger at the Green River ferry, now controlled by Mormons. He "drew his sword . . . and Pushed some of the [Mormon] men out of the haus and Cast his Robe on to the ground and Stamped it in anger."

Washakie scolded, "When our young men have been hunting, and got tired and hungry, they have come to the white man's camp and have been ordered to get out, and they are slapped, or kicked, and called 'd__d Injuns.' . . . I will tell you what I will do. Every white man, woman or child, that I find on this side of that water . . . at sunrise tomorrow I will wipe them out."[49]

Brigham Young wrote Washakie a conciliatory letter saying that Bridger should not have hidden from the posse, suggesting that he "probably would have been fined if he had not have fled. . . . Perhaps he might have got clear and not even been fined."[50] That was a risk that Bridger was not willing to take.

24

GUIDING GORE, WARREN, AND HAYDEN
1854–1856

After losing their fort to Mormon control, Bridger and Vasquez began planning for a new trading post along the Santa Fe Trail. While Bridger was in Washington, Vasquez began purchasing land in New Santa Fe, about nine miles south of Westport. They purchased more land there in 1854 and 1855. Advantageously situated at the intersection of the Santa Fe Trail and the Military Road, the property lay less than a quarter mile from the border of the state of Missouri and Kansas Territory.[1] With their neighbor Josiah Watts, they formed a partnership called Vasquez, Bridger, and Watts, and Watts helped establish and manage the daily operations.[2] Neighbor George Kemper was said to have helped build the log structures for the store.

Bridger and Vasquez were doing well financially. In December 1853 Bridger had deposited a draft with Campbell for $2,300 from Livingston and Kinkead for the sale of forty-six head of oxen valued at $50 a head. This was in addition to the $6,600 from Livingston and Kinkead the previous year, which was already earning 6 percent interest.[3] Bridger's home life was in order as well. In the winter of 1853–54 the Bridgers sent Virginia, age six, and John, age four, to Robert Campbell to be schooled at St. Charles, joining their brother Felix and sister Mary Josephine. Mary was taking care of their baby daughter, Mary Elizabeth, born in 1853.

The four oldest children were baptized at St. Charles Borromeo Catholic Church in St. Charles—Mary Josephine in April 1853, Felix in January 1854, and Virginia and John in May 1854. Mary Josephine left the convent school in November 1853 and went under the care of Susan Richard, the sister of John Richard Sr., who was very active in the Rocky Mountain trade. "Rocky Mountain Felix," as Father De Smet called him, was in a growth spurt, and De Smet arranged for new clothing for him.[4]

Robert Campbell probably was the one who connected Jim Bridger with Sir St. George Gore, an adventurer from Sligo, Ireland, who had been planning a hunting trip to the Rocky Mountains for some time. An avid hunter and traveler, Gore was fascinated with James Fenimore Cooper's Leatherstocking Tales (1823–41) and Francis Parkman's *The Oregon Trail* (1847), and he was determined to shoot game in the American West.

Gore had hunted the Scottish Highlands and probably the grounds of William Stewart's Murthly Castle in Perthshire. At Stewart's castle Gore would have seen Alfred Jacob Miller's romantic paintings of Indians, trappers, and buffalo and would have heard tales of Stewart's friend "Jem" Bridger. By May 1854 Gore was in St. Louis putting his outfit together for a lengthy hunt at the same time Bridger was expected to be in nearby St. Charles visiting his children in school. Bridger epitomized the western frontiersman that Gore was looking for.[5]

Sir St. George Gore was the eighth baronet of Gore Manor in Northern Ireland, and money was of little consequence. To fund his purchases, he wrote two drafts to Pierre Chouteau totaling £1,800. Gore assembled his enormous retinue in Bridger's new hometown of Westport and amazed onlookers as he set out with forty people to attend him—cooks and stewards to prepare his meals and serve his wines, fly-makers to tie his fishing hooks, tenders to care for his forty hunting dogs, and various secretaries and servants.

He hired Henri Chatillon as his hunter and Jim Bridger as his guide. One hundred seventy horses, oxen, and mules pulled twenty-one carts and six heavy wagons filled to the brim with provisions, including a giant green-and-white striped tent, chairs, and a bathtub. He also packed three tons of ammunition, as he intended to shoot as much game as he could. His passport from the U.S. Indian agency allowed him to travel in Indian lands beginning May 24, 1854.[6]

Bald on top but heavily whiskered on his cheeks, Gore lived a pampered life on the trail. He usually slept until noon, and then his servants heated pail after pail of water for his bath. They served him a meal of delicacies from his well-stocked larder, and only then did he set off on the day's hunt, often alone or with one or two others. He became quite animated whenever his bloodhounds caught the scent of game.

Sometimes Gore didn't return until ten in the evening, and then he invited Bridger to his tent for dinner. After a sumptuous meal with wine, Gore sat in a chair brought from St. Louis and read aloud. Bridger felt that some of Shakespeare's stories were "a leetle too highfalutin for him" and "that thar big Dutchman, Mr. Full-stuff, was a leetle bit too fond of lager beer." It would have been better if he had just drank whiskey.[7]

Both Bridger and hunter Henri Chatillon had their differences with the ostentatious Irishman. Chatillon spent eleven months with Gore and called him "a very disagreeable 'Jonnie Bull' [who] put on any amount of airs, had 18 blood hounds to chase the antelope, and played smash in general."[8] Bridger also had his disagreements with his employer. According to Capt. Randolph Marcy, who met Bridger after his stint with Gore, the Irishman once read Sir Walter Scott's description of the battle of Waterloo and asked Bridger if he didn't think that was "the most sanguinary battle he had ever heard of?"

Marcy said Bridger was quick to answer, and he paraphrased the mountain man's response. "Wall now, Mr. Gore, that thar must 'a bin a considdible of a skrimmage, dogon my skin ef it mustn't; them Britishers must 'a fit [fought] better thar than they did down to Horleans, whar Old Hickry gin um the forkedest sort o' chain-lightenin' that prehaps you ever did see in all yer born days." Gore was incredulous, and Bridger added, "You can jist go your pile on it, Mr. Gore—*you can*, as sure as yer born."[9]

Another time Gore read stories about Baron Munchausen, and Bridger said he'd "be dogond ef he swallowed every thing that thar *Baren* Mountchawson said, and he thout he was a durned liar." But when Gore asked Bridger to reflect on his own experiences with the Blackfeet, Bridger admitted his adventures would be equally marvelous "ef writ in a book."[10]

Whatever Bridger thought of Gore's personality and temperament, he enjoyed his arsenal of rifles, including one so unique it required special instructions for loading. Bridger thought it was "the best gun he ever handled." Gore later sold the rifle for $260 to the Blair family, who were friends to several presidents and owners of the Blair House, which serves today as a presidential guest house across from the White House.[11]

In 1854 Gore hunted his way across Kansas, Nebraska, and Colorado, including the headwaters of the North Platte River northwest of Denver. Nine years later a party crossed the trail made by "Sir George Gore . . . under the guidance of Jim Bridger [and saw] the names of himself and party rudely carved on trees bearing the date, 1854."[12] Subsequent travelers found a wagon axletree that Gore had abandoned on the Uinta River in the vicinity of Fort Bridger.

On September 23 Robert Campbell wrote a letter to Sir St. George Gore at Fort Laramie with sad news: "Tell Jim Bridger that his youngest son that was at St. Charles died about a month ago—his disease was bilious dysentery—his other children are well."[13] John Bridger had been buried at St. Charles cemetery on August 27, four weeks prior to Campbell's letter.

Bridger returned home to Westport to comfort Mary after the loss of their child while Gore and his party set up their winter camp about ninety miles west of Fort Laramie at the mouth of Box Elder Creek. There he could enjoy abundant grass, wood, water, and hunting. Bridger planned to join them again in spring 1855 to resume the hunt.

On March 22, 1855, Bridger purchased the old Thatcher farm, which sat about nine miles south of Westport and just north of New Santa Fe, all of which would eventually become part of Kansas City, Missouri. The farm had 287 acres, some in cultivation and some in timber. The northern boundary of Bridger's land was close to Indian Creek and Watts Mill in the small town of Dallas, Missouri. The property extended south for about two miles up the slope of the Indian Creek valley, almost to the town of New Santa Fe.[14] By summer 1855 Bridger had started construction on a new house to be built for him by Watts, who was authorized to draw on Bridger's account for expenses.[15]

This may have been when Bridger built the big farmhouse where Bridger would spend his final days. It had a two-story veranda across the front, a large central hall with two huge rooms on either side with fireplaces and two large rooms on the second floor, also with fireplaces. It was more like Old Bedlam, the spacious officers' quarters at Fort Laramie, rather than the small rooms he and his family had lived in at Fort Bridger. It stood on the crest of a ridge south of Indian Creek, the "sort of hilltop lookout a scout would naturally select for his home."[16]

In April 1855 Jim Bridger boarded a steamboat at Westport bound for St. Louis, intending to see his children, inform Robert Campbell of Gore's plans for 1855, and arrange for carts and other articles Gore and Bridger would take on that year's expedition. Bridger hadn't traveled very far on his journey down the Missouri when he contracted a severe case of pneumonia. He had to get off the boat at Sibley, Missouri, and was so sick his caretakers thought he might die. This same disease had killed his friend Tom Fitzpatrick the year before. Several days lapsed before Bridger was able to travel, and he finally boarded the boat for St. Charles to see his children. From there he went on to St. Louis to talk with Campbell about Gore's summer hunt.[17]

By summer 1855 Bridger was in the West again, guiding Gore. He must have wondered if the warrant for his arrest was still standing. Brigham Young had not eased his threats toward those who opposed him. Young called for blood atonement that year for those who had persecuted the Latter-day Saints: "If they had any respect for their own welfare, . . . they would be willing to have their [own] heads chopped off . . . for their sins." When asked about those who persecuted his people, Young said one "could take the same law they have taken, viz. mobocracy, and if any scoundrels come here, cut their throats."[18]

In October 1853, Capt. John Gunnison and several of his men were killed while exploring a railroad route in Utah near the Grand and Sevier rivers. Lt. Col. Edward Steptoe and several soldiers arrived in Salt Lake City the next year for survey work, and Steptoe was ordered to capture and help convict the perpetrators of Gunnison's murder. President Franklin Pierce appointed Steptoe to replace Brigham Young as governor of Utah Territory,[19] and congressional delegate Bernhisel bluntly told Young that the president had moved to replace him because "you defied the Federal Government, and [said] that you would declare war against it."[20]

The official investigation found no proof of Mormon complicity in Gunnison's murder. But Mormon authorities exerted little energy in arresting or properly charging the guilty parties.[21] Steptoe could see how difficult it would be to assume the governorship of Utah Territory, and he declined the president's appointment. When Steptoe and his soldiers left Utah, at least one hundred married and single women took that opportunity to leave the Mormon-controlled Salt Lake City with them.[22]

Given Young's violent rhetoric, there was little chance that Bridger could ever come back to live in Utah Territory. So in July he rode to Fort Bridger to see about selling. He met Green River County sheriff Bill Hickman, who tried to settle the matter. But Hickman found Bridger "verry carless and indeferent about Selling." The mountaineers encouraged Bridger to hold on, saying that "he had better keep the Place."

Lewis Robison, purchasing agent for the Mormon Church, arrived at the fort hoping to close the deal. Backed by church funds, Robison had made an arrangement with Young that he would receive one half of any profits that would materialize. He wanted to pay less than the $8,000 that they had talked of, but

Bridger "would not fall on his Price" and in fact wanted $600 or $800 more. Robison held firm; it would be $8,000 and "not another Dime would I give. An that was Double what he ever would git again."[23]

Robison wanted proof of title and had prepared a bill of sale to that effect. Bridger refused, saying he had "a first rate lawyer boarding with him that could do business up right," describing Vasquez's agent Hiram Morell. They finally agreed on $8,000: $4,000 in August 1855 and $4,000 in November 1856. Bill Hickman was one of the party that conveyed the heavy gold, which included forty-eight twenty-dollar gold pieces marked "United States Assay Office of Gold San Francisco California."[24]

Robison created an inventory of the present assets that the church was buying: 107 head of cattle and horses at $30 each; over $250 worth of cloth; two wagons; quantities of flour, beaver pelts, traps, beads, and vermilion; and a wagon and five oxen at Green River. The 1855 inventory of stock and goods added up to $4,726.30. The property taken from Fort Bridger in 1853 totaled $2,736.21, so the total of stock and goods for both years came to $7,463. The Mormons later agreed to pay an additional $1,000 in 1858, so their total purchase price was $9,000. When the value of the stock and goods is deducted from the amount paid, though, the Mormons gave only $1,537 for the fort, the land, and the business that had brought Bridger and Vasquez thousands of dollars of income each year.[25]

Bridger marked his X, and Morrell signed for Vasquez. Mormon official Heber Kimball wrote to a fellow believer in England: "The Church has bought out Bridger Ranch. . . . Bridger is gone."[26] Bridger rode away from his first adult home, a place he had lived for ten years, and from the fort that had brought him fame throughout the West. He carried a bitterness in his heart for the rest of his life.

After the sale Bridger resumed his role as Gore's chief guide, taking him to Pumpkin Buttes, then down the Powder River and up the Yellowstone to the mouth of the Tongue. There Gore constructed cabins for his second winter in the Rockies.[27] Again, hundreds of buffalo fell to Gore's precision rifles, their blood staining the snow.

Bridger spent the winter of 1855–56 with his family in Westport and then came back to guide Gore the following spring. In 1856 Bridger took Gore to the head of Rosebud Creek and then led him to a large village of Crow Indians, who were particularly fascinating to Gore. The Irish adventurer was one of the most horrific hunters in Rocky Mountain history, killing many more animals than his party could ever hope to use. Eventually he tired of the chase and began to

shoot from a fixed spot, using a brace for his rifle, and the buffalo dropped to
the ground one after another.

The range of the American bison had been shrinking for years, and while they
were not yet nearing extinction, many people viewed Gore's hunting practices as
irresponsible, particularly the Sioux. Indian agent Alfred Vaughan complained
to his superintendent in St. Louis that Gore had violated his passport and had
boasted that he and his men killed 105 bears, some 2,000 buffalo, and 1,600 elk
and deer purely for sport.[28]

Bridger was never known for excessive hunting, so Gore's behavior must have
seemed wasteful to him. As atrocious as Gore's buffalo kill was, it was a fraction
of the total number of buffalo slaughtered annually by commercial companies.
Charles Chouteau, manager of Pierre Chouteau Jr. & Co., told traveler Elias
Marsh that his company was purchasing fifty thousand buffalo robes every spring
and that the total number of buffalo killed commercially was ten times that.[29]

Finally, in 1856, Gore called an end to his hunt. His payment to Bridger for
the period between May 1, 1854, and June 10, 1856, came to $1,350 to be credited
to Bridger's account with Robert Campbell. The breakdown may have been one
hundred dollars a month for six months in 1854, five months in 1855, and two
and a half months in 1856. Vasquez also earned $400 for guiding Gore, some
of which he earned while Bridger was away finalizing the sale of Fort Bridger
with the Mormons.[30]

Bridger, Vasquez, and two others headed down the Yellowstone ahead of
Gore, and on June 30, 1856, they arrived at Fort Union, where the Yellowstone
flows into the Missouri. The water rose two feet in twenty-four hours and then
started to recede somewhat by July 1. Edwin Hatch visited Bridger on July 6 and
learned that it was their party that had been attacked by Blackfeet the previous
winter. He wrote that he "was very amused" at Bridger's tales of mountain life.[31]

Gore was ready to go home, and he ordered two flatboats built to float his
gear down the Tongue and then down the Yellowstone to the Missouri. He usually paid liberally but refused to have anyone take advantage of him. Because
of a financial disagreement, he ordered his winter houses at the Tongue River
destroyed, his wagons and carts burnt, and all the iron thrown in the river, as
he was "determined that no one should reap any benefit from them." Gore's
blacksmith secretly cached the iron, and a portion of it was used annually at Fort
Sarpy "to be worked into tomahawks, traps, and other articles in demand."[32]

A tremendous summer storm poured down on Bridger and the others at Fort
Union, followed by intense heat. That year the confluence of the Yellowstone

and the Missouri saw a convergence of scientists and topographers, traders and mountaineers, soldiers and Indians. The steamboat *St. Mary* arrived with annuities for the Indians as well as an expedition of surveyors and scientists led by topographer Gouverneur K. Warren and geologist Ferdinand Hayden. Survey crews tried to keep cool as they prepared the transit to take observations. The Assiniboines came in for their annuities, led by a long line of men riding abreast over the hill. They raised their heavy banners, and their outriders shot their guns and raced ahead. Then the chief appeared, followed by a cacophony of men, women, children, and dogs.[33]

That night they all suffered from another furious storm. Powerful winds howled from the northwest, ushering in frigid air. Lightning flashed and thunder shook their lodges. Then the rain fell in torrents. The next day the downpour continued, and winds blew with the rage of the gods. Tents reeled and staggered. Soon rainwater stood two inches deep across the plains.

Warren's schedule was delayed (although not by the weather), and he used the extra time to explore the Yellowstone River. He hired Bridger to be his guide at $100 a month, a bit more per month than the $1,000 annual salary that Ferdinand Hayden was earning. Warren also hired one of Bridger's men for $25 a month. He purchased two wagons from Gore to take up the Yellowstone as well as six mules and twelve horses. Two or three of the horses were good buffalo runners that Gore had purchased from the Crows.

The transition from the wealthy pleasure-seeker Gore to topographer Warren and geologist Hayden was a journey from the ridiculous to the sublime for Bridger. No longer witnessing the needless slaughter of animals, Bridger was now guiding one of the nation's most important scientific expeditions. Warren was the nation's leading topographer as well as an accomplished naturalist, and his trip up the Yellowstone was part of his effort to create the first comprehensive map of the trans-Mississippi West.

Ferdinand Hayden was even more prominent than Warren. Just a couple of years earlier, he had discovered the first Jurassic-age fossils in America; he had also found fossilized teeth from the Cretaceous period near the confluence of the Judith and the Missouri River, which the Academy of Natural Sciences in Philadelphia identified as dinosaur fossils. Hayden was also the first scientist to identify the Black Hills as an extension of the Rocky Mountains instead of a separate range.[34]

Warren and Hayden had prepared for their 1856 expedition in consultation with the leaders of the ten-year-old Smithsonian Institution. They were eager to learn more about the West's prehistoric life, its undescribed species, and its geologic mysteries. Secretary of the Smithsonian Joseph Henry was particularly enthusiastic to document new discoveries, as he harbored a fear that the Smithsonian would become merely a place to amuse the visitors and citizens of Washington.

Assistant Secretary Spencer Baird was also enthusiastic for the knowledge the expedition would bring to the fledgling institution, and he provided scientific instruments, shipping containers, and arsenic to preserve specimens. Baird's daughter once amusingly wrote, "No bride ever devoted more thought and attention to her trousseau than did my father to the fitting out of each of these explorers, and he watched the progress of each with anxious personal interest."[35]

Warren's team consisted of thirty-four men—scientists, topographers, cooks, mule drivers, fifteen soldiers, and "Jim Bridger the celebrated mountaineer and trapper as guide."[36] They purchased a yawl from the steamboat and paid Gore ten dollars for the use of his flatboat, using the vessels to cross to Bridger's side of the Missouri River. Another fierce storm drenched them that night, and they spent the next day drying what they could. Indian agent Alfred Vaughan and several men came to Warren's camp and "drank several glasses of Mountain dew" (moonshine) with St. George.[37] Colonel Vaughan's party continued in the same direction as Warren, Hayden, and Bridger's party for the next two days, and they camped together.

Finally, on July 24 the new party set out, everything still wet and heavy. Their wheels and axles clogged with clumpy black earth, and they only made three and a half miles. As they traveled, they collected specimens, made detailed sketches of the topography, and measured and surveyed the distance using a prismatic compass and odometer. For the next several days they averaged sixteen miles a day, collecting, measuring, and sketching whenever they could. They found plenty of elk, antelope, and bison for food. Swarms of "nocturnal enemies," accosted them so fiercely they could barely eat or sleep. When the mosquitoes let up, Warren attempted to take his first astronomical observations along the Yellowstone. But a storm arose and obscured the sky as if to bedevil him.[38]

On the fifth day, gullies began to block their path along the river, as Bridger knew they would. Cactus covered much of the ground, but Bridger found a good place to camp with plenty of grass, water, and even a bear for food. Warren was finally able to make good observations for latitude. The next day was ideal for travel, and they explored twenty-nine miles along the river.

High bluffs now flanked the banks of the river, as Bridger had foretold. He laid out their options. For the next twenty miles they could leave the river, take their wagons around the bluffs for three or four days, and then rejoin the Yellowstone. Alternately, they could leave some of the men with their wagons and specimens collected so far, and a small party could go ahead by horse and mule through the bluffs along the river in half the time. The scientists opted for the geologically promising and physically challenging route along the river. They wanted to continue amassing more scientific treasures.[39]

Bridger warned that they soon would be entering the battleground of the Blackfeet and the Crows. All remained in good spirits, though, which was fortunate because temperament could be as difficult as the terrain for both Warren and Hayden. Warren was surveying for the Corps of Topographical Engineers, while Hayden was collecting for the Smithsonian, and their objectives sometimes differed. In one argument Warren called Hayden a fool and accused him of lying. Hayden complained to Baird, "I intend now either to whip him or shoot him, or else consider myself no more as a gentleman."[40]

The party of seven set out at four P.M., including Bridger, Warren, Hayden, assistant topographer W. H. Hutton, and three others, all mounted on steady animals. Two sure-footed pack mules carried their goods. Bridger guided them along mountain sheep trails that he had used for decades, leading them across nearly perpendicular bluffs looming three hundred feet high. They climbed and slipped their way for a mile or so to reach the top of the first ridge. Then they careened down the other side to the river plain again. Several miles later, Bridger selected their camp, a small point of timber with excellent grass where a dry creek joined the Yellowstone. Though they had not set out until late afternoon, they still made twelve and a half miles that day.

The next day the small team again followed the narrow path along the river. Jutting red hills rewarded them with awe-inspiring craggy vistas. They likened the spectacular sight to the ruins of an ancient Egyptian city and were amazed by the "rounded dome-like appearance of the hills . . . the square mesa-like formation, [and] flat topped residences and conical temples all turned to stone & earth." Dark red hills intersected with giant seams of lignite, sometimes called brown coal. The outlying rock was a burnt-looking sandstone, and fragments covered the land an inch deep as if it was "an immense brickyard."[41]

Two creeks had turned into troublesome mud quagmires, and they again took to trails used by bighorn sheep, pulling their mounts up the steep paths and then leading them down the slippery slopes. After five tortuous miles they once again came to an unobstructed path along the Yellowstone. Bridger called camp near two old makeshift forts built by the Blackfeet during a battle against the Crows.

The next day they covered another fifteen miles and finally reached the mouth of the Powder. They were near the site of Henry's Caches, and Bridger recalled to them how Andrew Henry had cached goods there thirty-two years earlier, only to have the Crows ransack the underground hiding places and steal the goods.

They had traveled as far up the Yellowstone as Warren's time allowed, and Bridger gave an extensive description of what lay farther upriver. He painted a captivating picture of gushing geysers, exploding mud pots, and dramatic waterfalls. Warren and Hayden knew that if what Bridger told them actually existed, it would be one of the most spectacular sites in the world.

James Stevenson was an assistant naturalist under Ferdinand Hayden during this expedition, and he remembered Bridger saying that his first encounter with the thermal features of Yellowstone was after "he had had a fight with the Blackfeet and retreated far enough into the Yellowstone basin to come in sight of the geysers." Stevenson and Bridger "tented & hunted together, he for game as meat, & I in the capacity of Asst. Naturalist in quest of mammals and birds for the Smithsonian Institution." Stevenson took a professional interest in Bridger as well and said that he had studied Bridger "almost as an object of Natural History."[42]

Bridger entrusted Stevenson with all his domestic correspondence, and Stevenson later recorded:

> In this way many little and interesting features connected with his boyhood and early domestic life came to my knowledge. . . . [Bridger's] memory was an encyclopedia. He had a vivid, and evidently, accurate recollection of the details of events connected with his life and ventures and would, while sitting by the camp fire at night, recite hundreds of events that occurred. . . . There are so many anecdotes & funnyisms connected with my experiences while associated with him it would take days to record. I was with him on two occasions when the Indians attacked us & I had an opportunity to observe his tact and coolness, which satisfied me that his stories of the many fights he had with the Blackfeet, Bannocks & others were not colored or exaggerated.[43]

Bridger's enthusiasm fired up their curiosity. Warren planned "to penetrate the unknown but marvelous region of the Yellowstone Basin" at some later date, and Bridger agreed guide him. Hayden's curiosity bubbled over at Bridger's descriptions of Yellowstone's geologic and geothermal features, "wonderful tales, that had sharpened the curiosity of the whole party."[44]

Bridger led them back down the Yellowstone, and they collected specimens from a rich deposit of baculites, ammonites, and other fossils that resembled squid, octopus, and nautilus. At a bend in the Yellowstone where they halted to rest, Bridger agreed to build a boat so they could continue collecting and carrying more specimens. While Bridger directed the construction of the boat, the scientists prepared and arranged the skins and skeletons they had collected. Ultimately, they even packed a skeleton of a buffalo.[45]

Bridger designed an elongated bullboat, easier to paddle and capable of carrying more men and cargo than the round bullboat common to the Mandans. He had the soldiers cut small cottonwood and willow branches and insert both ends into the sand as an arch. These were the ribs, turned upside down. They covered the ribs with three buffalo hides, fur sides in, and stitched the hides together with sinew to form the bottom and sides. Then they melted buffalo tallow and mixed it with ash to cover the boat skin, allowing it to soak into the seams.

Within two days they had a boat eighteen feet long and four feet wide that drew only two inches. They cut heavy, green cottonwood poles to push off sand bars or to steer to the other side of the channel. The topographers marked the site as "Bull Boat Camp" on their maps. With Bridger as steersman, Hutton commanding, and soldiers poling, they launched the boat and averaged over twenty miles a day loaded with the valuable specimens. The scientists continued collecting on shore. Hayden put strychnine in the carcass of a buffalo as a lure to collect wolf specimens. If they had to leave the boat for a time, they left a shirt there, knowing that the scent of a human would keep wolves away.

Having guided them for a month, Bridger brought the party back to Fort Union. The boats for their trip down the Missouri were ready, and they loaded their specimens and gear on board. Warren, Hayden, and their crew headed home, eminently successful. Bridger rode downriver with them, and when they reached Westport, James Stevenson had the pleasure of meeting Bridger's wife, Mary.

During the summer of 1856, which included some of his time with Bridger, Hayden collected examples of 135 bird species, 80 new shells, skins and skeletons of all the large plains quadrupeds, and more than twice as many fossil plants as he had found previously.[46] Warren's topographic report was also a success, documenting vast stretches of previously unmapped land. His commanding officer, A. A. Humphreys, ultimately endorsed Warren's proposed two-year expedition to complete the exploration of the sources of the Yellowstone.

Bridger had described Yellowstone's wonders to Stansbury and Gunnison in 1849, to Father De Smet in 1851, and to Warren and Hayden in 1856. All five had recorded his accounts, but their reports and journals were not widely circulated, and Yellowstone remained almost universally unknown to most of America. When Bridger returned to Westport, he described Yellowstone to the editor of the *Kansas City Journal*, R. T. Van Horn.

Van Horn recorded Bridger's enthusiastic descriptions of the steaming geysers, bubbling paint pots, obsidian glass, thermal springs, and dramatic waterfalls, summing up with Bridger's declaration that Yellowstone was the "place where hell bubbled up." Then someone advised Van Horn he would be laughed out of town if he printed "any of old Jim Bridger's lies." The disappointed, doubting editor killed his own story.[47] Bridger continued to be one of the few voices describing this fantastic and unbelievable gem, but national and global awareness of Yellowstone would have to wait another decade.

Over the winter, Bridger traveled to St. Charles and St. Louis, and on March 25, 1857, he and Samuel Tullock met for the first time in eighteen years at Robert Campbell's counting house in St. Louis, and they recalled their trapping days together. Tullock was well liked and "called the Crane by all the Indians, on account of his extreme length and slenderness."[48] On that very day, Campbell received a letter from G. K. Warren asking who discovered Great Salt Lake, and Campbell had the letter read aloud to Bridger and Tullock.

The old trappers recalled how they had been wintering in 1824–25 in Cache Valley, called Willow Valley then, and how Bridger was selected to follow the Bear to settle the bet. Etienne Provost may have seen the lake from a distance in fall of 1824, before Bridger. But Bridger was the first Euro-American to taste the waters of Great Salt Lake in late 1824 or early 1825 and discover that the lake contained salty water.[49]

25

CHIEF GUIDE FOR THE UTAH WAR

1857–1858

In Utah Territory disputes between the Mormons and the U.S. government continued to fester. The Latter-day Saints were now open about their practice of polygamy, and the newly created Republican Party nominated John C. Frémont as its candidate for president in 1856, adopting a platform to abolish the "twin relics of barbarism: slavery and polygamy."[1] John A. Tyler, son of the former president, suggested, "We can supercede [sic] the Negro-mania question with the almost universal excitement of an anti-Mormon Crusade."[2]

Polygamy was a safer topic than slavery for the Democratic Party as well. Stephen Douglas, vying for the Democratic nomination, called plural marriage "an ulcer on the land that had to be cut out." His primary opponent, James Buchanan, was not as emphatic and won the Democratic nomination and ultimately the presidency, which he assumed March 4, 1857.

An often-stated Mormon goal was to supersede the United States' control of Utah with a government ruled by their religious leaders.[3] David Burr, the federally appointed Utah surveyor general, reported, "These people repudiate the authority of the United States . . . and are in open rebellion against the general government."[4] The *Chicago Tribune* reported that Brigham Young said he would "sooner see any Gentile from the States buried deep in hell before he would relieve him from starving; let them all die the death of dogs."[5]

These challenges to U.S. authority caused President Buchanan to appoint Alfred Cumming, who was not a Mormon, to be the new governor of the territory.

He ordered up to 2,500 troops to escort the new governor to Utah to see that Young relinquished his position peacefully. Mormon leader Heber Kimball exclaimed, "God almighty helping me, I will fight until there is not a drop of blood in my veins. Good God! I have wives enough to whip out the United States."[6] Young vowed, "If [Gen. William S.] Harney crossed the South Pass the buzards Should pick his bones. The feeling of Mobocracy is rife in the 'States' the constant cry is kill the Mormons. Let them try it."[7]

On July 16, 1857, the army hired Jim Bridger (at five dollars a day) to be chief scout for the expedition, which was the largest assembly of troops in the United States at that time.[8] The army mismanaged the timing of the campaign, though, and it was not until September 3, 1857, that Bridger set out for Salt Lake City leading Col. Edmund Alexander, eight companies of the Tenth Infantry, and a battery of artillery from Fort Laramie. They were soon followed by the Fifth Infantry and another battery of artillery.[9]

These were dangerous times in Utah, and Young's rhetoric not only condoned violence but seemed to require it. As a method of reform within his church, he preached the practice of "blood atonement" for faltering Mormons, declaring that some sins were so grievous that the sinner should beg their brethren "to have their blood spilt upon the ground . . . as an offering for their sins."[10] He asked his people, "Will you love that man or woman [who has committed sin] well enough to shed their blood? . . . This is loving our neighbor as ourselves." Concerning those who had violated church covenants, Young said, "The blood of Christ will never wipe that out; your own blood must atone for it."[11]

On September 11, 1857, as Bridger was leading the first federal troops toward the mountains, the Fancher and Baker wagon train from Arkansas was passing through Mountain Meadows in southern Utah. Local Mormons persuaded Paiutes to attack the train, but the travelers defended themselves well. Mormon John Lee was ordered to "decoy the emigrants from their position and kill all of them that could talk."[12] So Lee led a group of Mormon militia as if they were coming to the emigrants' rescue, and the emigrants lowered their rifles. Lee and fifty-three other Mormons opened fire on the wagon train. They killed 120 men and women and even those children who were old enough to testify against them. Toddlers who were too young to talk were parceled out to Mormon families.

Brigham Young denied any involvement, and no evidence connects him directly to the massacre. But Young's vitriolic rhetoric and his call to blood atonement created the conditions and atmosphere that fostered the outrage. Four years after the massacre, Young visited the site and saw a monument that read,

"Vengeance is mine . . . saith the Lord." Young then pronounced, "Vengeance is mine—and I have taken a little."[13]

On September 29, as Bridger guided Alexander closer to Utah, Young declared martial law to prepare for what he thought would be an approaching hostile force. He had been planning for an invasion for some time. In 1851 he had written to Samuel Colt looking for his "most powerful sophisticated, scope-equipped weapons . . . suited to mountain warfare." Latter-day Saints leaders also explored, however briefly, a weapon of massive destruction invented by Uriah Brown, one of Joseph Smith's secret Council of Fifty. It was "an invention of liquid fire to destroy an army & navy. . . . If pipes were laid in the kanyon [one] could destroy an army instantly without injuring the operator."[14] The concept never materialized. More recently, Young had planned an escape route for his people to Washington and Oregon Territories or to British Columbia and had recently made a thirty-three-day trip to explore a safe haven in the Flathead lands.[15]

While Bridger was guiding troops in western Wyoming, his oldest living daughter, Mary Josephine, died at St. Charles of unspecified causes. She was buried on September 7, 1857, at the St. Charles Borromeo Cemetery, though it is not known when Bridger received the news.[16] This was the second Bridger child to die at St. Charles.

Mary and the family were not well either. In September 1857 Westport physician Dr. Parker made four house calls to the Bridger home to attend to Felix and give him quinine, which was the common treatment for fevers caused by malaria and other diseases. Felix was home because he had finished one level of schooling. He had written to Father Verdin on June 2, 1857, asking for acceptance into St. Louis University, but university records do not show Felix's enrollment.[17]

Dr. Parker was also summoned to treat Mary Bridger three times in September 1857 to assist with fever and her late-term pregnancy. Mary gave birth to a boy, and they named him William. Dr. Parker's charges for the seven house calls came to $40, and Bridger paid the bill when he returned to the states the next year.[18] William was Bridger's seventh child. Felix, Virginia, and Mary Elizabeth were alive, and Mary Ann, Mary Josephine, and John were deceased.

Bridger guided Col. Edmund Alexander and his troops to Ham's Fork, then returned to Laramie to guide Col. Albert Sidney Johnston, the overall commander of the expedition. Johnston was a large, mustachioed Kentuckian who had fought in the Black Hawk War, the Mexican War, and on the Comanche frontier in Texas. He left Fort Laramie with forty mounted dragoons on October 6.[19] Following them was Lt. Col. Philip St. George Cooke with over a thousand soldiers and the new governor, Alfred Cumming, and his wife in the retinue. The expedition included some 2,600 supply wagons stocked with enormous quantities of pork, flour, and other food. The army troops and supply trains were spread out over the Oregon Trail, and if put in one continuous line would have stretched for many miles.

The travelers soon learned that snow came early to the mountains. Maj. Fitz John Porter, assistant adjutant general under Johnston, recorded, "Near the Rocky Mountains, snowstorms began to overtake us, but Bridger, the faithful and experienced guide, ever on the alert, would point in time to the 'Snow-boats' which, like balloons sailing from the snowcapped mountains, warned us of storms; and would hasten to a good and early camp in time for shelter before the tempest broke upon us. At South Pass a cold and driving snowstorm barred progress for a few days, but permitted the gathering of trains, which assured protection."[20]

They met Washakie at South Pass, who informed them that Brigham Young had tried to persuade the Shoshones to fight against the soldiers, saying the army might turn on them after they killed the Mormons.[21] Washakie offered his warriors to the army instead, and Johnston refused, advising Washakie to have nothing to do with the conflict.

Meanwhile Alexander was having troubles without Bridger by his side. He chose to forge ahead and followed Ham's Fork to Bear River, but the expedition found the roads impassable from snow. There was little grass, so the horses ate mostly sagebrush and could only sustain short marches. Alexander decided to retrace their route back to Ham's Fork, and his men joked that he changes "his mind as often as the wind blows."[22]

In contrast to the violence at Mountain Meadows—and in some of Young's rhetoric—the Mormon leader, now faced with a formidable threat, actually discouraged direct engagement with the federal troops. Young's orders were to "annoy them in every possible way. . . . Stampede their animals and set fire to their trains. Burn the whole country before them and on their flanks. Keep them from sleeping by night surprises, blockade the roads by falling trees and destroying fords. . . . Set fire to the grass on their windward."[23]

Lot Smith and his Mormon raiders burned most of the forage between South Pass and Fort Bridger, and they stopped and burned many of the U.S. advance supply trains and swept behind U.S. Army forces to burn more of their supply wagons. Smith and his men entered the camp of a federal supply train, and a U.S. Army captain exclaimed, "For God's sake don't burn the trains!" Smith answered, "It's for His sake I am going to burn them!"[24] Smith set fire to fifty-one wagons and all the supplies, leaving a single wagon for the personal property of the men. The fires blazed high, especially when bacon or gunpowder caught fire.

Two nights later Smith attacked another train and burned twenty-three wagons, leaving two for the men's personal property.[25] Smith burned a third wagon train on the Sandy River. Other Mormons manned the steep walls through Echo Canyon, ready to fire down on federal troops if they tried to go through the narrow passage.[26] One of the prominent raiders with the Mormon Nauvoo Legion was Joshua Terry, who had worked for Bridger shortly after he had come to Utah in 1847.[27]

Alexander united with Johnston and Bridger on November 3, and the force was again in good hands. Temperatures continued to drop, and with little shelter or forage at Ham's Fork, Bridger advised Colonel Johnston they should move to Black's Fork for less wind, better temperatures, and timber for their winter camp. It would be a horrendous march, but they would lose more animals if they did not get to a sheltered valley. Bridger was a frequent visitor to Johnston's tent, and that evening Colonel Johnston gave Bridger the title of major.[28]

On November 6 Bridger led the expedition out toward Black's Fork only to be assaulted by a blizzard. Temperatures dropped below zero, and even the grease on the wagon axels and caissons froze. Fierce winds tore at the men's skin, and Johnston's mustache turned into an icicle. Oxen and mules died, and horses became so weak they reeled; soldiers could count the ribs of their animals from twenty feet away.[29] The men made fires from sage brush, but they burned all too briefly. Animals lay down along the road to die.

Each night they made torches of hemp, tobacco, leather, and wild sage, holding the burning blazes under the noses of their horses to relieve their coughing and running. Every morning, fifty more animals were dead. The thermometer reached 16 degrees below zero, and the men suffered frostbite. But their old guide Bridger kept their spirits up. They must have thought surely if this man could live thirty-five years in this country, they certainly could last one winter.

It took over two weeks to reach Black's Fork, and by then they were near exhaustion. But not a man was lost. They saw that the Mormons had burned Fort Bridger to the ground so it could not be used by the army, and all that was left was the stone perimeter wall they had built. The Mormons had also burned their nearby Fort Supply, destroying a hundred log houses, a sawmill, gristmill, and thrashing machine.

Bridger had been forced to sell his fort, and he negotiated with the army to lease his land, not concealing the fact that the church had agreed to pay Vasquez

James Bridger (1804–1881) (1874), by William Henry Jackson. This charcoal sketch of Jim Bridger was created by photographer and artist William Henry Jackson. It was shown at the U.S. Centennial Exhibition in Philadelphia in 1876, which celebrated the hundredth anniversary of the signing of the Declaration of Independence. *Wisconsin Historical Society Archives 148096*

and him $8,000. The value of the stock and goods confiscated by the Mormons was $7,463. So as of 1857, the Mormons were paying only $537 for the fort, the land, and the yearly profits of the business, which had generated thousands of dollars of income each year. (The Latter-day Saints added $1,000 to the purchase price, bringing the total amount paid for the fort land and business to $1,537.) Chief Bugler William Drown recorded Bridger's feelings: "The Mormons . . . gave him his choice . . . $8,000 for his place here, leaving his cattle and everything as it was, or be forced to leave, although the stock [alone] he had here at the time was well worth the amount proffered."

Assistant quartermaster John Dickerson prepared a lease to pay $600 a year for ten years and included an option for the United States to purchase the land for $10,000, but all was payable only if Bridger provided proof of title. Bridger made his X in the presence of two witnesses. In a cover letter to his superiors, Dickerson wrote Bridger "bases his claim to the land on some Mexican or Spanish law, similar to the pre-emption laws of the United States. I think it exceedingly doubtful whether his title is good."[30]

Lt. Col. Philip St. George Cooke arrived at Black's Fork a few days after Bridger and Johnston's troops had settled in. Cooke was a wiry man with a thin face made thinner by the upsweep of hair above his high forehead and the mutton-chops that plunged downward along his jaws. His command had also suffered terribly on their winter journey, and they lost many of their horses and mules.

Cooke brought with him the new territorial governor, Alfred Cumming, a waddling man with a prodigious front porch who had worked as a post sutler and as superintendent of Indian affairs. His wife was described as one of the most intolerable talkers on earth but was pleasant enough to most people just the same. Johnston's command was united now.

November 19 was nearly clear with a gentle breeze from the southwest as Jim Bridger made his way up the banks to the army pickets overlooking the valley. The snow had melted rapidly, and Bridger gazed upon the trees along Black's Fork and, far beyond, saw the dim outline of the Wind River Mountains. Capt. John Phelps, Johnston's commander of artillery, had come up to admire the countryside and was moved when he saw the old mountaineer standing by himself looking pensively at the land that had once been his.

It is 35 years since [Bridger] first came here. . . . He traded with the Indians, sending the furs which they brought from the mountains to St. Louis once a year and returning with a supply of goods. . . . He was a perfect monarch of all he surveyed, at one time having the control of 500 men, and never dreamed that his kingdom would ever be disturbed by emigration in his day—so remote was it from the United States. . . . But the Mormons came. Mr Bridgers reign was ended. They seized upon this point and ejected its ancient owner.[31]

The soldiers had plenty of food, but no milk, butter, eggs, or salt. Young sent a wagonload of salt to relieve the "destitute soldiers," but the soldiers suspected it might be poisoned or laced with a dysentery agent. The colonel told the driver to take the salt back and promised he would hang the next such messenger.[32]

They had lost so many mules and horses that Colonel Johnston sent Captain Marcy and several soldiers and mountaineers to New Mexico to secure more animals. Marcy's party went astray, suffered frostbite, and contracted snow blindness, a very painful condition. Although guided by veterans Jim Baker, Tim Goodale, and Mariano Medina, it was a muleskinner among their party named Miguel Alona who showed them the way across the mountains to the San Luis Valley. One man died, but the rest were rescued. They didn't return to Black's Fork with the animals until June 9, more than six months after they had left.[33]

U.S. authorities feared the Mormons might recruit Ute Indians to their side, and in November 1857 the secretary of interior ordered Indian agent Kit Carson to keep them neutral and "to use all diligence, tempered with extreme caution, to ascertain the feeling of these bands of Utes . . . and secure their friendship." Carson spoke with the Ute bands in March 1858 and determined that they had indeed been contacted by the Mormons. The Utes understood that the Mormons said they "had a stream in their country . . . which the U.S. troops have to pass which causes instant death by their drinking of it, [but] for Indians it is healthy and the 'Good Spirit' will protect them."[34]

Over the long winter Johnston kept his soldiers busy rebuilding the fort and performing daily drills. Bridger told his stories and yarns, and sometimes it was hard to know which was which. Bridger told them it snowed seventy days straight in the winter of 1832, which killed off most of the buffalo west of the Divide. Bugler Drown wrote that Bridger is "allowed by all the Mountaineers to be the best and most experienced guide in the country."[35]

In early January 1858 Johnston selected Albert Browne, a correspondent for the *New York Daily Tribune,* John Hockaday, and four others to be part of a journey from Black's Fork to New York to deliver messages to army headquarters. Johnston swore the group to secrecy as they prepared for their midwinter trek. On January 7 they met at Johnston's quarters for dinner, with Jim Bridger there to instruct them on the route they would take to escape the patrolling Mormons. Browne thought Bridger was a marvelously interesting character, "a counterpart of Cooper's Leatherstocking . . . unbent by age . . . and lithe and sinewy as a willow wand."[36]

Browne and his fellow travelers planned to leave before dawn so they could get to Henry's Fork, where they would pick up their horses and pack mules. From there Bridger told them that instead of striking east, they should travel south along Green River to the mouth of Bitter Creek and follow that creek up as far as the snow permitted. Then they should go northeast across the tableland in the direction of the Wind River Mountains. When they reached the Sweetwater River, they would be on the Oregon Trail. Browne and his party left the next day while stars were still visible, and they successfully completed their mission.[37]

In March 1858 heavy winds gusted, and a violent downpour drenched them. Capt. Jesse Gove wrote to his wife: "Storm still raging. Old Bridger, who is Col. Johnston's guide and who was driven out from his place by the Mormons, says that this is the equinoctial storm, and may last for some days. Then comes the warm weather."[38]

Also in March 1858, back in Missouri, the Bridger household was dealing with a situation involving an enslaved person. Mary Bridger asked Robert Campbell what she should do with "the Negro Man." Campbell answered, "Mr. Vasquez or Mr. Watt will advise you." They must have sold the man, because Bridger's account with Campbell increased by $420 "for Negro man."[39] How and when this enslaved person came to the Bridger household is not clear. Bridger may have made the arrangement himself nine months earlier before he left for Utah. Equally likely, Vasquez or Watts, who each held slaves, made the decision while Bridger was with the Utah expedition, for Bridger gave them broad authority. For example, in 1855 Vasquez authorized Watts to freely draw on Bridger's account "for the purpose of building a house for Bridger."[40]

Two years later the census recorder came to the Bridger home while the mountain man was guiding Captain Raynolds in Montana and Wyoming. The recorder listed Ruth Scaggs as head of household as well as her two sons and the Bridger children. The recorder also listed an enslaved twenty-year-old woman and two toddler daughters who were housed in an adjacent structure. The slave owner was recorded as "Ruth Scaggs, housekeeper," followed by the words "employer James Bridger of Utah Territory."[41] While the ownership of the enslaved woman is ambiguously stated, the woman may have been with the Bridger family for four years, as Dr. Parker treated a black woman named Martha at the Bridger residence in September 1857 and also in March 1861.[42]

Bridger does not appear to have been a supporter of slavery. During the Civil War he served the Union Army on the Indian frontier, and his son Felix and his son-in-law Albert Wachsman also served in the Union Army, primarily in Missouri. Many of their neighbors, including Stubbins Watts, fought for the Confederacy.[43]

Mary Bridger's letter of March 1858 told Robert Campbell that she wanted to go back to Fort Bridger to be with her husband and her people. She also wanted to take their five-year-old daughter Elizabeth from the school at St. Charles to be with her. Campbell wrote to Mary: "I do not think it well for you to go out to Salt Lake this season without Mr. Bridger send for you. I do not think it would be well to send your daughter up at present but after Mr. Bridger comes back she can then doubtless go up with him."[44] Campbell also fulfilled a request from Mary and arranged for Felix's trunk to be sent to her through their neighbor, Stubbins Watts.[45]

The spring weather in Utah turned the soldiers' thoughts to the upcoming expedition to Great Salt Lake. Bridger helped Johnston strategize how and when to attempt the mountain passes. Brigham Young had been thinking of taking his flock to another land where they would start again and believed that escaping to the north was still a possibility. But on March 8 Young received news that the Bannocks and Northern Shoshones had attacked the Mormon outpost at Fort Lemhi, four hundred miles to the north, closing that avenue of refuge.[46]

From his command post at Black's Fork, Governor Cumming declared that the Mormons were in open rebellion and that those who continued their treason would be arrested and punished as traitors. The army ordered thousands more soldiers to Utah to add to Johnston's existing two thousand men. At the same time, President Buchanan sent commissioners from Washington to offer pardons if the Mormons agreed to submit to federal authority.

Young had stirred his flock into a frenzy, vowing he would never let the U.S. gentiles take their city. Yet with spring approaching, the passes were suddenly open and a substantial army waited just over the mountains, possibly guided by Young's nemesis, Jim Bridger. In the face of this overwhelming force, Young capitulated. He persuaded Governor Cumming to cross the mountains ahead of the soldiers and take office so it would not look like a military defeat. Meanwhile Young urged Dr. John Bernhisel to continue lobbying for statehood, a development that could return Young to power by popular vote.

Governor Cumming entered the city on April 12, 1858. Yet Johnston insisted on fulfilling the president's orders, so he still planned to march through Salt Lake City. Johnston sent Bridger with Captain Newton and thirty-one soldiers to see whether a northern route could be made to Cache Valley, which would enable Johnston's troops to enter Salt Lake City from the north and avoid any attack at Echo Canyon. Bridger guided him there, and Newton concluded the northern route was more canyon than tableland and therefore unsuited for the army march. He did recommend, however, that the best opportunity for a road might be along the eastern portion of the divide between Ogden's Hole and Cache Valley as well as through the canyon of Muddy Creek.

In the end Johnston marched his troops through Echo Canyon and found that the Mormons were no longer defending it.[47] Brigham Young was clearly defeated. He could no longer thwart federal authority or order his bishops to serve as civil and criminal judges. In a hollow attempt at protest, Young ordered the city evacuated, leaving only a handful of men to defend the property of the residents. The army marched through the virtually empty city from dawn to dusk, stretching out for miles, with the only sounds being "the music of the military bands, the monotonous tramp of regiments, and the rattle of the baggage wagons."[48] The army finished its march and ultimately camped on the west bank of the Jordan River. "With one broad sweep of its military fist, the federal government ended forever the Saints' dream of implanting a millennial society on the fringe of the frontier."[49]

Bridger was employed from June 12–30, when he was guiding Captain Newton; July 1–2 at Camp Floyd; and then from July 16–20 in the field.[50] About this time Solomon Hale met Bridger in Capt. William H. Hooper's office in Salt Lake, which also housed his bookkeeper, William Clayton. Bridger and Chauncey W. West came walking into the room, and Bridger and Hooper enjoyed each other's acquaintance and spoke about settling some land matters.

Bridger was wearing his buckskin coat with fringe down the sleeves, and he had a beard and long hair. "He spoke fluently and with great earnestness," remembered Hale. "One was readily impressed with the sincerity and honesty of the man. He was a man of character, embodying great courage and leadership. Very naturally he partook of the nature of his environment and life on the frontier, but he impressed me very strongly as being honest and dependable and

a leader among men. . . . He came readily into the association of big men, and
he was given by men of prominence courtesies and considerations that are not
usually extended to men of ordinary rank and character."[51]

Bridger may have been talking to Hooper, the secretary of Utah Territory,
about the second payment for Fort Bridger. By late July he had set out for home,
and traveler Richard Ackley saw him homebound near Chimney Rock on July 22,
1858.[52] Vasquez collected that final $4,000 payment in October 1858, along with
another $1,000 added for goods taken by the Mormons. (Bridger and Vasquez
had earlier hired Tim Goodale to collect the second payment, scheduled for
November 1856, but that never occurred.)[53]

26

THE SEARCH FOR
YELLOWSTONE
1859–1860

By the late 1850s Jim Bridger had a foot in two worlds. Though he was raised in the eastern settlements, he had reached manhood in the far West. He lived in Westport, Missouri, with his Shoshone wife and their children, but his heart lived in the mountains. He could not write his own name, but he could read Indian sign language and read the land in the mountains better than anyone.

In 1859 the government asked him to guide an expedition that intended to map lands containing the headwaters of the Yellowstone and Missouri rivers and many of their major tributaries. "The Exploration of the Yellowstone" was an eighteen-month topographical and scientific survey that was inspired in part by Bridger's descriptions of Yellowstone to G. K. Warren and Ferdinand Hayden during their 1855–56 expedition. Congress approved the survey and appropriated $60,000 for costs. Though Bridger and other trappers and traders had traversed these lands extensively, they had not been mapped or explored scientifically since Lewis and Clark's expedition of 1804–6.

Bridger joined the expedition by boarding one of the two steamboats, *Spread Eagle* and *Chippewa*, that stopped at Kansas City. The boats were heavily laden with Pierre Chouteau's Indian trade goods, treaty annuities that the expedition was to distribute to the Indians, and wagons, animals, and equipment for the survey. Ferdinand Hayden, the chief naturalist, was already on board with his scientists. Capt. William F. Raynolds, the expedition's commander and chief topographer, boarded a few miles upriver at St. Joseph. Hayden and other naturalists hurried ashore whenever the boat docked, hoping to find fossils or animal specimens.

At times the scientists, cartographers, and other interested passengers asked Bridger about animals in the West. They asked if he had ever seen a white buffalo, and Bridger answered that "in all his life he had only met with one white buffalo alive, though he has seen the skins." When questioned about "silk" buffalo robes and "beaver" buffalo robes, he told them they were the same thing, and that buffalo hair was long or short depending on the season.[1] They asked him if the Cross Fox, which Audubon had painted with two intersecting black bands on its back, was a distinct species, and Bridger said he only knew it as a crossbreed between the gray and red fox. Alexander Culbertson, who had been on the Upper Missouri since 1833, agreed.

Near Sioux City, Chief Smutty Bear and his key leaders representing the Yankton Sioux came peacefully on board in full regalia to arrange for receipt of the annual goods. The steamboats continued up the Missouri to Fort Pierre, where Raynolds met the angry representatives of the other nations of Sioux. Chief Bear Rib, a Hunkpapa Sioux, complained to Raynolds, "General Harney told us that no whites were going to travel through this country; but I see wagons loaded and you wish to go through."[2] Raynolds threatened to withhold their annuities, and the Sioux grudgingly agreed that the expedition could proceed and even provided an Indian guide for the first portion of their journey.

At Fort Pierre Raynolds's men unloaded their wagons, mules, and supplies and prepared for their overland trek. The district Raynolds was to explore under Bridger's guidance was within a 250,000-square-mile section stretching from the Missouri River to the Rockies and from the Platte River to the Canadian border.[3] Their goals were to determine the feasibility of wagon roads in the Powder River and Bighorn country; to explore the headwaters of the Yellowstone and the Missouri River; to map the Sioux, Cheyenne, and Arapaho region for the army; and, at Warren's regretful recommendation, to identify "the proper routes by which to invade their country and conquer them."[4]

Unlike Bridger, who lived among Indians and was used to their ways, Raynolds was repulsed by the High Plains tribes. "They had discarded their gaudy vestments and barbaric trappings, and with these their glory had departed. A filthy cloth about the loins, a worn buffalo robe, or a greasy blanket, constituted the only covering to their nakedness, . . . their whole air and appearance indicating ignorance and indolence . . . banishing all ideas of dignity in the Indian character, and leaving a vividly realizing sense . . . that the red men are savages."[5]

Disagreements between the two men arose due to Bridger's extensive knowledge of the West and Raynolds's reliance on woefully incomplete maps that did not show the obstacles presented by the terrain. At the outset of the expedition, Raynolds intended to march along the banks of the Missouri to the Cheyenne River, and Bridger and others immediately told him the shoreline along that stretch of river was nearly impassable.

In late June the expedition of topographers, scientists, and a guard of thirty soldiers set out on horses and wagons. Bridger pointed to signal fires on the distant hills, indications that the Sioux were tracking their movements and reporting to each other. The sun burned the white men's skin, and temperatures rose to well over 100 degrees. Lack of water was a problem: their thirst grew worse with each succeeding day, and soon even water tainted with buffalo waste was a welcome balm to their parched mouths. Bridger calmed their fears daily. A soldier saw three buffalo charging their camp and raised his hands in terror, shouting, "Elephants! Elephants! My God! I didn't know that there were elephants in this country!"[6]

Warren's advice to Raynolds, undoubtedly based on Bridger's counsel, was that they use only pack trains to traverse the rugged terrain.[7] But Raynolds chose wagons anyway, and the soldiers resented having to constantly raise and lower them with ropes or make temporary roads with picks and shovels. Raynolds also irritated the men by refusing to allow travel or work on Sunday. He called them to his own religious service every Sunday by firing his weapon three times in lieu of church bells. The first time Raynolds had them travel on a Sunday, he overheard two of the men arguing. One of the men insisted it was Sunday. But the other strongly disagreed, saying, "I tell you it ain't. Don't you know the Captain never moves on a Sunday."[8]

Raynolds tried to prohibit Hayden from collecting fossils on these Sabbath days of rest, causing Hayden to complain bitterly to the Smithsonian: "Capt. R is an old *Fogie*" and "is by no means the man we all supposed him to be."[9] Hayden led some men to explore Wolf Mountain in present-day Montana and didn't return until the next day. Bridger showed Hayden and his men Indian signal fires on the mountains, very likely at the same location where Hayden had been the day before.[10] Raynolds told Hayden he acted as if the expedition had been fitted out "simply to build up the Smithsonian."[11] Hayden retorted perhaps it was, and added that the nation would place was a higher value on his scientific discoveries than on Raynolds's topographic surveys.

Hayden's field of study was cutting edge for its time; Charles Darwin's *On the Origin of Species* was published that same year, 1859. At times Hayden fostered an exaggerated image of himself, stating that he was "frequently among hostile tribes of Indians, who watched his movements with great curiosity, and formed very absurd ideas of his sanity."

Indians once saw him scurrying from rock to rock and surrounded him, upending his precious collection sack. When they discovered it contained only fossils embedded in rock, they called him "the-man-who-picks-up-stones-running." Hayden himself described his strange appearance: "My pick in one hand, my bag in the other, my notebook in my side pocket, my bottle of alcohol in my vest pocket, my plant case around my neck, and with all these [I also] carry a gun to defend myself from bears and Indians."[12]

Raynolds generally admired Bridger's knowledge and praised him his journal. One day Bridger pointed out the distant junction of the Tongue and Yellowstone rivers. It surprised Raynolds that his map showed the location of Yellowstone fifteen miles in error, and he realized his map couldn't compete with the map in Bridger's head.

But the topographer was also headstrong, and the men disagreed on the route to the Yellowstone. Bridger told Raynolds he intended to lead them up the Tongue, cross over to the Rosebud and Immell's Fork, and then go down to the Yellowstone. This was not in Raynolds's preconceived plan, but Bridger told him that if they went Raynolds's way, they would be stopped by the bluffs. Raynolds ultimately agreed to "accept his advice out of deference to his remarkable knowledge of the country."[13]

When they reached the valley of the Yellowstone, Raynolds was amazed at the herds of buffalo and estimated their numbers in the hundreds of thousands. The expedition made its way to the Bighorn River, and again Bridger seemed to know every square mile. His skill with the rifle quickly added two buffalo cows to their depleted larder. Raynolds was moved by the Bighorn Canyon, calling it "one of the most remarkable sights upon the continent." Bridger regaled them with the story of his solo trip through the Bad Pass rapids thirty-four years earlier.

In September, along the waters that flowed into the Powder River, they experienced "a steady rain with the driving northwest wind. A thick fog closed around us shutting out all view of the country. . . . Our guide, however, did not falter but pointed out our course with every mark of complete self-confidence, and as cool as if on a broad Turnpike in clear weather."[14]

Bridger spoke of the thermal wonders of the Yellowstone country that they planned to see the following spring, describing "burning plains, immense lakes, and boiling springs [and a stream] which divides and flows down either side of the water-shed. . . . Near the headwaters of the Columbia River, in the fastnesses of the mountains, there is a spring gushing forth from the rocks near the top of the mountain . . . cold as ice, but it runs down over the smooth rock so far and so fast that it is hot at the bottom."[15] This story of the Firehole River, based on truth, lives on today as one of Bridger's classic tales about Yellowstone.

Bridger loved to hunt, and when Raynolds reported seeing a fine elk in a thicket, Bridger immediately rode out alone, despite the fact that an Indian had crept into their camp the night before and cut the ropes of four of their animals. Bridger returned just before dark and gave them directions to a spot a mile away, telling them to take a wagon as he had just shot one of the largest elks he had ever seen. Five men used their horses to lift the carcass onto the cart. It was too big to weigh in its entirety, but the combination of head, horns, hide, neck, shanks, and quarters totaled well over one thousand pounds, which would provide food for all of them for several days.[16]

Bridger was pleased that James Stevenson was one of the party, serving as assistant naturalist to Ferdinand Hayden as he had in their exploration of the Yellowstone River in 1856. Stevenson later became a highly respected naturalist and anthropologist for the Smithsonian Institution's Bureau of Ethnology. Stevenson later wrote that Bridger's "many wanderings among the mountains and over the plains had invested him with many of the instincts of the animals of that region, and he frequently exhibited them in the highest degree."[17]

Stevenson was once suffering with a huge boil on his face that had been "suppurating" for several days. Bridger had been telling stories about Yellowstone resembling "hell bubbling over," and on arising one morning he said to Stevenson, "Jimmy, what in the devil is the matter with you, boy? Your face has got a young geyser on it." Stevenson was amused and replied, "O Mr Bridger, it's only a boil." Bridger then joked, "No, that's not it. You're rotten, you beast you."

Another time a storm was imminent, and "lightening flashed & the thunder was especially loud." Bridger cast his eyes around the horizon a moment and commented, "Jimmy listen! Old Billy God and Jesus is *talkin;* Hell will come along after while."[18] Bridger frequently spoke to Stevenson about Marcus Whitman and his attempt to remove the arrowheads from his back. Bridger showed Stevenson the wounds, and Stevenson thought the one arrowhead would have been too close to the vertebrae to ever extract it. When Bridger experienced ongoing pain, Stevenson hypothesized that it might be related to the arrow point that he carried in his body for nearly three years.[19]

As winter neared, Bridger led Raynolds to Deer Creek, one hundred miles west of Fort Laramie. Raynolds settled in for the winter while Bridger headed for home, taking a cutoff he knew to Fort Laramie. There he met several old friends. The east-bound mail wagon rolled into Laramie on the afternoon of October 25, enabling Bridger to buy a ticket for the next day. That night, the west-bound mail wagon arrived, carrying a letter for Bridger from Stubbins Watts, a twenty-one-year-old lad living adjacent to the Bridger property. Bridger listened intently as it was read to him. He learned that Mary was dead.[20]

Dr. Parker had been called to attend to Mary on September 29, 1859, and she died unexpectedly. Knowing that Bridger was away, the *Missouri Republican* printed a notice on October 8 to help get word to him, stating, "Mrs. Mary Bridger, an Indian lady, died at her residence near Little Sante Fe, in this county. Her husband is out on Government business in some of the territories, and it is not known where a letter will reach him, hence it is desired that the sad occurrence be mentioned in your paper which reaches all parts of the western country."[21] It is not known if the newspaper ever reached Bridger at Fort Laramie.

Virginia Bridger Hahn recalled her stepmother's death. "I was only a little girl about 10 years old, when she died in 1859 in the fall, and was buried out on Mockbee farm, Jackson County, Missouri, where she was visiting." Neighbor Robert Steele remembered that she was buried in the front yard of the Mockbee house. In Bridger's absence, neighbors must have secured a caretaker for the children, a forty-five-year-old widow named Ruth Scaggs who came to live at the house with her two sons Andrew and John. Ruth Scaggs may have begun her role as caretaker for the children as early as 1857 or as late as summer 1860.[22]

Bridger arrived home in the fall of 1859 and must have enjoyed the time with his children. Raynolds wrote to Bridger over the winter, at one point asking him to go to Leavenworth to see if the scientific instrument he had ordered had arrived.[23] In spring of 1860 Bridger took the westbound stage to rejoin Raynolds at his winter camp at Deer Creek, west of Fort Laramie. Raynolds and Bridger set out for the second year of the expedition on May 10, 1860.

Just five weeks earlier Russell, Majors, and Waddell had launched the Pony Express, one of the most unique marketing ventures in American history. Their inaugural trip from Missouri to California took seventy-five horses and ten and a half days. Soon five hundred fast horses and eighty skinny young riders were carrying the mail, each one selected with an eye toward maximum speed.

The riders carried pistols, not rifles, to reduce weight, and the mail was wrapped in oiled silk and carried in leather saddlebags at a cost of five dollars an ounce. Riders changed horses every ten to fifteen miles. The route, soon to be famous, went from St. Joseph, Missouri, to Sacramento, California, with stops that included Laramie, Deer Creek, Fort Bridger, and Salt Lake City, delivering in ten days what the stagecoach had taken twenty to thirty days to deliver.[24]

Bridger led Raynolds, Hayden, Stevenson, and the others west along the Platte River, past the Red Buttes, and on to the Wind River. On May 26 Bridger was ill and reluctant to leave camp. But someone spotted movement across the river and, after finding the source, shouted, "Bear!" Bridger immediately perked up and in an instant went to the river with his rifle and swiftly dropped the bear. Some of the men crossed the river and brought back plenty of bear meat to refill their larder.[25]

Raynolds wanted to be at Three Forks, the headwaters of the Missouri, by June 30. From there he intended to ride eighteen days north into British territory to record a solar eclipse. But before then, he also wanted to find a wagon route from the headwaters of the Wind River to the headwaters of the Yellowstone. Bridger told him there was no such pass, and even if there were, it certainly would be difficult to find in May or June with heavy snow pack and raging streams. If Raynolds had used pack mules instead of wagons in 1859, as Warren and Bridger advised, they could have explored Raynolds's possible route from the Wind to the Yellowstone in the fall of 1859, when the passes were open.

Bridger was emphatic that the most feasible route from the Wind River to the Yellowstone was to cross to the west side of the Divide, go north, and then again cross the Divide to the east to reach the Yellowstone. Raynolds looked at his two-dimensional map, which had little notation of the intervening mountains and passes, and maintained it made no sense to cross the Divide twice. So against Bridger's warnings, Raynolds ordered the party to proceed northwest up the Wind River. The higher they climbed, the colder it got. Biting winds swept into their overcoats, and they huddled close to fires at night, watching ice freeze in their water buckets. Some suffered from severe colds acompanied by ague and fever.

The expedition continued its upward march, and soon Bridger could see the craggy, snow-capped peaks of the Wind River Range to their left. To their right he could see the Owl Creek Range of the Bighorns, and he pointed out Gray Bull Pass, a fine connector to the Bighorn River country. As usual, Raynolds held the party at rest on Sunday, May 27. The sky was overcast, and they heard thunder in the mountains. Then the rain poured down, dousing them all afternoon and through the night.

When the weather finally cleared on Monday, May 28, the lifting clouds revealed the mountains that blocked the path Raynolds hoped to travel. Snow blanketed the mountains all the way to the valley floor, as Bridger had known it would. They crossed from one side of Wind River to the other, struggling to keep their footing as the waist-high current pushed hard against them. The odometer cart had become a cursed burden, and they kept it upright by using ropes. Their barometer told them they were 6,100 feet above sea level; at this altitude cedars replaced cottonwoods, and weariness replaced enthusiasm. And the route they followed climbed higher still.[26] Rain pelted them again that night, and Bridger knew the river might continue to rise. What fell on them as rain at six thousand feet was falling as snow higher up the trail.

On May 29 they had to wade across the Wind River twice, the rushing water now pushing against their chests. They stationed a man every few feet to keep the animals moving through the water. At the forks of the Wind, Bridger guided them to the left, and they made two more wet crossings. The river was now 120 feet wide, and a pathway along its banks was almost nonexistent. They were in a steep gorge with high ridges on the south bank and colorful pinkish-red strata on the north bank. Bridger led them to what he called Otter Creek, and Raynolds was extraordinarily impressed, saying it was the best grass since they had left winter quarters.[27]

Raynolds knew the next day as May 30. Bridger knew it as the day Raynolds would realize the futility of his pursuit. Bridger tried again to steer his foolish commander by pointing to the pass they should take, today known as Union Pass. It would bring them over the Divide and then to lower elevations. Or they could take Togwotee Pass to the west side of the Divide. But Raynolds insisted they adhere to his route.

May 30 was chilly at six A.M. By seven a heavy nimbus cloud passed over the mountains heading northward. After several miles they reached the plateau that Bridger knew lay before them. Raynolds had them cross it. Then they came to a solid wall rising between 3,000 and 5,000 feet, again as Bridger knew they would. Crestfallen, Raynolds stared at the massive barrier in front of him. There was no notch or canyon offering a way to the Yellowstone. Bridger said, "I told you, you could not go through. A bird can't fly over that without taking a supply of grub along."[28]

Raynolds had no reply. He and Hayden had found other vertical walls in the Wind River valley ranging from 1,500 to 2,000 feet high, and Hayden surmised that these bluffs had never been scaled by an Indian or a white man.[29] Raynolds mentally conceded the accuracy of the "old man of the mountains."[30] He had no choice but to turn around and go back to the pass Bridger had pointed out the previous day (Union Pass).

The next day Bridger began their journey out of their predicament, hoping to cross the Divide before nightfall. In their first three miles they ascended a thousand feet. Another three miles brought them to a vast deadfall that they had to chop through and clamber over. Then they climbed again, tromping down the snow before them, until they reached the last ridge before the Divide. But the valley that separated them from the pass was deep in snow. Bridger led them on a circuitous route to the left, and due to the crusted snow, the men and horses traveled several feet above the ground. When they came to soft spots, they disappeared as if through a trap door, sinking to their shoulders and panicking as the snow shackled and almost entombed them. The horses floundered as well in this process known today as "post-holing."

Bridger advised that they stop, but Raynolds went ahead alone, crawling over the snowpack, his face close to the ground. When he sank, he had to roll and extend himself as wide as he could on top of the snow's surface to get out of the hole. He finally reached the pass, his clothes heavy with snow. Retracing his steps, he found that the party under Bridger had followed him and were already halfway caught up. They finally crossed the Continental Divide. In Raynolds's daily journal he did not mention "Union Pass" or "Union Peak" or describe any effort to make tea with water from both sides of the Divide. But he did write, "I had the satisfaction, however, of being the first to reach the summit," not mentioning that Bridger and many others had crossed it many times before. Many years later when Raynolds finally submitted his official report, he added the names "Union Pass" and "Union Peak."[31]

It was as if they were on top of the world, and in a sense they were, because a single cloud could drop rain that would flow to three different seas thousands of miles apart. Some drops would flow east, down the course of Jakeys Fork to the Wind, the Bighorn, the Yellowstone, the Missouri, the Mississippi, and into the Gulf of Mexico. Some drops would flow west, beginning along Fish Creek and running to the Gros Ventre, the Snake, the Columbia, and into the Pacific. And some drops would flow south, beginning along Raging Fork to the Green, the Colorado and its Grand Canyon, and into the Gulf of California.

They had already gone ten miles that day and they needed to get to shelter, so they started their descent down the other side of the Divide. They trudged another six miles before they found a patch of grass. It was the hardest day endured since their expedition began a year earlier. They were on the waters of the Gros Ventre River, which they could follow to the Snake River and then go upstream to the Yellowstone country. But Raynolds refused and instead determined that they would travel along the western edge of the Divide and try to find a way to cross to the east of the Divide again as soon as possible. For the next several days, Raynolds had them climbing ridges and ravines looking for a crossing back to the Atlantic side.

The odometer abruptly fell down a steep slope, the cart and mules rolling over and over before finally landing at the bottom. The men also had to pull out twenty-five mules that were mired in the mud. Tempers were as short as the snow was deep, and Raynolds finally admitted that his fondly cherished scheme "would result in the certain loss of our animals, if not of the whole party."[32] He later wrote that Bridger "told me that even if the snow was gone we could not get out of the pines for weeks."[33] Bridger was finally allowed to lead them down the Gros Ventre toward Jackson's Hole.

For their part, Hayden and his naturalists were thrilled to be on the west side of the Divide. Looking over the Snake River, Hayden saw land he described as covered with eruptive rocks and a "basaltic conglomerate composed of large angular masses cemented with the melted material."[34] Bridger told him these same formations occurred all along the Wasatch Range to Bear Spring (Beer Spring?) and Henry's Fork; down Snake River almost to Blackfeet Creek; and also in the valley of the Yellowstone River above and below the Yellowstone Lake. Hayden's team eagerly collected four unknown species of squirrels and eight new birds. Along the Gros Ventre River they collected several fossils that they thought might be from the early Jurassic to the late Cretaceous periods.

Ferdinand Hayden was a sponge for all Jim Bridger could tell him. He studied the angled strata of the rock formations and theorized on the meaning of different layers. Seeing the Tetons "piercing the clouds like needles," Hayden asked if any mountaineers had scaled these rugged peaks. Bridger told him that to his knowledge, "the trappers have never been able to get near them."[35]

Meanwhile, Captain Raynolds continued to make dangerous decisions. At Jackson's Hole the Snake River was in a torrential rage, still swollen with snowmelt so early in the season. Bridger immediately said they should make a bullboat. But Raynolds ordered the men to search for a place to ford instead. One of the men, Lance Corporal Bradley, was swept away by the angry torrent, and his body was never recovered.

Raynolds then decided to build a log raft and assigned just a few men to help Bridger construct the alternative bullboat. Raynolds put his log raft into the water and attempted to guide it by rope, but the current was so rapid they couldn't control it, and Raynolds declared it "a complete failure." The location for this fiasco was just east of present-day Wilson, Wyoming, south of the Wilson Bridge.[36] Finally, after the death of one man, twenty-five miles of river searched, a worthless raft destroyed, and two days wasted, Raynolds grudgingly assigned more men to help with Bridger's bullboat.

Bridger showed them how to tie willow poles together in bowl fashion with leather thongs to make the frame. He used their old gutta-percha blankets and wrapped them all with his own lodge skin for the boat skin, sealing the seams with resin from local pines. Bridger's boat was twelve-and-a-half feet long and three-and-a-half feet wide without a single nail or peg. The river had continued to rise and spread laterally, and it was now one hundred yards wide, pouring through three channels. But they made seventeen successful crossings over two days, each passage taking only two minutes. Then they swam the horses and mules across.[37]

Now Bridger led the expedition west over Teton Pass to Pierre's Hole, which Bridger thought "the finest valley in the world."[38] Snowcapped peaks surrounded them on all sides, including the western slopes of the Tetons. He pointed north toward another lofty peak that was the general area where the middle fork of the Jefferson began. From Pierre's Hole Bridger led them north to what would one day be known as Raynolds Pass. They reached Three Forks on July 3, too late for Raynolds to travel another five hundred miles to observe the eclipse on July 18.

The Raynolds's party started down the Missouri toward home with one more region to investigate. At Fort Benton, Raynolds sent Lt. John Mullins, Bridger, Hayden, and twenty other men on another exploration, telling Mullins, "The whole country between the Yellowstone and the Missouri is unknown." But it was certainly known to Jim Bridger. Ferdinand Hayden and James Stevenson collected fossils, Anton Schönborn served as artist and meteorologist, and W. D. Stuart was topographer. Four days into their journey, they met Little Robe's band of Blackfeet with fifty-four skin lodges and the American flag waving from the chief's tent. Several Flatheads were traveling with them, and with interpretation by Bridger, the Flatheads, and the Blackfeet, all parties could communicate.

Ten days later, the party spied a large band of Crows riding rapidly toward them. Soon a dozen of them rode to the crest of a hill, bows strung and rifles in hand. Bridger rode up alone to meet them and calmed them down. Mullins had the horses hobbled, ordering seven of his soldiers to guard them and the other seven to stay with the camp. Bridger led the small party of Indians into camp, and three of them fired their rifles into the air, shouting something in their Absaroka (Crow) tongue, which Bridger translated as "Our hearts are bad."[39]

At the same time 250 warriors rode down upon them, yelling and guns blazing. They fired thirty shots into camp, perforating one of the tents and trampling another with their horses. Their chief, Great Bear, remained in a furious state, and Bridger translated. Since the Horse Creek treaty nine years earlier, the Sioux had driven the Crows to the west side of the Bighorn, so the Crow annuities were being delivered to land now controlled by the Oglala Sioux. "The white man [soldiers] has set our enemies upon us; some of our warriors have been killed, and we have lost many horses. . . . Now our hearts being black, we have come out to fight you."[40]

With great difficulty, Bridger was able to calm them and assure them they would eventually get their annuities. This was the second time Stevenson had seen Bridger withstand a possible attack with "tact & coolness," convincing Stevenson that Bridger's stories of battle with Indians were not "colored or exaggerated."[41]

The Raynolds expedition came to a close in October 1860. They had documented much of the Powder River country as well as areas west of the Divide, and the naturalists had collected many valuable specimens for the Smithsonian Institution. They had even discovered gold in three places—in the Black Hills between the forks of the Cheyenne River, in the Bighorn Range, and in the valley of the Madison River near the Three Forks. Bridger related that he was stooped to drink from a small stream in the Black Hills when he "was attracted by the curious appearance of . . . small yellow pebbles." Both Raynolds and Hayden confirmed it was gold, and Raynolds insisted he throw it away and not let anyone know.[42] Raynolds worried that his own disgruntled soldiers would desert and become "irresponsible adventurers," as they were already carrying all the tools needed for mining: picks, shovels, and blasting powder.[43]

Bridger was disappointed that Captain Raynolds's unwillingness to accept his advice had cost them the exploration of the Yellowstone geothermal area. It was no mystery to Bridger where the wonders of Yellowstone were or how to get there. In his encyclopedic mind, Yellowstone was already charted. It was just unknown to topographical engineers, scientists, travelers, and just about everyone else. And so it would remain for several more years. Once back in the states,

Raynolds regretted they had not verified Bridger's "marvelous tales," writing "I am prepared to concede that Bridger's 'Two Ocean river' may be a verity."[44]

One major task remained for Raynolds. That was to create the maps and write the reports that would make their two years' work accessible. The Civil War effectively curtailed Raynolds's efforts, and his delay would create a significant challenge to the nation.

27

AMERICA'S GUIDE AND STORYTELLER
1861–1863

By 1860 Jim Bridger had become the most able scout and guide of his era and certainly one of America's greatest frontier heroes. He embodied the skill, bravery, and individualism that the nation treasured, scouting unknown paths and protecting travelers from attack, starvation, freezing, drowning, and other calamities on the western frontier. Daniel Boone's explorations were told in print and legend. Davy Crockett's life was portrayed in popular fiction and even on stage. Kit Carson rose to fame through Frémont's widely read publications about his expeditions, which in turn made Carson the hero of many dime novels.

While Bridger could not write and did not collaborate with anyone to tell his story, he was part of the American identity. Alfred Jacob Miller had featured him in his dramatic Western paintings, and Washington Irving had depicted him in *The Adventures of Captain Bonneville*. Schoolbooks described Bridger and his fort, and newspapers chronicled his exploits as a frontiersman, scout, and guide.

Though he could not read, Bridger was news for daily and weekly newspapers. Denver's *Rocky Mountain News* actually reported Bridger's death in 1860. But the event had been "greatly exaggerated," and on December 12, 1860, the paper stated: "This old mountaineer, whose reported death we published some time since, is neither dead nor sleeping. He has recently returned to the Kansas

234

settlements, as we are informed by Capt. [Jim] Beckwourth, who has received a letter from him within a day or two past. He reports having found a new gold mining region—the exact whereabouts of which will not be published just yet— which far exceeds in richness anything ever before found in North America. Capt. Beckwourth has written to him in reply, and will learn by due course of mail the locality of this new Eldorado."[1]

Bridger wrote to Beckwourth on Christmas Eve, 1860, with the help from someone who did not spell very well but did capture Bridger' s cadence and phrasing.

I Have received yours of the 8th instant which cosed me agradill [a great deal] of pleasure to here from you and know that you are well etc. We certainly found gold in three places and in two of the places gold is very planty. I intand going to pikes peack in the Spring. On my way their [there] I want a small company of our friends to go along. I think that it will pay us well.

And if silver ore is worth any thing I found agodill in Montana. But as for myself I want nothing lest then gold. Know [now] understand I dont want to [pay?] any one to go their but I want every one for themselves etc.

You are aware that I Loane[d] A. P. Vasquez & Co. Seven Hundred dollars to pay their debts down here. I want you to exert yourself to git it for me.

The [w]hole country is up side down here. Since the Election of Lincole for the Presidency the State of South Carolinia has ceceded and their [there] is Several States that will follow her. So for the present we have no Government.

I want you to inquire for a man by the name of John D. Lee an old Georgia miner that went up with me in the Stage last Spring. If you see him tell him to write to me. I want him to go along with me.

> Old Vasquez sends you his best compliment
> Yours Truly
> James Bridger[2]

Bridger was asking Beckwourth to collect money due him from A. P. Vasquez & Co., a Denver store owned by Louis Vasquez's nephew. Between October 1858 and April 1861, Bridger's account at Robert Campbell's counting house had grown from $2,710 to $5,500, due in large measure to the sale of Fort Bridger, his partnership with Vasquez ($3,405), and his pay for guiding Raynolds ($570).[3]

Captain Raynolds was having trouble finishing his maps, and he wrote to Bridger asking for help on March 28, 1861. Hugh Campbell, Robert's brother, wrote back on Bridger's behalf:

> Our friend Mr. Jas Bridger . . . is exceedingly desirous to impart to you every thing he knows about the Yellow stone region and if you will send me a sketch of your map, with queries, he will do all he can, to meet your wishes. . . . He is willing to go on at once to Washington (his expenses being paid) and give you verbally all the information he possesses. Mr. Bridger regrets that he is a poor scribe and a worse draughtsman, for he seems to be sincerely desirous of obeying your request, while he feels incapable of doing so with any credit to himself, or benefit to you, unless he has either a sketch of the country before him, or yourself at his elbow.[4]

Hugh Campbell sent the letter on April 12, 1861; that same day Confederate forces fired on Fort Sumter, marking the beginning the Civil War. As a West Point graduate and officer, Raynolds was swept up into the war and did not finish his maps or report for several years, and then he did so without the assistance of Bridger. When his report of the expedition was finally published, Ferdinand Hayden claimed the earlier survey by Raynolds was wildly inaccurate (by 15 to 20 degrees longitude) and pointed out that his map omitted the Jefferson River, a mistake that Bridger would have readily caught.[5]

Warren, Raynolds, and Stansbury had all stayed loyal to the Union, as did Bridger, who spent the rest of his active life guiding Union forces on the Indian frontier. Col. Albert Sidney Johnston fought for the Confederates and was one of their highest-ranking generals until he was killed in the Battle of Shiloh in 1862.[6] During the war the army substantially pulled out of Fort Bridger. William Carter, who had come out with Johnston's army as sutler, organized local mountain men and Shoshone chief Washakie to protect the fort from repossession by Mormon interests.[7]

The government never paid Bridger for the lease of Fort Bridger because he never showed proof of title. The government also never allowed the Mormons to inhabit the fort, even though they had paid Bridger and Vasquez $7,463 for the stock and goods and $1,537 for the fort, land, and business. The government's reasoning was the same: the Mormon claim was invalid because Bridger had never validated his claim.

By the spring of 1861 seven southern states had seceded, and Congress canceled the Butterfield Overland Mail and stage contract, which ran through Missouri and the rebel states of Arkansas and Texas. Mail and passengers would be carried by the new Central Overland California and Pikes Peak Express from Missouri to California through land loyal to the Union. This million-dollar contract to move daily mail did not map out the route, but it did require that Denver and Salt Lake City be supplied by the main or branch lines.

The coach and mail service had previously gone through South Pass, but the company wanted to route it though Bridger Pass instead. The main line would only go through Denver if Colorado citizens agreed to build new way stations from Denver north up the Cache la Poudre River, the Laramie plains, Bridger Pass, and then on to Fort Bridger. The company hired Jim Bridger to lay out that route.[8]

Bridger arrived in Denver by stage on May 8, 1861, and met with Beckwourth. He gave him power of attorney to sell a lot he owned fronting on Ferry Street measuring twenty feet wide and running one hundred thirty-two feet back to the alley.[9] The *Rocky Mountain News* was eager to hear about gold, but Bridger told them that back in his trapping days "beaver was the best paying gold they wanted to mine for in those creeks and rivers."[10]

The community was so enthusiastic for a direct stage line west from Denver that the Central Overland line reassigned Bridger, Tim Goodale, and others to go with engineer Edward Berthoud to search for a route across the Rockies. Bridger, Berthold, and ten men set out on May 10, going up Clear Creek valley and stopping the first night at what Berthoud named "Camp Bridger." The next day Berthoud and two men tried to cross the range to the north, but they gave it up because the terrain was so steep. The following day Bridger, Goodale, and a Captain Emory set out to find a possible pass near Tarryall in South Park, while Berthoud and a few others took the north fork of Clear Creek.

By the merest chance, Berthoud found a low spot that they decided would be their best choice. The discovery of Berthoud Pass inspired the stage line to enlarge its vision and support the western route across Colorado. William Russell, who had established the Pony Express, raced to Leavenworth and convinced his board to "dispatch Major Bridger and E. L. Berthoud immediately to review, locate, and mark out this proposed new route through Colorado from Denver all the way to Great Salt Lake City."[11] Bridger and Berthoud departed Denver on July 6 to survey the new Denver, Golden City & Great Salt Lake Wagon Road, which would traverse terrain Bridger had explored first during his trapping days and later as a trader at Fort Bridger.

From Hot Sulphur Springs they traveled to the headwaters of the Yampa, followed that river down to the mouth of the Little Snake, then on to the White

River, where Berthoud was stunned by awesome, weather-worn sandstone bluffs. They ferried across the Green River and went up the Uinta River, crossed the Wasatch Range, and followed the Provo River to Provo and then Salt Lake City.[12] Berthoud was convinced that this new wagon road could be built quickly and at low grade.

As they camped, Bridger told the party of the time he rode above the canyons of the Colorado and Grand rivers. As thirsty as he was, it was impossible to get a drink of the water that ran hundreds of feet below in the steep canyons.[13] Bridger also told them he had explored the wilderness that eventually became Denver and saw the area totally flooded, including the entire bottom of Cherry Creek and the Platte River. It took him nine days before he was able to make the crossing. For that reason he was selling his land on Ferry Street in Denver for a low price because it might flood again.[14]

None of the party argued with him, but all thought he was just telling a tale and exaggerating the threat. Yet less than three years later, on May 19, 1864, the properties along Cherry Creek were destroyed by a horrendous flood that carried boulders, trees, and buildings in its wake, causing the loss of several lives and an estimated loss of one million dollars.[15]

Bridger and Berthoud guided the party as they retraced and surveyed the trail going west to east. Two teams of chainmen leap-frogged each other to measure the entire route from Provo to Golden City using a thirty-three-foot and a sixty-six-foot chain each day and an "excellent compass." They saw stunning canyons and mesas and enjoyed forests cedar and pinon. The new road measured 427 miles, which would cut more than 200 miles off the Overland route, and Berthoud estimated it could be built for $100,000.[16]

But the Colorado stage line never materialized; Berthoud Pass was almost four thousand feet higher than Bridger Pass, and deep snow drifts made it impassable during winter months. At least the new route between Atchison, Kansas, and Denver could be shortened by 130 miles. Bridger boarded the eastbound stage at Denver and arrived at Atchison on Thursday, September 24, 1861.[17] From there it was just a short trip to his farm on the banks of Indian Creek in near Westport, Missouri.

Bridger spent winter with his family at Westport. Their store in New Santa Fe was selling a variety of goods to both travelers and local residents. In 1859 Bridger purchased riverfront property at Westport Landing (Kansas City), the new principal point for offloading livestock and merchandise and setting out on the Santa Fe Trail. In 1860 and 1861 he purchased land in the north and west portions of Westport.[18] Before he went back West, Bridger asked Campbell to order a subscription to the *Tri-Weekly Republican*, and Campbell wrote, "We hope you will enjoy your trip to the mountains and return in improved health. You act very properly in encouraging your family to read and amuse themselves."[19]

In spring of 1862 the army called Bridger to guide troops through the war-torn Indian lands along the Oregon Trail. The peace from the great treaty at Horse Creek, where Bridger had helped set the boundaries, had first been broken in 1854 when a young Miniconjou Sioux killed and butchered a wayward cow from a migrant train, and the soldiers at Fort Laramie refused to take several horses as compensation for the animal. Lt. John Grattan, twenty-nine soldiers, and one drunk interpreter marched into the Brulé camp with rifles, a twelve-pound howitzer, and a twelve-pound mountain gun. The Brulés refused to surrender the cow killer, and the soldiers killed their chief, Conquering Bear. The Sioux reacted with fury, killing Grattan and all of his men.[20]

After the Grattan fight, the Brulé Sioux left Fort Laramie and began raiding, and the next year, 1855, Col. William Harney and six hundred troops killed seventy Brulé men, women, and children at Ash Hollow in what is now western Nebraska. The Grattan and Harney attacks ignited a blaze that would not be extinguished for decades. Among the witnesses to the Grattan battle were Red Cloud and Man Afraid of His Horses, both Oglalas, and a ten-year-old Miniconjou later known as Crazy Horse.

Technology was rapidly changing the world, and the country wanted speed. Even the Pony Express was not fast enough. In a monumental feat, between July and October 1861, Edward Creighton and Western Union strung telegraph wire from Omaha to Sacramento, creating the Transcontinental Telegraph and enabling instant communication between the Atlantic and the Pacific. By October 24, 1861, the talking wire, which followed the Oregon Trail/South Pass route, now delivered dots and dashes in minutes, and it put the Pony Express out of business after only eighteen months.[21]

The telegraph lines crossed lands that had been granted to the Indians by the Horse Creek Treaty, and increased emigration along the Oregon Trail only added to the tribes' anger at broken promises. The Sioux, Arapahos, and Cheyennes soon learned they could "cut the white man's tongue" by throwing a rope over the talking wire and pulling it down. They also raided the telegraphic relay stations along the Oregon Trail, and in the summer of 1862 Bridger was called to Fort Laramie to guide soldiers along the trail. They were tasked with protecting the telegraph and its battery-powered relay stations, which were from fifty to seventy-five miles apart.

Col. William Collins arrived at Fort Laramie on May 30, 1862, and within days Bridger was guiding him and his solders west to establish small military outposts set twenty-five to fifty miles apart. Greenhorn soldiers practiced shooting at targets, nervously preparing for possible battle.[22] Bridger usually scouted at the beginning of each day and then rejoined the main column to shepherd the soldiers to a safe camp each night.

It was terribly cold for June, and at Independence Rock fierce winds put a chill in Bridger's bones. Gusts blew rain into their faces, and then hailstones, and Colonel Collins called a halt. The next morning the storm was still blowing, and Bridger saddled his mount and headed into the mountains, telling those nearby that he was going "to get in some canyon and make a large fire."[23]

Caspar Collins, who was travelling with his father to restore his health, liked to sketch, and he made a drawing of a mountaineer wearing a "coat of buck or antelope skins trimmed fantastically with beaver fur, buffalo breeches with strings hanging for ornament along the side, a Mexican saddle, moccasins, and spurs with rowels two inches long . . . a heavy rifle, a navy revolver, a hatchet, and a Bowie knife. They all have a rawhide lasso tied to one side of the saddle with which to catch and tie their ponies."[24]

On the last Sunday in June the party was at camp. Some soldiers were hunting in the hills, while others were cleaning rifles or rearranging equipment. A rider raced into camp shouting, "Indians! Indians!" He threw himself off his horse and pleaded for help, telling the soldiers that Indians had ambushed their wagon train at a point five miles distant. One of the wagons had been lagging behind, making an easy target, and two men were already dead. The rest of the wagons had circled.

Colonel Collins called "Boots and Saddles," and Bridger, Collins, and one hundred men galloped to the scene. They found armed men standing vigilantly around the circled emigrant train, and women and children gathered around warming fires in the center and tending to the horses. Bridger and the rescue party continued over a long hill to the wagon that had straggled some one hundred yards behind. First they came to the body of an old man with three arrows protruding grotesquely from his body. Bridger pulled the arrows out and saw the telltale creases in the arrowheads that allowed the blood to flow. Arapahos and Cheyennes, he announced. He studied the tracks and determined that the man jumped off the wagon when the Indians attacked, trying to run to the rest of the party.[25]

Bridger saw that the Indians had cut the harness straps to steal the horses. The ground was littered with flour, sugar, rice, and coffee spilled as they scrambled for booty. The younger man who had been killed, an invalid traveling to California for his health, lay near the wagon. Three bullets had torn through his clothes, and blood was splattered around each black circle. He had been scalped and mutilated, and more than a dozen arrows were sticking out from his body. Bridger grasped the boy's right hand, which still clutched a Colt revolver in a death grip. The marauding Indians had tried unsuccessfully to cut the gun from his hand.

Bridger peered into the chamber of the revolver and saw that the boy had gotten off four shots. He circled the perimeter and stopped to examine a piece of sagebrush. Then he widened his search and spotted another bit of sagebrush with a speck of blood on it and stooped to break it off. He widened his search more and found more drops of blood. "The boy hit one of the scamps, anyway," he said. Bridger concluded there had been about twenty attackers. They had ridden off toward the Sweetwater and were likely far beyond the river by now. Collins sent a detachment out on the Indians' trail. They returned five days later with no sign of the raiders.[26]

Colonel Collins was interested in mapping the West, and in July, Bridger led Collins and his men on a hunting, fishing, and scouting expedition to the Wind River Mountains, Green River, Horse Creek, and Wind River. They cut their way through five miles of pine forests, and all hands were needed to lower the wagons down a two-hundred-foot slope that was too steep for the mules and horses to descend.

Bridger became a favorite of seventeen-year-old Caspar Collins, who was amazed to see the mountain man cook a whole jackrabbit and an eighteen-inch trout on sticks over the fire, then eat them both without a particle of salt. Bridger washed his meal down with a quart of black coffee and told Caspar that when he was young, he could eat the whole side ribs of a buffalo, which was likely true— Hudson's Bay men often ate twelve pounds of buffalo a day.[27]

In the summer of 1862 continued trouble with the Plains tribes led the postmaster general to order the Overland Mail company to abandon the North Platte–Sweetwater portion of the route through Fort Laramie (the Oregon Trail–South Pass route) and adopt the more southerly Overland Trail through Bridger Pass and Julesburg. One of Bridger's jobs was to guide the soldiers as they relocated to the new Overland Trail. The mail line was transferred to the Overland Trail in the fall.[28]

In the last week of September, Bridger led Colonel Collins, his son Caspar, several soldiers, a wagon master, a teamster, and a cook on an exploratory trip from Fort Laramie to Fort Halleck on the Overland Trail. The old route went by way of Laramie River, Sybille Creek and Canyon, back to Laramie River, then crossed Rock Creek and Medicine Bow River, and on to Fort Halleck.

The soldiers had brought no tents, and they slept in the rain and sleet with nothing but blankets to burrow into. On the first two nights they ate nothing but salt pork. Then they dropped two antelope and supplemented their larder with prairie chickens, grouse, hares and rabbits, and ducks. Caspar Collins was amazed at the many languages Bridger could speak, at least a bit: French, Spanish, Shoshone, Bannock, Crow, Salish, Nez Percé, Pend Oreille, and Ute.[29]

When Bridger and the soldiers arrived at Fort Halleck, they saw nine bears together outside the gates. Bridger may have told the soldiers his famous story about the time he was surrounded by such a group of bears. He put a serious look on his face and said he was in a little nook cooking his breakfast when he looked up and saw under the trees around him in a great circle about 250 bears sitting down and watching him. They had smelled the meat frying and had come in as near as they dared.

"Well, what did you do?' asked one.

"Oh, didn't do nothing," said Bridger.

"Well, what did the bears do?"

"Oh, they did nothing, only they just sot around," said Bridger. That soon became a favorite expression among some of the men at the Western forts. When asked what they did the night before, they drawled like Bridger and said they did nothing, "only just sot around."[30]

"Of all these guides, Bridger was the most interesting. . . . Every night, he was out in front of the sutler store sitting on the benches, and telling stories of his adventures," one soldier later recalled.[31]

On the route back to Fort Laramie, Bridger guided them "on a new road never before travelled by any body except Indians."[32] The first part of the journey was the same, crossing and camping at Rock Creek and Medicine Bow River. But then Bridger led them on a more direct path with a "night camp on mountain, night camp at cliff and spring, noon in impassable canyon, [and] night camp in mountain prairie on Laramie slope." From there they followed the Laramie River to Fort Laramie. The distance was reduced from 125 miles on the way there to

Bridger-Collins Map (1863), *detail*. Bridger first drew a rough version of this map in the sand or earth with a stick and then replicated it on an animal skin with charcoal. Col. William Collins used that to create this map. The portion shown here depicts a new, direct line from Fort Halleck to Fort Laramie that Bridger blazed in 1862. *American Heritage Center, University of Wyoming, Laramie*

108 miles on the way back, and a line drawn on the Bridger-Collins map roughly shows this shorter route.[33]

At frontier posts like Fort Laramie, officers tried to relieve monotony among the troops. They sponsored amateur entertainments, charades, readings, miniature dramas, even extemporized operas.[34] Scouts and interpreters often told stories. Bridger made an entertaining tale out of his frustrating time with Raynolds, telling A. J. Shotwell how he had offered to make a bullboat but "was curtly told he was employed only as a guide." Only after one soldier drowned and the officer's log raft didn't work did the officer finally appeal to Bridger. When his boat got them across safely, the officer "fell on his knees, and in a loud voice thanked the Lord God of Hosts for bringing the troops over in safety." Then, in a humorous twist, Bridger reportedly added, "And darn his sanctimonious skin, he never mentioned Bridger once, and I felt as if I had something to do with that plan myself."[35]

Bridger wasn't egotistical in his stories, and he usually connected them to some natural wonder or oddity or the ways of Indians or animals. He would begin with a kernel of truth and build a tale around that geographic or geologic wonder. "He rarely talked of his own adventures and never relayed stories that involved any heroism on his part. His stories had a philosophic and scientific bent."[36]

Once, on a "scientific" train of thought, he told Lieutenant Eugene Ware that "Court House Rock had grown up from a stone which he threw at a jack rabbit." Then he suggested "rocks grew just as trees and animals, only they grow larger and for a longer time." He often said that "mountains were considerable larger and higher than when he first came."[37]

Many soldiers whiled away the hours asking Bridger questions. John Hunton, a clerk at the Fort Laramie sutler store who shared the store bunk room with Bridger in later years, remembered that Bridger answered queries as truthfully as he could and was a good listener and talker when the topic interested or pleased him. But sometimes when he felt comments about somebody or something were made in ignorance or malice, he would curl his upper lip in a sneer and leave, saying he did not like to sacrifice his feelings, intelligence, or personal pleasure "when it was such an easy matter to walk away from a damn fool talking."[38]

One day Ware told Bridger he saw Indians eating animal entrails dipped in gall. Bridger told him, "I have cleaned up that kind of stuff and eaten it myself, when I had to." Some Indians ate all parts of animals, for that nourished or cured that same part in them, which resulted in some revolting stories. Another time, Ware met a man named Morgan on the preliminary survey of the Union Pacific Railroad who had just run a trial line up past Laramie when he met Bridger. The old scout told him Cheyenne Pass at the head of Lodgepole was a lower pass, and it proved to be so.[39]

Some of his best stories focused on Yellowstone and its geysers, and through time, those tales have made him more famous in the annals of the West. "I saw a couple of Indians coming along down through the grass on the other side of the creek," wrote Ware in paraphrasing Bridger. "They hadn't gone very far before the crust of the earth gave way under them, and they and their ponies went down out of sight, and up came a great powerful lot of flame and smoke."[40] That story may have been based on another event, real or composed, from his trapping days.

Another story said that six Blackfeet came across Bridger, who was alone one night reconnoitering the area. They let fly with arrows at short range and saw him fall flat to the ground. They ran forward with knives drawn to take his scalp and were shocked to see him rise without a single arrow in him. They thought they were seeing a ghost. But Bridger had tripped and fallen at the exact moment they shot, and their arrows passed through the space he had just occupied. He killed three of the Blackfeet and wounded another, and the survivors ran to their people with their story.[41]

Captain J. Lee Humfreville roomed with Bridger at Fort Laramie and recalled that Bridger ate and slept whenever he felt like it. He often rested in the afternoon and rose in the evening to roast his dinner at the fire. He was thin and strong, and his diet was almost exclusively meat. When he was up at night, Bridger sang "Injun," accompanying himself with a tin pan as a drum.[42]

One winter Bridger complained of vermin in his buckskin clothing. Humfreville told him to take off his buckskin jacket and breeches and wrap himself in buffalo robe. The captain poured a ridge of powder down the seams and lit the powder and watched the vermin burn. Unfortunately, he burned the leather too. The charred legs curled up like a half moon. "I'm goin to kill you for that," swore Bridger.

Humfreville tried to straighten the clothes out, but the burnt leather was so brittle it cracked when he stretched it. Bridger had to stay wrapped in his buffalo robe until a new outfit could be made for him. And every time he saw his curled-up clothes, he said, "The next time you want to rid me an' my clo's of varmints don't you do it with a doggon'd trail of gun powder."[43]

Bridger liked to spin a dramatic yarn and he once told a dozen listeners about the time when he had a very difficult scrape. He was riding alone when six Sioux came bearing down on him. All he had was a six-shot revolver, and he spurred his horse, but the Indians' mountain ponies were gaining on him. He turned in the saddle and shot the first pursuer on the run. Soon the second one was riding at his back, and he turned and killed him too. Same with the third, fourth, and fifth. Then it was just the last one. Try as he might, he couldn't shake him.

"We wus nearin' the edge of a steep and wide gorge," said Bridger, according to Captain Humfreville. "No horse could leap over that awful chasm an' a fall to the bottom meant sartin death. I turned my horse suddint an the Injun was upon me. We both fired at once, and both horses wus killed. We now engaged in a han'-to-han' conflict with butcher knives. He wus a powerful Injun—tallest I ever see. It wus a long and fierce struggle. One moment I have the best of it, an' the next the odds was agin me. Finally . . ."

Here Bridger paused as if to catch his breath.

"How did it end?" asked one of the breathless listeners.

Bridger replied with slow deliberation. "*The Injun killed me.*"[44]

But when Bridger guided soldiers through Native lands, he was always true to his word.[45] One person remembered the time that General Grant and a party were on an inspection trip along the route of the Northern Pacific Railroad, and General Harney sent for Bridger to come down from Fort Laramie, as he wanted General Grant and party to hear him lie. Bridger had been known to say that Bridger's Peak had "slewed around" about 1,200 feet since he first went there.[46]

While Bridger was guiding America's soldiers and emigrants, his children were growing up. His daughter, Virginia, who sometimes went by Jane or Jennie, was fifteen and would soon marry. Bridger received a letter from an army lieutenant named Albert Wachsman asking for Bridger's consent to marry his daughter. Wachsman had enlisted in the Union army in June 27, 1862, and by January 20, 1864, was serving with rank in the Second Regiment Missouri Light Artillery. Felix Bridger enlisted as a private in that same regiment on January 25, 1864.[47]

A fellow traveler named David Deaver remembered riding with Bridger on their way from Fort Leavenworth, Kansas, to Fort Laramie. When Bridger got the letter, Deaver teased him "that he had promised the girl to me. He laughed and told me I was 'too slow.'"[48] Deaver wrote the letter for Bridger in which he gave his consent and also ceded some property he owned to his daughter as a wedding present. Virginia Bridger married Albert Wachsman on February 24, 1864.[49]

BLAZING THE BRIDGER TRAIL
1864

Gold is a secret rarely kept. In the American West the Indians knew it caused problems with the whites. Black Elk called it "the yellow metal that they worship and that drives them crazy."[1] That yellow metal was about to cause a war between the United States and the Sioux, Cheyennes, and Arapahos. Bridger had a plan to avert that.

The precious ore turned Grasshopper Gulch into Bannack City and Alder Gulch into Virginia City, and by the spring of 1864, twenty thousand people had come to the western Montana mines. Boosters brought huge gold nuggets to Washington, D.C., to show President Lincoln and Congress, and by May, Congress had carved Montana Territory out of Idaho Territory.[2]

At first, most would-be miners traveled the Oregon Trail to Salt Lake City, then went north. But those wanting to get to the goldfields faster opted for a new route called the Bozeman Trail. John Bozeman had come to the diggings when he was twenty-five, abandoning his wife and three children just as his father had abandoned him during the gold rush of 1849. He chose a cutoff route that left the Oregon Trail northwest of Fort Laramie and skirted the eastern slope of the Bighorn Mountains, land Bridger had explored decades earlier.

The Bozeman Trail took miners through the Powder River country, which was claimed by the Sioux, Cheyennes, and Arapahos. The Northern Cheyennes and Sioux stopped Bozeman's first wagon train in 1863, threatening to kill the travelers if they didn't turn back. Most did, but Bozeman and nine others forged ahead and reached Virginia City. By 1864 Bozeman was gearing up to lead a major migration along the same route.

Jim Bridger and Colonel Collins worried. Collins telegraphed his superiors: "Immigration is coming rapidly. . . . It should be sifted, controlled, and guided on designated routes; not permitted to run wild and make trouble."[3] But the U.S. government didn't agree. The Civil War had already created an unprecedented $2.76 billion in national debt, and Washington was desperate for gold to shore up the treasury.[4] Montana gold would back up the newly printed federal paper currency, called greenbacks because of the color of the ink on the back of the bills.

Bridger knew that whites trespassing across Indian land on the eastern side of the Bighorns could lead to all-out war. If he could steer emigrants and gold-seekers west of the Bighorns, they might preserve the peace and save countless lives. What became known as the Bridger Trail passed through Crow and Shoshone land, and the Crows missed Bridger. Just a year earlier they had asked traveling miners why Jim Bridger never came to see them anymore.[5] In contrast, the Sioux stopped miners on the Bozeman Trail, telling them to turn around and adding that if they went "by the Blanket Road" (Bridger's Crow name), the Sioux would let them pass.[6]

Collins released Bridger from duty so he could guide miners on the newly designated Bridger Trail.[7] As miners arrived at Fort Laramie that spring, parties formed for both trails. Bridger's party left first, on May 20, and thanks to confidence in Bridger's reputation and skill, it numbered about three hundred men and one hundred wagons, including the Stateler train from Denver.[8] The going rate for joining the train was five dollars per wagon.

Each morning Bridger scouted for Sioux or Blackfeet or the occasional horse-stealing Crows. Only then did he signal the men to let their stock out to graze. When breakfast was done, the animals were brought in, harnessed, and yoked. Then the long line of wagons began moving, guarded front and back by mounted lookouts. Bridger had been over this land many times, but mostly on horseback. Now he had to select a path that would accommodate wagons in addition to his normal routine of scouting for Indians, finding fords, locating watering holes, picking midday rest spots, and selecting the evening campsite.

He kept the wagons traveling until three or four o'clock each day, then circled them at the campsite he had selected. They brought the front wheels of each wagon close to the hind wheels of the next, providing a barricade of sorts. In the early evening they let their horses and oxen out to graze under heavy guard, while others gathered wood, filled water buckets, and prepared supper. After dinner, they greased the wagon wheels. At dark, the livestock were brought into the wagon enclosure and Bridger had guards surround the camp. Invariably there was music and dance. The first seventy miles were dry, and they managed by sinking shallow wells in streambeds.[9]

Before they reached the Bighorns, a large band of Indians came in during the night and camped within a mile of the train. From that distance neither group could tell the identity or intent of the other. Bridger selected a few men and instructed them to come with him, unarmed. As they approached, a small party of Indians rode forward to meet them. When they saw who it was, they were instantly animated and cried, "Bridger! Bridger!" It was Chief Washakie and his Shoshones on a buffalo hunt, and Bridger had the families prepare a feast for them. The children in the train had a rare treat to see Indians so close. Bridger gave Washakie a paper showing that his band was friendly. Washakie was pleased and led the Shoshone out the next morning in good spirits.[10]

Bridger's route led the wagons around the southern end of the Bighorn Mountains and across Badwater Creek; from there the trail followed a creek (known today as Bridger Creek) and crossed over the Bridger Mountains, though the range was not so called at the time. The trail then followed and crossed the Bighorn River. The Bighorn was too full to ford or swim, so Bridger had men fell trees, and he oversaw the hurried construction of a ferry of hewn logs that was large enough to cross one wagon at a time.[11] The cattle, horses, and oxen swam across. When they were all safely on the far bank, Bridger ordered the ferry partially buried to preserve it in case they or anyone else needed it.

After Bridger left Fort Laramie, John Jacobs hung back to assemble another wagon train to follow Bridger; While Jacobs had earlier promoted the Bozeman Trail, he now was collecting five dollars for each of the seventy-two wagons that signed on with him. They used Bridger's ferry boat to cross 66 wagons, 218 men, and 250 head of stock in eleven hours.[12]

Those in Jacob's train resented him for drinking and swearing too much, for selecting poor grazing and watering sites, and for his dictatorial ways. They caught up to Bridger by mid-June, and by the first week of July most of Jacobs's wagons had abandoned him and joined Bridger's party. Two additional wagon trains took Bridger's new trail after Jacob's party.

Bridger's enlarged train continued along the west side of the Bighorn, fording the Grey Bull and Shoshone rivers. Then they followed Clarks Fork to the Yellowstone, a river he had first traveled with Andrew Henry and John Weber in the 1820s.[13] Day after day they moved west, Bridger constantly looking for more cutoffs to shorten the route. The wagon trains that followed Bridger all arrived at the Yellowstone by July 4, catching up to Bridger's train. This brought the assembly to about four hundred wagons, either directly under Bridger's charge or generally following him.

Sidelined by his Civil War duties, Captain Raynolds was still trying to complete his map and report. Despite this proof by Bridger that this was a viable wagon route, Raynolds inexplicably wrote in his report four years later that the valley of the Bighorn "is totally unfit for either rail or wagon roads."[14]

In this inaugural wagon trek of 1864, Bridger pioneered a crossing of the Yellowstone and used the common custom of moving diagonally upstream so the strong current would not take them sideways or backwards. It became known as Bridger's Ford and was used by emigrants from both the Bridger Trail and the Bozeman Trail. Two years later John Bozeman operated a ferry there for a brief time, but many travelers just crossed Bridger's Ford instead of paying a fee to Bozeman. Four miles northwest was a mineral hot spring that Bridger had visited in the 1830s. The spring is now known as Hunters Hot Springs and the crossing as Yellowstone Ford.[15]

Once the wagons on the Bridger Trail crossed what became known as the Bridger Mountains in Montana, they broke free, racing to get ahead of others. They all crossed the Gallatin River and then followed the valley of the Madison River southwest to Virginia City, arriving at various times in July. A total of ten wagon trains followed Bridger's route that summer, with Bridger leading the first and the last.[16]

Meanwhile, John Bozeman led his wagons from Joseph Bissonette's trading post at Deer Creek and traversed Sioux country on the east side of the Bighorns. The train left a little later than Bridger's and arrived at the gold fields about the same time. But the notion that there was a race between the two trails has been disproven.[17]

Bridger, who had been in the region when it was wilderness, now walked the streets of Virginia City taking it all in. Streets were "thronged," stores were "choked," saloons were "crowded," theaters were "packed," beds were "hardly available," gaming tables were "shining with yellow gold," and hurdy-gurdy houses were "filled with visitors, ranging from judges to blacklegs."[18] There were four large gaming houses, and cockfights on the street provided opportunity for more betting. Nevada City, just a quarter mile away, presented the same picture. Everyone had come to find their fortune. Some succeeded.

A miner named Ira Meyers met Bridger that summer on the streets of Virginia City and was impressed by the energetic mountaineer with long brown hair brown and keen gray eyes telling a story about petrified forests.[19] That evening Bridger again entertained a large crowd with stories of Yellowstone:

> Up there is one of the strangest mountains that I ever did see. It is a dia-
> mond mountain, shaped something like a cone. I saw it in the sun for two
> days before I got to it, and then at night I camped right near it. I hadn't
> more than got my horse lariated out—it was a little dusky—when I saw a
> camp-fire and some Injuns right through the mountain on the other side.
> So I didn't build any fire, but I could see them just as plain as if there hadn't
> been anything but air. In the morning I noticed the injuns were gone, and
> I thought I would like to see it the other side of the mountain. So, I rode
> around the other side and it took me half a day.[20]

Bridger returned to the Laramie area in August, where he met with an unfortunate encounter with a rowdy mount. A soldier at a nearby fort reported on August 16, 1864, from Fort Laramie, "Old Maj. Bridger is in Fort Meguire badly hurt by being thrown from a pony. Sent to the hospital."[21] John Hunton also later recalled that Bridger "had been bucked against the saddle by the mule he was riding." The incident "culminated in a stricture which [caused] constant and sometimes great pain."[22]

But Bridger's injury did not incapacitate him. On September 18 he guided the tenth and final wagon train up the Bridger Trail that year. It included ten wagons and twenty-five men, one of them an Indian agent, Maj. John Owen. They made improvements to the trail as they went. On November 1 they reached the Shoshone River, and snow soon caught them on the Yellowstone. Owen wrote that he was not able to get his wagons farther than Bozeman City. Bridger may not have gotten much farther. In late fall or early winter, Bridger was one of the wayfarers who "spread his blanket on the ground, and slept beneath the roof" at the log house of Capt. Frederick Fridley in Bozeman City.[23]

The Bridger Trail was far more popular than the Bozeman Trail in 1864, undoubtedly because of the reputation of the celebrated Jim Bridger. An estimated six hundred wagons took the Bridger Trail that year, accompanied by approximately 2,500 men and scores of women and children.[24] One thousand fewer emigrants took the Bozeman Trail in 1864, including the train that Bozeman guided and four trains that followed him, for a total of 1,500 emigrants.

The Bozeman Trail did indeed prove to be more dangerous. The third train on that trail was attacked by Sioux and Northern Cheyennes on the Powder River, and four emigrants were killed. Two more of that party were killed when they strayed from the train.[25] While the Bozeman Trail offered more water and grass for animals, the Bridger Trail was safer for the miners. But the critical point was that the Bozeman Trail would lead to war, and the Bridger trail would preserve the peace. The gold-hungry miners and the truculent military both preferred the Bozeman Trail even though the Sioux, Arapaho and the Cheyenne would wage war against them for their choice.

Meanwhile in Colorado, the Cheyennes were in near-constant battle with citizens and emigrants. Colorado Volunteers killed four blameless Cheyennes in April, believing they had stolen cattle. Fighting escalated through the summer and fall, and Cheyennes and Sioux also raided emigrant trains and settlements along the South Platte, closing the road to Denver, killing over fifty civilians, and taking seven captives.[26] As a sign of peace, the Cheyennes returned four captives, and Chief Black Kettle and his people separated themselves from the raiders and camped on Sand Creek awaiting a promised peace council.

But John Chivington, a fire-breathing minister-turned-soldier, wanted blood instead and preached, "The Cheyenne will have to be soundly whipped. . . . If any of them are caught in your vicinity, kill them, as that is the only way."[27] The Colorado volunteers rode out in search of Indians with instructions from Chivington to take no prisoners.

On November 29, 1864, the Cheyennes at Sand Creek saw armed white men racing toward them, and they ran from their lodges. Black Kettle raised an American flag and a white flag beneath it, for they were there under the presumed protection of the army. White Antelope stood in front of his skin lodge singing his death song, and the soldiers cut him down. The soldiers rushed the creek, and many Cheyenne Indian women opened their shirts to let the soldiers know they were women. But the soldiers shot indiscriminately, killing women and children.

One attacker shot Medicine Woman Later, Black Kettle's wife, and then other attackers put eight more bullets into her. But miraculously she survived. When darkness fell, the volunteer militia rode through the village one final time to kill any who were still alive, taking their scalps and female body parts as souvenirs. Volunteers who participated in the massacre generally estimated from seventy-five to two hundred killed, but Chivington claimed they killed several leading chiefs and "between 400 and 500 other Indians."

Back in Denver, Chivington arrogantly boasted as if he were a hero and reportedly said, "Posterity will speak of me as the great Indian fighter. I have eclipsed Kit Carson." To that Carson angrily retorted, "To think of that dog Chivington, and his hounds, up thar at Sand Creek! Whoever heerd of sich doings among Christians! . . . I never yit drew a bead on a squaw or papoose and I loathe and hate the man who would."[28] A wave of revulsion rippled across the nation. While Denver's *Rocky Mountain News* praised the raid, newspapers throughout the East condemned it as a massacre.

The U.S. House of Representatives, a joint committee of the House and Senate, and the U.S. Army each conducted investigations. A remorseful Jim Beckwourth, who guided Chivington to the site, testified against him. Chivington was disgraced and escaped a court-martial only because he was no longer part of the army.[29]

The Sand Creek Massacre set the plains on fire. All the apologies and outrage the whites could muster could not quell the anger and bitterness in the Indian world. The Cheyennes sent a pipe to the Sioux and Arapahos asking them to join in war against the whites. They formed a huge alliance to defeat the whites—on the Bozeman Trail, the South Platte, and the North Platte. The Indians believed they were fighting for their very survival. They tore down telegraph wires to silence the white voice and raided the mails to destroy their written words. They stole their stock and destroyed their way stations. They killed men and mutilated their bodies, captured women to misuse them, and took children to raise as Indians.[30]

Travelers from the Rockies to the Missouri and from Canada to Colorado were on high alert. In January 1865 a thousand Sioux, Cheyennes, and Arapahos raided the small town of Julesburg, 180 miles east of Denver and a way station on the Overland Trail. They sacked the town, then killed fourteen soldiers from nearby Fort Rankin. Less than four weeks later they attacked Julesburg again, burning the town. Colonel Collins rushed his men to battle, meeting the raiders at Mud Springs and Rush Creek. The sheer number of warring Sioux and Cheyennes was shocking, and Collins did not have enough men to pursue them.[31]

29

THE POWDER RIVER
CAMPAIGN
1865

Jim Bridger saw the body hanging in chains even before he reached Fort Laramie. The corpse was not a soldier or a Southern sympathizer but a Cheyenne Indian named Big Crow. Bridger had left Montana and arrived at the fort on April 29, 1865, five days after the hanging. Soldiers had arrested Big Crow in February for his role in the Julesburg raid in January, and he had languished in the Fort Laramie jail since then. When Indians killed a soldier a mile and half west of Fort Laramie, Gen. Patrick E. Connor ordered Lt. Col. William Baumer to "take Big Crow to the place where soldier was killed yesterday, erect a high gallows, hang him in chains and leave the body suspended."[1]

The soldiers tied Big Crow's hands in front of him, and he sang his death song as they brought him to the gallows. When soldiers drove the wagon out from under him, Big Crow grabbed the chain around his neck and climbed up to a gallows crosspiece and sat there. Soldiers shouted, "Shoot him!" but Connor's orders had said he was to hang, so a soldier climbed the scaffold and wrestled with Big Crow. Both fell from the crosspiece; the soldier landed on the ground, and Big Crow abruptly hanged. They left his body hanging from the scaffold. Eventually the weight of the heavy ball shackled to his ankle pulled off his rotting leg. Bridger knew the whites would pay dearly for leaving the body hanging like that.

On May 3 Bridger guided Col. Thomas Moonlight and five hundred cavalry-men to Wind River and Bighorn country hoping to find a camp of three hundred

254

lodges of Cheyenne raiders. Moonlight had assumed command of Fort Laramie after Colonel Collins left for Colorado Territory. They stopped at Sweetwater Station, giving hope to a private stationed there, who wrote, "Major Bridger, an old mountaineer is their guide. If there is any man in the west who can find the Indians, he can."[2] Though it was May, it snowed for two days straight, and they suffered miserably. Bridger said that he had never seen the region more barren.[3] He eventually found Indian tracks and surmised they had circled to the Sweetwater Mountains and then to Powder River. As Bridger led the soldiers back to Fort Laramie, they heard that Indians had stolen a number of horses from Deer Creek Station. Bridger had a horse there, and Moonlight telegraphed the station for him, asking, "Was Mr. Bridgers horse taken by Indians?"[4]

At Fort Laramie, Bridger saw new prisoners in the guardhouse: Oglala leaders Two Face and Black Foot, who stood accused of abusing a white woman named Lucinda Eubanks.[5] They boasted they had killed white men and would do so again if released, and Moonlight ordered the two Sioux to be hanged and the corpses be left hanging.[6] Bridger warned that this public display would lead to disaster.

So did post trader William G. Bullock, who told Moonlight it might prompt a massacre. Moonlight retorted, "Well, Colonel, you think there will be a massacre. Let me tell you there will be two Indians who will not take part in it."[7] Moonlight hanged the two prisoners on May 26 next to Big Crow. Each Indian stood on a dry goods box on the back of a wagon, and as the wagons pulled forward one Indian jumped backward to die by his own actions while the other stayed on the box as long as he could to prolong his life. Moonlight left the corpses rotting in public next to the corpse of Big Crow.[8] Again Bridger knew that this would have grave consequences for the whites.

That spring Secretary of War Edward Stanton ordered the relocation of 1,500 friendly Sioux Indians from the outskirts of Fort Laramie to Fort Kearny in Nebraska. As they were traveling, a hostile group among the Indians gunned down the commander of the escort, Capt. William D. Fouts, and then killed four of the soldiers who pursued them. Colonel Moonlight led more than two hundred men from Fort Laramie to apprehend the hostile Sioux, only to see the Sioux run off seventy-five of his horses during a rest break. Moonlight led his men back to Laramie in defeat, most of the men walking. The outraged Connor ordered that Moonlight be mustered out of the army for his blunders.[9]

General Connor was made commander of the newly established District of the Plains, and he moved his headquarters to Fort Laramie on June 22. From there he planned to launch a major offensive, the Powder River Expedition,

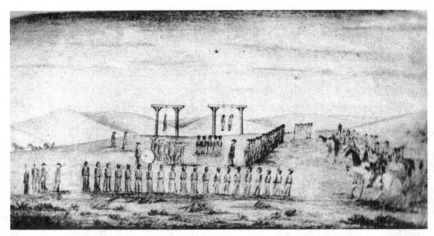

Hanging of the Chiefs (1865), by Ira Taber. This gruesome sketch shows the hanged bodies of Two Face and Black Foot next to the previously hanged body of Big Crow. Bridger
rightly predicted this desecration would lead to increased hostilities between whites and
the Plains Indians. *Yale Collection of Western Americana, Beinecke Rare Book and Manuscript
Library, Yale University*

against the Sioux, Arapahos, and Cheyennes. On July 6 they hired Jim Bridger as
chief guide at a wage of ten dollars a day. Working under him were several other
guides, including Nick Janis and an Arapaho man named Friday whom Tom
Fitzpatrick had befriended many decades earlier when the Indian was a boy.[10]

The guides played a crucial role in the expedition. Captain Raynolds still
had not created his maps of the area, and Warren's maps, made between 1856
and 1858, did not have the detail needed for a military operation. Maj. General
Grenville Dodge, commander of the Department of the Missouri and Connor's immediate supervisor, had to telegraph simple questions such as "Where
is Powder River and how far from Julesburg?" Dodge even paid out of his own
pocket to make photographic reproductions of a map he had found of the area.[11]
The places and knowledge of the terrain that Bridger had shared with Raynolds
had not yet been printed in maps, so the U.S. officers in the area had to rely on
the best map available—the one in Jim Bridger's head.

Equally challenging for Connor was the incredible shortage of soldiers, weapons, supplies, and animals. The Civil War had ended in April, and while the
army had well over a million volunteer soldiers on May 1, over the summer and
fall 800,963 of them were discharged. The government did not even finalize the

contracts for goods for the Powder River expedition until May 1, and the contrac-
tors had until December 1 to make delivery.[12] Yet the pressure on Connor was
relentless. Dodge wrote, "You will clear out those Indians. Do not, therefore,
fail to do it."[13]

Connor's force of twenty-five hundred men and two thousand horses comprised the largest offensive against the Plains Indians up to that time. The effort
to keep and feed their animals was enormous, and Connor had already requested
"six traveling forges, 5,000 shoes and nails for horses and same number for
mules."[14] Connor split his expeditionary force into three prongs, and Connor
and Bridger rode out on July 27 with the left prong, which consisted of 800 men
and 185 wagons.[15] Col. Samuel Walker led the troops in the center prong, and
they left Fort Laramie July 5 with pack animals instead of wagons. Col. Nelson
Cole led the right prong, setting out from Omaha on July 1 with 1,400 men and
140 wagons.[16]

An unnamed soldier at Fort Laramie vividly remembered Bridger during that
time, writing: "I knew scores of hunters, scouts, and trappers of great and less
repute, none of whom were worthy to sit at the same table with Jim Bridger. To
me, the simplicity, gentleness, kindliness and absolute truthfulness of his character marked him as a man above the common. . . . There wasn't an Indian on the
Overland Trail that doubted Bridger's word." When the soldier first encountered
Bridger, he viewed him as "a tall, well built man in plain civilian garb, with
nothing in his make up to mark him apart from men as they appeared back
east. A man who quietly went his way. . . . Imagine my surprise on being told
that this was Jim Bridger, the greatest of scouts in his time. . . . A man invaluable to the government . . . —in fact, an oracle in all that pertained to the vast
country surrounding."[17]

Bridger rose early every morning and had a quick cup of coffee and some
jerked meat. He saddled up and rode to General Conner's headquarters to go over
the route for the day, relaying the distance to the next camp, the contour of the
route, and where to find good water and grass. Then he rode off alone or with a
handful of men to look for Indian sign and plan their route for the following day.
Often he didn't return until late and would immediately report to Conner. Then
he cooked his frugal meal and found a place to sleep away from everyone else.[18]

When they reached La Bonte crossing, the Platte was fast and full. Floodwaters
had washed away the crossing that had been used a month earlier. Finally, they
found a fresh buffalo crossing and forty teamsters made a road with picks and

shovels during the night.[19] The next day, August 4, Bridger led the column away from the Platte River onto a new, untraveled route that followed Sage Creek, which was dry.[20] Bridger kept his scouts out all day searching forward as well as both flanks. He found a two-day-old trail of maybe a thousand Indians, and he presumed they were the ones who attacked the Platte Bridge in July.[21] Bridger estimated that this combined hostile force numbered over three thousand warriors.

The next night careless soldiers accidentally torched the grass, and the wind turned it into a prairie fire. Soldiers raced through the flames to drag two wagons full of gunpowder away from the fire. Indians as far away as the Bighorns now knew their location, if they had not known it already. This fork of the Cheyenne was dry, as Bridger had warned, but they sank empty cracker boxes into the sand to serve as spring boxes, and soon they could dip in their water buckets and fill them.[22]

An eighteen-year-old soldier named J. E. Spicer later recalled, "Bridger seemed to know every foot of the way in the country we went through. He was a very shrewd man and rather rough. He understood the ways of the Indians very well and seemed to be able to make friends even with the warriors. I supposed he was a Colonel [Major] as he was always known as such and we saluted him as an officer."[23] Connor and two officers went on a buffalo hunt accompanied by guides Bridger, Nick Janis, and James Brannan. They followed Bridger's old wagon trail from the Gore expedition ten years before, and Connor decided to adopt it as his wagon trail, too. At midday they went in search for water and got separated, "old Maj" [Bridger] going up it [the trail], while we went down."[24]

Connor was under orders to build a fort on Powder River, and Bridger picked a mesa one hundred feet above the river and five miles from the bluffs. What it lacked in grazing, it made up for in defense. It was named Fort Connor in honor of their commander. As they began construction of the fort, word came that Caspar Collins, who had risen to the rank of second lieutenant, had been killed by the Sioux and Cheyennes at Platte Bridge Station on the Oregon Trail. He had tried to rescue one of his men and was horribly outnumbered.[25] It was a grisly end for the lad who had begged Bridger for stories of the West.

Connor had given disturbing orders for his entire command. "You will not receive overtures of peace or submission from Indians, but will attack and kill every male Indian over twelve years of age."[26] Not long after, a courier from Fort Laramie arrived with an urgent telegram from Gen. John Pope. "These instructions are atrocious, and are in direct violation of my repeated orders. You will please take immediate steps to countermand such orders. If any such orders as

General Connor's are carried out it will be disgraceful to the government, and will cost him his commission, if not worse. Have it rectified without delay."[27]

While the fort was still under construction, Bridger led Capt. Frank North and some of his Pawnees to scout the road to Tongue River. About noon the next day, they returned and a diarist recorded, "Major Bridger says the Indians are moving in the direction of Powder River & from the general appearance along Old Woman's Fork [Crazy Woman's Fork], thinks there must have been at least 1500 Lodges in that vicinity lately."[28]

The next day several Indians appeared on the bluffs overlooking the fort, and Captain North and forty-eight Pawnees rode out to search for them. After traveling all night, they found their camp, and the Pawnees rushed into the fight half naked, killing and scalping all twenty-four Cheyennes, including one woman. The Cheyennes had indeed been raiders; among their possessions were found clothing from white women and children, two infantry coats, ten government horses and mules, one Overland Stage horse, two government saddles, and various letters written to soldiers.[29]

When the expedition finally left Fort Connor, Bridger scouted out an Indian camp four days old. Then he found a fire with red coals only two hours old and told the soldiers with him, "Go into camp and wait until I return and keep still and show no lights after dark." One of the soldiers was overwhelmed to be with the legendary Bridger and described him as "the greatest Indian scout that ever lived, not even excepting Kit Carson or Daniel Boone. [He] carried an extraordinary long double-barreled rifle with which he could plug the center at five hundred yards off hand. He was one of the most unassuming men I ever saw, but when he said anything he meant it."[30]

Connor was a gruff commander and had reservations about Bridger. Two years earlier, Connor had led the California Volunteers in a horrific massacre of nearly three hundred Northern Shoshones at Bear River in what is now Idaho. Among the dead were ninety women and children.[31] Connor had also wired John Chivington an urgent telegram just a month before the Sand Creek Massacre asking, "Can we get a fight out of Indians this winter?"[32]

Connor was well aware that Bridger had lived among the Shoshones and might be partial to Indians, and as they approached a dangerous canyon, Connor began to consider the possibility of an ambush. The general wheeled in his saddle and addressed Bridger. "Jim, if you lead me into an ambuscade, b—G [by God], you're the first who's going to die," emphasizing his point by slapping his hand on his holster. Chaplain Thomas Ferril was nearby, and he defended

Bridger's skill and loyalty. "Hell, beg pardon, Chaplain," replied Connor. "It is not profane to be damned emphatic."[33]

Bridger had developed a companionship with Capt. Henry Palmer, a Westport neighbor of the Bridgers and a good friend of Albert Wachsman, who had married Bridger's daughter, Virginia, the year before. Palmer had even contributed to help Jenny, as she was then called, and the rest of the family. He was Conner's acting quartermaster, and on August 26, four days after leaving the newly constructed Fort Connor, Bridger and Palmer set out early from Piney Fork. They were a mile or more ahead of the command and halted when they reached the dividing ridge between the Powder and the Tongue River. Bridger raised his hand to shield his eyes while Palmer raised his field glasses. "Do you see these 'ere columns of smoke over yonder?" asked Bridger.

"Where, Major?" asked Palmer.

"Over by that saddle," said Bridger, indicating a depression between two hills.

Palmer raised his field glasses again, but only saw a smoky haze in the distance and no columns. To avoid an argument, Palmer said they should wait for the general to come up. When Connor arrived, Palmer reported Bridger's discovery. The general raised his field glasses and scanned the horizon intently and said there was nothing to be seen. Bridger quietly turned his horse and rode away. Connor looked again and said there were no columns of smoke. Palmer caught up with Bridger in time to hear him swearing about "these damn paper collar soldiers" telling him there were no columns of smoke.[34]

Palmer thought Bridger was telling one of his tall tales and wrote, "The joke was too good to keep. . . . I don't believe the Major saw any columns of smoke," but he knew the location was a favorite place for Indian encampments.[35] It is possible, however, that Bridger may have actually seen smoke thirty-five miles distant. Objects could be seen much farther in the West, according to mathematician Orson Pratt, who recorded, "Chimney Rock, though forty miles distant, can be seen from the bluffs"; and "With our glasses, Chimney Rock can now be seen at a distance of 42 miles up the river."[36]

Bridger always seemed to have an interesting story or helpful advice. Later that day Bridger led the main body down Peno Creek, explaining to Palmer that the creek was named for a French trapper who had wounded a buffalo bull that chased him to the steep bank of the creek and then butted him on his rear. Peno tumbled fifteen or twenty feet into the creek, and the bull tumbled in after him so violently that Peno escaped. The next day Bridger warned the soldiers they would cross a small spring that was poison and neither they nor their stock should drink from it.[37]

Two days later one of the scouting parties found a fresh Indian trail and fires still smoldering. Connor sent Captain North and twenty of his men to follow the trail, which led to the spot where Bridger said he had seen columns of smoke. Two of North's scouts came back to the camp that night and excitedly reported a large Indian camp lay just twelve miles from where the soldiers had camped the night before.[38] "Bridger was all animation," wrote one of them, "and after a hasty consultation, two hundred and fifty men . . . were in the saddle, and with General Connor at the head, set off on a night's ride to reach the band of warriors before break of day. . . . The long column of silent men wound through rocky defiles and over stretches of grassy plains until the way seemed impossible, but all [were] confident in our guide."[39] Finn Burnett recalled that the column was led by Bridger, North, and the Pawnees, while others do not mention Bridger in this battle.

With the first light of day they saw an Arapaho Indian camp of about two hundred skin lodges under the leadership of Black Bear and Medicine Man, who had raided white settlements earlier that summer.[40] The Indians were gathering ponies and striking teepees. Connor told his men they should not kill women and children, and if they got into close quarters, they should group into fours and each save one charge in their revolvers for themselves.[41] Connor allowed no noise above a whisper, and the soldiers advanced right up to the village without being spotted. Then he rode his horse in full view of the Indians with his cavalry in a crescent behind him. Conner fired, followed by a volley from the entire command. Howitzers raked the village, the bugle sounded charge, and it was every man for himself racing towards the camp.

Rifle barrels clashed against tomahawks. Attackers were struck down from behind. Some soldiers fired only at warriors, while others fired at every brown skin they saw. A Pawnee scooped up a young Arapaho boy and said, "I kill him maybe," but a soldier stopped him. An Indian woman came out of hiding, pleading for peace but with a hatchet hidden behind her back. One soldier howled open-mouthed because an arrow had lodged in the root of his tongue. A young bugle boy riding a nervous cream-colored horse took a ball between the shoulders.[42]

The Arapahos tried to escape up Wolf Creek, and Connor galloped after them but was driven back to the camp. Connor ordered the men to gather the abandoned Indian lodges as well as their possessions and food, and they burned everything in a raging blaze. Knowing he did not have time to bury his fallen soldiers, he had their bodies put on top of the burning pile. As the Indians' lodges and soldiers' bodies went up in flames, the Arapahos counterattacked, and Connor retreated down Tongue River, greatly outnumbered.

The soldiers' attack on the village had lasted two hours; they then spent the next twelve hours defending themselves from a fierce resistance. Connor led his men in retreat while the Arapahos harassed the soldiers, firing on them from the crest of hills and daring them to attack. They used spectacular horsemanship to try to lure the soldiers back into battle. Eventually only forty soldiers had enough ammunition to even return fire. The Pawnees herded 1,100 captured ponies, but the Arapahos recaptured many of their horses. Connor and his men had killed sixty-three Indians and taken eighteen women and children captive. But he soon set the captives free and rode back to his full command.[43]

For the next several days, hundreds of wolves followed the soldiers, as they had since the column left Fort Laramie. On September 1, four nights after the attack on Tongue River, Bridger was alarmed by a strange and hideous howl, and he told those around him it was a "medicine wolf . . . a supernatural sort of an animal, whose howling is sure to bring trouble to the camp." Bridger and guides Nick Janis and Rulo were so alarmed they took up their blankets and struck out for a new camp. They found a spot about a half mile downriver and camped in the timber by themselves, "the only way of escaping from the impending danger."[44]

That danger soon befell the column under the command of Col. Nelson Cole, whose troops included Bridger's son. Felix was twenty-three and a private in the Second Missouri Light Artillery, which had fought in Missouri and Tennessee during the Civil War, as did his brother-in-law, Albert Wachsman.[45] They were equipped as cavalry and armed with seven-shot Spencer repeating rifles.[46]

On September 1, the same night as Bridger's medicine wolves, several hundred Indians raided livestock a mile from Cole's camp. Cole's entire command rode after them, recovering most of the stock and engaging them in battle. They killed twenty-five of the Indian raiders but lost six soldiers.[47] Later that evening two soldiers of the Second Missouri, Felix's unit, were tomahawked and mutilated.[48]

On September 3 a terrible storm swept over them, killing 225 horses and mules—so many that Cole had to order the soldiers to destroy the stores along with many of their wagons because there were not enough stock to pull them. On September 6 Cole's force was accosted by over a thousand warriors covering the hills, divides, and bluffs surrounding them. Then the combined forces of Cole and Walker were again attacked by thousands of warriors. Another storm began, which again pelted them with snow, sleet, and rain for thirty-six hours. They lost 414 more animals. The men were so hungry that as soon as an animal fell, the half-starved soldiers fell upon it and devoured what flesh they could.[49] When ordered to stop, a soldier gave a vacant stare and said, "Colonel, I can not help it; I am starving."[50] The beleaguered soldiers had to burn their saddles, harnesses, and implements to prevent them from falling into the hands of the Indians.

Meanwhile in eastern Wyoming Territory there were still more Indian skirmishes. Surveyor James Sawyers and his road crew had struggled that summer as they charted a wagon road from Sioux City, Iowa, to Virginia City. Cheyennes killed Nathaniel Hedges in the Sawyers party on August 13. Two day later Cheyenne leaders Bull Bear and Dull Knife and Oglala leader Red Cloud led an attack against the Sawyers party near Pumpkin Buttes. At noon the Indians called for a truce, and Bull Bear and Dull Knife demanded that Sawyers change his road to the Bridger Trail farther west along the Bighorn River. Sawyers argued that the Bridger road was too long and tried to appease them with supplies. Those Indians who did not receive supplies attacked and killed two more in the Sawyers party.[51]

Then, coincident with Bridger's medicine wolf howling, Indians killed a soldier scout with the Sawyers party on August 31 and two wagon drivers on September 2. The depleted road crew was immobile until September 13, when Connor sent reinforcements commanded by Capt. Albert Brown and accompanied by Winnebago leader Little Priest and his men. (Finn Burnett later claimed, inaccurately it seems, that Bridger had guided the Sawyers crew across the Bighorns through Pryor's Gap in order to reach Crow country.)[52]

Connor's men had fared well with Bridger as guide, but the same cannot be said for the other two prongs, whose commanders laid the blame on incomplete maps and incompetent scouts. Colonel Cole's chief guide was George Sard, a former clerk from Chicago who had been in the West only briefly. One of Cole's other guides directed them up Cedar Creek and then deserted, leaving them among impossible bluffs. Another time the guides led Cole's party five miles off course, and in yet another incident, their guide led them over difficult hills, ravines, and broken ground. Cole was so angry he threatened to hang the guide.[53]

Walker's contingent also suffered from incompetent guides. On the Cheyenne River several men in the command were allowed to drink from brackish water, which sickened large numbers of them and killed several. On the North Cheyenne, the frustrated Walker wrote, "Our guides knew nothing of the country from this out and our horses were getting weak. . . . Scouts returned and reported no grass and an impracticable road."[54]

Connor returned to Fort Laramie on September 29, disgraced in the eyes of his superiors, who thought he had not punished the Indians effectively, had issued inhumane orders, and had lost a thousand horses in a severe storm.[55] The Indians were more defiant than ever. Effective August 22, 1865, Connor was reassigned to the District of Utah, and he received the word that he was to cease hostilities in late September. Brig. General Frank Wheaton became the new commander for the District of the Plains, and Col. Henry Maynadier assumed command of Fort Laramie. By that time, some factions in Washington were pushing for peace.[56]

By October all forces had finally returned to Fort Connor or Fort Laramie. Jim Bridger finally met up with his son Felix. Lyman Bennett, an engineering officer with Cole's eastern prong, recorded that he "was introduced to Maj Bridger, the old mountaineer I have always heard of from boyhood. He has a son in the 2nd Mo. and they met at Fort Connor. The old man was displeased to see his son in the ranks a common soldier."[57] Lyman did not say whether Bridger's displeasure was with the command or with Felix.

Bridger went to Fort Laramie and remained there for a while. Cold weather descended on them as early as October 11 and they hunkered down. "Tonight we sit by a snug fire, listening to old Maj. Bridger's gold stories and we all conclude to go with him to the gold regions the next spring," wrote one. On December 15 the temperature showed "a difference of 40° between yesterday and today. We had a good time in our room tonight. Maj. Bridger and Gunn created lots of fun with Indian dances."[58]

30

RED CLOUD
FIGHTS BACK
1866

Hundreds of lives and millions of dollars depended on which route to the Montana gold fields the army chose to protect in 1866. Congressman James Ashley, a Republican abolitionist from Ohio, asked the secretary of war which of three routes to Virginia City should be selected: a wagon road from the Missouri River at the mouth of the Musselshell; the Bridger Trail along the west side of the Bighorns; or the Bozeman Trail on east side of the Bighorns through the Powder River country. On December 16, 1865 Col. Henry Maynadier asked Bridger to help him prepare a response to be forwarded to the secretary of war and Congressman Ashley. Maynadier wrote, "I am fortunate in having by me while I write Mr. Jas. Bridger, with whom I have just traced the route on the map." He added that Bridger was the most reliable source he knew.[1]

Bridger described in detail the route from the Missouri River and said it was entirely practical.[2] But Maynadier commented about the cost of steamboat transportation up the Missouri for the miners, though it was a pittance compared to the millions that would be spent if the military had to go to war in Indian lands. Bridger clearly thought that the trail he opened west of the Bighorns was the safest and the least expensive, but Maynadier gave it little attention in his letter.

With or without Bridger's awareness, Maynadier wrote. "This [Bridger Trail] is no longer a matter of opinion. The [Bozeman] road exists and has been passed over by a great many wagons." He concluded that the Bozeman Trail was the shortest and most direct route. The army thus perpetuated its ill-fated decision to go right through lands the Indians had shown they would fight to protect, foolishly ignoring advice from the nation's foremost Western plainsman and geographer.

Congressman Ashley also had asked where military forts might be situated to supplement Fort Connor, now renamed Fort Reno. Maynadier recommended two additional forts—perhaps with Bridger's input. One should be built on the Bighorn and one at Clark's Fork on the Yellowstone River.[3] Both of these locations were in Crow country and not in the heart of Sioux, Cheyenne, and Arapaho lands.

The Civil War was over. The nation had enormous debt, and the army ordered commanders to dismiss all citizen employees not sanctioned by higher authority. Bridger stayed at Laramie for another two weeks hoping to be rehired, but no such order arrived. About Christmas Day he set out for his home in Westport, finding room in the mail wagon with two homeward-bound soldiers, A. J. Shotwell and William McFadden.

"Where are you boys going?" he asked.

"To Julesburg, then by Overland stage to the [Missouri] River."

Bridger smiled and said. "So am I, and if we travel together, I guess it's best to be sociable." As they made themselves comfortable among the mail sacks and baggage, young Shotwell noticed that Bridger was "made of heroic stuff every inch." He was "straight as an Indian, muscular and quick in movement." He had the piercing eye of an eagle which seemed to "flash fire when narrating an experience that had called out his reserve power."[4]

At Julesburg the Overland stages were booked for at least ten days, so the trio found space in an empty wagon that was part of a train on its way to Fort Kearny in Nebraska and then on to the Missouri River. They bought enough hay to cover the wagon bed six inches deep and spread their blankets over it. The first night out from Julesburg, the wagon train halted at one of the roadhouses catering to travelers. The proprietor spotted Bridger and exclaimed. "Of all the men, who have we here if not Old Jim Bridger. Come right in, Jim. The place is yours as long as you care to stay."

"Here are two soldier boys traveling with me," said Bridger. "I stay with them."

"All the same," said the proprietor, opening his arms. "Bridger and his friends included." They enjoyed a bountiful meal, a place to sleep, breakfast, and a packed lunch for the next day, all at no charge.[5]

At Fort Kearny Bridger encouraged Shotwell and McFadden to come home with him, but their time was limited and they moved on. Bridger sojourned at the Overland House, and the editor of the Kearny *Semi-Weekly Herald* inter-viewed him there, a rare scoop. Bridger told him he still resented the loss of his fort and home and said next year, when his ten-year lease to the army expired, he was tempted to "return home and wake up the foes" who drove him away.

Bridger offered his opinion that the army's method of moving men and sup-plies with wagons was "simply absurd," resulting in heavy loss of animals and unnecessary exposure of troops. He said he could do much better with a group of experienced frontiersmen, "Dodgers." Bridger strongly felt that "if they will let him select a party of men, he will follow the Indians on foot, week after week, faring as they do, and will eventually overtake and surprise their villages."[6]

Bridger continued by stage to Atchison, Kansas, near his home in Westport, and Frank Root, who worked for the Overland stage, met "the jolly old frontiers-man," whom he thought was "uncouth in dress, not overly polite, a good talker, with a wonderful memory."[7] Bridger had a brief respite in Westport with his children, but his time home was short-lived, as Gen. Grenville Dodge expected him in nearby Leavenworth. Dodge ordered Bridger's reinstatement on Janu-ary 22, 1866, and the next day Gen. Frank Wheaton charged his underlings, "Do not drop from the rolls James Bridger, District Guide, Charles [Nick] Janis, Interpreter, and Rafael [Gallegos], Post Guide. Bridger was put on the payroll from January 25 to January 31 to meet with Dodge to discuss his strategy for 1866.

Dodge found Bridger "spare, straight as an arrow, agile, rawboned and . . . powerful."[8] Bridger undoubtedly spoke frankly, advising the general to establish a temporary base and use pack mules from there to supply the men, punctuat-ing it with this: "If the men can have some sense in dealing with these Indians, they can keep their lives."[9]

Dodge told Col. Henry Carrington, who was to choose the locations for the new forts: "Take with you James Bridger, who is the most reliable and most competent man you can get as a guide. He has good judgment and knows that country as well as we do our A.B.C.'s."[10] Dodge also told Carrington, "Make the posts neat, compact so that the garrison can defend themselves against all comers." He was likely referencing the kind of forts that Bridger had built when under attack by the Blackfeet twenty years earlier.

Dodge insisted that the army put Jim Bridger to work right away, and by mid-February, General Wheaton in Omaha was frantically looking for the old scout. Wheaton sent a telegram to Laramie: "Have not heard from Bridger. Don't know his whereabouts. I have directed the qm. [quartermaster] at Laramie to employ him as guide when ever Bridger reports at Laramie. Where is he now?"[11]

Bridger was in Westport buying a building for an emigrant outfitting business located on Main and Shawnee streets, now Pennsylvania Avenue and Westport Road. Cyprian Chouteau had erected the building in 1850 and sold it to Bridger on February 20, 1866, for $1,500.[12] It had thirty-seven feet of frontage and was next door to the general store that had been operated by Albert G. Boone, a grandson of Daniel Boone. The army finally found Bridger three days later and told him to report to Fort Laramie. That same day Robert Campbell passed the news on to Seth Ward that the army had ordered Bridger "to meet Genl. Wheaton at Fort Laramie on 5th March to make a treaty there with hostile Indians."[13]

Bridger arrived at Fort Laramie by stage on March 4 as chief guide for the army's newly formed Mountain District. After talking to his friend Bridger, the post trader W. G. Bullock wrote to Dodge offering to partner with him in a gold and silver venture in lands where Indians had found ore.[14] The suggestion went no further.

While the Department of Indian Affairs was planning to negotiate a treaty, the War Department was planning to take soldiers into their lands, by force if necessary, to build forts and open the road for civilians. Dodge was embarrassed and annoyed by this "imbecile half war and half peace policy."[15]

Red Cloud, Man Afraid of His Horses, and other leaders came to Fort Laramie with 150 Oglala warriors at the invitation of the Department of Indian Affairs, and they gathered under the pavilion where the Stars and Stripes had been replaced with a white flag of truce.[16] The army had arranged for Edward Taylor, the head of the Northern Indian superintendency (who could not be there in person), to address Red Cloud directly through the telegraph. Red Cloud was hesitant to enter the office where the dits and dashes of the "singing wire" beat like tiny drums. By telegram, Taylor assured Red Cloud that the "Great Father in Washington" wanted peace, and the commissioners would arrive in June with presents to negotiate a treaty.[17]

The army asked Bridger to build a ferry across the North Platte at La Bonte's crossing, fifty-five miles west of Fort Laramie, where Connor and his forces had difficulty crossing the year before. On May 16, Maynadier ordered: "The buildings at the [stage] station formerly occupied at Horse shoe creek will be removed to Bridger's Ferry. Mr. James Bridger is authorized to take such material belonging to the U.S. as may now be at Horse shoe and [use them?] as he may require erecting a house at the Ferry."[18]

Bridger designed his ferry with adjustable cables and pulleys so that with just a few minor alterations, the force of the river would propel the boat across in either direction. His ferry performed like clockwork, taking just eleven minutes for each round trip. The ferry buildings were on the north side of the Platte, while the telegraph line was on south bank.[19]

Bridger had acquired the territorial license for ferries across the Platte, Big Horn, and Yellowstone rivers and discussed that with General Dodge during his January meeting. Dodge agreed that the army would furnish the rope and tackle then at Laramie and the army would cross for free. Bridger's man, Ben Mills, a trader for Seth Ward, would operate the ferry and collect fares from the public, assisted by his wife Sally No Fat, an Oglala Sioux from Red Cloud's band, and their three children.[20]

The long-awaited treaty council began at Fort Laramie on June 5, 1866, in front of Old Bedlam, the fort headquarters and living quarters, with pine benches set up under a bower of fresh evergreens. There were nineteen chiefs in total, representing twenty-one bands of Sioux, Cheyennes, and Arapahos. Red Cloud came in with fifty to sixty selected warriors. Many of the key Indian leaders left in anger by June 8, having heard that the whites intended to come through their land no matter what. Red Cloud said he would never allow the Wasichus on the Bozeman Trail. The peace commission continued to negotiate with the Indians who remained.[21]

In the midst of this squabble, Col. Henry Carrington arrived in the Laramie area on June 13 with seven hundred troops and the equipment needed to build the new forts. Civilian teamsters drove 226 mule teams pulling wagons loaded with potatoes and onions for planting, grass-mowing machines, and machines to make shingles and bricks. The wagons also carried rocking chairs, churns, washing machines, windows with locks, sewing chairs, live turkeys and chickens, and canned oysters and fruits. Along with the wagons and the troops, the caravan included a herd of one thousand cattle and a brace of swine. Some officers, including Carrington, even brought their wives, as Gen. William Tecumseh Sherman had suggested.[22] Carrington's "Overland Circus" was obviously planning to build long-term installations.

Shortly after Carrington made camp, Standing Elk, a leader of the Brulé Sioux, came asking for gifts. As the sun set, Carrington went through the ceremonial presentation of tobacco. When he told Standing Elk they were going on the white man's road, Standing Elk told him they would have no peace, because "the fighting men in that country have not come to Laramie, and you will have to fight them. They will not give you this road unless you whip them."[23]

Carrington sent wagons over to Fort Laramie requesting one hundred thousand rounds of ammunition, but the quartermaster only gave him one thousand rounds. How could they protect the road and build three forts with so little ammunition? Alarmingly, Bridger had seen Indian ponies on the riverbanks loaded with kegs of gunpowder from the fort. Some of it was already heading to the Indians on Powder River. Carrington fared better with his request for food and other supplies, getting twenty-six wagons full. But the flour was musty and caked, riddled with mice and insects. The pilot bread was dark and nearly inedible, and the soldiers had to break it with a metal tool.[24]

The officers and their wives made a trip to the sutler's store. Crackers crunched under their feet as they entered, and they caught the smell of herring and cheese. Bullock, who lived in the gothic cottage nearby, was bustling about with his assistants, trading with Indians and whites. Some of the Indians wore red blankets over their shoulders; others were less concerned about modesty. The movement and talk of the buyers reminded Margaret Carrington of a busy store in a city like Omaha. Indians lined up to buy knives, tobacco, and brass nails. Others traded for glass beads and candy. One tall Indian delightedly sucked at the tall sticks of peppermint candy he had purchased. Indian women made the front of their skirts into pouches to carry rice, sugar, coffee, or flour. Excited sounds mingled in the air, and Indians exclaimed "Wash-ta-la," very good, or grunted "Wan-nee-chee," no good.[25]

Carrington wired for permission to remain at Fort Laramie until the peace treaty was completed. He was denied and told to march at once.[26] The War Department was deaf to the trail Bridger had blazed two years earlier, deaf to Indian protests, and deaf to the Department of Indian Affairs' efforts for peace. Treaties were completed with the Indians who had stayed, using replacements for the chiefs who had left.

But the Oglalas and Cheyennes from Powder River refused to touch their hands to the pen. One said, "In two moons the command would not have a hoof left." Another said, "Great Father sends us presents and wants new road, but white chief goes with soldiers to *steal* the road before Indian say yes or no."[27] General Dodge was told that Red Cloud would not give up any land above the North Platte, and if the army built the new road to Montana, "he would line it with dead soldiers."[28] An Indian messenger was sent out by the peace commission to talk to the Cheyennes, but Red Cloud's Bad Faces knocked him off his horse, whipped him, talked saucily, and sent him back to Laramie.

On June 17 Bridger led Carrington's train out from Fort Laramie with Henry Williams as assistant scout and Jack Stead as chief interpreter. As was his custom, Bridger dressed in plain clothes and a low-crowned, soft felt hat. His habits were also plain and sensible, though he continued to demonstrate an uncanny understanding of Indian ways and customs, adopting the Indian way of seeing without being seen.[29] Most of the soldiers were raw and scared. They were marching on foot into a land where warfare was conducted on horseback.

The officers had serious concern about their weapons. Most of the troops carried old muzzle-loading Springfields, and, since the regimental band had not yet been armed, they received the new breech-loading Spencer carbines that carried seven-shot cartridges. Carrington then had the members of the band give the Spencers to the better marksmen and take muzzle-loading Springfields in their place. They were also perilously low in ammunition. In addition, Carrington requested more troops, and Philip St. George Cooke approved it, but the request was sent up the ladder and ignored. Congress was trying to maintain the military in the Reconstruction South, and the federal budget screamed for reductions elsewhere.[30]

One day as they entered a steep gorge, Bridger kept a vigilant eye against ambush. Two men led their wives on a side trip to a canyon to hunt for agates. Before long they were shouting and shooting their pistols to hear their echoes reverberate through the gorge. Bridger warned that they could get "sculped" if they were not careful, but they scoffed, for there was not an Indian in sight.

Bridger was emphatic. "Better not go *fur*. There is *Injuns* enough lying under wolf skins or skulking on them cliffs, I warrant! They follow ye always. They've seen ye, every day, and when ye don't see any of 'em about, is just the time to look for their devilment."[31] The same day that Bridger issued this warning, Red Cloud and his Bad Faces raided Bridger's ferry just nine miles away and stole several animals.

Bridger led them into red and rocky terrain. The South Fork of the Cheyenne was dry, but he had them dig, and water soon pooled before them. The mountain man energizing them by opening a shortcut that shaved five miles off Bozeman's original trail. Soon they got their first views of the Bighorns and felt their cooling breezes.

As they approached Fort Reno (previously Fort Connor), Bridger picked up Indian sign all about. Carrington ordered that emigrant trains on the trail had to wait until they had thirty armed men among their numbers. On June 30 Indians raided the sutler's stock at Fort Reno, stealing twenty-seven mules and seven horses. Fifty soldiers gave chase, but they didn't return until the next morning, and they failed to recover any of the stolen animals. They did capture one Indian pony, which still carried supplies the Indians had been given at the Laramie peace council.[32]

The food at Fort Reno was as bad as it had been at Laramie. Mice had tunneled through the flour and bacon, and the men had to use a burlap sack as a sieve to remove the feces and dead animals. Fortunately they could boil an airtight pack of desiccated vegetables and make several gallons of rich soup. For their animals, over a million pounds of grain were scheduled to be delivered by rail to Omaha and then by wagon to the fort.[33]

Carrington left two companies to staff Fort Reno and marched on with four other companies. Maynadier's recommendation with Bridger at his side had been to erect one fort at the Bighorn and the second farther west on Clark's Fork.[34] But that plan had not prevailed, and Carrington's orders were to build the first of the two new forts near the Big Piney or Little Piney, in the heart of Sioux land, and the second at the Bighorn River.

July 9 was the hottest day of the year so far: the thermometer read 112° at Crazy Woman Creek. The wagon train had not gone far when Indians appeared first on one hill, then another. Bridger rode out to meet them and found they were Sioux claiming to be looking for the Shoshones. But Bridger knew they were counting the number of soldiers and wagons and planning their attack. At Clear Creek, army wives set up camp chairs to relax, only to discover that three rattlesnakes were curled under their chairs. An orderly quickly mangled them.[35]

At Rock Creek, Bridger's scouts found a message written in pencil on cracker boxes. Two emigrant trains had been attacked during the past week and their stock run off. Carrington increased the watch and dispensed with hourly rest breaks. By midafternoon they reached Little Piney Creek. Colonel Carrington thought it a perfect spot for Fort Phil Kearny. An elevated grassy plateau was situated between two streams, and it was out of shooting range from the neighboring hills. Carrington intended to build a wooden palisade three thousand feet in perimeter and then construct over two dozen wooden buildings.

Both Bridger and assistant guide James Brannan strongly encouraged Carrington to build the fort on Goose Creek or in Tongue River Valley. Carrington rode out to examine those sites but did not take Bridger along to help pick a spot. The colonel returned and stuck with his original choice on the Little Piney. While it had plenty of grass and water, its distance from timber would prove to be a fatal flaw.[36]

While Carrington was away, Cheyenne leader Black Horse sent a messenger to the army camp asking, "Does the White chief want peace or war?" When Carrington returned, he and Bridger decided that Black Horse and some of his men should visit the camp "when the sun is overhead, after two sleeps."[37]

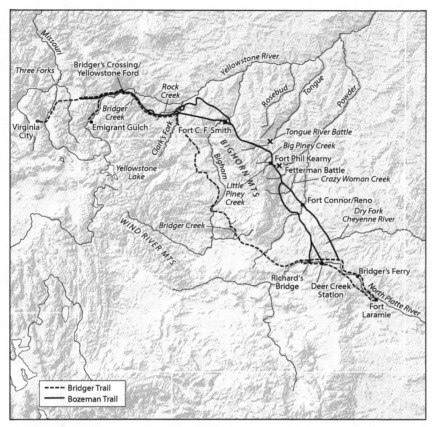

The Bridger Trail, Bozeman Trail, Battles, and Forts, 1864–1868

Meanwhile Carrington's soldiers used the mowing machines they had carried from Omaha to clear a footprint six hundred by eight hundred feet. The parade ground was to be four hundred feet square. It was as if they were creating a small village, and they laid out "streets" to accommodate officers' quarters, soldiers' quarters, storehouses, a sutler's store, quarters for the band, a guardhouse, and other buildings.[38]

July 16 was the day set for the Indian parley. Some Cheyennes came in full ornament and arms, wearing grizzly necklaces or presidential medallions handed down from their fathers. One arrived wearing nothing but a breechcloth, moccasins, and a large gaily-colored umbrella.[39] Bridger told Carrington to make a show of power, and Carrington ordered his men to fire the howitzer, "the gun that shoots twice." It impressed the Cheyennes when the cannon shot the canister and doubly impressed them when the canister exploded above its target with iron projectiles raining down onto the earth.

The Cheyennes and the soldiers assembled to begin their talk. Margaret Carrington recorded, "In front of them all, and to the left of the table," sat Jim Bridger, "elbows on his knees and chin buried in his hands." His "forty-four years upon the frontier had made him as keen and suspicious of Indians as any Indian himself could be." He was known as Big Throat to the Sioux because his neck was enlarged from goiter, the swelling of the thyroid gland probably caused by the lack of iodine in snowmelt streams. He was universally respected by the Indians, and yet of all the men assembled that day, his scalp would be the proudest trophy to the Cheyenne and Sioux alike. Margaret Carrington wrote: "To us he was invariably straightforward, truthful, and reliable. His sagacity, knowledge of woodcraft, and knowledge of the Indian was wonderful, and his heart was warm and his feelings tender wherever he confided or made a friend."[40]

Black Horse cast his buffalo robe from his shoulders and spoke for the 176 lodges of the Cheyennes. They did not want war with the whites. But he warned that other Cheyennes were riding with Red Cloud and had been following the soldiers since they left Laramie. Red Cloud had five hundred warriors, and more were coming. They would cut off any further travel and stop all supplies from reaching the forts.

When Black Horse and his Cheyennes left the soldiers' camp, they were accosted by the Sioux, who demanded to know if the soldiers were going to turn back. Black Horse told them no and said, "The white chief wished all the Arapahos and Sioux, and all the other Indians of that country, to go to Laramie and sign the treaty and get their presents." The Sioux were infuriated and unslung their bows, whipping the Cheyennes and crying "Coo" to humiliate them.[41]

HUNDRED
IN THE HAND
1866

Red Cloud was ready to fight back. He led the Sioux, Cheyennes, and Arapahos on a nine-day scourge against the soldiers and emigrants. On July 17, the morning after the Sioux counted coup on the Cheyennes, they sneaked past the army picket at Fort Phil Kearny and stole the bell mare and 174 head of livestock. Two dozen infantry gave chase, and the Sioux circled back as was their plan, firing bullets and arrows into the now-retreating soldiers.

When it was over the soldiers counted the losses. Two soldiers and one teamster were dead and five were wounded, some by poison arrows. On the way back the soldiers found the dead and mutilated bodies of French Pete Cazeau and four of his men, who had been trading with the friendly Cheyennes. The soldiers found another man with his throat cut.[1] Then, on July 18, three hundred Sioux stole thirty-four mules from a wagon train on the Bighorn River.

On July 20 Bridger was guiding Capt. Thomas Burrowes and a wagon train from Fort Phil Kearny back to Fort Reno. Bridger—dressed in his buckskin reinforced pants, buckskin coat, and broad-brimmed hat—would typically mount his gray mare, slide his musket across the saddle, and ride out in a slow walk.[2] But he was ever watchful, and when approaching high ground he would ride very slowly toward the crest then cut quickly either right or left to reach the top so that if an Indian lay in wait the guide would have a fifty-fifty chance of evading attack.[3]

On this day Bridger's keen eyes caught Indian sign at Clear Creek: a message painted on buffalo skulls telling other Indians to come to Crazy Woman's Fork to fight the whites. Bridger reported what he saw to Burrowes, who doubted what Bridger told him.[4]

Captain Burrowes had intended to camp at Clear Creek that night, but Bridger insisted, so the soldiers continued on toward Crazy Woman's Fork, following Bridger's lead. There they found a party of thirty-seven, including soldiers escorting an emigrant train of men, women, and children on the trail between Fort Reno and Fort Phil Kearny. Lt. George Templeton and Lt. Napoleon Daniels, who led the train, were attacked by Indians when they had ridden ahead to scout out a camp. Daniels was killed, and Templeton barely escaped back to his party. They corralled their wagons, and soon a hundred Indians encircled them.

Several civilians began to pray in earnest. David White, the new chaplain for Fort Phil Kearny, grabbed a weapon and told them, "There is a time for praying, and . . . a time for fighting. . . . Now stop Praying!" The fighting continued until dusk, and soon they were down to seven rounds per man.[5] One of the men, Samuel Peters, reported that two men made it through the Indian lines in an effort to get to Fort Reno for help. Then the soldiers and civilians spotted a solitary rider silhouetted against the darkening sky coming toward them from the direction of Fort Phil Kearny. They ordered the figure to halt. Peters recalled that the rider stopped and called out that he was a friend.

"What's your name?" they asked.

"Jim Bridger."

A cheer rose from the embattled men. Bridger picked his way across the ravine and rode into the camp to their tremendous relief. "I knew there was hell to pay here to-day at Crazy Woman," Bridger told them. "I could see it from the signs the Indians made on the buffalo skulls. But cheer up, boys, Captain Burroughs [Burrowes] and . . . [his] soldiers are coming down the road here, about two miles away."[6]

Fighting continued along the Bozeman Trail throughout the rest of July. Red Cloud was tightening the vise and rallying the Sioux, Cheyennes, and Arapahos to fight to the end. If they were going to die, they preferred to die fighting. The Sioux scorned the ways of the Wasichus who brought machines to turn grass into hay and trees into boards. They carried animal food in sacks. Did they not know that horses could forage for their own food and eat the bark of the cottonwood?

As construction of Fort Phil Kearny neared completion, Carrington sent Bridger farther west with two companies under Capt. Nathaniel Kinney to build the final fort. Carrington's fighting force was now spread out among three forts, and 560 of the 640 soldiers were inexperienced recruits. The construction

Red Cloud, photographed by William Henry Jackson. Red Cloud fought the U.S. Army for building forts on the Bozeman Trail, telling them to use the recently opened Bridger Trail instead. *History Nebraska RG2845 PH 3-4*

detail left on August 4. Two days out of Fort Phil Kearny, they came to Hugh Kirkendall's train of 110 wagons, and they decided to travel together.

Bridger led them across Peno Creek, Goose Creek, Tongue River, the Little Bighorn, Grass Lodge, and Rotten Grass Creek. Finally, they reached the Bighorn River and selected the site for Fort C. F. Smith two miles from the mouth of Big-horn Canyon, where Bridger had rafted Bad Pass for William Ashley forty-one years earlier. This spot on the trail was 91 miles northwest of Fort Phil Kearny and 281 miles east of the much-ballyhooed Virginia City.[7]

Wagons were backed up on both sides of the Bighorn waiting to cross. Although Mitch Boyer and others had repaired and operated the ferry there earlier that year, it was now in sorry shape, with rough planks corked with rags. The firm of Smith and Leighton had the sutler's contract for the store; Bridger, having the ferry license, began to stretch the rope and fix the ferry.[8]

Hugh Kirkendall and his 110 wagons were impatient though and wanted to cross immediately, not willing to waiting for Bridger's repairs. They searched for a shallow crossing, but each place they tried was too deep. They tested one more location and were caught in an eddy in the fast-moving river. Their horses were being sucked down, and the men scrambled off of them. One of the men, George MaGee, disappeared, and it was hours before his body was recovered. He was buried the next day, the same day construction began on Fort C. F. Smith.[9]

Bridger and his scout, Henry Williams, had orders to lay out and shorten the road to Virginia City, and they agreed to let Kirkendall's wagon train travel with them. Other wagon trains followed, often querying Bridger on the best route. Bridger piloted them through shortcuts and away from dangerous routes. One of his improvements was to go down the east side of Rosebud Creek to the Stillwater and cross just above present-day Absarokee, Montana. This allowed travelers to avoid the treacherous Sanborn Hill, which had required them to lower their wagons with chains and ropes held fast by a snubbing post at the top of the hill.[10]

This was still a perilous country for those who separated from the protec-tion of their wagon train, but three miners did just that. The train came upon their bodies near Bridger Creek and Yellowstone River. Rev. William Thomas was found near the rear wheels of his wagon with thirteen arrows in his body, and his eight-year-old son Charley lay near the front wheels with three arrows. Both had been scalped, and wolves had eaten away at the boy's body. The body of the third man, James Schultz, was in the river, but he had not been mutilated. The men debated whether the attack had been perpetrated by the Sioux or the

Crows, but Bridger said it was Blackfeet, since Schultz's body was in the river and Blackfeet "would not molest a body that lay in the water."[11]

The *Montana Post* covered Bridger's arrival in Virginia City in early September, and Bridger was emphatic that "if the authorities in Washington will furnish him the means, he will 'clean out' all the hostile tribes in one summer."[12] He was one of the few alive who could make such a claim. In August Bridger met with the Crows in their village between Clark's Fork and the Bighorn. He asked them to meet quietly with Red Cloud to determine his intentions, but the Crows told Bridger the startling news that the Sioux had already gathered a large alliance to fight the whites. The Crows reported to Bridger:

> The Man afraid of his horses, Red Cloud, and Iron Shirt and several other Chiefs . . . were in their Village and smoked with them, for the purpose of getting them to join them to fight the whites. They said they had already formed an alliance with the Assiniboines, Crees, Grosvents of the Prairie, and black Feet and now wanted the Crows, Flat Heads, Nisperses and Snakes to join them and then they would have all the . . . people. Then they said they would move up and down the road and compell the Whites to leave it.[13]

The Crows also told Bridger there were fifteen hundred Sioux, Cheyennes, and Arapahos already gathered on the Tongue River—so many it would take half a day to ride through their villages. The assembled warriors promised to destroy the two new forts, and while the Crow leaders said they wanted peace, some of their young men wanted to fight either the Sioux or the whites, whichever would help them regain the Powder River country.[14]

Crow leader Iron Shell told Bridger that they had met peace commissioners on the steamboat *Ben Johnson* who promised to pay $25,000 in goods if the Crows would allow the United States the rights to use the Blanket Road (the Bridger Trail). The Crows also told Bridger they were willing to negotiate a price for the western end of the Bozeman Trail, which the Crows controlled from Fort C. F. Smith to Virginia City. At Bridger's request the Crows came to Fort C. F. Smith on August 27 to tell the army commander these things.[15]

Bridger relayed this news to Colonel Carrington. He also had a letter written on his behalf to his friend William Bullock at the sutler store at Fort Laramie, saying, "Now, Major, if the government ever intends to do anything with them, they better be moving, for the Indians are all assembling down on Tongue River and they mean mischief. I think next summer the Indians will make a desperate struggle against the Troops and Emigrants on all the roads to the Mountains."[16] Bullock shared Bridger's letter with Maj. James Van Voast, who was then in command at Fort Laramie. Van Voast forwarded the information to his superior with the comment, "I do not believe much of what Mr. Bridger says—He exaggerates about Indians."[17] Van Voast and other doubters were about to learn a difficult lesson.

In less than two months Bridger helped establish Fort C. F. Smith, fixed the ferry across the Bighorn, secured the loyalty of the Crows, and shortened the route to the gold fields near Virginia City by twenty miles, with another thirty-mile reduction possible. He returned to Fort C. F. Smith on September 29. On October 23 he rode east with several officers to report to Carrington, who needed his services at Fort Phil Kearny.[18]

The distance the troopers had to travel to cut wood was Fort Phil Kearny's weak point. Almost daily the Indians harassed the cutting parties, which were set up several miles away from the fort. Bridger regularly scanned the nearby hills and sometimes caught the glint of mirrors from Indian signals. Both the army and the Indians used signal flags, mirrors, and spyglasses to communicate. If the army scout on Pilot Knob saw Indians, he would signal back to the fort by circling his horse, ending with his horse facing in the Indians' direction.[19]

On November 3 Capt. William J. Fetterman arrived at Fort Phil Kearny along with Lt. Horatio Bingham and sixty-three additional soldiers. Fetterman did not know much about Indians but was confident of his own abilities. Full of bravado from Civil War action, he boasted only two days after he arrived, "A company of regulars could whip a thousand Indians and a regiment could whip the whole array of hostile tribes."[20] Fetterman's boast was seconded by Capt. Frederick Brown and Lt. Francis Grummond. That very night Fetterman tried to show his skill by picketing mules outside the fort as a trap. He stayed on watch for hours but the Indians didn't take the bait, instead making off with a herd a mile away. Bridger struggled to make them realize the seriousness of their plight.[21]

Bridger thought that Fetterman and his men "who fought down South are Crazy! They don't know anything about fighting Indians."[22] But Fetterman soon learned the danger. On December 6 Carrington, Fetterman, Grummond, and others fought a harrowing battle. The Sioux attacked a party of twenty-five soldiers and civilians who were headed for the wood camp. Carrington sent Fetterman to lead the rescue party, and Carrington himself led another party to go beyond Lodge Trail Ridge to catch the Sioux by surprise.

Through a series of misfortunes and miscommunications, there were several casualties. Three soldiers died and six were wounded. About ten Sioux were also killed.[23] Margaret Carrington recorded that Fetterman "has learned a lesson" and now knew that "this Indian war has become a hand-to-hand fight, requiring the utmost caution." Fetterman also added that "he wants no more of such risks."[24]

Van Voast did little to support Carrington and his three undermanned and under armed forts, and he continued to doubt the severity of the threat. He suggested he himself could lead an expedition to punish the Indians with his abundance of ten companies at Fort Laramie, Camp Mitchell, and Bridger's Ferry. The commander of the Department of the Platte, General Cooke, also did not take Bridger's cautions seriously. On November 25 Cooke wrote impatiently to Carrington, "Turn your earnest attention to the possibility of striking the hostile band of Indians by surprise in their winter camps," pointing out that they had a "large arrear of murderous and insulting attacks . . . to settle."[25] Carrington promised to do so when the weather confined the Indians to their villages.

After a council with the Crows on October 31, Lieutenant Templeton at Fort C. F. Smith worried, "If the government does not take decided measures very soon in regards to the Sioux," the Crows will join them and "for the first time make war with the whites." Carrington responded on November 16, ordering Bridger to go back to Fort C. F. Smith to keep the Crows loyal. The army had hired Jim Beckwourth on August 13, though in Carrington's estimation, "He talks much; I doubt his influence with them."[26]

Beckwourth fell ill and his nose would not stop bleeding. He died on October 29, and the Crows laid his body on a platform in a tree a few miles north of the Yellowstone. Jim Beckwourth, the Black Chief of the Crows, also known as Antelope or Medicine Calf, was home.[27]

As Bridger prepared to go back to Fort C. F. Smith, Carrington sent specific orders to give to the commander there. "If the Crow chiefs shall visit this post [Fort Phil Kearny], Mr. Bridger will return with them as interpreter during their stay."[28] Red Cloud was determined to stop the soldiers, killing them if necessary. Bridger was equally determined to keep the soldiers alive, but he could not be at two forts at once.

Bridger arrived at Fort C. F. Smith on November 28 with the last mail from Fort Phil Kearny of the season.[29] Some soldiers doubted Bridger's estimation of the number of Indians in Red Cloud's coalition. Others didn't understand the battle skills of Plains Indians and thought Bridger was just an aging mountain man living on past accomplishments. But Bridger was exactly in the right place—a remnant of an America that was fast disappearing. This Powder River country resembled the West that Bridger had first seen in 1822, with no railroads and no cities, just rolling hills occupied by thousands of Indians who considered the land theirs by right of claim or treaty.

Department of the Platte headquarters in Omaha ordered Carrington to discharge several civilians, including Bridger. Carrington wrote back asking if the order required him to discharge "James Bridger and other citizen guides who are familiar with the country."[30] Frances Carrington (whom the colonel married after Margaret's death) stated that her husband wrote on the back of the order, "Impossible of Execution."[31]

The country at large knew little of the looming disaster. President Andrew Johnson incorrectly told Congress in his written State of the Union address on December 3, 1866: "Treaties have been concluded with the Indians, who . . . have unconditionally submitted to our authority and manifested an earnest desire for a renewal of friendly relations."[32]

The truth was that Indians had carried out fifty-one separate attacks on the Bozeman Trail from July to November 1866, causing the loss of ninety-one soldiers and fifty-eight civilians, as well as 750 animals. Bridger's cautions were borne out to some of the men at Fort Phil Kearny when they saw "the enemy was increasing in force and watchful of every exposure or recklessness of parties leaving the fort."[33]

The conflict had come to a climax. Miniconjou chief White Swan addressed his people: "I have tried to keep you from fighting the whites, but now I am going to die. If you want to fight the whites, collect together and go and satisfy yourselves—fight them once more. This is all I have to say."[34] The Miniconjou High Back Bone led the effort, inviting the Oglalas, Brulés, Two Kettles, Hunkpapas, Cheyennes, and Arapahos to join them. Between 1,500 and 2,000 warriors, most equipped with bows and arrows and lances, agreed to fight the Wasichus. In the Lakota world, December was known as the moon of deer shedding horns.

Black Elk, an Oglala Sioux who was just a boy in 1866, remembered hearing that "the Wasichus were coming and that they were going to take our country and rub us all out and that we should all have to die fighting. . . . Crazy Horse was only about 19 years old then, and Red Cloud was still our great chief. . . . He called together all the scattered bands of the Sioux. . . . Many of our friends, the Shyela (Cheyenne) and the Blue Clouds (Arapaho), had come to help us fight."[35]

But some were hesitant. A spirit person came forth—a Hee-man-eh, half man and half woman, connected to the spirit world. Wearing a black cloth over his face, he rode out in a zigzag pattern blowing a whistle to look for the enemy. He came back to the Sioux leaders and said, "I have ten men [enemies], five in each hand. Do you want them?" "No, we do not wish them," a leader said. "Look at all these people here. Do you think ten men are enough to go around?"[36]

The Hee-man-eh rode off again, veering from one side to the other, then returned, saying, "I have ten men in each hand, twenty in all. Do you wish them?" The same leader said, "No, I do not wish them; there are too many people here and not enough enemies." The half man half woman came back again. "I have twenty in one hand and thirty in the other. The thirty are in the hand on the side which I am leaning." Still the leader said no. A fourth time the Hee-man-eh returned, riding fast. He stopped his horse and fell to the ground. "Answer me quickly," he said. "I have a hundred or more." The guttural yells from the Sioux and Cheyenne warriors could be heard over the distant hills. That was enough of an enemy to die. They prepared for a battle that they would call the "hundred in the hand."[37]

An Oglala Sioux named Fire Thunder remembered, "We started out on horseback just about sunrise [on December 21], riding up the creek toward the soldiers' town on the Piney for we were going to attack it. The sun was about halfway up when we stopped at the place where the Wasichu's road came down a steep, narrow ridge and crossed the creek. It was a good place to fight, so we sent some men ahead to coax the soldiers out." The decoys were six Sioux, two Cheyennes, and two Arapahos.[38] By this time a larger force of Indians had attacked the wood party. Colonel Carrington ordered Capt. William Fetterman to take several men to relieve the wood party, giving specific instructions not to go cross Lodge Trail Ridge.

Fire Thunder said:

We divided into two parts and hid in the gullies on both sides of the ridge and waited. After a long while we heard a shot up over the hill, and we knew the soldiers were coming. So we held the noses of our ponies that they might not whinny at the soldiers' horses. The decoys came back, some walking and leading their horses so that the soldiers would think they were worn out. The soldiers on horseback followed, shooting. When they came to the flat at the bottom of the hill, the fighting began all at once. . . . The soldiers were falling all the while they were fighting back up the hill.[39]

Oglala warrior American Horse remembered that he "ran his horse directly at Fetterman at full speed, knocking him over. He jumped on the army commander and cut his throat with his knife. Captain Brown was killed by a small pistol ball to his left temple."[40] The soldiers "fought very hard until not one of them was alive. . . . Dead men and horses and wounded Indians were scattered all the way up the hill, and their blood was frozen, for a storm had come up and it was very cold and getting colder all the time." The Indians "left all the dead lying there, for the ground was solid, and we picked up our wounded and started back."[41]

Red Cloud had led the opposition to the forts along the Bozeman Trail, and American Horse attested that "Red Cloud was there" at the fight known as the Hundred in the Hand. "I saw him before the fight, I saw him after the fight." White Face, Rocky Bear, and Red Fly also stated that Red Cloud was at the scene.[42]

Fetterman and his command were entirely wiped out. For those inside Fort Phil Kearny, the night of December 21, 1866, was a fearful and tragic episode. The soldiers laid the bodies wherever they could find room—in a spare ward of the hospital, in two hospital tents, and in a double cabin. Troopers donated their best uniforms to dress the dead. They dug a mass grave fifty feet long and seven feet deep, but it was so cold they could work only in fifteen-minute shifts. Soldiers and civilians alike pulled out or cut off arrows and carefully joined bodies together. They numbered and arranged a long line of pine coffins near the hospital, recording both the names of the dead and the location of their coffins in case of future reburial.[43]

Carrington penned a frantic message and an urgent repetition of his plea for men, horses, and arms. "Expedition now with my force impossible. . . . I have had today a fight unexampled in Indian warfare. My loss is ninety-four (94) killed. . . . I need prompt reinforcements and repeating arms. I am sure to have, as before reported, an active winter, and must have men and arms."[44] Portugee Phillips and William Baily volunteered to ride through the night to the telegraph station at Laramie to send the news. They rode through snow-covered plains to Fort Laramie, arriving during the Christmas Ball, and the officers' celebration was no more.[45]

The annihilation of the soldiers by Indians hit the country hard. There had been nothing like this in the West since the Alamo. General Sherman could not understand how the soldiers had suffered such a defeat. Debate raged across the country in newspapers and in general stores. Those in the chain of command did not want to reveal how they had ignored Carrington's pleas for soldiers, ammunition, and horses.

Many continued to disagree with Jim Bridger's estimate that there were thousands of Indians gathered in defiance. Very few were talking about the folly of the original decision to support the Bozeman Trail over the safer Bridger Trail.

But Margaret Carrington concluded that the events unfortunately affirmed "the value and integrity of Major Bridger and his statements."[46]

President Johnson upbraided Secretary of War Stanton, who came after General Grant, who leaned on General Sherman, who could not get any information from Brigadier General Cooke due to the intense snow. Cooke turned on Colonel Carrington, and Carrington put the blame on Captain Fetterman. Over the years Fetterman has been falsely criticized by many historians and writers, including the Carringtons. (Colonel Carrington, his wife Margaret, and his second wife, Frances Grummond Carrington, wrote descriptions of the events that impugned Fetterman).[47] But in truth a raft of poor decisions led to the horrific loss of lives.

Bridger had tried to avert a war by blazing the Bridger Trail, but the army chose the Bozeman Trail instead. Against Bridger's recommendations, the army built an elaborate fort at Phil Kearny miles away from a source of timber. Overconfident officers disregarded Bridger's hard-earned advice on how to fight Indians. This latter, fatal error was repeated ten years later by George Armstrong Custer, close to the same place and by the same Indian decoy tactic.

One soldier summarized it succinctly: "James Bridger was with us all the summer of 1866 up until late in the fall. If Colonel Carrington and the officers had followed the advice of Bridger I do not think there would have been nearly as many of our men killed. He told the officers not to follow the Indians and to send more men on escort duty, but they thought he was old and did not know anything about Indian warfare."[48]

32

"THE CROWS WOULD NOT PERMIT BRIDGER TO BE ENDANGERED"
1867–1868

In December 1866 Bridger and the others at Fort C. F. Smith were unaware of the tragedy at Fort Phil Kearny. Blizzard conditions and the threat of another Indian attack continued to paralyze and isolate the three posts on the Bozeman Trail. A week after the fight, the Crows came to Fort C. F. Smith with the news that the Sioux alliance had killed ninety-seven men at Phil Kearny and mutilated their bodies, even cutting off the soldiers' noses and storing them in a buffalo robe. Another Crow came the next day, reporting that 1,500 Indians took part in the battle.[1]

Lt. Col. Innis Palmer, commander at Fort Laramie, reported to Omaha on January 2, 1867, that eleven different bands of Indians had joined together in the attack. Palmer shared the startling news that "Fort C. F. Smith was to be attacked boldly, but the Crows were living near there and Bridger was there, and the Crows would not permit Bridger to be endangered, and so the expedition failed."[2]

The soldiers at C. F. Smith were worried that the Crows might join with the Sioux. "The Crow are in a quandary about the Sioux," wrote Lt. George Templeton within ten days of Fetterman's defeat. "They have received orders from them to leave our vicinity and they are afraid to disobey, and yet would like to remain and help the whites."[3] There had been no mail at C. F. Smith since Bridger had arrived six weeks earlier, and he was worried about the lack of news from the other forts.

The thermometer plunged to 23 degrees below zero. Then it reached 38 below. But that did not stop a Crow man named Iron Bull from walking past the commander's house every morning with an ax so he could chop a hole in the ice of the Bighorn River for his daily bath.[4] The soldiers were in a precarious position, having about two hundred men and very few provisions; they had to boil grain meant for the animals just to stay alive.

On February 2, 1867, Bridger and others were excited to see twenty-two-year-old John Richard (pronounced Reshaw) and his men arrive with two wagons from Virginia City carrying potatoes and butter. John was the nephew of Rosalie and Susan Richard, who had cared for Bridger's daughters in St. Charles. The fort had not enjoyed fresh vegetables for some time and had not even a pound of flour. Their hardtack was nearly exhausted and mostly inedible. Capt. Nathaniel Kinney bought all that he could and agreed to buy as much as ten more wagonloads of flour.[5]

As the only guide at Fort C. F. Smith, Bridger was pleased to see Mitch Boyer arrive with Richard. Boyer was twenty-eight, the son of a French Canadian trapper and a Santee Sioux woman. A superb scout, he was said to be a protégé of Bridger's. The army hired Boyer as an additional guide at five dollars a day.[6]

Five days later two couriers arrived from Phil Kearny with the fort's first mail in months, including official confirmation of what had happened on December 21. The road between C. F. Smith and Phil Kearny was now open, and it was vital that Captain Kinney send Bridger's and Boyer's assessment of Indian strength to Phil Kearny. The two guides listed twelve Indian bands with a total of 2,270 lodges, including 490 Oglala lodges, 430 Miniconjou lodges, and 300 Hunkpapa lodges. By mid-March 1,800 lodges of Sioux were camped within thirty-five miles of Fort C. F. Smith waiting for the weather to moderate.[7]

On April 8 Colonel Palmer at Fort Laramie wrote an urgent message to C. F. Smith asking to hear from Bridger immediately. "I think it highly important that some of the friendly Crows who know of the circumstances . . . should come down [to Laramie]. They will be liberally paid for so doing. I very much hope that Mr. Bridger will come down as I fancy that he could give more real information than any man in the Country."[8]

Knowing Bridger was sixty-two and had some physical limitations, Palmer added, "If he could come as far as Fort Phil Kearny on horseback, he could obtain [a wagon] there to bring him here, and I would see that he was provided with comfortable conveyance. If Mr. Bridger cannot come, will you please get all the information you can from him and give everything you can to throw light on the subject."⁹ Hearing from Bridger and the Crows "will be worth more than any statement the Commissioners are able to get in this part of the country."

Despite Palmer's urging, the Crows and therefore Bridger did not go to Fort Phil Kearny until June. Meanwhile Boyer went to Phil Kearny and on his return in the first week of May, he learned from the Crows that the Sioux were gathering with the Arapahos and Gros Ventres on the Powder to dance the Sundance. They were planning a "war of extermination against the whites" that included a major attack on Fort C. F. Smith in June.¹⁰

Congress demanded answers regarding the Fetterman Fight and the continued unrest, and President Johnson and Department of the Interior established a Joint Indian Commission to investigate.¹¹ With a scribe's help, Bridger wrote a detailed letter to the *Army and Navy Journal* dated May 5, 1867, which was published June 29.

> In June last a so-called treaty was made at Fort Laramie. . . . I . . . told the commissioners that the treaty would not amount to anything, but that all the Indians wanted was to receive presents and procure a supply of powder and lead, and then they would take to the war path, and would plunder trains and murder emigrants going over the road. . . . None of the Cheyennes, Arapahoe, or principal Sioux chiefs who live in the country through which the road runs signed the treaty.
>
> The Indians had been hanging around the fort every day, stealing stock on every opportunity, attacking the trains going to the woods, and even stealing up at night and shooting men connected with passing trains. . . . The intention was to attack Fort Phil Kearny first, and if they were successful to then attack Fort. C. F. Smith. At the present time the entire tribe of Northern Sioux are collecting on Powder River, below the mouth of Little Powder River, and their avowed intention is to make a vigorous and determined attack on each of the three posts, and on all trains that may come along the road. . . .
>
> I have been in this country among these Indians nearly forty-five years, and am familiar with their past history, and my experience and knowledge of them is greater than can be gained by any commissioners during the sittings of any council that may be held. I know that these Indians will not respect any treaty until they have been whipped in it.¹²

On June 11 long-awaited supplies and reinforcements from Fort Laramie arrived at C. F. Smith, filling out the garrison to three companies. Bridger guided the return party to Fort Phil Kearny with orders to report to the command-ing officer of the Mountain District. Bridger blazed yet another cutoff on their journey east, creating a new route for cavalry and light wagons. His cutoff left the emigrant road about two miles south of the present-day Montana state line and rejoined the route at the base of what would be called Fetterman Ridge or Massacre Hill. The "Cutoff," as it was known, appeared on military maps that summer and was increasingly popular. Heavier wagons continued to use the older route.[13]

On their way to Fort Phil Kearny, Bridger's column passed 121 lodges of Crows and 9 lodges of Nez Percé. Bridger arrived at the fort on June 16 and met with John Kinney, a member of the Joint Indian Commission, to advise him how to keep the Crows friendly.[14] When five lodges of Crow Indians arrived at Phil Kearny, the Sioux quickly stole all forty-three of their horses. The day after Bridger arrived, the Sioux tried to decoy soldiers out of the fort and into an ambush, but the soldiers were not fooled by the trick.[15] By June 21 the number of friendly Crows at Phil Kearny had grown to 1,800.

Alson Ostrander, recently discharged from the army, remembered meeting Bridger for the first time in the sutler's store at Fort Phil Kearny.

> When I first saw him he was tilted back in a chair with one arm on the counter. His once light-colored hat, now dingy and smoky, was pulled down so that it hid nearly half his face. His face, tanned by Wyoming winds, was somewhat wrinkled, and he wore a stubby beard. His square-set jaw and his keen eyes showed real character and intelligence.
>
> Nearly everyone who came in said, "Hello, Jim!" or "Howdy, Jim!" and he replied, "How!" or merely nodded his head in acknowledgement. So I knew this was old Jim Bridger, the most noted plainsman, scout, trapper, and guide in the Rocky Mountains.[16]

While Colonel Palmer and Commissioner Kinney treasured the wisdom of Jim Bridger, Col. John Smith, the new commander of the Mountain District, protested Bridger's transfer to Phil Kearny. "He is not needed here, one guide for this post being enough." On September 17 Smith wrote he had twenty mounted men for scouting, and "I pay no heed to rumors about attacks on posts, except to put the Post in good condition as possible for a fight."[17]

The commander was wrong to think there would be no attacks. The Sioux raided near Fort Phil Kearny on July 12, 17, and 19. Then on August 2 more than a thousand Sioux attacked a small group of woodcutters from the fort. Fortunately, the soldiers now had new .50-caliber Springfield breech-loading rifles and were able to hold them off, losing only three men. The battle became known as the Wagon Box Fight. Indian losses at the fight were considerable.[18]

A day earlier hundreds of Cheyennes had attacked the haymakers around Fort C. F. Smith, perhaps emboldened because Bridger had left that fort. The Indians boxed in the men and forced them into a desperate eighty-four-hour fight. They killed three men and wounded three. But these soldiers were also armed with the new Springfield repeating rifles, and the bulk of the party survived against overwhelming odds.[19]

Bridger received a temporary discharge in September 1867 to "recuperate his enfeebled condition."[20] He had lived frugally, hardly touching his pay, and post records showed he was due a balance of $2,730 as of June 30, 1867.[21] On November 16 the *Kansas City Advertiser* noted that he was in town and gave a brief update of his recent role a guide.[22]

After a rest Bridger returned to Fort Laramie. He was always welcome at the officers' clubroom, and he spent considerable time on the double-deck veranda at Old Bedlam, which housed the officers. This had become home to him. He bunked in the sutler store building along with employees John Hunton, John Boyd, and Hopkins Clark. He also made a few trips to Cheyenne and Fort D. A. Russell for the army, none of them over ten days.[23]

With the rapid completion of the Union Pacific Railroad, the United States didn't need the Bozeman Trail anymore. Red Cloud sent word that he would stop his war if Forts Phil Kearny and C. F. Smith were abandoned. In May 1868 the United States agreed, promising to leave the Powder River country. Red Cloud and his people were the only Indians to win a war against the U.S. government in its near hundred-year history. Unfortunately, the Crows, who had remained friendly to the whites, ended up having their land reduced from thirty-eight million acres to eight million acres in the 1868 Laramie Treaty.[24]

Bridger guided three companies building a road from Fort Fetterman to Medicine Bow in May 1868. It was a direct road meant for summer use but was unusable during winter snows.[25] At the same time, a treaty gathering was planned at Fort Bridger with the Shoshone and Bannock Indians, and Gen. John Sanborn wrote to the superintendent of Indian affairs at Fort Bridger, F. H. Head, "Do you desire the assistance of Mr. Bridger. If so we will Send him at once to you."[26] Head said that was unnecessary and added that one of their primary concerns was feeding the Indians who came to the peace treaty.

Bridger may have later expressed some concerns about the results of that treaty, though the details are not known. In January 1869 James Van Allen Carter, an interpreter for Superintendent Head, wrote, "I am quite fearful that Major B's influence is not in the interests of the indians upon other matters. He is much dissatisfied with the treaty made here in July last & has, I have heard, used his influence to awaken opposition to it upon the part of the settlers in their country."[27]

The army hired Bridger from May 23 to July 21, 1868, to guide those troops closing the forts on the Bozeman Trail.[28] May 23 was also the day that Bridger's old friend Kit Carson died in his home a few miles from the former site of Bent's Fort in southern Colorado. Carson, fifty-eight, had been heartbroken over the recent death of his wife, and that may have contributed to his death from heart disease. The apprentice who had run away from saddle-making to become one of the most celebrated scouts in U.S. history never forgot his trapping days with Old Gabe.[29]

To close the forts, Bridger was guiding Gen. Henry A. Morrow and a considerable number of soldiers and teamsters driving two hundred wagons. They would transfer useable property from the Bozeman Trail forts to Fort D. A. Russell near Cheyenne. Bridger's role, as usual, was keeping the soldiers safe from Indians, poisonous water, and other dangers. The army sold forty buildings at auction, along with 150 stoves, several wagons, and huge amounts of paint, nails, and shoes for both horses and men.[30]

In 1866 Bridger had been quite spry, but by 1868 his eyesight was showing signs of weakening—he was not always the expert shot he had been.[31] Yet teamster Finn Burnett remembered, "He seemed to never forget a trail that he had ever traveled, or the distance between streams or watering places, whether good water or bad, and also whether there was wood, and if there was good feed for the stock. So we always knew what sort of camp the one ahead would be, and what kind of country we would travel over in order to reach it."[32] On July 21, 1868, Bridger was "paid and discharged" by the army for the last time.[33]

SO MUCH FARTHER
1868–1881

The painful injury Jim Bridger sustained in 1864 when he was bucked by a mule continued to bother him. All the same, when he heard in 1868 that Gen. Philip Sheridan was preparing a winter campaign against the Indians south of the Arkansas River, he took a train on his own initiative and expense to speak to the general at Fort Hays, Kansas. Sheridan intended to "fall upon the savages relentlessly for in that season their ponies would be thin, and weak from lack of food."[1] The general was set on a harsh winter campaign, even if it ended with the "utter annihilation of these Indians."[2]

Bridger met with Sheridan as he had with General Dodge, hoping to stop the army from making a foolish mistake. He told Sheridan, "You can't hunt Indians on the plains in winter, for blizzards don't respect man or beast."[3] Sheridan went ahead with his plan anyway, and he seemed to be pleased that "Mr. James Bridger, the famous scout and guide of earlier days," made a special effort "to discourage the project. Bridger even went so far as to come out . . . to dissuade me."[4]

Sheridan left Fort Hays on November 15, 1868. On the first night out, a blizzard struck them so hard it carried away their tents. Sheridan reported: "Shivering from wet and cold, I took refuge under a wagon and there spent such a miserable night that, when at last the morning came, the gloomy predictions of Old Man Bridger and others rose up before me with greatly increased force."[5]

Sheridan's command included Lt. Col. George Armstrong Custer, who in the previous year had been court-martialed and suspended for a year for misconduct and mistreatment of soldiers. With rampant ambition and carelessness, on November 27 Custer led seven hundred men in a brutal attack on Black Kettle's Southern Cheyenne village on the Washita River, killing over a hundred men, women, and children, including Black Kettle and his wife Medicine Woman Later.[6] For this Custer was again put under court-martial, this time for not properly assessing the strength of the enemy and for abandoning a fellow officer and eighteen of his men.

Bridger didn't want retirement. In February 1869, a month shy of his sixty-fifth birthday, Bridger asked his old friend Robert Campbell to sponsor his application to be Indian agent to the Crows. He was certainly experienced in Crow culture, and the assignment would take him back to the West he loved. He had proven at Fort Bridger that he could manage the distribution of food, supplies, and clothing, and he could help the Crows when they dealt with other Indians or dishonest whites. Robert's brother, Hugh, called on General Nichols and General Randolph Marcy and told Bridger that Marcy promised to "do all he can to have you appointed. . . . The officers here are all favourable to you. But the appointment does not belong to them."[7]

Robert Campbell wrote to General Sherman, commander of all U.S. forces, asking him to use his influence to procure Bridger's appointment. Campbell thought highly of Bridger and remembered, "Just 40 years ago, we passed the winter together in the village of the Crow Indians, on Wind River." Campbell made his case to Sherman in a careful and logical manner. "Politicians who know nothing about the Indians . . . have done much to cause our Indian Wars. James Bridger is the well known Guide, who has been in the employ of the U.S. Gov. for many years, and is well known to all the Army Officers who have visited the Rocky Mountains."[8]

Sherman formally approved Bridger's nomination on the "Presidential Applicant" form from army headquarters on March 19, 1869, and referred it to the secretary of the interior.[9] Campbell relayed the news to Bridger, stating, "We firmly believe that if we succeed, we will have given to the country the best appointment that can be made of a first class Indian Agent." But then the news came that "the Indian Commission deemed it imprudent to recommend any one for office in the Indian Department. . . . There will be no agent appointed (except Quakers) [or] Army officers."[10]

In his memoirs Sherman specifically recalled Bridger in his discussion about Western campfires as a source of "living radiant truth." After mentioning Kit Carson, the Bent brothers, and others, he concluded, "Bridger always at a campfire carried off the palm." Then Sherman told of Bridger's story of the petrified forests of Yellowstone.[11]

In a private letter, General Sherman quoted Robert Campbell in stating that Bridger was "a man of the strictest integrity and truthfulness." Sherman knew Bridger was also a consummate storyteller. "Nothing delighted the trappers . . . more than after supper to sit round the camp-fire, each trying to outdo the others in his tales of fights with Indians, bears, and buffaloes, and Jim's reputation stood high for this sort of romancing."[12]

In 1869 Albert Wachsman petitioned the secretary of war for payment of the ten-year lease for Fort Bridger. A lawyer followed up on the Bridger family claim in 1873, stating that Bridger was robbed of property valued at more than $100,000, which was a gross exaggeration. This pursuit of compensation for the army's use of the Fort Bridger site continued long after Bridger's death, although with lesser claims of $10,000. On January 24, 1889, Congress finally authorized payment of $6,000 to the Bridger family "for the Relief of the Heirs of Jim Bridger, deceased." Ironically, the payment was not for the lease of Bridger's land or property but for improvements to the property: namely the stone wall that had been built by the Mormons.[13]

At home in Westport Bridger relied on his two daughters, Virginia and Mary Elizabeth. It was a "great place for dances and neighbors often gathered there for parties and holidays" and Mary Elizabeth taught dance steps.[14] In August 1870 Virginia and Mary Elizabeth hosted the wedding of John Brum and Elizabeth Spaulding at the Bridger house.[15] Virginia and Albert lived in Westport, looking after Bridger's store at 504 Westport Road and operating Wachsman's Hall on the second floor, where Felix sometimes tended bar.[16]

There are varying accounts of Bridger's home/s. As previously stated, he had purchased 287 acres at Indian Creek–Dallas in February 1855, and he authorized Josiah Watts to build a house for him in July of that year. This may have been the large frame house often referred to. Alternately, there are traditions that Bridger's grand house was built in the 1860s with lumber from a house that a man named William Bernard had dismantled.[17]

Bridger sold many of his properties between 1866 and 1872: in 1866 he sold one of his New Santa Fe properties; in 1871 he sold three properties, including the Bridger store; and in 1872 he sold two more.[18] On April 8, 1872, Bridger deeded his farm, 287.5 acres, to Virginia, which was the total acreage he had purchased there in 1855. Bridger described Virginia's payment as "One Dollar and love and affection I bear towards her as my daughter."[19]

As he grew older, Bridger retained his frontier ways, squatting on his heels and rarely sitting in a chair if a stump or a rail was handy. When he visited the Vasquez family, he usually climbed up on the fence. He was proud of his apple orchard and sent bushels of apples to his neighbors. When someone asked Bridger how his crops were doing, he would reply, "Perfect damn failure! Perfect damn failure!"[20]

Bridger lived his final thirteen years in Westport, spending many days on his long veranda. Occasionally a young newspaper reporter would visit, seeking to delight readers with a look back into the Old West. They almost always doubted his stories about Yellowstone. "Called me the damndest liar ever lived," Bridger would swear.[21]

Indigenous people had been in Yellowstone for centuries. Many trappers saw Yellowstone at the same time Bridger did. But it was Bridger more than anyone else who spread word of its wonders and shared its little-believed secrets with travelers, curiosity seekers, engineers, cartographers, and scientists. In a very real sense, Jim Bridger was the grandfather of Yellowstone National Park, having described it to Stansbury, Gunnison, De Smet, Raynolds, and Hayden. These officers, scientists, and missionaries all recorded his observations in their reports or letters; Raynolds declared that Yellowstone was "the most interesting unexplored district in our widely expanded country."[22]

In the 1860s and early 1870s there were a few attempts to explore Bridger's Yellowstone. In 1866, when he was in Virginia City, Montana, Bridger described to Nathaniel Langford the river that flowed so rapidly from a descending ledge that the water was "warm at the bottom." Bridger also told Langford that "he had seen a column of water as large as his body, spout as high as the flagpole in Virginia City, which was about sixty (60) feet high." Langford was part of an exploratory party in 1870, and when he actually felt warmth under his feet in the middle of a stream, he excitedly exclaimed, "Here is the River which Bridger said was hot at the bottom."[23]

Ferdinand Hayden led the first federally funded geological survey of Yellowstone in 1871, joined by Thomas Moran, who painted the fantastic landscapes, and William Henry Jackson, who photographed them. Their effusive reports soon led to petitions to Congress. On March 1, 1872, Yellowstone National Park was established, the first national park in the world.

Bridger must have taken satisfaction when his "lies" were proven to be true. In fact, in May 1879 the *Kansas City Journal* printed an apology to Bridger, which must have been a thrill for his children to see. Editor and publisher Robert Van

Horn had "heard from Bridger's own lips his account of those wonders and had written it out for publication, but had suppressed it because some of his friends laughed at it as utterly incredible."[24] When a lecturer spoke about Yellowstone before the Kansas City Academy of Sciences, Van Horn remembered how he had killed his story about Bridger thirty years earlier, which led to his public apology.

In 1874 famed photographer and artist William Henry Jackson drew a charcoal sketch of Bridger on a heavy, matte-surfaced paper. The image Jackson used as a base for his drawing was an 1857 photograph of Bridger taken in St. Louis, perhaps when Bridger was visiting Robert Campbell.[25] Jackson's portrait of Bridger was exhibited at the 1876 Philadelphia Centennial Exposition to celebrate the hundredth anniversary of the Declaration of Independence. By 1886 the portrait was at the Smithsonian.[26]

Felix Bridger was said to have served in Texas under Custer.[27] In 1876 George Armstrong Custer and over two hundred men were lured to their death at the Little Bighorn, much the same way that Fetterman had been decoyed in 1866. Among the fallen was Bridger's friend and protégé Mitch Boyer, who "bore the reputation of being, next to the celebrated Jim Bridger, the best guide in the country."[28]

Twenty-five days later, on July 19, Felix died at the age of thirty-four.[29] Jim Bridger was seventy-two, and his son's death undoubtedly reminded him of the time they had laid his own mother in the grave in 1816, followed quickly by his brother and then his father. He may have thought of Felix's mother and the two other two children they had together: Mary Ann, who died in the aftermath of the Whitman Massacre, and Mary Josephine, who had died at school in St. Charles, Missouri. He would have remembered Chipeta, his Ute wife who had died in 1848, and Mary, his Shoshone wife, who had died in 1859. He had three remaining children: Chipeta's daughter Virginia, who was twenty-eight; and Mary's offspring, Mary Elizabeth, twenty-three, and William, nineteen.

By the late 1870s Bridger's eyesight had faded, but he still recognized people by the sound of their voices. He tried to combat the loss with glasses. He must have fingered his sterling silver watch and listened to the chimes that played every quarter hour, a handy device for someone who could no longer see.[30] Made in 1867 by the National Watch Company, it had roman numerals and a hunters-case with a spring-hinged metal cover.

Charles Harrington, who lived directly across from Bridger, described something of his final years: "Daughter Jennie keeps house for him," his daughter Mary Elizabeth "visits her father's room several times each night to make sure he is covered up and comfortable," and his son William "resides on his portion of the farm." Bridger "frequently visits the little town of Sante Fe" and "feels his way with a heavy staff with a club on the end." Visitors "come from far and near to hear him spin his wonderful yarns about the West and the events of his thrilling life. . . . He can still out talk any seven men. . . . He is as anxious to live West as ever, and declares he would not stay East a day if he could only have the use of his eyes."[31]

Even with his impaired vision, Bridger still liked to ride a roan horse with a white face and two white feet. He would rise from his stoop on the veranda and call to Virginia, "I wish you would go saddle Old Ruff for me. I feel like riding around the farm." Bridger would ride off, letting Ruff pick the way, his dog Sultan alongside. He would go out to the fields, kneel on the ground, and feel how high the wheat was with his hands. If they got lost, Bridger would wait atop the horse, while Sultan ran home barking.[32]

At times he would say to Virginia, "I would give anything in the world if I could see some of the old Army officers once more, to have a talk with them of olden times; but I will not be able to see any of my old time mountain friends any more. I know that my time is near. I feel that my health is failing me very fast, and see that I am not the same man I used to be."[33]

Children loved to come and sit with him on his porch. He sometimes used colorful language, and Lizzie Watts Cummins remembered she overheard Bridger cuss his horse when she was about five. Her older brother Edgar later talked to his pony that way and got a "good tanning" from his mother.[34] Bridger had grandchildren by then, including Virginia's daughter, Louise, who was born in 1875.[35]

"I shall always remember Bridger's kindly, blue-gray eyes," remembered a woman who was ten or twelve when she knew him.

> I would often go over to see Mr. Bridger. He was always very hospitable, and liked to have the children of the neighborhood come to see him. His son, Bill, played the violin, and the whole neighborhood used to come to dance at the Bridger home. I often saw him riding on horseback or walking over his land, feeling his way along with his stick, accompanied by two or three of his fox hounds. If they started a rabbit, the Old Man would get greatly excited, and halloo the hounds onto the chase.[36]

Even as Bridger's health deteriorated, the chocolate river nearby called Missouri continued its course to the sea. Its waters still flowed down from Bridger's fabled Yellowstone and picked up snowmelt from the Winds and the Bighorns.

It swept up the flow of the Tongue and the Powder, the Laramie and the Platte. It flowed past Westport and on to St. Louis, the place Bridger had left for the mountains fifty-nine years earlier.

The Missouri joined the Mississippi there, and the great river flowed past the American Bottom where his mother, father, and brother had died and where he had worked for Philip Creamer. The waters from the mountains and the muddy Mississippi entered the Gulf of Mexico, where the flow was picked up by the Gulf Stream, moving around Florida and up the Atlantic seaboard past Virginia, eventually turning eastward toward England where his family had come from centuries earlier.

Jim Bridger died on July 17, 1881. He was buried in the Watts's cemetery, his grave marked with a modest tombstone. Watts remembered the burial brought together a fairly large crowd for a country funeral. He didn't remember a minister, "just a friendly neighbor to say a few words and a prayer."[37] Remnants of Bridger's apple orchards can still be found on his former property.

In his final years Jim Bridger would frequently sit on his veranda, resting his chin on his cane with his face toward the West. Nearly blind, suffering from some internal rupture, and afflicted with other infirmities, he liked to talk of his life on the plains. He would often say, "I wish I was back there among the mountains again. You can see so much farther in that country."[38]

EPILOGUE

Jim Bridger's obituary appeared in newspapers across the county, featuring glowing (and sometimes inaccurate) descriptions of his life. One obituary printed several times incorrectly credited him with being a guide for Frémont. For the next several decades many people wrote about when and where they had met Bridger (even if they hadn't).

Wyatt Earp claimed to have talked with Bridger about 1863 or 1864 when Earp was sixteen and traveling with a wagon train in Utah led by his brother.[1] Writer Phillip Rollins claimed that he asked Bridger in 1874 how scouts could survive such dangerous times, and Bridger told him good scouts "preserved their scalps by tying them to their brains."[2]

Three of Bridger's seven children survived him. William, the youngest, was twenty-three at the time of his father's death, and he lived in a log house near present-day Wornall Road and 103rd Street. He died of consumption on July 12, 1887, at the age of twenty-nine, and was buried alongside Felix at the Stubbins Watts farm.[3]

Mary Elizabeth was twenty-eight when Bridger died, and on November 9, 1881, just months after her father's death, she married Abraham Carrol. They lived on the farm at Wornall Road and 103rd Street and had eight children. Mary Elizabeth died on September 19, 1922, from heart trouble.[4] Long after Jim Bridger was gone, his family treasured their memories of him. Mary Elizabeth's descendants recounted a family tradition that her father's Shoshone name was Peejatowahooten (Pe-ja-to-wa-hooton), meaning Mysterious Medicine Man.[5]

Virginia was thirty-two when her father died. Within two years her husband Albert Wachsman was also dead, and she soon remarried. She worked as a seamstress, among many other jobs, and she later receive a plot of land on the Uintah reservation, which she sold for $500 to help support herself in Kansas City.[6]

In 1923 the Famous Players–Laskey Corporation and Paramount Pictures Corporation created a film titled *The Covered Wagon*, based on Emerson Hough's book by the same name. Virginia was horrified that the popular movie inaccurately portrayed her father as a heavy drinker who was living with two Indian women at the same time. She exclaimed, "Pa was never like that."

Virginia filed a million-dollar suit against the movie company as well as another suit for the same amount against Sam S. Shubert Theater Corporation. News of the lawsuit spread across the country, and historians gathered testimonials to counter the impressions made by the movie. The cases were dismissed because a civil libel suit could not be filed for damages to a deceased person.[7]

Many years after her father's death, Virginia kept his glasses on a center table or dresser. A friend of Virginia's, Minnie Brown, recalled, "I have often put them on when in a playful mood with her and I call[ed] myself her Pa—I called her Chiptia [Chipeta] as that was her mother's name. Her father called her that if he wanted her to hurry or obey him when she was a child."[8] Virginia died March 7, 1933, at the age of eighty-four.

Grenville M. Dodge believed that Jim Bridger was the most distinguished of all the mountain men and scouts in the West, yet he saw that his grave was little-visited, and there was no substantial record of Bridger's life. In 1904 Dodge organized a memorial service and a new burial site and monument for Jim Bridger at Mount Washington Cemetery in Kansas City.[9] Dodge wrote a twenty-seven-page tribute to his friend and onetime guide, who "was without an equal." He concluded, "Unquestionably, Bridger's claims to remembrance rest upon the extraordinary part he bore in the exploration of the west."[10]

Eight-year-old Marie Louise Lightle, Virginia's granddaughter and Jim's great-granddaughter, pulled the cord that unveiled the granite memorial. The marker was revealed in strong inclement weather, "which kept all but the determined persons away from the unveiling"[11] The monument remains on view today in Mount Washington Cemetery.

Bridger was among the first Western heroes proposed to have his likeness carved at what would become Mount Rushmore. In 1923 South Dakota state historian Doane Robinson had the idea to commission colossal statues carved in the granite formations in the Black Hills. In a letter to a sculptor, Robinson described what the monument might look like: "Near the summit is a little park through which the highway passes. . . . It is studded with column after column of these pinnacles and in my imagination I can see all the heroes of the Old West peering out from them; Lewis and Clark, Fremont, Jed Smith, Bridger, Sa-kaka-wea, Red Cloud, and in an equestrian statue [Buffalo Bill] Cody and the overland mail."[12] The concept was later changed to recognize presidents Washington, Jefferson, Lincoln, and Theodore Roosevelt.

Today Bridger's name is preserved at Fort Bridger State Historic Site and the Bridger Wilderness within the Bridger-Teton National Forest. His name graces mountains, trails, lakes, a canyon, towns, streets, creeks, schools, monuments, an energy plant—and at one time a liberty ship. The Museum of the Mountain Man in Pinedale, Wyoming, and the Montana Historical Society Museum each have a Jim Bridger rifle in their collections.

Bridger has been recognized in popular culture over the years as well, including a ballad by Johnny Horton and songs by singer/songwriter Bobby Bridger. Bridger has also been featured as a character in television's *Wagon Train* and *Death Valley Days* and in the movies *Bridger* (1976), *Kit Carson and the Mountain Men* (1977), *Tomahawk* (1951), and most notably *The Revenant* (2015). In the movie *Jeremiah Johnson* (1972), Will Geer's character says he is "blood kin to the grizz that bit Jim Bridger's ass," and in *Inglourious Basterds* (2009), Brad Pitt's character says, "I'm the direct descendant of the mountain man Jim Bridger. That means I got a little Injun in me."

Jim Bridger is often viewed as America's greatest frontier scout of his era. His knowledge of the West was uncanny, and his frontier survival skills were unparalleled. He could read the land at a moment's glance and recall thousands of miles of past trails in an encyclopedic recital. His contributions to Western exploration and history are enormous, though the details are often forgotten today.

He discovered Great Salt Lake when he was twenty and ran the Bad Pass rapids at twenty-one. He led Rocky Mountain fur trappers, including Kit Carson, throughout the West, and interpreted and mapped for the great Horse Creek Treaty of 1851. He built Fort Bridger on the Oregon and California trails and helped chart Bridger Pass and the Overland route that became the preferred route across the Rockies.

Bridger guided more trappers, emigrants, miners, engineers, scientists, and soldiers than any scout in American history. He was chief scout for noted cartographers and scientists such as Stansbury, Warren, Hayden, and Raynolds, and he guided major military expeditions for Johnston, Collins, Connor, and Carrington.

Equally significant, Bridger was a friend and ally to the Shoshone, Crow, Flathead, Nez Percé, and Ute Indians. He was widely respected by the Cheyennes, Sioux, Arapahos, and other indigenous peoples and could invariably treat with them to avoid conflict. He blazed the Bridger Trail and advocated for its use to try to prevent the bloody war with the Sioux, Cheyennes, and Arapahos that lasted from 1865 to 1868. When the Army foolishly selected the Bozeman Trail instead, he tried to protect the lives of soldiers who built their forts in Indian lands.

Bridger went west at eighteen and lived among the Indians and the mountains. He had a sense of family when he traveled with the fur brigades. Then he married and had his own family with the Flathead woman, Cora; the Ute woman, Chipeta; and the Shoshone woman, Mary. When he had to leave Fort Bridger, his only permanent home in the West, he settled in Westport, Missouri, but he also lived on the road as a scout for more than a dozen expeditions. When he wasn't guiding, he often found a bunk at forts Laramie, Phil Kearny, and C. F. Smith.

All of Bridger's life he searched for home. In that journey he found America and helped shape it.

NOTES

Chapter 1

1. Dodge, *James Bridger*, 1, names the parents "James and Schloe," while Chittenden, *American Fur Trade*, names them "William and Chloe," 1:255.

2. H. J. Clayton, *San Francisco Daily Alta California*, April 21, 1872.

3. *Native America: A State-by-State Historical Encyclopedia*, ed. Daniel S. Murphree (Boston: Greenwood, 2012), 436.

4. Ferguson, *Illinois in the War of 1812*, 55–56, 65–71.

5. Edmunds, *The Potawatomis*, 166–69.

6. Ferguson, *Illinois in the War of 1812*, 4, 13.

7. Ibid., 159, 43.

8. Stevens, "Illinois in the War of 1812," 69–70.

9. Ferguson, *Illinois in the War of 1812*, 20–21, 108, 199.

10. Ibid., 32, 10.

11. Ibid., 82–86, 158–59.

12. Philbrick, *Laws of Illinois Territory*, 25:177–78.

13. Dodge, *James Bridger*, 5.

14. Favour, *Old Bill Williams*, 50–55.

15. Marcy, *Army Life*, 404.

16. Schilling, "Chronology of Monks Mound," 14–28.

17. Hodge, *Handbook of American Indians*, 2:241.

18. Previous Bridger biographers, particularly J. Cecil Alter (*James Bridger* [1925] and *Jim Bridger* [1962]) and Stanley Vestal (1946), err in describing the youthful Bridger as suffering inferiority, loneliness, "tongue-tied timidity," and "frustrating shyness." No documentation supports Alter's suggestion that Bridger had a canoe that was later put

on the bow of Henry's keelboat ascending the upper Missouri. See Enzler, "Tracking Jim Bridger," 2–4.

19. Dodge, *James Bridger*, 5.

20. Ibid.

21. Ibid., 6.

22. *History of Madison County*, 124–25.

23. Reynolds, *Pioneer History of Illinois*, 295.

24. Johnson and Paul, *Philip Creamer*, 3.

25. Brackenridge, *Recollections*, 263.

26. Richard Graham to the secretary of war, St. Louis, September 20, 1816, in Carter, *Territorial Papers*, 17:396.

27. Richard Graham to acting secretary of war, St. Louis, April 7, 1817, ibid., 493–96.

28. Acting Secretary of War George Graham to Governor Edwards, March 26, 1817, ibid., 493–95.

29. Johnson and Paul, *Philip Creamer*, 5.

30. Edmunds, *The Potawatomis*, 225.

31. Carter, *Territorial Papers*, 17:434–36.

32. Ibid., 398–401.

33. Ferguson, *Illinois in the War of 1812*, 4, 207.

34. Receipt of U.S. Indian Agency to R. Graham, July 4, 1817, Graham Papers, Missouri History Museum Archives.

35. Dickson, "Joseph Dickson," Family History Library, Salt Lake City.

36. U.S. Census, 1820: Cahokia, St. Clair County, Ill., p. 135, NARA, Roll M33 12, image 132; burial records from Holy Family Catholic Church, Cahokia, Belleville Public Library, 34, 42, 46. Paul, "(Young) Old Jim," 5–11.

37. "[Ill.] State Capitol and Official State Symbols," 106, www.cyberdriveillinois.com /publications/handbook/statecapsym.pdf.

38. Reynolds, *Pioneer History of Illinois*, 279.

39. Ibid., 295.

40. White, "St. Louis," 9, Missouri Historical Society.

41. U.S. Census, 1820: Cahokia, St. Clair County, Ill., p. 136, NARA, Roll M33 12, image 133.

42. Johnson and Paul, *Philip Creamer*, 14–15.

43. Ibid., 8.

Chapter 2

1. Morgan, *West of William Ashley*, 1.

2. White, "St. Louis," 2, Missouri Historical Society.

3. Reynolds, *Pioneer History of Illinois*, 295.

4. Morgan, *West of William Ashley*, 3–4.

5. Receipt of U.S. Indian Agency to R. Graham, July 1817, Graham Papers, Missouri Historical Society, St. Louis.

6. Dodge, *James Bridger,* 6.

7. Clokey, *Ashley,* 35, 52, 64.

8. Morgan, *West of William Ashley,* 3–4.

9. Clyman, *Journal,* 9; Morgan, *West of William Ashley,* 4–5.

10. McDermott, *Early Histories of St. Louis,* 67–71.

11. Bonner, *Beckwourth,* 18–20, 541; Wilson, *Beckwourth,* 15.

12. White, "St. Louis," 5–7, Missouri Historical Society.

13. Morgan, *West of William Ashley,* 1.

14. Ibid., 6.

15. White, "St. Louis," 8, Missouri Historical Society.

16. McDermott, *Early Histories of St. Louis,* 67–71.

17. Morgan, *West of William Ashley,* 6–7.

18. Ibid., 3–4.

19. White, "St. Louis," 9, 6–7, Missouri Historical Society.

20. Ibid., 2.

21. Blair and Meine, *Mike Fink,* 179–80.

22. Mark St. John Erickson, "Decrypting Old Bones: Archaeologists Investigate St. Luke's Church-Floor Grave for the Information Hidden in A Wealthy Colonist's Bones," *Isle of Wight Daily Press,* January 30, 2007.

23. Letter to John Hunton, Hebard Collection, American Heritage Center, University of Wyoming, Laramie.

24. *History of Nodaway County,* 82.

25. Morgan, *Jedediah Smith,* 36.

26. Morgan, *West of William Ashley,* 248n205.

Chapter 3

1. Morgan, *West of William Ashley,* 7.

2. Catlin, *O-Kee-Pa,* 6–10.

3. Morgan, *West of William Ashley,* 70–72.

4. Chittenden, *American Fur Trade,* 1:250.

5. Clokey, *Ashley,* 63.

6. James, *Three Years,* 46.

7. Morgan, *West of William Ashley,* xxxvi.

8. Ibid., 40, 9–11.

9. Morgan, *Jedediah Smith,* 33.

10. Morgan, *West of William Ashley,* 40.

11. Ibid., 19, 15.

12. Morgan, *West of William Ashley,* 38–39; Hafen, "John H. Weber," 9:379, 383–84.

13. Landry, "Trappers' Cache," 22.

14. Victor, *River of the West,* 64–65; Bonner, *Beckwourth,* 62.

15. James, *Three Years,* 30–33.

16. Morgan, *Jedediah Smith,* 45.

17. Potts letter, July 16, 1826, in Frost, *Notes on General Ashley,* 57.

18. Ibid.

19. Potts letter, July 7, 1824, in Morgan, *West of William Ashley,* 40.

20. Ewers, *The Blackfeet,* 5–9, 45.

21. Ibid., 39, 46; "Madison Buffalo Jump State Park," Montana State Parks, accessed May 28, 2020, http://stateparks.mt.gov/first-peoples-buffalo-jump/.

22. De Smet, *Western Missions and Missionaries,* 84.

23. Morgan, *West of William Ashley,* 41, 70–72.

24. Ibid., 42.

25. Ibid., 70, 42.

Chapter 4

1. Blair and Meine, *Mike Fink,* 235–39, 181.

2. Clyman, *Journal,* 9–10; errors are in the original.

3. Morgan, *West of William Ashley,* 22.

4. Ibid., 25–27, 70–71.

5. Ibid., 25–27, 70–72.

6. Ibid., 45–46.

7. Ibid., 52.

8. Ibid., 53–55.

9. Ibid., 57–58.

10. Clokey, *Ashley,* 115.

11. Morgan, *West of William Ashley,* 11, 70.

12. Clyman, *Journal,* 22.

13. Morgan, *West of William Ashley,* 78.

14. Ibid., 68–69.

15. Clyman, *Journal,* 18–19.

16. Cooke, *Scenes and Adventures,* 139–51.

17. *St. Louis Enquirer,* June 7, 1824, qtd. in Morgan, *West of William Ashley,* 76.

18. Hall, "Missouri Trapper," 304–5.

19. Edmund Flagg Papers, Missouri Historical Society.

20. Flagg, "Adventures at the Head Waters," 326.

21. Enzler, "Tracking Jim Bridger," 8–14.

22. Jesse Applegate, "Hunted and Haunted: The Tragic Mystery in the Life of Old Jim Bridger." *Helena Independent,* October 13, 1882.

23. Chittenden, *American Fur Trade,* 2:694.

24. James Stevenson to James D. Butler, February 28, 1886, Butler Papers, Wisconsin State Historical Society Archives.

Chapter 5

1. Morgan, *West of William Ashley,* 68–69, 44, 238–39, 297n255.

2. Ibid., 84.

3. Clokey, *Ashley,* 132.

4. Denig, *Five Indian Tribes*, 152–53, 187.

5. Irving, *Captain Bonneville*, 122; Daniel Potts to Robert Potts, July 16, 1826, in Frost, *Notes on General Ashley*, 58.

6. Hafen, *Broken Hand*, 339.

7. Clyman, *Journal*, 37–38, 27–29.

8. Anderson, *Journals*, 387.

9. Morgan, *West of William Ashley*, 146.

10. Ferris, *Life in the Rocky Mountains*, 144.

11. Humfreville, *Twenty Years*, 445.

12. Chittenden, *American Fur Trade*, 2:770.

13. Irving, *Adventures of Bonneville*, 118; Bonner, *Life of Beckwourth*, 62.

14. Russell, *Journal of a Trapper*, 82.

15. Morgan, *Jedediah Smith*, 143, 400n11.

16. Potts letter, July 16, 1826, in Frost, *Notes on General Ashley*, 58.

17. Warren, *Report of Explorations*, 35–36.

18. Gen. Henry A. Morrow to James D. Butler, January 27, 1886, Records of the Office of the Chief of Engineers, Letters Received, 1871–86, NARA, RG 77, Entry 52.

19. *Rocky Mountain News*, May 15, 1861, in Anderson, *Journals*, 260.

20. Hafen, "Weber," 9:384.

21. Ogden, *Snake Country Journals*, xlii.

22. Morgan, *West of William Ashley*, 118.

23. Morgan, *Jedediah Smith*, 402–3.

24. Ogden, *Snake Country Journals*, 51, 234–35.

25. Ibid., xli.

26. Ogden, *Snake Country Journals*, 53, 234–35.

27. Caspar Collins to Catherine Collins, October 8, 1862, Caspar Collins Papers, American Heritage Center, University of Wyoming.

28. Morgan, *West of William Ashley*, 98, 100–104.

29. Ibid., 106.

30. Gowans, *Rocky Mountain Rendezvous*, 10–12.

31. Morgan, *West of William Ashley*, 118.

32. Ibid.

33. Clyman, *Journal*, 33.

34. Morgan, *West of William Ashley*, 126.

35. Morgan, *Jedediah Smith*, 172.

Chapter 6

1. Morgan, *West of William Ashley*, 129–30.

2. Ibid.

3. Bonner, *Beckwourth*, 77–79.

4. Ibid., 79.

5. Bearss, *Bighorn Canyon*, 37–38.

6. David, *Finn Burnett*, 200.

7. Bearss, *Bighorn Canyon*, 68.

8. Morgan, *West of William Ashley*, 296.

9. Ibid., 297.

10. Morgan, *Jedediah Smith*, 189.

11. Hafen, *Broken Hand*, 59.

12. Bonner, *Beckwourth*, 93–94; Hafen, *Broken Hand*, 60.

13. Ogden, *Snake Country Journals*, 146.

14. Victor, *River of the West*, 80.

15. Ferris, *Life in the Rocky Mountains*, 47–48, loosely quoting Byron's *Childe Harold's Pilgrimage*.

16. Bonner, *Beckwourth*, 93–98.

17. Ibid., 94.

18. Irving, *Adventures of Bonneville*, 114; Morgan, *West of William Ashley*, 304n313.

19. William Clayton, *Daily Record*, 272.

20. Frémont, *Expeditions*, 2:381–82. Wheat suggests this might be the Bruneau River, eighteen miles southwest of Mountain Home; see *TransMississippi West*, 2:136; Frémont-Smith-Gibbs map, https://collections.lib.uwm.edu/digital/collection/agdm/id/868/.

21. Bonner, *Beckwourth*, 107.

22. Morgan, *West of William Ashley*, 137–38.

23. Potts letter, July 16, 1826, in Frost, *Notes on General Ashley*, 60.

24. Morgan, *West of William Ashley*, 149–52.

25. Frost, *Notes on General Ashley*, 134; Morgan, *West of William Ashley*, xxiii.

Chapter 7

1. Daniel Potts to Robert Potts July 8, 1827 in Haines, *Yellowstone Story*, 1:41–42.

2. Mattes, *Colter's Hell*, 7; Hardee, *Pierre's Hole*, 11.

3. Haines, *Yellowstone Story*, 1:41–42.

4. De Smet, *Life, Letters and Travels*, 182.

5. Haines, *Yellowstone Story*, 1:41–42.

6. Ibid., 1:5.

7. Ibid., 1:38.

8. Mattes, *Colter's Hell*. 2.

9. Irving, *Adventures of Bonneville*, 9–10.

10. Campbell, *Narrative*, 26.

11. Sunder, *Bill Sublette*, 35. Sublette was also known as "Straight Walking Rain" and "Fate"; see Field, *Prairie and Mountain Sketches*, 96; Bonner, *Beckwourth*, 24.

12. Haines, *Yellowstone Story*, 1:41–42; Campbell, *Narrative*, 32.

13. Morgan, *Jedediah Smith*, 215.

14. Ibid., 232–33; Daniel Potts to Dr. Lukens, July 8, 1827, in Gowans, *Rocky Mountain Rendezvous*, 34.

15. Field, *Prairie and Mountain Sketches*, 65.

16. Campbell, *Narrative*, 41–42; Morgan, *Jedediah Smith*, 295; Sunder, *Bill Sublette*, 74.

17. Daniel Potts to Robert Potts, October 13, 1828, in Campbell, *Narrative*, 33–34, 54n35; Morgan, *Jedediah Smith*, 341–45.

18. Berry, *Majority of Scoundrels*, 228.

19. Gowans, *Rocky Mountain Rendezvous*, 42; Anderson, *Journals*, 272; Leonard, *Adventures*, 228; Morgan, *Jedediah Smith*, 305.

20. Campbell, *Narrative*, 37, 55n41; Gowans, *Rocky Mountain Rendezvous*, 56; Morgan, *Jedediah Smith*, 239–40, 268–69.

21. Morgan, *Jedediah Smith*, 307; Alter, *Jim Bridger*, 109. Alter mistakenly cites Meek's recollection of fall 1830 to document Bridger's presence in fall 1829.

22. Victor, *River of the West*, 77–79.

23. Morgan, *Jedediah Smith*, 309–10.

24. Victor, *River of the West*, 82.

25. Ibid., 83–85.

26. Ibid., 88, 280.

27. Walker and Hardee, "Phillip Covington," 35.

Chapter 8

1. Victor, *River of the West*, 89.

2. Sunder, *Bill Sublette*, 83.

3. Berry, *Majority of Scoundrels*, 254, 262–63.

4. Humphries, "(Peg-Leg) Smith," 323–24.

5. Ibid., 320.

6. Anderson, *Journals*, 312.

7. Hafen, *Broken Hand*, 87, 90–91.

8. Newell, *Memoranda*, 31.

9. Victor, *River of the West*, 97–98; Newell, *Memoranda*, 32.

10. Morgan, *West of William Ashley*, 193–94.

11. Newell, *Memoranda*, 32.

12. Victor, *River of the West*, 99–100.

13. Newell, *Memoranda*, 32.

14. Ferris, *Life in the Rocky Mountains*, 124; Gowans, *Rocky Mountain Rendezvous*, 70.

15. Morgan, *Jedediah Smith*, 329–30, 436.

16. Hafen, *Broken Hand*, 97–98.

17. Ferris, *Life in the Rocky Mountains*, 126.

18. Anderson, *Journals*, 274.

19. Roberts, *Kit Carson*, 54–55.

20. Ferris, *Life in the Rocky Mountains*, 89.

21. Waldman, *Dictionary of Native American Terminology*, 79.

22. Newell, *Memoranda*, 32.

23. Victor, *River of the West*, 103.

24. Ibid., 104–7.

25. Raynolds, *Report*, 96.

Chapter 9

1. Irving, *Adventures of Bonneville*, 50; Victor, *River of the West*, 107–8.
2. Ferris, *Life in the Rocky Mountains*, 178.
3. DeVoto, *Wide Missouri*, 24.
4. Leonard, *Adventures*, 219–20.
5. Victor, *River of the West*, 110–11.
6. John Wyeth, *Oregon*, 10–13, 24.
7. Berry, *Majority of Scoundrels*, 276, 297–300.
8. Hardee, *Pierre's Hole*, 187–88.
9. Irving, *Adventures of Bonneville*, 38–40.
10. Robert Campbell to Hugh Campbell, July 18, 1832, *Rocky Mountain Letters*, 42.
11. Ibid.
12. Leonard, *Adventures*, 71–72.
13. Irving, *Adventures of Bonneville*, 41.
14. Hardee, *Obstinate Hope*, 89.
15. Hafen, *Broken Hand*, 123–24.
16. Ibid.
17. Victor, *River of the West*, 131.
18. Ferris, *Life in the Rocky Mountains*, 176–77.
19. Irving, *Adventures of Bonneville*, 63.
20. Victor, *River of the West*, 133.
21. Southesk, *Saskatchewan and the Rocky Mountains*, 160–62.
22. Catlin, *Letters and Notes*, 1:30, 34, plate 14. Catlin describes him as a Piegan, but Southesk reported he was a Blood.
23. Southesk, *Saskatchewan and the Rocky Mountains*, 161; Victor, *River of the West*, 124-25.
24. Spring, *Caspar Collins*, 126.
25. Irving, *Adventures of Bonneville*, 64–65; Victor, *River of the West*, 133–34.
26. Hafen, *Broken Hand*, 124.
27. Nester, *Mountain Man*, 61; Hafen, *Broken Hand*, 124.
28. Southesk, *Saskatchewan and the Rocky Mountains*, 161.

Chapter 10

1. Newell, *Memoranda*, 32.
2. Victor, *River of the West*, 93.
3. Stansbury, *Exploration*, 250; Landry, "Hugh Glass," 10–13.
4. Hafen, *Broken Hand*, 126.
5. Anderson, *Journals*, 303, 313.
6. Larpenteur, *Forty Years*, 29, 25.
7. Anderson, *Journals*, 273
8. Ibid., 313–14.
9. Stewart, *Edward Warren*, 3.

10. Madsen, *Great Salt Lake*, 688–91.

11. Gowans, *Rocky Mountain Rendezvous*, 117–18.

12. Berry, *Majority of Scoundrels*, 348–49.

13. Hardee, *Obstinate Hope*, 365–66, 389.

14. Hafen, *Broken Hand*, 135–36.

15. Ibid., 136–37; Victor, *River of the West*, 158.

16. Lecompte, "John Hawkins," 4:141.

17. Gowans, *Rocky Mountain Rendezvous*, 118.

18. Barry, *Beginning of the West*, 251–52.

19. Hafen, *Broken Hand*, 136–37.

20. Carson, *Autobiography*, 33–37.

21. Pagnamenta, *Prairie Fever*, 27; Stewart, *Edward Warren*, v.

22. Stewart, *Edward Warren*, 429; Anderson, *Journals*, 354.

23. Stewart, *Edward Warren*, 429; Victor, *River of the West*, 141; Bonner, *Beckwourth*, 280.

24. Stewart, *Edward Warren*, 429.

25. Ibid., 2–3.

26. Carson, *Autobiography*, 39.

27. Hardee, *Hope Maintains*, 25–26.

28. Ibid., 46–47.

29. Alter, *Jim Bridger*, 145.

30. Townsend, *Narrative*, 149.

31. Hardee, *Hope Maintains*, 67–68.

32. Anderson, *Journals*, 109.

33. Ibid., 134–35, 138–39.

34. Ibid., 314.

35. Berry, *Majority of Scoundrels*, 397–98.

36. Gowans, *Rocky Mountain Rendezvous*, 118.

Chapter 11

1. Victor, *River of the West*, 164.

2. Hafen, *Broken Hand*, 142–43.

3. Irving, *Adventures of Bonneville*, 110.

4. Anderson, *Journals*, 152–53, 168–69; Marsh, *Four Years in the Rockies*, 70.

5. Victor, *River of the West*, 176.

6. Ibid., 176.

7. Alter, *James Bridger*, 518; Caesar, *Jim Bridger*, 162–63.

8. Anderson, *Journals*, 160–63; Victor, *River of the West*, 177.

9. Anderson, *Journals*, 160–63.

10. Farrar was the first person known to duel on Bloody Island, and he used pistols obtained from Creamer's gun works in 1810; see Johnson and Paul, *Philip Creamer*, 4.

11. Carson, *Autobiography*, 39–40; Newell, *Memoranda*, 33.

12. Enzler, "Otholoho," 60–65.

13. Marsh, *Four Years in the Rockies*, 70–75; Victor, *River of the West*, 141.

14. Victor, *River of the West*, 141

15. Marsh, *Four Years in the Rockies*, 73.

16. Carson, *Autobiography*, 42.

17. Hafen, *Broken Hand*, 148.

18. Anderson, *Journals*, 110, 128, 310.

19. Drury, *Marcus and Narcissa Whitman*, 1:64, 119, 122–24.

20. (Boise) *Idaho Statesman*, May 13, 1876.

21. Drury, *Marcus and Narcissa Whitman*, 1:84, 120, 123, 160.

22. (Boise) *Idaho Statesman*, May 13, 1876.

23. Parker, *Journey*, 80–81.

24. Stewart, *Edward Warren*, 427n40.

25. Parker, *Journey*, 81; Stewart, *Edward Warren*, 427.

26. Parker, *Journey*, 84; Carson, *Autobiography*, 42–44.

27. Carson, *Autobiography*, 44.

28. Roberts, Kit Carson, 72.

29. Victor, *River of the West*, 186–87; Parker, *Journal of an Exploring Trip*, 87–88.

30. Russell, *Journal of a Trapper*, 30–31; Victor, *River of the West*, 168.

31. Marsh, *Four Years in the Rockies*, 60.

32. Russell, *Journal of a Trapper*, 162n68.

33. Ibid., 33–34, 39.

34. Turney-High, "Flathead Indians of Montana," 66.

35. Morgan and Harris, *Journals*, 265–66.

Chapter 12

1. Russell, *Journal*, 39.

2. Ibid., 39, 162n78.

3. Ibid., 40–41.

4. Hafen, *Broken Hand*, 151–52; Anderson, *Journals*, 368, 293.

5. Drury, *First White Women*, 1:19; Drury, *Marcus and Narcissa Whitman*. 1:158, 161n40, 107.

6. Drury, *Marcus and Narcissa Whitman*, 1:166; Drury, *First White Women*, 1:185n5, 3:311.

7. Victor, *River of the West*, 205–6.

8. Miller, *West of Alfred Jacob Miller*, opposite plate 150.

9. Hafen, *Broken Hand*, 156.

10. Anderson, *Journals*, 310, 264–65; Hafen, *Broken Hand*, 152–53, 246.

11. Hafen, *Broken Hand*, 160.

12. Russell, *Journal*, 45.

13. Ibid., 48–49.

14. Ibid., 43, 47–48, 49–50.

15. Quotes and events described in these paragraphs are from Victor, *River of the West*, 189–94.

16. Russell, *Journal*, 51.

17. Victor, *River of the West*, 172–73.

18. Marsh, *Four Years in the Rockies*, 142.

19. Carson, *Autobiography*, 57.

20. Russell, *Journal*, 52; Marsh, *Four Years in the Rockies*, 137.

21. Doyle, *Journeys to the Land of Gold*, 2:536–37.

22. Carson, *Autobiography*, 57.

23. Russell, *Journal*, 153–53.

24. Marsh, *Four Years in the Rockies*, 144–45; Russell, *Journal*, 53.

25. Russell, *Journal*, 54; Carson, *Autobiography*, 58; Marsh, *Four Years in the Rockies*, 144–46.

26. Russell, *Journal*, 54; Marsh, *Four Years in the Rockies*, 147.

27. Russell, *Journal*, 54.

28. Ibid.; Carson, *Autobiography*, 58.

Chapter 13

1. Victor, *Joe Meek*, 179–80.

2. Russell, *Journal*, 54–59.

3. Ibid., 59.

4. Victor, *Joe Meek*, 197–98. Meek erroneously listed this event as 1836, not 1837, and said the Bannock who confronted Bridger was a chief. He also said the cook for the booshways was a black man who was "greatly elated" at his "signal feat."

5. Russell, *Journal*, 60.

6. Hardee, *Obstinate Hope*, 386–88.

7. David Brown, *Rocky Mountains*, 12.

8. Miller, *The West*, opposite plate 159.

9. Ibid.

10. Victor, *Joe Meek*, 238; Stewart, *Edward Warren*, 171, 173.

11. William Gray, "Unpublished Journals," *Whitman College Quarterly* (June 1913): 102.

12. David Brown, *Rocky Mountains*, 19–20.

13. Carson, *Autobiography*, 48–49.

14. T. Brown, "Smallpox Blankets."

15. Noel, *Witnessing America*, 487.

16. Ewers, *The Blackfeet*, 65–66.

17. Carson, *Autobiography*, 50.

18. Russell, *Journal*, 86–87.

19. Carson, *Autobiography*, 50.

20. Ibid., 51; Victor, *Joe Meek*, 230.

21. Russell, *Journal*, 87–88.

22. Ibid., 88, 169n139.

23. Ibid., 89.

24. Victor, *Joe Meek*, 231–32.

25. Drury, *On to Oregon*, 2:101; Russell, *Journal*, 90.

26. Drury, *Elkanah and Mary Walker*, 40.

27. Gowans, *Rendezvous*, 221–22.

28. Carson, *Autobiography*, 50; Gowans, *Rendezvous*, 221–22.

29. Victor, *Joe Meek*, 234.

30. Gowans, *Rendezvous*, 208.

31. Anderson, *Journals*, 264–65.

32. Newell, *Memoranda*, 37.

33. Anderson, *Journals*, 362, 374.

34. Russell, *Journal*, 91.

35. Wislizenus, *Journey*, 89.

Chapter 14

1. DeVoto, *Year of Decision*, 58.

2. Humphries, "Peg-Leg Smith," 328.

3. Hafen and Hafen, *Old Spanish Trail*, 236–42.

4. Newell, *Memoranda*, 39.

5. Raynolds, *Report*, 77.

6. Campbell, *Narrative*, 23.

7. H. J. Clayton, *San Francisco Daily Alta California*, April 21, 1872.

8. Johnson and Paul, *Philip Creamer*, 5–7.

9. H. J. Clayton, *San Francisco Daily Alta California*, April 21, 1872.

10. Anderson, *Journals*, 314; Hafen, "Henry Fraeb," 3:135–36.

11. Sunder, *Bill Sublette*, 158.

12. Anderson, *Journals*, 265.

13. Gowans, *Rocky Mountain Rendezvous*, 252–53.

14. Alter, *Jim Bridger*, 196.

15. Stansbury, *Valley of the Great Salt Lake*, 51.

16. Anderson, *Journals*, 118–19.

17. De Smet, *Letters and Sketches*, 99.

18. Hardee, *Obstinate Hope*, 270, 275.

19. De Smet, *Letters and Sketches*, 141.

20. De Smet, *Life, Letters and Travels*, 1:262.

21. Ibid., 4:1488–89, 3:1010–12.

22. Newell, *Memoranda*, 39; Anderson, *Journals*, 328.

23. Anderson, *Journals*, 178–79.

24. E. Willard Smith, *Journal*, 272.

25. Victor, *River of the West*, 264–65.

26. Leonard, *Adventures*, 129; Field, *Prairie and Mountain*, 110–11; Talbot, *Journals*, 41–42.

27. Hafen and Hafen, *Old Spanish Trail*, 242–43.

28. Ibid., 184, 243; Hafen, "Henry Fraeb," 137; Anderson, *Journals*, 265, 381.

Chapter 15

1. Hafen, *Broken Hand*, 177.

2. Hafen and Hafen, *To the Rockies and Oregon*, 42.

3. Hafen, "Henry Fraeb," 3:138.

4. Ibid.

5. Stansbury, *Exploration of the Great Salt Lake*, 239–40; Frémont, *Expeditions*, 1:221

6. Narcissa Whitman to Jane Prentiss, October 1, 1841, in N. Whitman, "Letters and Journals."

7. Anderson, *Journals*, 265–66.

8. St. Charles Borromeo Baptismal Register, State Historical Society of Missouri, 11; Caesar, *Jim Bridger*, 304.

9. McLoughlin, *Letters*, 225–26.

10. Simpson, quoted in *Certain Correspondence*, 2:59–60.

11. Ibid.

12. Bagley, *So Rugged*, 101.

13. Alex C. Anderson to George Simpson, February 13, 1844, HBC Archives, D.5/10, FO. 222, Archives of Manitoba, Winnipeg.

14. Schoolcraft, *American Indians*, 233–34; Enzler, "Bridger Challenges the HBC," 121.

15. Tate et al., *Great Medicine Road*, 175–82.

16. Bagley, *So Rugged*, 185.

17. Tate et al., *Great Medicine Road*, 179.

18. McDonald, *Fur Trade Letters*, 225.

19. Newell, *Memoranda*, 39; Victor, *River of the West*, 259–60.

20. McLoughlin, *Letters*, 82.

21. Hafen and Hafen, *Rockies and Oregon*. 265–66; Bagley, *So Rugged*, 183.

22. Hafen and Hafen, *Rockies and Oregon*, 270.

23. Frémont, *Expeditions*, 1:221; Preuss, *Exploring*, 26; Hafen and Young, *Fort Laramie*, 65; Anderson, *Journals*, 108.

24. Hafen, *Broken Hand*, 180; Frémont, *Expeditions*, 1:222, 223.

25. Frémont, *Expeditions*, 1:237; Preuss, *Exploring*, 21, 25.

26. Frémont, *Expeditions*, 1:214. Frémont was not present for the events recorded on pages 212–18 and expanded on Preuss's daily journal during that period.

27. Ibid., 1:214.

28. Preuss, *Exploring*, 21–22.

29. Ibid., 50.

30. Frémont, *Expeditions*, 1:229, 224.

31. Ibid., 1:223–24n43.

32. Ibid., 1:224, 241.

33. John P. Sarpy affidavit, June 20, 1843, https://www.donaldheald.com/pages/books/24188/jim-bridger; Andrew Drips account book, 1819–20, cited in Alter, *James Bridger*, 204.

34. Anderson, *Journals*, 266; Sunder, *Sublette*, 162.

35. Anderson, *Journals*, 375.
36. Ibid.
37. Tate et al., *Great Medicine Road*, 177.
38. Morgan and Harris, *Rocky Mountain Journals*, 375.
39. Mattes, *Indians, Infants, and Infantry*, 58.
40. Clayton, *Journal*, 285.
41. Gardner, "Fort Bridger."
42. Ibid.
43. Ibid.
44. Chittenden, *American Fur Trade*, 1:xxvii.

Chapter 16

1. Robinson, *Fort Pierre*, 189.
2. Richard Grant to George Simpson, March 15, 1844, HBC Archives, D.5/10, folios 425–428, 2, Archives of Manitoba, Winnipeg.
3. Stewart, *Edward Warren*, vii.
4. Field, *Mountain Sketches*, xxx–xxxi, 126.
5. Ibid., 147.
6. Ibid., 138–39.
7. Talbot, *Journals*, 42.
8. Frémont, *Expeditions*, 1:462–63n40.
9. Field, *Mountain Sketches*, 138–39.
10. Frémont, *Expeditions*, 1:467; Morgan and Harris, *Journal*, 266; Talbot, *Journals*, 41.
11. Talbot, *Journals*, 41.
12. Laidlaw to Chouteau, December 1843, Chouteau-Walsh Collection, Missouri Historical Society.
13. Larpenteur, *Forty Years*, 182.
14. Audubon, *Journals*, 2:73–74.
15. Alter, *Jim Bridger*, 209–10; Bridger to Chouteau, December 10, 1843, Chouteau-Walsh Collection.
16. Ibid., 210–11.
17. Ibid.
18. Larpenteur, *Forty Years*, 182.
19. Ibid., 185.
20. Samuel Allen Rogers, 1891–92, A-1682, Utah State Historical Society, Salt Lake City.
21. Bryant, *California*, 143.
22. Palmer, *Journal*, 32.
23. Lillian Schlissel, *Women's Diaries*, 55.
24. Minto, "Reminiscences," (2.2), 124.
25. Ibid., 165–66.
26. Ibid., 163; Sager, *Whitman Massacre*, 15–16.

Chapter 17

1. Bullock, *Pioneer Camp*, 210.

2. Schoolcraft, *American Indians*, 233–34.

3. DeLand, *Fort Tecumseh and Fort Pierre*, 209–10; Alter, *James Bridger*, 200; Keep, *Common Seashells*, 34.

4. Clayton, *Journal*, 276; Morgan, *Great Salt Lake*, 192–93.

5. Bullock, *Pioneer Camp*, 211; Morgan, *Jedediah Smith*, 200.

6. Jacobs, eds., The Record of Norton, 63-64, cited in Bullock, *Pioneer Camp*, 207.

7. Bouis to Picotte, in DeLand, *Fort Tecumseh and Fort Pierre*, 206.

8. DeLand, *Fort Tecumseh and Fort Pierre*, 206; Bryant, *What I Saw*, 109.

9. Morgan, *Overland in 1846*, 1:30–31.

10. Hastings, *Emigrants' Guide*, 135–38.

11. Morgan, *Overland in 1846*, 1:30–35.

12. Clyman, *Journal*, 255–56.

13. St. Charles Borromeo Baptismal Register, State Historical Society of Missouri, 7.

14. W. T. Brazille to Charles T. Kemper, December 1941, Typescript Collection C995 #679, State Historical Society of Missouri.

15. Morgan, *Overland in 1846*, 2:757n90; Parkman, *Oregon Trail*, 85, 97–98; Bryant, *What I Saw*, 142–43.

16. Clyman, *Journal*, 249, 253, 267–68.

17. Wallis, *Best Land under Heaven*, 39, 44.

18. Murphy, "Across the Plains," 409–10, 412; Alter, *James Bridger*, 188; Korns and Morgan, *West from Fort Bridger*, 201–2.

19. Morgan, *Overland in 1846*, 1:260–61.

20. Barry, *Beginning of the West*, 644; Morgan, *Overland in 1846*, 1:372n33; Bryant, *What I Saw*, 145.

21. Korns and Morgan, *West from Fort Bridger*, 194.

22. Morgan, *Overland in 1846*, 1:279–80.

23. Ibid., 1:237, 240, 243.

24. Ibid., 1:279–80.

25. Stewart, *Ordeal by Hunger*, 13.

26. Gowans and Campbell, *Fort Bridger*, 22; Morgan, *Overland in 1846*, 1:54, 263, 434n40.

27. Morgan, *Overland in 1846*, 1:445n96, 447n114.

28. Wallis, *Best Land under Heaven*, 205–6.

29. Morgan, *Overland in 1846*, 1:310.

30. Jacob, *Mormon Vanguard*, 190.

31. Korns and Morgan, *Fort Bridger*, 204n10.

32. Morgan, *Overland in 1846*, 1:304.

Chapter 18

1. Morgan, *Overland in 1846*, 1:279–80.

2. Wheeler, "James Gemmell," 331.

3. Bullock, *Pioneer Camp*, 209.

4. Joseph Smith Jr., Church History, *Times and Season* 3:9:707, https://www.josephsmithpapers.org/.

5. Bigler and Bagley, *Mormon Rebellion*, 19.

6. Arrington, *Brigham Young*, 98–103, 111.

7. Bagley, *Whites Want Every Thing*, 59.

8. Arrington, *Brigham Young*, 123; Beam, *American Crucifixion*, 254.

9. Saunders, *Morgan on the Mormons*, 58.

10. Arrington, *Great Basin Kingdom*, 41–42.

11. Bullock, *Pioneer Camp*, 210.

12. Ibid., 211n20.

13. Frémont, *Expeditions*, 2:381–82, 422.

14. Bullock, *Pioneer Camp*, 211; William Clayton, *Journal*, 272–78.

15. Alter, *James Bridger*, 196–97.

16. Ibid., 198.

17. Ibid., 191, 198.

18. George Albert Smith, "Notes October 1913," A-1682, Utah State Historical Society.

19. Bullock, *Pioneer Camp*, 210.

20. Turner, *Brigham Young*, 215.

21. Alter, *James Bridger*, 195.

22. Saunders, *Morgan on the Mormons*, 299–300.

23. Turner, *Brigham Young*, 76.

24. Ward, et al. *The West*, 106

25. Bagley, *So Rugged*, 363.

26. "Notes on Virginia Bridger Hahn," WPA, Colorado Historical Society, 87–88; Varnell and Hanson, *Women of Consequence*, 32–33.

27. A. G. Brackett in Gowans and Campbell, *Fort Bridger*, 9; Bagley, *So Rugged*, 281-82.

28. B. Roberts, *Comprehensive History*, 331.

29. Alter, *Jim Bridger*, 225

30. Bagley, *Whites Want Every Thing*, 59.

31. Jim Bridger Box 20.7, Church Archives, Church of Jesus Christ of Latter-day Saints, Salt Lake City.

32. Journal History of the Church of Jesus Christ of Latter-day Saints, May 7, 1849, 1; May 12, 1849, 1; May 13, 1849, 2, Church History Library. Hereafter cited as Journal History.

33. Journal History, June 15, 1849, 1.

34. Cain and Brower, *Mormon Way-Bill*.

35. Kimball and Kimball, *Mormon Trail*, 47.

36. George Washington Brown, "Reminiscences," MS 18129, folder 27, Church History Library, SLC.

37. Golda Louise Rideout Soffe, "The Descendants of Joshua Terry," BYU Provo: Grant Stevenson, ca 1965, LDS Church History Library microfilm, MS 16673; MacKinnon, *At Sword's Point*, 2:472.

38. Arrington, *Brigham Young*, 169.

39. Arrington, *Great Basin Kingdom*, 81; Alter, *Jim Bridger*, 579.

Chapter 19

1. Victor, *River of the West*, 1:238.

2. N. Whitman to Prentiss, March 1, 1842, "Letters and Journals."

3. Sager, *Whitman Massacre*, 20.

4. Drury, *Marcus and Narcissa Whitman*, 2:128–29, 148–50.

5. N. Whitman to Prentiss, March 1, 1842, "Letters and Journals."

6. Drury, *Marcus and Narcissa Whitman*, 2:128; Narcissa to Marcus, October 4, 1842, "Letters and Journals."

7. Whitman to Prentiss, March 1, 1842, "Letters and Journals."

8. Ibid.

9. Sager, *Whitman Massacre*, 20.

10. Drury, *Marcus and Narcissa Whitman*, 2:122.

11. Ibid., 2:148–49.

12. Ibid., 2:210–13.

13. Ibid., 2:224–25.

14. Ibid., 2:174–76, 225.

15. Ibid., 2:231–34.

16. Ibid., 2:265, 271, 274.

17. Ibid., 2:289, 285.

18. Ibid., 2:291–92.

19. Victor, *River of the West*, 2:196–98, 215.

20. Drury, *Marcus and Narcissa Whitman*, 2:299, 315; *Oregon Spectator*, March 23, 1848, 4.

21. U.S. Census Records, 1850, 1860, 1870, 1880, St. Charles Borromeo Baptismal Records, 12, State Historical Society of Missouri.

22. Virginia Bridger Hahn, "The Life of James Bridger," MSS 204, American Heritage Center, University of Wyoming, Laramie.

23. Wislizenus, *Journey to the Rocky Mountains*, 55.

24. Caesar, *King of the Mountain Men*, 221–24; Dodge, *James Bridger*, 21–22.

Chapter 20

1. Ted Bagglemann and Willard Thompson, "John Sutter's Journey, 1834–39," *Golden Notes* 3 (1987): 3, Sacramento, Calif.: Sacramento County Historical Society, www.schs.sacramentohistory.info.

2. "John Augustus Sutter," New Perspectives on the West, www.pbs.org/weta/thewest/people/s_z/sutter.htm.

3. DeLand, *Fort Tecumseh and Fort Pierre Letter Books*.

4. "Fort Benton Journal, 1854–56"; "Fort Sarpy Journal, 1855–56," *Contributions to the Montana Historical Society* 10:277–78; "Trapper in the '40's," September 11, 1899, *Santa Cruz Evening Sentinel*.

5. Ibid.

6. Ibid.

7. Homen, "Jim Bridger as I Remember Him," A2147, Utah State Historical Society, Salt Lake City.

8. Mattes, *Great Platte River Road*, 62.

9. Johnston, *Overland to California*, 94, 132.

10. William Kelly, *Excursion to California*, 205–6.

11. Unruh, *Plains Across*, 137.

12. Homen, "Jim Bridger as I Remember Him."

13. Unruh, *Plains Across*, 248.

14. Ibid., 248, 408–10.

15. Johnston, *Overland to California*, 106–7.

16. Ibid.

17. The quotes and descriptions in this paragraph and those below are from H. J. Clayton, *San Francisco Daily Alta California*, April 21, 1872.

18. Stansbury, *Exploration*, 74.

19. Ibid., 74–75.

20. Ibid., 228.

21. Gunnison, *The Mormons*, 150.

22. Ibid., 151–52.

23. Stansbury, *Exploration*, 229.

24. Ibid., 75–76.

25. Alter, *Jim Bridger*, 235.

26. Stansbury, *Exploration*, 76–78.

27. Bullock, *Pioneer Camp*, 210.

28. Stansbury, *Exploration*, 78.

29. Ibid., 79.

30. Madsen, *Exploring the Great Salt Lake*, 149n14.

31. McChristian, *Fort Laramie*, 40–41.

32. Stansbury, *Exploration*, 81–82.

33. Ibid., 84.

34. Ibid., 227.

35. Clayton, *Daily Alta California*, April 21, 1872.

36. Stansbury, *Exploration*, 85.

37. Ibid., xiii, 84.

Chapter 21

1. Fergusen, *Experiences of a Forty-Niner*, 62.

2. William Carter Papers, June 15, 1924, Box 5, Fd. 24, Bancroft Library, University of California, Berkeley.

3. Christy, *Road across the Plains*, 6–7; Unruh, *Plains Across*, 119–20.

4. Langworthy, *Scenery of the Plains*, 65, 68.

5. Bigler and Bagley, *Mormon Rebellion*, 43.

6. Stansbury, *Exploration*, 217.

7. Madsen, *Exploring the Great Salt Lake*, 268, 633.

8. Ibid., 627.

9. Stansbury, *Exploration*, 230.

10. Ibid., 231–32, 233.

11. Ibid., 233–34.

12. Ibid., 237.

13. Ibid., 240.

14. Ibid., 242.

15. Ibid., 241–42, 247.

16. Ibid., 250.

17. Gunnison, *The Mormons*, 151.

18. Stansbury, *Exploration*, 252.

19. Ibid., 253–54.

20. Ibid., 254.

21. Madsen, *Exploring the Great Salt Lake*, 686, 692–93.

22. Ibid., 686–91.

23. Stansbury, *Exploration*, 336–49.

24. Ibid., 261.

25. Madsen, *Exploring the Great Salt Lake*, 647.

Chapter 22

1. Hafen, *Broken Hand*, 279, 284–85.

2. Brigham Young to J. M. Holeman, August 11, 1851, Utah Indian Affairs, NARA, RG 75.

3. Stephen B. Rose to Luke Lee, August 16, 1851; H. R. Day to Luke Lea, August 12, 1851, NARA, RG 75.

4. H. R. Day to Luke Lea, January 2, 1852, *The Utah Expedition* (Washington, D.C.: U.S. War Department, 1858), 130–32.

5. Bullock, *Pioneer Camp*, 243–44.

6. Hafen, *Broken Hand*, 274.

7. Lowe, *Five Years a Dragoon*, 79–80.

8. McChristian, *Fort Laramie*, 62.

9. Lowe, *Five Years a Dragoon*, 79–81.

10. Ibid., 81–82.

11. Hafen, *Fort Laramie*, 190–91; Terrell, *Black Robe*, 100, 105–9, 250–51, 262.

12. B. Gratz Brown, October/November *Missouri Republican* typescript, Fort Laramie National Historic Site Archives, Fort Laramie, Wyoming.

13. Kurz, *Journal*, 221.

14. Mattes, *Colter's Hell*, 77–80.

15. Haines, *Yellowstone Story*, 1:77, 122, 149, 345n78.

16. Brown, November 9, 1851, *Missouri Republican* typescript, Fort Laramie National Historic Site Archives.

17. Lowe, *Five Years a Dragoon*, 91.

18. Hafen, *Broken Hand*, 299.

19. Ibid., 300–7.

20. Bigler and Bagley, *Mormon Rebellion*, 35.

21. Arrington, *Brigham Young*, 224.

22. *Territory of Utah, Acts*, 162–63, 84–88, 166–67.

23. Utah State Archives and Records Service, Series S373, Bridger Box 1, Folders 6, 10, 11.

24. Robert Campbell Papers, Letterbook 1:07, p. 444; 1:10 p. 465, Mercantile Library, St. Louis.

25. De Smet, *Life, Letters and Travels*, 4:1483.

26. Ferris, *Mormons at Home*, 83–85.

27. Gowans and Campbell, *Fort Bridger*, 178–79, 59.

28. Ferris, *Mormons at Home*, 83–85, 206–7.

29. Campbell Papers, Letterbook 1:07, p. 566; 1:10, p. 95; De Smet, *Life, Letters and Travels*, 4:1484–85.

Chapter 23

1. Bigler and Bagley, *Mormon Rebellion*, 35, 48–49.

2. Bigler, "Lion in the Path," 9.

3. Gowans and Campbell, *Fort Bridger*, 43.

4. Bigler and Bagley, *Mormon Rebellion*, 40.

5. Holeman to Lee, March 29, 1852, *The Utah Expedition* ex. doc 71, 139, 142.

6. Bailey, *Holy Smoke*, 38.

7. Moorman, *Camp Floyd*, 9; Bigler and Bagley, *Mormon Rebellion*, 37.

8. *Territory of Utah, Acts*, First Session, 162–63; Second Session, 17–18.

9. Gowans and Campbell, *Fort Bridger*, 49.

10. "Agreement . . . between Wm. J. Hawley, J. A. Thompson, and John MacDonald and . . . Jas. Bridger and Louis Vasquez, Bridgers Fort, May 21, 1853," Ken Rendell Collection.

11. "1853 November 29 Statement of Settlement" and "1855 February 21 Letter to William J. Hawley," Brigham Young Center, http://brighamyoungcenter.org.

12. *Bridger, Hawley, Thompson & Co. vs. Dennis, et al.*, and *Bridger, Hawley, Thompson & Co vs. Sweeney et al.*, Utah State Archives, Series 25011, Box 1, folders 58–59.

13. Ibid.

14. Piercy, *Route from Liverpool*, 98.

15. Stuart, *Montana As It Is*, 52.

16. *U.S. vs. James Bridger*, 1853, Utah State Archives and Records Service, Territorial First District Court, Case Files, Series 25011. (Gowans and Campbell misquoted this as "1st day of 1853" instead of "1st day of August 1853, in *Fort Bridger*, 50).

17. Hickman, *Brigham's Destroying Angel*, 91.

18. Young to Ferguson, August 20, 1853, Correspondence and Orders 1850–56, MS 17205, LDS Archives, https://catalog.churchofjesuschrist.org/assets?id=98a50659-9219-4e8e-9959-1f293a75b957&crate=0&index=7.

19. *Journal History*, May 7, 1849, 1.

20. Gowans, "Fort Bridger and the Mormons," 53.

21. Gray, *Custer*, 13.

22. Kimball to Ferguson, August 27, 1853, Utah Territorial Militia Records, 1849–1877, Series 2210, Utah State Archives and Records Service, 308. (Hereafter cited as UTMR.)

23. Gowans, *Rocky Mountain Rendezvous*, 53.

24. Ferguson to Young and Wells, August 28, 1853, UTMR, 1361.

25. Gowans and Campbell, *Fort Bridger*, 56.

26. Hickman, *Brigham's Destroying Angel*, 92.

27. Ibid.; Kimball and Ferguson to Wells, UTMR, 370; *Bridger, Hawley, Thompson & Co vs. Sweeney et al.*, Series 25011, Box 1, folder 59, Utah State Archives.

28. Hickman, *Brigham's Destroying Angel*, 92–93.

29. Kimball to Wells, August 29, 1853, UTMR, 363; Gowans and Campbell, *Fort Bridger*, 52–53, 56.

30. Blair to Young, August 30, 1853, UTMR, 368.

31. Young to Ferguson, August 23, 1853, UTMR, 1366.

32. Gowans and Campbell, *Fort Supply*, 15.

33. Liberty (Missouri) *Weekly Tribune*, October 8, 1853; *L.D.S. Millennial Star*, December 10, 1853, A5308, Utah State Historical Society, Salt Lake City.

34. Gowans and Campbell, *Fort Bridger*, 59; *Louisville Courier-Journal*, November 1853; *Washington* (D.C.) *Sentinel*, December 13, 1853; Barry, *Beginning of the West*, 1183.

35. *Kansas City Star*, June 26, 1922. C1-2.

36. Campbell to Vasquez, December 31, 1853, Letterbook 1:10, p. 95, Mercantile Library, St. Louis.

37. Hafen, *Broken Hand*, 317.

38. *Evening Star* (Washington, D.C.) January 6, 1854, p. 4.

39. Cushing to Davis, March 23, 1854, Archives, Church of Jesus Christ of Latter-day Saints, Salt Lake City.

40. Hafen, *Broken Hand*, 317.

41. Campbell to Joseph Bissonette, February 20, 1854, Letterbook 1:10, p. 529, Mercantile Library, St. Louis.

42. MacKinnon, "Like Splitting a Man," 107–8.

43. Ibid., 108.

44. Ibid. Thanks to historian William P. MacKinnon for sharing this transcription by genealogist-historian Ardis E. Parshall.

45. Ibid.

46. "The Utah Expedition," in *Executive Documents, U.S. House of Representatives, 1857–1858*.

47. Cushing to Davis and Davis to Bridger, Church Archives, Church of Jesus Christ of Latter-day Saints.

48. Unruh, *Plains Across*, 294, 490n104, 314.

49. Bagley, *Whites Want Every Thing*, 397–98.

50. "Brigham Young–Chief Washakie Indian Farm Negotiations," ed. Rhett S. James, *Annals of Wyoming* 39, no 2 (1967): 246.

Chapter 24

1. Honig, *James Bridger*, 128.

2. All or part of lots 7, 8 and 10, New Santa Fe, Jackson County, Missouri, Recorder instruments #1854C0002224, #1854I0022537, #1855I0023541, and #1855I0024104.

3. Campbell Papers, Letterbook 1-07:566, 1-10:465.

4. St. Charles Borromeo Baptismal Records, 7, 11, 34, State Historical Society of Missouri; De Smet, *Life, Letters and Travels*, 4:1488.

5. Pagnamenta, *Prairie Fever*, 102; De Smet, *Life, Letters and Travels*, 4:1488–89, 3:1010.

6. Alfred J. Vaughan, quoted in Roberts, *Lord Gore*, 163–64.

7. Marcy, *Thirty Years of Army Life*, 403.

8. Gray, *Custer's Last Campaign*, 13.

9. Marcy, *Thirty Years of Army Life*, 404.

10. Ibid.

11. Equivalent to $7,350 today. Campbell Papers, Letterbook 1-13:663, Mercantile Library, St. Louis.

12. Gray, *Custer's Last Campaign*, 14.

13. Campbell Papers, Letterbook 1-06:294, Mercantile Library, St. Louis.

14. Jackson County, Missouri, Recorder instrument #1855I0024046.

15. Campbell Papers, Letterbook 1-12:321–22, Mercantile Library, St. Louis.

16. Purchased from James W. and Elizabeth Manion, April 2, 1855, E. R. Schauffler, *Kansas City Star*, March 2, 1941.

17. Campbell Papers, Letterbook 1-12:125, 1-12:191, Mercantile Library, St. Louis.

18. Young, *Journal of Discourses*, February 18 and July 8, 1855, 2:186, 311.

19. MacKinnon, *At Sword's Point*, 1:47–48.

20. Arrington, *Brigham Young*, 243, 247.

21. Bigler and Bagley, *Mormon Rebellion*, 63–64.

22. MacKinnon, *At Sword's Point*, 1:48–49.

23. Gowans and Campbell, *Fort Bridger*, 63, 176–77.

24. Ibid., 74.

25. Ibid., 57, 71, 175.

26. Ibid., 76.

27. Gray, *Custer's Last Campaign*, 15.

28. Roberts, *Lord Gore*, 164.

29. Marsh, "Journal: Account of a Steamboat Trip," 82.

30. Campbell Papers, Ledgerbook Roll 17, folder 2-19, Mercantile Library, St. Louis.

31. Edwin Hatch and Family Papers, Journal P1537, Gale Family Library, Minnesota Historical Society.

32. Gray, *Custer's Last Campaign*, 16–17. F. G. Heldt errs depicting this happening at Fort Union after a dispute between Gore and Culbertson; see "Sir George Gore's Expedition," *Contributions to the Historical Society of Montana*, vol. 1, Helena, Mont., 1876, 144–48.

33. Hanson, *Little Chief's Gatherings*, 122, 136, 118.

34. Foster, *Strange Genius*, 66–68, 79.

35. Viola, *Exploring the West*, 122, 125, 127.

36. Hanson, *Little Chief's Gatherings*, 137.

37. Roberts, *Lord Gore*, 165.

38. Hanson, *Little Chief's Gatherings*, 122, 137.

39. Ibid., 122, 138–139.

40. Foster, *Strange Genius*, 80.

41. Hanson, *Little Chief's Gatherings*, 138–39, 122–23.

42. Stevenson to Butler, February 28, 1886, Butler Papers, Wisconsin Historical Society Archives, Madison.

43. Stevenson to Butler, February 28, 1886, Butler Papers, Wisconsin Historical Society Archives, Madison.

44. Hayden, *Fifth Annual Report of Progress*, 7.

45. Hanson, *Little Chief's Gatherings*, 123, 139–40.

46. Foster, *Strange Genius*, 75.

47. Chittenden, *Yellowstone*, 48–49.

48. Larpenteur, *Forty Years*, 38.

49. Warren, *Explorations in Nebraska*, 35–36; Anderson, *Journals*, 39, 194–95, 244–48, 344.

Chapter 25

1. Moorman, *Camp Floyd*, 15.

2. MacKinnon, *At Sword's Point*, 1:124.

3. Bigler and Bagley, *Mormon Rebellion*, 5–11.

4. Bigler, "Lion in the Path," 15–16.

5. Moorman, *Camp Floyd*, 13.

6. Hafen and Hafen, *Mormon Resistance*, 183–84.

7. Young, *Diary, 1857*, 49.

8. Vestal, *Jim Bridger*, 318; Hebard and Brinninstool, *Bozeman Trail*, 1:81. Hebard and Brinninstool err in stating Bridger had a ferry at La Bonte from 1857–59.

9. Alter, *Jim Bridger*, 266; Hafen and Hafen, *Mormon Resistance*, 58–61, 87.

10. Walker, Turley, and Leonard, *Massacre at Mountain Meadows*, 24–25.

11. *Journal of Discourses*, 4:219–20, https://contentdm.lib.byu.edu/digital/collection/JournalOfDiscourses3/id/540/rec/4.

12. Brooks, *Mountain Meadows Massacre*, 81.

13. Walker, Turley, and Leonard, *Massacre at Mountain Meadows*, xiv, 3.

14. MacKinnon, *At Sword's Point*, 1:45–46.

15. Bigler, "Lion in the Path," 16–18.

16. St. Charles Borromeo burial records, 79, State Historical Society of Missouri.

17. St. Louis University Historical Records, Letterbook 30, 1857.

18. Parker, Medical Journal, 157, Missouri Valley Special Collection, Kansas City Public Library.

19. Bailey, *Holy Smoke*, 76.

20. W. Johnston, *Albert Sidney Johnston*, 211.

21. Bigler and Bagley, *Mormon Rebellion*, 14.

22. Alexander's Summary Report, November 17, 1857, in Hafen and Hafen, *Mormon Resistance*, 87; Hafen and Young, *Fort Laramie*, 291.

23. Hafen and Hafen, *Mormon Resistance*, 161–62.

24. Bigler and Bagley, *Mormon Rebellion*, 212.

25. Bailey, *Holy Smoke;* 93.

26. Saunders, *Morgan on the Mormons,* 72.

27. MacKinnon, *At Sword's Point*, 2:472.

28. Alter, *Jim Bridger*, 267.

29. W. Johnston, *Albert Sidney Johnston*, 243.

30. Alter, *Jim Bridger*, 268, 289.

31. John Wolcott Phelps, Diary, November 19, 1857, MssCol 2399, New York Public Library Archives and Manuscripts.

32. Alter, *Jim Bridger*, 268–69.

33. MacKinnon, *At Sword's Point* 2:45, 49, 557.

34. Ibid., 1:57–58, 2:60.

35. Alter, *Jim Bridger*, 268.

36. *Atlantic Monthly*, June 1877, vol. 39: 697–700; MacKinnon, *At Sword's Point*, 2:97–99.

37. *Atlantic Monthly*, June 1877, vol. 39: 697–700; MacKinnon, *At Sword's Point*, 2:97–99.

38. Hafen, *Mormon Resistance*, 279.

39. Campbell Papers, Letterbook 1-13:585; Ledgerbook 2-037:87, Mercantile Library, St. Louis.

40. Campbell Papers, Letterbook 1-12:322, Mercantile Library, St. Louis.

41. U.S. Census, Kansas City, Missouri, 1860.

42. Parker, Medical Journal, 157, Missouri Valley Special collection, Kansas City, Missouri, Public Library.

43. Crotty, *Watts Mill*, 5.

44. Campbell Papers, Letterbook 1-13:585, Mercantile Library, St. Louis.

45. Campbell Papers, Ledgerbook 2-021:61, and Letterbook 1-27:903, Mercantile Library, St. Louis.

46. MacKinnon, *At Swords Point*, 2:316.

47. *Message from the President of the United States to the Two Houses of Congress*, vol. 2, *Report of the Secretary of War, 1858* (Washington, D.C.: James B. Steedman, 1858), 202–6.

48. Vestal, *Jim Bridger*, 202.

49. Moorman, *Camp Floyd*, 4.

50. Alter, *James Bridger*, 313; Vestal, *Jim Bridger*, 318.

51. Hale, "Jim Bridger," Utah State Historical Society.

52. Ackley, "Across the Plains," *Utah Historical Quarterly* 9 (July-October 1941): 198–99.

53. Gowans and Campbell, *Fort Bridger*, 76–77, 56.

Chapter 26

1. Marsh, "Journal: Account of a Steamboat Trip," 79–86; Lawrence and Cottrell, *Steamboats West*, 62.

2. Raynolds, *Report*, 20.

3. Ibid., 6.

4. Warren, *Explorations in Nebraska*, 53–54.

5. Raynolds, *Report*, 48.

6. Ibid., 34.

7. Warren, *Exploration in Nebraska*, 11.

8. Raynolds, *Report*, 67.

9. Foster, *Strange Genius*, 85.

10. Raynolds, *Report*, 45.

11. Viola, *Exploring the West*, 143.

12. Foster, *Strange Genius*, 60–61, 63.

13. Raynolds, *Report*, 41.

14. Ibid., 45, 54–55, 64.

15. Ibid., 77.

16. Ibid., 57.

17. Stevenson to Butler, February 28, 1886, Butler Papers, Wisconsin Historical Society Archives, Madison.

18. Ibid.

19. Ibid.

20. Raynolds, Journals, October 22 and 25, 1859, Yale Collection of Western Americana, Beinecke Library; William Carter Papers, June 15, 1924, Box 5, Fd. 24, Bancroft Library, University of California, Berkeley.

21. Parker, Medical Journal, 157; *Missouri Republican*, "Border Correspondence," October 12, 1859, 1.

22. A. B. MacDonald, "Brothers Born in Old House Saw the Start of Kansas City," *Kansas City Star*, June 26, 1922; U.S. Census, 1860, Kansas City, Missouri.

23. Raynolds, Journals, December 3, 1859, January 9, February 9, March 15, 1860, Yale Collection of Western Americana, Beinecke.

24. Hafen, *Overland Mail*, 174–81.

25. Raynolds, *Report*, 84.

26. Raynolds, Journals, May 28, 1860, Yale Collection of Western Americana, Beinecke.

27. Raynolds, *Report*, 85.

28. Ibid., 86–87.

29. Hayden, *Fifth Annual Report of Progress*, 135.

30. Raynolds, Journals, May 30, 1860, Yale Collection of Western Americana, Beinecke.

31. Raynolds, *Up the Winds and Over the Tetons*, 42–43, 83–85.

32. Raynolds, *Report*, 91.

33. Foster, *Strange Genius*, 87.

34. Hayden, *Sixth Annual Report*, 21.

35. Ibid.

36. Raynolds, *Report*, 94.

37. Raynolds, *Up the Winds and Over the Tetons*, 103n73.

38. Raynolds, *Report*, 96.

39. Ibid.,166–67.

40. Ibid.

41. Stevenson to Butler, Butler Papers, February 28, 1886, Wisconsin Historical Society Archives, Madison.

42. Alter, *James Bridger*, 333–34.

43. Raynolds, *Report*, 14.

44. Ibid., 10–11.

Chapter 27

1. Mumey, *Beckwourth*, 71–72.

2. Ibid., 71–74.

3. Campbell Papers, Ledgerbook 2-037:87, Mercantile Library, St. Louis.

4. Ibid., Letterbook 1-17:943.

5. Merrill, *Yellowstone: Hayden Expedition*, 21–22, 83, 194.

6. W. Johnston, *Albert Sidney Johnston*, 292, 614.

7. Gowans and Campbell, *Fort Bridger*, 121–22.

8. Hafen, *Overland Mail*, 217–19.

9. Mumey, *Beckwourth*, 72–73.

10. *Rocky Mountain News*, May 15, 1861.

11. Hafen, *Overland Trail*, 220–22.

12. E. L. Berthoud, "Field notes of the Denver, Golden City & Great Salt Lake Wagon Road 1861," NARA, RG 17, entry 161, Field survey records, file #2-2-1-1m, Box 24.

13. Berthoud, cited in Dellenbuach, *Fremont and '49*, 23.

14. (Denver) *Weekly Commonwealth*, June 1, 1864.

15. Ibid.

16. Hafen, *Overland Trail*, 220–22.

17. Remsburg, "Snatched from the Wayside," 19–20.

18. Jackson County, Missouri, Recorder instruments #1855I0024046, #1860I0034106, and #1861I0037385.

19. Campbell Papers, Letterbook 1-15:858, Mercantile Library, St. Louis.

20. Unruh, *Plains Across*, 214–15.

21. Hafen, *Overland Mail*, 187.

22. McDermott, *Circle of Fire*, 9.

23. Spring, *Caspar Collins*, 116–17.

24. Ibid., 121.

25. Brackett, "Bonneville and Bridger," 194–97.

26. Ibid.

27. Spring, *Caspar Collins*, 126.

28. Hafen and Young, *Fort Laramie*, 307–8.

29. Spring, *Caspar Collins*, 143–44.

30. Ware, *Indian War of 1864*, 214–15.

31. Ibid., 203.

32. Caspar Collins to his mother, October 8, 1862, Hebard Papers, American Heritage Center, University of Wyoming, Laramie.

33. Spring, *Caspar Collins*, 142–43.

34. Mattes, *Indians, Infants, and Infantry*, 46.

35. Hebard and Brinninstool, *Bozeman Trail*, 2:240–41.

36. Ware, *Indian War of 1864*, 204.

37. Ibid.

38. Hebard and Brinninstool, *Bozeman Trail*, 2:233.

39. Ware, *Indian War of 1864*, 253–54, 203–4.

40. Ibid., 205–6.

41. Shotwell letter to *Freeport Press*, Hebard Collection, American Heritage Center, University of Wyoming, Laramie.

42. Humfreville, *Twenty Years*, 467.

43. Ibid., 468–69.

44. Ibid., 466.

45. Hebard and Brinninstool, *Bozeman Trail*, 2:241–42.

46. C. R. Tyler to Neil B. Judd, April 19, 1924, Judd Papers, National Anthropological Archives, Smithsonian Institution.

47. Enrollment Records, NARA.

48. *Atchison Weekly Globe*, April 3, 1924, 3.

49. Honig, *James Bridger*, 119.

Chapter 28

1. Neihardt, *Black Elk Speaks*, 9.

2. Doyle, *Journeys*, 137.

3. Lowe, *Bridger Trail*, 88.

4. McDermott, *Red Cloud's War*, 1:1.

5. Stuart, "Yellowstone Expedition," 193.

6. LeForge and Marquis, *Memoirs of a White Crow Indian*, 8.

7. Lowe, *Bridger Trail*, 88.

8. Doyle, *Journeys*, 142.

9. Lowe, *Bridger Trail*, 193–94.

10. Stanley, *Life of Stateler*, 180–81.

11. Lowe, *Bridger Trail*, 23, 247.

12. Ibid., 246.

13. Ibid., 23.

14. Raynolds, *Report*, 13.

15. Doyle, *Journeys*, 752–53, 768.

16. Lowe, *Bridger Trail*, 23, 135–37, 94.

17. Ibid., 292.

18. McDermott, *Red Cloud's War*, 12–13.

19. Ira Meyers, *The Powder River County Examiner and the Broadus* [Mont.] *Independent*, December 16, 1921, 5.

20. Ware, *Indian War of 1864*, 206.

21. Hull, "Soldiering on the High Plains." Hull may have meant Fort McKay, Camp Mitchell, or Camp Marshall.

22. Hunton to Hebard, November 22, 1915, Hebard Collection, American Heritage Center, University of Wyoming; see also "Old Bridger [Death of a Celebrated Scout and Guide]," *Kansas City Mail*, July 1881.

23. Lowe, *Bridger Trail*, 143–44.

24. Ibid., 93–94, 206.

25. Ibid., 150–51.

26. Wagner, *Patrick Connor's War*, 22.

27. Hoig, *Sand Creek Massacre*, 83.

28. Roberts, *A Newer World*, 282–83.

29. Wilson, *Beckwourth*, 175–80.

30. Wagner, *Patrick Connor's War*, 25–26.

31. McDermott, *Red Cloud's War*, 17.

Chapter 29

1. McDermott, *Circle of Fire*, 57.

2. Unrau, *Talking Wire*, 240.

3. Rogers, *Soldiers of the Overland*, 151.

4. Moonlight report to Deer Creek commanding officer, May 21, 1865, NARA, RG 393, part 3, entry 614.

5. McDermott, *Circle of Fire*, 60.

6. Wagner, *Patrick Connor's War*, 38.

7. McDermott, *Circle of Fire*, 62.

8. Hebard and Brinninstool, *Bozeman Trail*, 1:151–52.

9. McDermott, *Circle of Fire*, 69–73; Wagner, *Patrick Connor's War*, 42–44.

10. Gray, *Custer's Last Campaign*, 29; Hafen, *Broken Hand*, 326–27.

11. Wagner, *Powder River Odyssey*, 247; Dodge, *Personal Biography*, 456.

12. McDermott, *Circle of Fire*, 159, 161.

13. Pope to Dodge, June 3, 1865, *War of the Rebellion*, part 2, vol. 48:756.

14. Connor to Dodge June 6, 1865, ibid., 48:799.

15. Hafen and Hafen, *Powder River*, 104, 107–8.

16. Hafen, *Fort Laramie*, 338.

17. Hebard and Brinninstool, *Bozeman Trail*, 2:241–42.

18. Ibid., 2:235.

19. Hafen and Hafen, *Powder River*, 110–12.

20. Wagner, *Patrick Connor's War*, 82.

21. Hafen and Hafen, *Powder River*, 172.

22. Ibid., 114–15.

23. J. E. Spicer to Herbert S Auerbach, June 19, August 20, 1924, COLL CAINE MSS 028, Utah State University, Logan.

24. Hafen and Hafen, *Powder River Campaign*, 176.

25. McDermott, *Circle of Fire*, 93.

26. *War of the Rebellion*, part 2, vol. 48:1048–49, quoted in Rogers, *Soldiers of the Overland*, 168.

27. Pope to Dodge, Dodge to Connor/Price, August 11, 1865, *War of the Rebellion*, part 1, vol. 48:356.

28. Wagner, *Patrick Connor's War*, 108.

29. Connor to Pope, August 21, 1865, *War of the Rebellion*, part 1, vol. 48:358.

30. Quinn, "Soldering on the Plains in 1865," Hebard Papers, B-C762, American Heritage Center, University of Wyoming.

31. Hafen and Hafen, *Powder River*, 24–25.

32. Hoig, *Sand Creek Massacre*, 134.

33. Ferril, "Sixteenth Kansas Cavalry," 857.

34. Hafen and Hafen, *Powder River*, 125–26.

35. Ibid., 127.

36. Pratt, "Interesting Items Concerning the Journeying of the Latter-day Saints," May 22, 30, 1847, https://history.churchofjesuschrist.org/overlandtravel/sources/4442/pratt-orson.

37. Hafen and Hafen, *Powder River*, 127, 211.

38. Wagner, *Patrick Connor's War*, 154–55.

39. Hebard and Brinninstool, *Bozeman Trail*, 2:235.

40. Shotwell Papers, 3, Hebard Collection, American Heritage Center, University of Wyoming.

41. McDermott, *Circle of Fire*, 112.

42. Hafen and Hafen, *Powder River*, 133.

43. Ibid., 128–36.

44. Ibid., 139.

45. Soldiers and Sailors database, Civil War, www.nps.gov/civilwar/soldiers-and-sailors-database.htm; Springer, *Soldiering in Sioux Country*, 67.

46. Wagner, *Powder River Odyssey*, 43; Springer, *Soldiering in Sioux Country*, 17.

47. Hafen and Hafen, *Powder River*, 73.

48. McDermott, *Circle of Fire*, 131–32.

49. Hafen and Hafen, *Powder River*, 74–81.

50. Rogers, *Soldiers on the Overland*, 237.

51. Grinnell, *Fighting Cheyennes*, 208–9; McDermott, *Circle of Fire*, 121–23.

52. Hafen and Hafen, *Powder River*, 260–64, 335, 214.

53. Wagner, *Powder River Odyssey*, 48, 52, 75, 90, 111.

54. Hafen and Hafen, *Powder River*, 92–94.

55. Young, "Journals of Travel," 382.

56. Wagner, *Powder River Odyssey*, 52; Hafen, *Fort Laramie*, 340.

57. Wagner, *Powder River Odyssey*, 232.

58. Young, "Journals of Travel," 382.

Chapter 30

1. Maynadier to John Lewis, Correspondence, West Subdistrict of Nebraska, December 16, 1865, Correspondence 1865–66, NARA, RG 393.

2. Ibid.

3. Ibid.

4. A. J. Shotwell, quoted in the *Freeport Press*, May 16, 1916, Hebard Papers, American Heritage Center, University of Wyoming, Laramie.

5. Ibid.

6. Legh R. Freeman, (Kearny, Nebraska) *Semi-Weekly Herald*, January 6, 1866.

7. Alter, *James Bridger*, 387.

8. Wheaton to Maynadier, Report of Persons Hired, Fort Laramie, 1866, NARA, RG 393; Gray, *Custer's Last Campaign*, 43; Alter, *James Bridger*, 522.

9. Freeman, (Kearny) *Semi-Weekly Herald*, January 6, 1866.

10. Dodge, *Personal Biography*, 475–76.

11. Frank Wheaton to Sam E. Mackey, Telegraph, February 16, 1866, No. 94, NARA, RG 393.

12. Jackson County Recorder instrument #1866I004615.

13. Robert Campbell to S. E. Ward, Campbell Papers, Letterbook 1:17, 943, Mercantile Library, St. Louis; McDermott, *Red Cloud's War*, 1:70.

14. Dodge, *Personal Biography*, 469.

15. *Omaha Daily Herald*, January 1866, cited in Pyper, "Grenville Mellen Dodge," 28, unpublished thesis, Council Bluffs, Iowa, Library.

16. Gray, *Custer's Last Campaign*, 36.

17. McDermott, *Red Cloud's War*, 1:35–36.

18. Maynadier, Headquarters District of the Platte, Fort Laramie, D.T., May 16, 1866, NARA, RG 393.

19. Mattes, *Indians, Infants, and Infantry*, 39; M. Carrington, *Ab-sa-ra-ka*, 84–85.

20. Doyle, *Journeys to the Land of Gold*, 2:743; Dodge, Personal Biography, Leighton correspondence.

21. McDermott, *Red Cloud's War*, 1:51–54.

22. Ibid., 1:57, 47; M. Carrington, *Ab-sa-ra-ka*, 42–46.

23. Henry B. Carrington, "History of Indian Operations on the Plains, 1867," Sen. Ex. Doc. 33, 50th Congress (Washington, D.C.: Government Printing Office, 1888), 5.

24. M. Carrington, *Ab-sa-ra-ka*, 75–76.

25. Ibid., 76–77.

26. McDermott, *Red Cloud's War*, 1:57.

27. M. Carrington, *Ab-sa-ra-ka*, 79–80.

28. Dodge, *Personal Biography*, 482.

29. McDermott, *Red Cloud's War*, 1:71.

30. Ibid., 1:208–9.

31. M. Carrington, *Ab-sa-ra-ka*, 83.

32. McDermott, *Red Cloud's War*, 1:83–84.

33. Ibid., 1:91.

34. Maynadier to John Lewis, acting assistant adjutant general, Correspondence, West Subdistrict of Nebraska, December 16, 1865, Correspondence 1865–66, NARA, RG 393.

35. McDermott, *Red Cloud's War*, 1:82, 86; M. Carrington, *Ab-sa-ra-ka*, 101.

36. M. Carrington, *Ab-sa-ra-ka*, 103; McDermott, *Red Cloud's War*, 1:88.

37. McDermott, *Red Cloud's War*, 1:88–89.

38. M. Carrington, *Ab-sa-ra-ka*, 106.

39. McDermott, *Red Cloud's War*, 1:92.

40. M. Carrington, *Ab-sa-ra-ka*, 113, 114.

41. Ibid., 121.

Chapter 31

1. McDermott, *Red Cloud's War*, 1:94–95.

2. Ostrander, *An Army Boy*, 260.

3. Caleb Henry Carlton, quoted in McDermott, *Red Cloud's War*, 1:72.

4. F. Carrington, *My Army Life*, 80–81.

5. McDermott, *Red Cloud's War*, 1:98–103.

6. F. Carrington, *My Army Life*, 73–81.

7. McDermott, *Red Cloud's War*, 1:115, 123.

8. McDermott, *Red Cloud's War*, 1:65; Gray, *Custer's Last Campaign*, 30; Doyle, *Journeys to the Land of Gold*, 2:567, 682–83, 765.

9. Spear Family, *Bozeman Trail Scrapbook*, 52.

10. Doyle, *Journeys to the Land of Gold*, 2:680, 684, 764.

11. Ibid., 2:536–37; McDermott, *Red Cloud's War*, 1:124.

12. *Montana Post*, September 15, 1866.

13. James Bridger to William Bullock, November 5, 1866, NARA, RG 393, part 1.

14. M. Carrington, *Ab-sa-ra-ka*, 130–31.

15. Rzeckowski, "The Crow," 35.

16. Bridger to William Bullock, November 5, 1866, NARA, RG 393, part 1.

17. Van Voast, September 17, 1866, NARA, RG 393, part 1, E3731 DP, LR, 1866 (N-Y) Box 1A.

18. M. Carrington, *Ab-sa-ra-ka*, 252; McDermott, *Red Cloud's War*, 1:158.

19. Hebard and Brinninstool, *Bozeman Trail*, 2:89–110.

20. F. Carrington, *My Army Life*, 119.

21. McDermott, *Red Cloud's War*, 1:172.

22. F. Carrington, *My Army Life*, 253.

23. McDermott, *Red Cloud's War*, 1:184–93.

24. M. Carrington, *Ab-sa-ra-ka*, 195.

25. S. Smith, *Give Me Eighty Men*, 85–87.

26. Rzeckowski, "The Crow," 36; Special Orders No. 43, Headquarters, District of the Platte, August 8, 1866, NARA, RG 393; Alter, *Jim Bridger*, 325.

27. Wilson, *Beckwourth*, 184.

28. Col. H. B. Carrington, Special Order No. 68, Fort Philip Kearny, November 16, 1866, NARA, RG 393.

29. McDermott, *Red Cloud's War*, 1:182.

30. H. Carrington, Fort Philip Kearny, December 3, 1866, NARA, RG 393.

31. F. Carrington, *My Army Life*, 129.

32. D. Brown, *Fort Phil Kearny*, 159.

33. F. Carrington, *My Army Life*, 135.

34. McDermott, *Red Cloud's War*, 1:202

35. Neihardt, *Black Elk Speaks*, 8, 9, 10.

36. White Elk, quoted in Grinnell, *Fighting Cheyennes*, 237–38.

37. Ibid.

38. Neihardt, *Black Elk Speaks*, 11; McDermott, *Red Cloud's War*, 1:208–9.

39. Fire Thunder, quoted in Neihardt, *Black Elk Speaks*, 11–12.

40. American Horse and Dr. Samuel Horton, quoted in Monnett, *Fetterman Fight*, 56–57.

41. Fire Thunder, quoted in Neihardt, *Black Elk Speaks*, 12–13.

42. Monnett, *Fetterman Fight*, 73–75.

43. M. Carrington, *Ab-sa-ra-ka*, 211–13.

44. H. Carrington to Cooke and Grant, quoted in McDermott, *Red Cloud's War*, 1:238.

45. McDermott, *Red Cloud's War*, 1:241–45.

46. M. Carrington, *Ab-sa-ra-ka*, 209.

47. O'Connell, *Fierce Patriot*, 193; Smith, *Give Me Eighty Men*, 111–13.

48. Murphy, "Forgotten Battalion," 401.

Chapter 32

1. McDermott, *Red Cloud's War*, 1:295.

2. Innis Palmer to H. G. Litchfield, Fort Laramie, Letters Sent, January 2, 1867, NARA, RG 98.

3. Rzeckowski, "The Crow," 36–37.

4. Mattes, *Indians, Infants, and Infantry*, 15.

5. McDermott, *Red Cloud's War*, 1:298.

6. Gray, *Custer's Last Campaign*, 54, 59; McDermott, *Red Cloud's War*, 1:298.

7. McDermott, *Red Cloud's War*, 1:296, 298–302, 2:330.

8. Innis Palmer to Commanding Officer, Fort C. F. Smith, Fort Laramie Letters Sent, NARA, RG 98.

9. Ibid.

10. Gray, *Custer's Last Campaign*, 64.

11. McDermott, *Red Cloud's War*, 1:315–17.

12. Ibid., 2:361–63.

13. Ibid., 1:303.

14. Gray, *Custer's Last Campaign*, 66.

15. J. F. Kinney to N. G. Taylor, June 17, 1867, Selected Documents, Upper Platte Indian Agency, NARA, RG 75.

16. Ostrander, *Army Boy of the Sixties*, 191–92.

17. Mattes, *Infants, Indians, and Infantry*, 134.

18. McDermott, *Red Cloud's War*, 2:371, 411, 419.

19. Ibid., 379–95.

20. John Hunton, Hebard Collection, B.B764-j, American Heritage Center, University of Wyoming, Laramie.

21. Persons and articles hired, Fort C. F. Smith, June 30, 1867, NARA, RG 98.

22. *Kansas City Advertiser*, November 16, 1867, cited in Alter, *Jim Bridger*, 335.

23. Hunton to Hebard, November 22, 1915, Hebard Collection, American Heritage Center, University of Wyoming, Laramie.

24. McDermott, *Red Cloud's War*, 2:502–3

25. Robrock, "Fort Fetterman," 19–20.

26. Morgan, "Washaki," 66.

27. Ibid., 87.

28. McDermott, *Red Cloud's War*, 2:516–18.

29. Roberts, *Newer World*, 284.

30. McDermott, *Red Cloud's War*, 2:517–19.

31. Murphy, "Forgotten Battalion," 401; Hebard and Brinninstool, *Bozeman Trail*, 2:245–46.

32. Hebard and Brinninstool, *Bozeman Trail*, 2:245–46.

33. Vestal, *Jim Bridger*, 318–19.

Chapter 33

1. Sheridan, *Memoirs*, 307, 297.

2. Hutton, *Phil Sheridan*, 53.

3. Rister, *Border Command*, 92.

4. Sheridan, *Memoirs*, 307.

5. Ibid., 310–11.

6. Rister, *Border Command*, 94–95, 100–4.

7. Hugh Campbell to Bridger, February 8, 1869, Campbell Papers, Letterbook 644, Mercantile Library, St. Louis.

8. Robert Campbell to W. T. Sherman, March 19, 1869, Field Office Appointment Papers, 1849–1879, NARA, RG 48, Entry 15.

9. Field Office Appointment Papers, 1849–1879, NARA, RG 48, Entry 15 MT.

10. Campbell to Bridger, June 8, 1869, Campbell Papers, Letterbook 1-19:873, Mercantile Library, St. Louis.

11. Fletcher, *Reminiscences of General Sherman*, 457–59.

12. "James Bridger," 31, unpublished manuscript (one of two), Butler Papers, Mss KK, Wisconsin Historical Society Archives, Madison.

13. S. 480, 50th Congress 1st Session, 1887; Alter, *James Bridger*, 483–92.

14. E. R. Schauffler, *Kansas City Star*, March 2, 1941.

15. Marriage Records, State of Missouri, County of Jackson.

16. Adrienne T. Christopher, "What I Remember of Virginia Bridger Wachsman," *Westport Historical Quarterly* (September 1968): 11–12.

17. Honig, *James Bridger*, 128–29.

18. Jackson County, Missouri, Recorder instruments 1866I0045430, 1871I0087295, 1871I0088279, 1872I0096059, and 1872I0096349.

19. Warranty Deed, James Bridger to Virginia [Bridger] Wachsman, April 8, 1872, Fort Bridger State Historic Site, Fort Bridger, Wyoming.

20. Alter, *Jim Bridger*, 338.

21. Schauffler, *Kansas City Star*, March 2, 1941.

22. Raynolds, *Report*, 11.

23. Langford, *Discovery of Yellowstone Park*, xxix, xxvi, 113; Whittlesey, *Storytelling in Yellowstone*, 109–10.

24. Whittlesey, *Storytelling in Yellowstone*, 30–31.

25. Alter, *Jim Bridger*, 262.

26. James D. Butler papers, Mss KK, Wisconsin State Historical Society, Madison.

27. Honig, *James Bridger*, 114; A. B. MacDonald, *Kansas City Star*, June 26, 1932.

28. Gen. John Gibbon, quoted in Gray, *Custer's Last Campaign*, 139.

29. Vital Historical Records of Jackson County, Missouri, 1826–76, Kansas City, 370–71. Felix Francis Bridger's tombstone records he died at age thirty-four on July 19, 1876.

30. Collections, donated by Minnie Brown, a friend of Virginia, Union Pacific Railway Museum, Council Bluffs, Iowa.

31. Glendale [MT] *Atlantis*, December 1, 1880, quoted in *Montana Magazine*, Summer, 1954, 63.

32. Virginia Bridger Wachsman to Grenville M. Dodge, cited in Alter, *Jim Bridger*, 339–40.

33. Ibid.

34. Schauffler, *Kansas City Star*, March 2, 1941.

35. U.S. Census 1880, Jackson County, Missouri, Kansas City.

36. "The Real 'Jim' Bridger A Leather-Stocking Character," *Kansas City Star*, January 18, 1924.

37. Schauffler, *Kansas City Star*, March 2, 1941.

38. "The Real 'Jim' Bridger," *Kansas City Star*, January 18, 1924.

Epilogue

1. Glavin, *Dodge City*, 35.

2. Rollins, *The Cowboy*, viii, 315.

3. E. R. Schauffler, "Only a Hole Marks the Spot," *Kansas City Star*, March 2, 1941; Mrs. W. T. Brazille letter, January 21, 1942, Utah Historical Society, Salt Lake City; Honig, *James Bridger*, 121.

4. Brazille letter, Utah Historical Society.

5. Honig, *James Bridger*, 121; Billie [Brazille] Duncan (Bridger's great-granddaughter) to Gene Caesar, June 1958, American Heritage Center, University of Wyoming, Laramie; Virginia Bridger to W. M. Camp, 1923, Sheridan [Wyo.] Library.

6. "Notes on Virginia Bridger: Summary of WPA interview with Virginia Bridger Hahn," Colorado Historical Society, 87–89.

7. "Pa Was Never like That," *Kansas City Star Magazine*, January 18, 1925.
8. Minnie Brown to B. B. Brooks, July, 1933, Fort Bridger State Historic Site.
9. *Kansas City Times,* December 12, 1904.
10. Dodge, *James Bridger*, preface, 25–26.
11. *Kansas City Times*, December 12, 1904.
12. Smith, *The Carving of Mount Rushmore*, 26.

BIBLIOGRAPHY

Manuscripts and Archival Sources

Brazille, W. T., to Charles T. Kemper, December 1941. Typescript Collection C995 #679. State Historical Society of Missouri, St. Louis.

Bridger, James. Jim Bridger Box 20.7. Church Archives, Church of Jesus Christ of Latter-day Saints, Salt Lake City.

Brown, B. Gratz. Typescript from October–November, *Missouri Republican*. Fort Laramie National Historic Site Archives, Fort Laramie, Wyo.

Brown, George Washington. "Reminiscences." MS 18129, Folder 27. Church History Library, Salt Lake City.

Bullock, William G. Letters from W. G. Bullock. Seth Ward Collection, FF23. Denver Public Library.

Burial Records, Holy Family Catholic Church, Cahokia, Belleville [Illinois] Public Library.

Butler, James D. Papers. Mss KK. Wisconsin Historical Society Archives, Madison.

Caesar, Gene. Papers. American Heritage Center, University of Wyoming, Laramie.

Campbell, Robert. Family Papers. Mercantile Library, St. Louis.

Carter, William Alexander. Papers. BANC MSS 99/75 p. Bancroft Library, University of California, Berkeley.

Collins, Caspar. Papers. B.6692-c. American Heritage Center, University of Wyoming, Laramie.

Dickson, Clair C. "Joseph Dickson: First on the Yellowstone." Manuscript, 921.73 A1 No. 657. Family History Library, Salt Lake City.

Dodge, Grenville M. "Personal Biography of Major General Grenville M. Dodge from 1831 to 1871." Council Bluffs [Iowa] Public Library.

Flagg, Edmund. Papers. Missouri Historical Society, St. Louis.

Graham, Richard. Papers. Illinois River Agency Papers. Missouri Historical Society, St. Louis.

Hahn, Virginia Bridger. Papers. Hebard Collection. MSS 204 and B-H124-vb. American Heritage Center, University of Wyoming, Laramie.

Hahn, Virginia Bridger. Letters 1926–32. RG1050.AM. Nebraska State Historical Society, Lincoln.

Hale, Sol. H. "Jim Bridger as I Remember Him." A2147d. Utah State Historical Society, Salt Lake City.

Hatch, Edwin. Journal, June 7–October 13, 1856. Edwin Hatch and Family Papers, P1537. Gale Family Library, Minnesota Historical Society.

Homen, W. H. "Jim Bridger as I Remember Him." A2147. Utah State Historical Society, Salt Lake City.

Hunton, John. Papers. Hebard Collection, B.B764-j. American Heritage Center, University of Wyoming, Laramie.

Judd, Neil M. Papers. 4036, Box 14. National Anthropological Archives, Smithsonian Institution, Washington, D.C.

Medical records. Fort Laramie National Historic Site Archives, Fort Laramie, Wyo.

National Archives and Records Administration, Washington, D.C.

Parker, Dr. James W. Medical Journal. Missouri Valley Special Collections, Kansas City [Mo.] Public Library.

Phelps, John Wolcott. Diary. MssCol 2399. New York Public Library Archives and Manuscripts.

Pyper, Walter W. "Grenville Mellen Dodge and Nineteenth-Century America: Growing Pains of a Man and a Nation." Unpublished thesis, Council Bluffs [Iowa] Public Library.

Quinn, P. P. "Soldering on the Plains in 1865: Recollections of General Connor's Indian Expeditions," Carlisle, Pa., 1897. B-C762PP. Hebard Papers. American Heritage Center, University of Wyoming.

Raynolds, William. Papers, Journals. Yale Collection of Western Americana, Beinecke Library, New Haven, Conn.

Shotwell, A. J. Papers. Hebard Collection. American Heritage Center, University of Wyoming.

Simpson, George. Hudson's Bay Company. Archives of Manitoba, Winnipeg.

Smith, George Albert. "Notes October 1913." A-1682. Utah State Historical Society, Salt Lake City.

Spicer, J. E. Correspondence concerning Jim Bridger and Louis Vasquez, 1924. COLL CAINE MSS 028. Utah State University, Logan.

St. Charles Borromeo Baptismal Records. State Historical Society of Missouri, Columbia.

St. Louis University Historical Records. Letter Book 30, 1857.

Sterns, Abel. Collection. SG Box 27, 61. Huntington Library, San Marino, Calif.

Utah State Archives and Records Service. Utah Territorial Militia Records (UTMR), 1849–1877. Series 2210. http//familysearch.org.

Utah State Archives and Records Service. District Court (First District) Case Files.

Warren, Gouverneur Kemble. Papers, 1848–82. SC6681. New York State Library, Albany.

White, James Haley. "St. Louis and Its Men Fifty Years Ago." Missouri Historical Society, St. Louis.

Published Works

Ackley, Richard Thomas. "Across the Plains in 1858." *Utah Historical Quarterly* 9 (July–October 1941): 198–228.

Allen, John H. "Maps and the Mountain Men." In *The Mountains West: Explorations on Historical Geography,* edited by William Wycloff and Larry M. Dilsaver. Lincoln: University of Nebraska Press, 1995.

Allen, Michael. *Western Rivermen, 1773–1861.* Baton Rouge: Louisiana State University Press, 1990.

Alter, J. Cecil. *James Bridger, Trapper, Frontiersman, Scout, and Guide: A Historical Narrative.* [1925.] Reprinted, Columbus, Ohio: Long's College Book Co., 1951.

——. *Jim Bridger.* Norman: University of Oklahoma Press, 1962.

Anderson, William Marshall. *The Rocky Mountain Journals of William Marshall Anderson.* Edited by Dale Morgan and Eleanor Towles Harris. San Marino, Calif.: Huntington Library, 1967.

Arrington, Leonard J. *Brigham Young: American Moses.* New York: Knopf, 1985.

——. *Great Basin Kingdom: Economic History of the Latter-Day Saints, 1830–1900.* Lincoln: University of Nebraska Press, 1966.

Audubon, Maria R. *Audubon and His Journals.* Annotated by Elliott Coues. New York: Charles Scribner's Sons, 1897. Guttenberg Project EBook #39979.

Bagley, Will. *So Rugged and Mountainous.* Norman: University of Oklahoma Press, 2010.

——. *South Pass.* Norman: University of Oklahoma Press, 2014.

——, ed. *The Whites Want Every Thing: Indian-Mormon Relations, 1847–1877.* Norman, Okla.: Arthur H. Clark, 2019.

Bailey, Paul. *Holy Smoke: A Dissertation on the Utah War.* Los Angeles: Westernlore Books, 1978.

Barry, Louise. *The Beginning of the West: Annals of the Kansas Gateway to the American West, 1540–1854.* Topeka: Kansas State Historical Society, 1972.

Beam, Alex. *American Crucifixion: The Murder of Joseph Smith and the Fate of the Mormon Church.* New York: PublicAffairs, 2014.

Bearss, Edwin C. *Bighorn Canyon National Recreation Area, Montana-Wyoming. History Basic Data.* 2 vols. Washington, D.C.: U.S. Office of History and Architecture, Eastern Service Center, 1970.

Berry, Don. *A Majority of Scoundrels: An Informal History of the Rocky Mountain Fur Company.* Sausalito, Calif.: Comstock, 1981.

Bettelyoun, Susan Bordeaux, and Josephine Waggoner. *With My Own Eyes: A Lakota Woman Tells Her People's History.* Lincoln: University of Nebraska Press, 1998.

Bidwell, John. *Echoes of the Past.* New York: Arno Press, 1973.

Bigler, David L. "A Lion in the Path: Genesis of the Utah War, 1857–1858." *Utah Historical Quarterly* 76.1 (2008): 4–21.

Bigler, David L., and Will Bagley. *The Mormon Rebellion.* Norman: University of Oklahoma Press, 2011.

Blair, Walter, and Franklin J. Meine. *Mike Fink: King of the Keelboatmen.* New York: Holt, 1933.

Bonner, Thomas D. *The Life and Adventures of James P. Beckwourth.* Lincoln: University of Nebraska Press, 1981.

Brackenridge, Henry Marie. *Recollections of Persons and Places in the West.* 2nd ed. Philadelphia: J. B. Lippincott, 1868.

Brackett, William S. "Bonneville and Bridger." *Contributions to the Montana Historical Society* 3 (1900): 175–200.

Brooks, George W. *The Southwest Expedition of Jedediah S. Smith.* Glendale, Calif.: Arthur H. Clark, 1977.

Brooks, Juanita. *Mountain Meadows Massacre.* Norman: University of Oklahoma Press, 1962.

Brown, David L. *Three Years in the Rocky Mountains.* Fairfield, Wash.: Ye Galleon Press, 1975.

Brown, Dee. *Fort Phil Kearny: An American Saga.* Lincoln: University of Nebraska Press, 1962.

Brown, Thomas. "Did the U.S. Army Distribute Smallpox Blankets to Indians?" In *Fabrication and Falsification in Ward Churchill's Genocide Rhetoric.* Ann Arbor: MPublishing, University of Michigan Library, 2006.

Bryant, Edwin. *What I Saw in California.* Lincoln: University of Nebraska Press, 1985.

Bullock, Thomas. *The Pioneer Camp of the Saints: The 1846 and 1847 Mormon Trail Journals of Thomas Bullock.* Edited by Will Bagley. Spokane, Wash.: Arthur H. Clark, 1997.

Caesar, Gene. *King of the Mountain Men: The Life of Jim Bridger.* New York: E. P. Dutton, 1961.

Cain, Joseph, and Arieh C. Brower. *Mormon Way-Bill, to the Gold Mines.* Great Salt Lake: W. Richards, Printer, 1851.

Campbell, Robert. *A Narrative of Colonel Robert Campbell's Experiences in the Rocky Mountain Fur Trade from 1825 to 1835.* Fairfield, Wash.: Ye Galleon Press, 1999.

———. *The Rocky Mountain Letters of Robert Campbell.* Printed for Frederick W. Beinecke, 1955.

Carson, Christopher. *Kit Carson's Autobiography.* Edited by Milo Milton Quaife. Lincoln: University of Nebraska Press, 1966.

Carrington, Frances C. *My Army Life and the Fort Phil Kearney Massacre.* Lincoln: University of Nebraska Press, 2004.

Carrington, Henry B. "History of Indian Operations on the Plains." [1867.] Sen. Ex. Doc. 33, 50th Cong., 1st Sess. Washington, D.C.: Government Printing Office, 1888.

Carrington, Margaret Irvin. *Ab-sa-ra-ka: Home of the Crows.* Lincoln: University of Nebraska Press, 1983.

Carter, Clarence Edwin, ed. *The Territorial Papers of the United States, The Territory of Illinois, 1814–1818, Volumes 16–17.* Washington, D.C.: Government Printing Office, 1950.

Catlin, George. *Letters and Notes on the Manners, Customs, and Conditions of the North American Indians.* New York: Dover Publications, 1973.

———. *O-Kee-Pa: A Religious Ceremony and Other Customs of the Mandans.* Edited by John C. Ewers. New Haven, Conn.: Yale University Press, 1967.

Chittenden, Hiram Martin. *The American Fur Trade of the Far West.* 2 vols. Lincoln: University of Nebraska, Press, 1964.

———. *The Yellowstone National Park.* Edited by Richard A. Bartlett. Norman: University of Oklahoma Press, 1986.

Christy, Thomas. *Thomas Christy's Road across the Plains, 1850.* Edited by Robert Becker. Denver: Old West Publishing, 1969.

Clayton, William. *Journal: A Daily Record of the Journey of the Original Company of "Mormon" Pioneers from Nauvoo, Illinois, to the Valley of the Great Salt Lake.* Salt Lake City: Clayton Family Association, 1921.

Clokey, Richard M. *William H. Ashley: Enterprise and Politics in the Trans-Mississippi West.* Norman: University of Oklahoma Press, 1990.

Clyman, James. *Journal of a Mountain Man.* Edited by Linda M. Hasselstrom. Missoula, Mont.: Mountain Press Publishing, 1984.

———. *James Clyman, American Frontiersman, 1792–1881.* Edited by Charles L. Camp. San Francisco: California Historical Society, 1928.

Cooke, Philip St. George. *Scenes and Adventures in the Army.* Philadelphia: Lindsay & Blakiston, 1857.

Crotty, Bill. *Watts Mill.* Kansas City, Mo.: Watts Mill's Journals, 1985.

David, Robert Beebe. *Finn Burnett, Frontiersman.* Mechanicsburg, Pa.: Stackpole Books, 2003.

Davis, James E. *Frontier Illinois.* Bloomington: Indiana University Press, 1998.

DeLand, Charles Edmund, ed. *Fort Tecumseh and Fort Pierre Journal and Letter Books.* Pierre, S.D.: South Dakota Historical Collections 9, 1918.

Dellenbuach, Frederick S. *Fremont and '49.* New York: Knickerbocker Press, 1913.

Denig, Edwin Thompson. *Five Indian Tribes of the Upper Missouri.* Norman: University of Oklahoma Press, 1961.

De Smet, Father Pierre-Jean. *Letters and Sketches: With a Narrative of a Year's Residence among the Indian Rocky Mountains.* Philadelphia: M. Fithian, 1843.

———. *Life, Letters and Travels of Father Pierre-Jean De Smet, S. J.* Edited by Hiram Martin Chittenden and Albert Talbot Richardson. 4 vols. New York: Francis P. Harper. 1905.

———. *Western Missions and Missionaries: A Series of Letters.* Shannon: Irish University Press, 1972.

DeVoto, Bernard. *Across the Wide Missouri.* Boston: Houghton Mifflin, 1947.

———. *The Year of Decision, 1846.* Boston: Little, Brown, 1943.

Dodge, Grenville. *Biographical Sketch of James Bridger, Mountaineer, Trapper and Guide.* New York: Unz & Co., 1905.

Doyle, Susan Badger, ed. *Journeys to the Land of Gold: Emigrant Diaries from the Bozeman Trail, 1863–1866.* 2 vols. Helena: Montana Historical Society Press, 2000.

Drury, Clifford M. *Elkanah and Mary Walker: Pioneers among the Spokanes.* Caldwell, Idaho: Claxton Printers, 1940.

——. *First White Women over the Rockies: Diaries, Letters, and Biographical Sketches of the Six Women of the Oregon Mission Who Made the Overland Journey in 1836 and 1838.* 3 vols. Glendale, Calif.: Arthur H. Clark, 1963–66.

——. *Marcus and Narcissa Whitman and the Opening of Old Oregon.* 2 vols. Seattle: Northwest Interpretive Association, 1994.

——, ed. *On to Oregon: The Diaries of Mary Walker and Myra Eells.* Lincoln: University of Nebraska Press, 1963.

Edmunds, R. David. *The Potawatomis: Keepers of the Fire.* Norman: University of Oklahoma Press, 1978.

Enzler, Jerry. "Jim Bridger Challenges the Hudson's Bay Company." *Rocky Mountain Fur Trade Journal* 9 (2015): 110–25.

——. "Otholoho and Grohean: Two Fast Horses, One Set of Tracks." *Rocky Mountain Fur Trade Journal* 11 (2017): 60–65.

——. "Tracking Jim Bridger: Finding the Trail of Old Gabe." *Rocky Mountain Fur Trade Journal* 5 (2005): 1–19.

Ewers, John C. *The Blackfeet: Raiders of the Northwestern Plains.* Norman: University of Oklahoma Press, 1958.

Favour, Alpheus. *Old Bill Williams.* Norman: University of Oklahoma Press, 1962.

Ferguson, Charles D. *The Experiences of a Forty-Niner in California.* New York: Arno Press, 1973.

Ferguson, Gillum. *Illinois in the War of 1812.* Urbana: University of Illinois Press, 2012.

Ferril, Will C. "The Sixteenth Kansas Cavalry in the Black Hills in 1865." *Collections of the Kansas State Historical Society* 17 (1928): 855–58.

Ferris, Mrs. B. G. *The Mormons at Home: With Some Incidents of Travel from Missouri to California, 1852–3, in a Series of Letters.* New York: Dix & Edwards, 1856. http://archive.org/stream/mormonsathomewitooferr#page/n3/mode/2up.

Ferris, Warren Angus. *Life in the Rocky Mountains.* Edited by P. C. Phillips. Denver: F. S. Rosenstock, the Old West Pub. Co., 1940.

Field, Matthew C. *Prairie and Mountain Sketches.* Edited by Kate L. Gregg and John Francis McDermott. Norman: University of Oklahoma Press, 1957.

Field, Timothy. "Mike Fink: The Last of the Boatmen." *Western Monthly Review.* Cincinnati: E. H. Flint, 1830.

Flagg, Edmund. "Adventures at the Head Waters of the Missouri." *Louisville Literary News-Letter,* September 7, 1839.

Fletcher, Thomas C. *Life and Reminiscences of General Wm. T. Sherman.* Baltimore: R. H. Woodward, 1891.

Foster, Mike. *Strange Genius: The Life of Ferdinand Vandeveer Hayden.* Niwot, Conn.: Roberts Rinehart, 1994.

Frémont, John C. *The Expeditions of John Charles Frémont.* 3 vols. Edited by Marilee Spence and Donald Jackson. Urbana: University of Illinois Press, 1984.

Frost, Donald McKay. *Notes on General Ashley: The Overland Trail and South Pass.* Barre, Mass.: Barre Gazette, 1960.

Gardner, A. Dudley. *Fort Bridger.* Rock Springs: Western Wyoming College, 2014.

Glavin, Tom. *Dodge City: Wyatt Earp, Bat Masterson, and the Wickedest Town in the American West.* New York: St. Martin's Press, 2017.

Gowans, Fred R. "Fort Bridger and the Mormons." *Utah Historical Quarterly* 42.1 (1974): 49–67.

———. *Rocky Mountain Rendezvous.* Layton, Utah: Peregrine Smith Books, 1985.

Gowans, Fred R., and Eugene E. Campbell. *Fort Bridger: Island in the Wilderness.* Provo, Utah: Brigham Young University Press, 1975.

———. *Fort Supply: Brigham Young's Green River Experiment.* Provo, Utah: Brigham Young University Press, 1975.

Gray, John S. *Custer's Last Campaign: Mitch Boyer and the Little Bighorn Reconstructed.* Lincoln: University of Nebraska Press, 1991.

———, ed. "Young Fur Trapper—Phillip Covington's Travels to the Rockies with William Sublette." *Colorado Heritage* 1.2 (1982): 10–25.

Gray, William. "Unpublished Journals of William H. Gray." *Whitman College Quarterly,* June 1913.

Grinnell, George Bird. *The Fighting Cheyennes.* Norman: University of Oklahoma Press, 1956.

Gunnison, J. W. *The Mormons, or Latter Day Saints.* Philadelphia: Lippincott, Grambo & Co., 1852.

Hafen, Leroy R. *Broken Hand: The Life of Thomas Fitzpatrick, Mountain Man, Guide, and Indian Agent.* Lincoln: University of Nebraska Press, 1973.

———. "Henry Fraeb." In Hafen, *Mountain Men and the Fur Trade of the Far West,* vol. 3: 131–39.

———. "John H. Weber." In Hafen, *Mountain Men and the Fur Trade of the Far West,* vol. 9: 379–84.

———. "The Last Years of James P. Beckwourth." *Colorado Magazine* 5.4 (1928): 131–39.

———, ed. *The Mountain Men and the Fur Trade of the Far West.* 10 vols. Glendale, Calif.: Arthur H. Clark, 1965–72.

———. *The Overland Mail.* Glendale, Calif.: Arthur H. Clark, 1926.

Hafen, LeRoy R., and Ann W Hafen, eds. *Mormon Resistance: A Documentary Account of the Utah Expedition, 1857–1858.* Lincoln: University of Nebraska Press, 2005.

———. *Old Spanish Trail: Santé Fe to Los Angeles.* Glendale, Calif.: Arthur H. Clark, 1954.

———. *Powder River Campaigns and Sawyers Expedition of 1865.* Glendale, Calif.: Arthur H. Clark, 1951.

———, eds. *To the Rockies and Oregon, 1839–1842.* Glendale, Calif.: Arthur H. Clark, 1955.

Hafen, Leroy R., and Francis Marion Young. *Fort Laramie and the Pageant of the West, 1834–1890.* Lincoln: University of Nebraska Press, 1938.

Haines, Aubrey. *The Yellowstone Story.* 2 vols. Yellowstone National Park: Yellowstone Library and Museum Association, 1977.

Hall, Frank. *History of the State of Colorado.* La Crosse, Wis.: Brookhaven Press, 2000.

Hall, James. "The Missouri Trapper." In *Letters from the West.* Gainesville, Fla.: Scholars' Facsimiles & Reprints, 1967.

Hanson, Charles E., Jr., and Veronica Sue Walters. "The Early Fur Trade in Northwestern Nebraska." *Nebraska History* 57.4 (Fall 1976): 291–314.

Hanson, James A. *Little Chief's Gatherings, the Smithsonian Institution's G. K. Warren 1855–1856 Plains Indian Collection, and the New York State Library's 1855–1857 Warren Expedition Journals.* Crawford, Neb.: The Fur Press, 1996.

Hardee, Jim. *Hope Maintains Her Throne: The Western Expedition of Nathaniel J. Wyeth, 1834–1838.* Vol 2. Pinedale, Wyo.: Museum of the Mountain Man, 2018.

———. *Obstinate Hope: The Western Expeditions of Nathaniel J. Wyeth.* Pinedale, Wyo.: Museum of the Mountain Man, 2013.

———. *Pierre's Hole: The Fur Trade History of the Teton Valley, Idaho.* Pinedale, Wyo.: Museum of the Mountain Man, 2010.

Hastings, Lansford Warren. *Emigrants' Guide to Oregon and California.* [1845.] Reprinted, Bedford, Mass.: Applewood Books, 1994.

Hayden, Ferdinand V. *Preliminary Report of the United States Geological Survey of Montana, and Portions of Adjacent Territories: Being a Fifth Annual Report of Progress.* Washington, D.C.: Government Printing Office, 1872.

———. *Sixth Annual Report of the United States Geological Survey of the Territories.* Washington, D.C.: Government Printing Office, 1873.

Hebard, Grace Raymond, and E. A. Brinninstool. *The Bozeman Trail: Historical Accounts of the Blazing of the Overland Routes into the Northwest, and the Fights with Red Cloud's Warriors.* Cleveland, Ohio: Arthur H. Clark, 1922.

Hickman, William. *Brigham's Destroying Angel: The Life, Confession, and Disclosures of Bill Hickman.* Bedford, Mass.: Applewood Books, 1872.

History of Madison County, Illinois. Edwardsville, Ill.: W. R. Brink & Co., 1882.

History of Nodaway County, Missouri. St. Joseph, Mo.: National Historical Company, 1882.

Hodge, Frederick Webb, ed. *Handbook of American Indians North of Mexico.* Smithsonian Institution Bureau of American Ethnology Bulletin 30. 2 vols. Washington, D.C.: Government Printing Office, 1910.

Hoig, Stan. *Sand Creek Massacre.* Norman: University of Oklahoma Press, 1962.

Honig, Louis O. *James Bridger: The Pathfinder of the West.* Kansas City, Mo.: Brown-White-Lowell Press, 1951.

Hudson, John. *A Forty-Niner in Utah: With the Stansbury Exploration of Great Salt Lake.* Edited by Brigham D. Madsen. Salt Lake City: University of Utah Library, 1981.

Hull, Lewis B. "Soldiering on the High Plains: The Diary of Lewis Byram Hull, 1864–1866." Edited by Myra E. Hull. *Kansas Historical Quarterly* 7.1 (1938): 3–53.

Humfreville, J. Lee. *Twenty Years among Our Hostile Indians.* Mechanicsburg, Pa.: Stackpole Books, 2002.

Humphries, Alfred Glen. "Thomas L. (Peg-Leg) Smith." In Hafen, *Mountain Men and the Fur Trade of the Far West,* vol. 4: 311–30.

Hunton, John. *Diary.* Edited by L. G. Flannery. Lingle, Wyo.: Guide-Review, 1956.

Hutton, Paul Andrew. *Phil Sheridan and His Army,* Norman: University of Oklahoma Press, 2013.

Irving, Washington. *The Adventures of Captain Bonneville.* [1837.] Santa Barbara: Narrative Press, 2001.

Jackson, John C. *Shadow on the Tetons: David E. Jackson and the Claiming of the American West.* Missoula, Mont.: Mountain Press, 1993.

Jacob, Norton. *The Mormon Vanguard Brigade of 1847: Norton Jacob's Record.* Edited by Ronald O. Barney. Logan: Utah State University Press, 2005.

James, Thomas. *Three Years among the Indians and Mexicans.* Lincoln: University of Nebraska Press, 1984.

Johnson, Curtis L., and Victor A. Paul. *Philip Creamer: "The Most Celebrated Gunsmith in All the West."* Washington, Mo.: Obscure Place Publishing, 1992.

Johnston, William G. *Overland to California.* Oakland, Calif.: Bio Books, 1948.

Johnston, William Preston. *The Life of General Albert Sidney Johnston: Embracing His Services in the Armies of the United States, Republic of Texas, and the Confederate States.* New York: D. Appleton and Co., 1878.

Keep, Josiah. *Common Seashells of California.* San Francisco: Upton Bros., 1881.

Kelly, Charles, and Dale Morgan. *Old Greenwood.* Georgetown, Calif.: Talisman Press, 1965.

Kelly, Mark William. *Lost Vices on the Missouri: John Dougherty and the Indian Frontier.* Leavenworth, Kans.: Sam Clark Publishing, 2013.

Kelly, William. *An Excursion to California.* London: Chapman and Hall, 1951.

Kimball, Stanley B., and Violet T. Kimball. *Mormon Trail: Voyage of Discovery.* Las Vegas, Nev.: KC Publications, 1995.

Korns, J. Roderic, and Dale L. Morgan. *West from Fort Bridger.* Revised and updated by Will Bagley and Harold Schindler. Logan: Utah State University Press, 1994.

Kurz, Rudolf Friederich. *Journal.* Translated by Myrtis Jarrell, edited by J. N. B. Hewit. Lincoln: University of Nebraska Press, 1970.

Landry, Clay J. "Hugh Glass: The Rest of the Story." *Rocky Mountain Fur Trade Journal* 10 (2016):1–17.

———. "Trappers' Cache: Trade Goods, Equipment, and Clothing of the William Ashley and Jedediah Smith Trapping Ventures." *Rocky Mountain Fur Trade Journal* 2 (2008):14–29.

Langford, Nathaniel Pitt. *Discovery of Yellowstone Park: Journal of the Washburn Expedition to the Yellowstone and Firehole River in 1870.* Lincoln: University of Nebraska Press, 1972.

Langworthy, Francis. *Scenery of the Plains, Mountains and Mines.* Edited by Paul C. Phillips. Princeton, N.J.: Princeton University Press, 1932.

Larpenteur, Charles. *Forty Years a Fur Trader on the Upper Missouri.* Edited by Milo Milton Quaife. Chicago: R. R. Donnelley & Sons, 1933.

Larson, Lawrence H., and Barbara J. Cottrell. *Steamboats West: The 1859 American Fur Company Missouri River Expedition.* Norman, Okla.: Arthur C. Clark, 2010.

Latter-day Saints Millennial Star. Vol. 34. Liverpool: A. Carrington, 1872. https://contentdm.lib.byu.edu/digital/collection/MStar/id/25727/rec/34.

Lecompte, Janet. "John Hawkins." In Hafen, *Mountain Men and the Fur Trade of the Far West,* vol. 4: 141.

LeForge, Thomas H., and Thomas Marquis. *Memoirs of a White Crow Indian*. New York: Century Co., 1928.

Leonard, Zenas. *Adventures of a Mountain Man: The Narrative of Zenas Leonard*. Lincoln: University of Nebraska Press, 1978.

Little, James A. *From Kirtland to Salt Lake City*. Salt Lake City: Self-published, 1890.

Lowe, James A. *The Bridger Trail*. Spokane, Wash.: Arthur H. Clark, 1999.

Lowe, Percival. *Five Years a Dragoon, 1849–1854*. Kansas City: Privately printed, 1906.

MacKinnon, William P. *At Sword's Point: A Documentary History of the Utah War*. 2 vols. Norman, Okla.: Arthur H. Clark, 2008, 2016.

———. "Like Splitting a Man Up His Backbone: The Territorial Dismemberment of Utah, 1850–1896." *Utah Historical Quarterly* 71.2 (Spring 2003): 100–124.

Madsen, Brigham D., ed. *Exploring the Great Salt Lake: The Stansbury Expedition of 1849–50*. Salt Lake City: University of Utah Press, 1989.

———. *Gold Rush Sojourners in Great Salt Lake City*. Salt Lake City: University of Utah Press, 1983.

Marcy, Randolph B. *The Prairie Traveler: A Hand-Book for Overland Expeditions, with Maps, Illustrations, and Itineraries of the Principal Routes between the Missouri and the Pacific*. [1859.] Reprinted, Bedford, Mass.: Applewood Books, 1993.

———. *Thirty Years of Army Life on the Border*. New York: Harper, 1874.

Marsh, Elias J. "Journal of Dr. Elias J. Marsh: Account of a Steamboat Trip on the Missouri River, May–August, 1859." *South Dakota Historical Review* 1 (1936): 79–127.

Marsh, James B. *Four Years in the Rockies, or, the Adventures of Isaac P. Rose*. New Castle, Pa.: Printed by W. B. Thomas, 1975.

Mattes, Merrill J. *Colter's Hell and Jackson's Hole*. Washington, D.C.: Yellowstone Library and Museum Association and Grand Teton Natural History Association, 1962.

———. *The Great Platte River Road: The Covered Wagon Mainline via Fort Kearny to Fort Laramie*. Lincoln: University of Nebraska Press, 1987.

———. *Indians, Infants, and Infantry: Andrew and Elizabeth Burt on the Frontier*. Lincoln: University of Nebraska Press, 1960.

McChristian, Douglas C. *Fort Laramie: Military Bastion of the High Plains*. Norman: University of Oklahoma Press, 2009.

McDermott, John D. *Circle of Fire: The Indian War of 1865*. Mechanicsburg, Pa.: Stackpole Books, 2003.

———. *Red Cloud's War: The Bozeman Trail*. 2 vols. Norman, Okla.: Arthur H. Clark, 2010.

McDermott, John Francis. *Audubon in the West*. Norman: University of Oklahoma Press, 1965.

———, ed. *The Early Histories of St. Louis*. St. Louis: St. Louis Historical Documents Foundation, 1952.

McDonald, Lois Halliday. *Fur Trade Letters of Francis Ermatinger, 1818–1853*. Glendale, Calif.: Arthur H. Clark, 1980.

McLoughlin, John. *The Letters of John McLoughlin from Fort Vancouver to the Governor and Committee, Second Series, 1839–44*, edited by E. Rich. Toronto: Champlain Society for the Hudson's Bay Records Society, 1943.

Merrill, Marlene Deahl, *Yellowstone and the Great West: Journals, Letters, and Images from the 1871 Hayden Expedition*. Lincoln: University of Nebraska Press, 1999.

Meyers, John. *The Saga of Hugh Glass: Pirate, Pawnee, and Mountain Man*. Lincoln: University of Nebraska Press, 1963.

Miller, Alfred Jacob, with Marvin C. Ross. *The West of Alfred Jacob Miller*. Norman: University of Oklahoma Press, 1968.

Minto, John. "Reminiscences of Experiences on the Oregon Trail in 1844." *Oregon Historical Quarterly* 2.2 (1901): 119–67; 2.3 (1901): 209–54.

Monnett, John H., ed. *Eyewitness to the Fetterman Fight: Indian Views*. Norman: University of Oklahoma Press, 2017.

———. *Where a Hundred Soldiers Were Killed*. Albuquerque: University of New Mexico Press, 2010.

Moorman, Donald R., with Gene A. Sessions. *Camp Floyd and the Mormons: The Utah War*. Salt Lake City: University of Utah Press, 1992.

Morgan, Dale. *Jedediah Smith and the Opening of the West*. Lincoln: University of Nebraska Press, 1964.

———. *The Great Salt Lake*. Lincoln: University of Nebraska Press, 1986.

———. *Overland in 1846: Diaries and Letters of the California-Oregon Trail*. 2 vols. Georgetown, Calif.: Talisman Press, 1963.

———. "Washakie and the Shoshoni." *Annals of Wyoming* 30.1 (1958): 66–87.

———, ed. *The West of William H. Ashley*. Denver: F. S. Rosenstock, Old West Publishing, 1964.

Morgan, Dale, Richard L. Saunders, and Gregory E. Smoak. *Shoshonean Peoples and the Overland Trail*. Logan: Utah State University Press, 2007.

Mumey, Nolie. *James Pierson Beckwourth, 1856–1866: An Enigmatic Figure of the West*. Denver: Fred A. Rosenstock, Old West Publishing, 1957.

Murphy, Virginia Reed. "Across the Plains with the Donner Party." *Century Magazine* 42 (1891): 409–26. https://digital.library.upenn.edu/women/reed/donner/donner.html.

Murphy, William, "The Forgotten Battalion." *Annals of Wyoming* 7.2 (1930): 383–401.

Mutti Burke, Diane. *On Slavery's Border: Missouri's Small-Slaveholding Households, 1815–1865*. Athens: University of Georgia Press, 2010.

Neihardt, John G. *Black Elk Speaks: Being the Life Story of a Holy Man of the Oglala*, Lincoln: University of Nebraska Press, 1961.

Nester, William R. *From Mountain Man to Millionaire*. Columbia: University of Missouri Press, 1999.

Nevill, Morgan. *Missouri Intelligencer,* September 4, 1829.

Newell, Robert. *Robert Newell's Memoranda: Travels in the Territory of Missourie. . . .* Edited by Dorothy O. Johansen. Portland, Ore.: Champoeg Press, 1959.

Noel, Rae. *Witnessing America: The Library of Congress Book of Firsthand Accounts of Life in America, 1600–1900*. New York: Stonesong Press, 1996.

O'Connell, Robert L. *Fierce Patriot: The Tangled Lives of William Tecumseh Sherman*. New York: Random House, 2014.

Ogden, Peter Skene. *Snake Country Journals, 1824–25 and 1825–26.* Edited by E. E. Rich. London: Hudson's Bay Record Society, 1950.

O'Leary, Mrs. James L. "Henry Chatillon." *Missouri Historical Society Bulletin* 22 (January 1966): 123–42.

Ostrander, Alson B. *An Army Boy of the Sixties: A Story of the Plains.* New York: World Book Company, 1924.

Pagnamenta, Peter. *Prairie Fever: British Aristocrats in the American West, 1830–1890.* New York: Norton, 2012.

Palmer, Joel. *Journal of Travels over the Rocky Mountains.* Fairfield, Wash.: Ye Galleon Press, 1983.

Parker, Samuel. *Journey of an Exploring Tour Beyond the Rocky Mountains.* New York: J. C. Derby & Co., 1948.

Parkman, Francis. *The Oregon Trail.* Garden City, N.Y.: Doubleday, 1946.

Parrish, Randall. *Historic Illinois.* Chicago: A. C. McClurg, 1906.

Paul, Victor A. "Searching for (Young) Old Jim." *Museum of the Fur Trade Quarterly* 26.4 (1990): 5–11.

Peterson, Levi S. "The Development of Utah Livestock Law, 1848–1896." *Utah Historical Quarterly* 32 (1964): 198–216.

Philbrick, Francis S., ed. *The Laws of Illinois Territory, 1809–1818.* Collections of the Illinois State Historical Society. Vol. 25. Springfield: Illinois State Historical Library, 1950.

Piercy, Frederick Hawkins. *Route from Liverpool to Great Salt Lake Valley.* Liverpool: Franklin D. Richards, 1855.

Preuss, Charles. *Exploring with Fremont: The Private Diaries of Charles Preuss, Cartographer for John C. Fremont on His First, Second, and Fourth Expeditions to the Far West.* Edited and translated by Erwin G. Gudde and Elizabeth K. Gudde. Norman: University of Oklahoma Press, 1958.

Proceedings of the Academy of Natural Sciences of Philadelphia, vol. 8 (1856).

Raynolds, William. *Report of Captain W. F. Raynolds' Expedition to Explore the Headwaters of the Missouri and Yellowstone Rivers.* Washington D.C.: Government Printing Office, 1868.

———. *Up the Winds and Over the Tetons: Journal Entries and Images from the 1860 Raynolds Expedition.* Edited by Marlene Deahl Merrill and Daniel D. Merrill. Albuquerque: University of New Mexico Press, 2012.

Remsburg, George J. "Snatched from the Wayside." *The Trail* 20 (September 1927).

Reynolds, John. *Pioneer History of Illinois.* Chicago: Fergus Printing Co., 1887.

Rister, Carl C. *Border Command: General Phil Sheridan in the West.* Norman: University of Oklahoma Press, 1944.

Roberts, Brigham H. *A Comprehensive History of the Church of Jesus Christ of Latter-day Saints.* 6 vols. Salt Lake City: Church of Jesus Christ of Latter-day Saints, 1930.

Roberts, David. *A Newer World: Kit Carson, John C. Frémont, and the Claiming of the American West.* New York: Simon & Shuster, 2000.

Roberts, Jack. *The Amazing Adventures of Lord Gore: A True Saga from the Old West.* Silverton, Colo.: Sundance Publications, 1977.

Robrock, David P. "A History of Fort Fetterman." *Annals of Wyoming* 48.1 (1976): 19–20.

Rogers, Fred B. *Soldiers of the Overland: Being Some Account of the Services of General Patrick Edward Conner and His Volunteers in the Old West*. San Francisco: Grabhorn Press, 1938.

Rollins, Phillip A. *The Cowboy, His Characteristics, His Equipment, and His Part in the Development of the West*. Skyhorse Publishing, 1974.

Ruggles, Richard I. *A Country So Interesting: The Hudson's Bay Company and Two Centuries of Mapping, 1670–1870*. Montreal: McGill-Queen's University Press, 1991.

Russell, Osborne, *Journal of a Trapper, 1834–1843*. Edited by Aubrey L. Haines. Lincoln: University of Nebraska Press, 1955.

Rzeckowski, Frank. "The Crow Indians and the Bozeman Trail." *Montana: The Magazine of Western History* 49 (Winter 1990): 30–47.

Sager, Catherine, Elizabeth Sager, and Matilda Sager. *The Whitman Massacre of 1847*. Fairfield, Wash.: Ye Galleon Press, 2002.

Saunders, Richard L. *Dale Morgan on the Mormons: Collected Works Part 1, 1939–1951*. Norman, Okla.: Arthur H. Clark, 2012.

Sawyers, James A. "Niobrara–Virginia City Wagon Road: Report of James A. Sawyers, Superintendent." *South Dakota Historical Review* 2:1.

Schilling, Timothy. "The Chronology of Monks Mound." *Southeastern Archaeology* 32:1. 14–28. www.tandfonline.com/doi/abs/10.1179/sea.2013.32.1.002.

Schoolcraft, Henry R. *The American Indians, Their History, Condition and Prospects*. Buffalo, N.Y.: George H. Derby and Co., 1851.

Sheridan, Philip H. *Personal Memoirs of P. H. Sheridan*. New York: Charles L. Webster & Co., 1888.

Simmons, Virginia McConnell. *The Ute Indian of Utah, Colorado, and New Mexico*. Boulder: University Press of Colorado, 2000.

Simpson, George. "Geo. Simpson to the Governor, Depy Govr. & Committee of the Honble. Hudson's Bay Company, November 25, 1841." In *Certain Correspondence of the Foreign Office and of the Hudson's Bay Company Copied from Original Documents, London, 1898*. Ottawa: Government Printing Bureau, 1899.

Smith, E. Willard. "Journal of E. Willard Smith While with the Fur Traders, Vasquez and Sublette, in the Rocky Mountain Region 1839–1840." *Oregon Historical Quarterly*, September 1913.

Smith, Rex Alan. *The Carving of Mount Rushmore*. New York: Abbeville Press, 1985.

Smith, Shannon D. *Give Me Eighty Men: Women and the Myth of the Fetterman Fight*. Lincoln: University of Nebraska Press, 2010.

Southesk, Earl of (James Carnegie). *Saskatchewan and the Rocky Mountains: A Diary and Narrative of Travel, Sport, and Adventure During a Journey through the Hudson's Bay Company's Territories in 1859 and 1860*. Toronto: James Campbell and Son, 1875.

Spear Family. *Bozeman Trail Scrapbook: The Books and Photos of Elsa Spear*. [Wyo.]: Fort Phil Kearny/Bozeman Trail Association, 1993.

Spring, Agnes Wright. *Caspar Collins: The Life and Exploits of an Indian Fighter of the Sixties*. Lincoln: University of Nebraska Press, 1927.

Springer, Charles H. *Soldiering in Sioux Country: 1865*. Edited by Benjamin Franklin Cooling III. San Diego: Frontier Heritage Press, 1971.

Stanley, E. L. *Life of Rev. L. B. Stateler*. Nashville: M. E. Church, 1916.

Stansbury, Howard. *Exploration of the Valley of the Great Salt Lake*. Washington, D.C.: Smithsonian Institution Press, 1988.

Stevens, Frank E. "Illinois in the War of 1812–1814." In *Transactions of the Illinois State Historical Society*. Springfield: Phillips Bros. State Printers, 1904.

Stewart, George R. *Ordeal by Hunger: The Story of the Donner Party*. Lincoln: University of Nebraska Press, 1960.

Stewart, William Drummond, *Edward Warren*. Edited by Bart Barbour. Missoula, Mont.: Mountain Press Publishing, 1986.

Stone, Elizabeth Arnold. *Uinta County: Its Place in History*. Glendale, Calif.: Arthur C. Clark, 1924.

Stuart, Granville. *Montana as It Is*. New York: C. S. Wescott & Co., 1865.

Stuart, James. "The Yellowstone Expedition of 1863." In *Montana Historical Society Contributions* (1876): 1.

Sunder, John E. *Bill Sublette: Mountain Man*. Norman: University of Oklahoma Press, 1987.

Talbot, Theodore. *The Journals of Theodore Talbot*. Edited by Charles H. Carey. Portland, Ore.: Metropolitan Press, 1931.

Tarbell, Ida. *The Life of Abraham Lincoln*. New York: MacMillan, 1928.

Tarbell, J. *The Emigrant's Guide to California*. Keokuk, Iowa: Whig Book and Job Office, 1853.

Tate, Michael L., ed., with Will Bagley and Richard L Rieck. *The Great Medicine Road: Narratives of the Oregon, California, and Mormon Trails, Part 1: 1840–1848*. Norman: University of Oklahoma Press, 2014.

Terrell, John Upton. *Black Robe*. New York: Doubleday, 1964.

Territory of Utah, Acts, Resolutions, and Memorials, First Annual Session. Great Salt Lake City: Brigham H. Young, Printer, 1852.

Territory of Utah, Acts and Resolutions, Second Annual Session. Great Salt Lake City: George Hales, Printer, 1853.

Townsend, John Kirk. *Narrative of a Journey across the Rockies to the Columbia River*. Vol. 21 of *Early Western Travels*, edited by Rueben Gold Thwaites. Cleveland: Arthur H. Clark, 1905.

Turner, John G. *Brigham Young: Pioneer Prophet*. Cambridge, Mass.: Belknap Press of Harvard University, 2012.

United States National Park Service. *Draft Comprehensive Management and Use Plan and Environmental Assessment, Santa Fe National Historic Trail*, 1989.

Unrau, William E. ed. *Tending the Talking Wire: A Buck Soldier's View of Indian Country, 1863–1866*. Salt Lake City: University of Utah Press, 1979.

Unruh, John D., Jr. *The Plains Across*. Urbana: University of Illinois Press, 1993.

"The Utah Expedition." In *Executive Documents, U. S. House of Representatives, 1857–58*. Washington, D.C.: James B. Steedman, 1858.

Utley, Robert M. "The Bozeman Trail before John Bozeman: A Busy Land." *Montana: The Magazine of Western History* 53.2 (Summer 2003): 20–31.

———. *Frontiersmen in Blue*. Lincoln: University of Nebraska Press, 1967.

Varnell, Jeanne, and M. L. Hanson. *Women of Consequence: The Colorado Women's Hall of Fame*. Boulder, Colo.: Johnson Press, 1999.

Vestal, Stanley. *Jim Bridger: Mountain Man*. Lincoln: University of Nebraska Press, 1970.

Victor, Frances Fuller. *The River of the West: The Adventures of Joe Meek*. 2 vols. Missoula, Mont.: Mountain Press Publishing, 1983.

Viola, Herman J. *Exploring the West*. Washington, D.C.: Smithsonian Books, 1987.

Wagner, David E. *Patrick Connor's War: The 1865 Powder River Indian Expedition*. Norman: Arthur H. Clark, 2010.

———. *Powder River Odyssey: Nelson Cole's Western Campaign of 1865: The Journals of Lyman G. Bennett and Other Eyewitness Accounts*. Norman, Okla.: Arthur H. Clark, 2009.

Waldman, Carl. *The Dictionary of Native American Terminology*. New York: Castle Books, 2009.

Walker, Ardis M. "Joseph R. Walker." In Hafen, *Mountain Men and the Fur Trade of the Far West*, vol. 5: 361–80.

Walker, Ronald W., Richard E. Turley, Jr., Glen M. Leonard. *Massacre at Mountain Meadows*. New York: Oxford University Press, 2011.

Walker, Scott, and Jim Hardee. "Philip Covington: A Year in the Mountains, 1827–28." *Rocky Mountain Fur Trade Journal* 14 (2020): 1–43.

Wallis, Michael. *The Best Land under Heaven: The Donner Party in the Age of Manifest Destiny*. New York: Liveright Publishing, 2018.

The War of the Rebellion: Official Records of the Civil War. 128 vols. Washington, D.C.: Government Printing Office, 1880–1901.

Ward, Geoffrey C., Stephen Ives, Ken Burns, and Dayton Duncan. *The West: An Illustrated History*. Boston: Little, Brown, 2006.

Ware, Eugene F. *The Indian War of 1864*. Edited by Clyde C. Walton. Lincoln: University of Nebraska Press, 1960.

Warren, G. K. *Preliminary Report of Explorations in Nebraska and Dakota in the Years 1855, -'56, -'57*. Washington, D.C.: Government Printing Office, 1875.

———. *Reports of Explorations and Surveys, to Ascertain the Most Practicable and Economical Route for a Railroad from the Mississippi River to the Pacific Ocean*. Washington, D.C.: Beverly Tucker Printer, 1855.

Wheat, Carl I. *Mapping the TransMississippi West, 1540–1861*. 6 vols. Mansfield Centre, Conn: Martino Publishing, 2004.

Wheeler, William F. "The Late James Gemmell." *Contributions to the Montana Historical Society* 2 (1896): 331–36.

White, Elijah. "St. Louis." In *Ten Years in Oregon (1838–1847): Travels and Adventures of Dr. E. White and Lady, West of the Rocky Mountains. . . .* Ithaca, N.Y.: Mack, Andrus & Co., 1848.

Whitman, Narcissa. "Letters and Journals of Narcissa Whitman." *The West*. http://www
.pbs.org/weta/thewest/resources/archives/two/whitman2.htm.

Whittlesey, Lee H. *Death in Yellowstone: Accidents and Foolhardiness in the First National
Park*. Lanham, Md.: Roberts Rinehart, 2014.

——. *Storytelling in Yellowstone: Horse and Buggy Tour Guides*. Albuquerque: University
of New Mexico Press, 2007.

Wislizenus, F. A. *A Journey to the Rocky Mountains in 1839*. Fairfield, Wash: Ye Galleon
Press. 1992.

Wyeth, John B. *Oregon*. Ann Arbor, Mich.: University Microfilms, Inc., 1966.

Wyeth, Nathaniel J. *The Journals of Captain Nathaniel J. Wyeth's Expedition to the Oregon
Country, 1831–1836*. Edited by Don Johnson. Fairfield, Wash.: Ye Galleon Press, 1984.

Young, Brigham. *Diary of Brigham Young, 1857*. Edited by Everett L. Cooley. Salt Lake
City: Tanner Trust Fund, 1980.

Young, Brigham, and His Counselors, the Twelve Apostles, and Others. *Journal of Dis-
courses*. Reported by G. D. Watt. Liverpool: S. D. Richards, 1855. Brigham Young
University Digital Collections. https://contentdm.lib.byu.edu/digital/collection
/JournalOfDiscourses3/id/540/rec/4.

Young, Will E. "Journals of Travel." *Annals of Wyoming* 7.2 (1930): 378–82.

INDEX

References to images or their captions appear in italic type.

Palmer, Henry, 260
Palmer, Innis, 286, 287–88
Paramount Pictures Corporation, 300
Parker, Samuel, 89, 91
Parkman, Francis, 150, 197
passports for Mexican territory, 119, 133
Peejatowahooten (Pe-ja-to-wa-hooton),
    Bridger's Shoshone name, 300
Peh-tó-pe-kiss, 70. *See also* Eagle Ribs
    (Blackfeet warrior)
*Peh-tó-pe-kiss, Eagle's Ribs, a Piegan
    Chief* (Catlin), *70*
pelts (beaver), quantities/value of: 1825,
    Henry and Ashley's company, 40;
    1826, Ashley and Smith, 47; 1827,
    Smith, Jackson, and Sublette, 52;
    1828 and 1829, Smith, Jackson, and
    Sublette, 53; 1830, Smith, Jackson, and
    Sublette, 57; 1832, Rocky Mountain
    Fur, 65; 1833, Rocky Mountain Fur, 77;
    American Fur pricing scheme, 81
Pend Oreilles, 92
Peoria, Ill., 2–3, 5
Perpetual Emigrating Fund, 188–89
Peters, Samuel, 276
Phelps, John, 215–16
Philadelphia Port-Folio, 27
Picotte, Honoré, 133
Piegans, Blackfeet people, 22, 69, *70*,
    109, 110
Pierce, Franklin, 200
Pierre's Hole, *14*, 48, 52, 62, *176*, 231
Pike, Zebulon, 8
Pilcher, Joshua, 23, 26, 96
Pitt, Brad, 301
Plains Indian alliances, conflicts with:
    1840s attacks by, 120–21, 123–24;
    Bozeman Trail *vs.* Bridger Trail,
    247–48, 252–53, 265–66, 284–85;
    destruction of telegraph lines, 239;
    early 1860s incidents, 239–41; and
    Horse Creek Treaty negotiations,
    177, 178; "Hundred in the Hand"

battle, 282–85; parley requested by
    Black Horse, 272–74; Powder River
    Expedition, 255–64; railroad and
    obsolescence of Bozeman Trail,
    290; Red Cloud alliance offensives,
    269, 270, 271, 275–76, 280–84; treaty
    council attempt 1866, 268, 269, 270
poison: bad water pools, 142, 261, 263;
    bullets/arrows, 92, 99, 100, 275
Polk, James, 148, 151
polygamy among Mormons, 147,
    188, 209
Ponto, Glaud, 55
Pony Express, 226–27, 239
Pope, John, 258–59
Popo Agie River, *14*, 32
Porter, Fitz John, 212
Potawatomis, 2–3, 5
Potts, Daniel: crippling injury, 22; on
    dangers of Blackfeet, 48; desertion
    of, 17; on geysers, 49; on Hugh Glass
    incident, 29; on poor profit margins
    of trapping, 52; return to expedition,
    19, 21; Wind River Mountain
    crossing, 33
Powder River, *14–15*, *176*, *273*. *See also*
    Plains Indian alliances, conflicts with
Powder River Campaign/Expedition,
    255–64
Powell, John Wesley, 137
Pratte, Bernard, 58. *See also* Bernard
    Pratte and Company; Pratte,
    Chouteau & Company
Pratte, Chouteau & Company, 87, 96.
    See also Chouteau (&) Company
Preparing for a Buffalo Hunt
    (Miller), *79*
Preuss, Charles, 125
Provost, Etienne, 35, 208
Pueblo de Los Angeles, 52, 113, 119

Queaterra. *See* Coyoterra ("Queaterra")
    region